# A MILTON ENCYCLOPEDIA

# A MILTON ENCYCLOPEDIA

VOLUME 5 Le–N

*Edited by*

William B. Hunter, Jr., *General Editor*

John T. Shawcross *and* John M. Steadman, *Co-Editors*

Purvis E. Boyette and Leonard Nathanson,
*Associate Editors*

*Lewisburg*
*Bucknell University Press*
*London: Associated University Presses*

© 1979 by Associated University Presses, Inc.


Associated University Presses, Inc.
Cranbury, New Jersey 08512


Associated University Presses Ltd.
Magdalen House
136–148 Tooley Street
London SE1 2TT, England




A Milton encyclopedia.
Includes bibliographical references.
1.  Milton, John, 1608–1674—Dictionaries, indexes, etc.
I.  Hunter, William Bridges, 1915–
PR3580.M5        821'.4        75–21896
ISBN 0–8387–1838–8

# SYSTEM OF REFERENCES

Organization of the material in this Encyclopedia is alphabetical with cross-referencing achieved in two ways. First, a subject may appear as an entry in the main alphabet, with citation of another entry under which that subject is treated. Second, subjects mentioned in an entry that are also discussed in other entries are marked with asterisks, with the exception of certain ones appearing too frequently for such treatment to be practical : the titles of all of Milton's works, each of which has a separate entry; the various named characters who appear in the works; and the names of Milton and his family, including his wife Mary Powell and her family, and his sister Anne Phillips and her family.

Titles of articles in serials have been removed, as have the places of publication of modern books. The titles of Milton's various works have been uniformly abbreviated in forms to be found in the front matter, as have references to the major modern editions and biographical works. All quotations of his writing are taken, unless otherwise indicated, from the complete edition published by the Columbia University Press (1931–1938).

# SHORT FORMS USED
# IN THIS ENCYCLOPEDIA

| | |
|---|---|
| *AdP* | Ad Patrem |
| *Animad* | Animadversions upon the Remonstrant's Defense |
| *Apol* | An Apology |
| *Arc* | Arcades |
| *Areop* | Areopagitica |
| *BrM* | Bridgewater Manuscript |
| *BN* | Brief Notes upon a Late Sermon |
| *Brit* | The History of Britain |
| *Bucer* | The Judgement of Martin Bucer |
| *CarEl* | Carmina Elegiaca |
| *Carrier 1, 2* | On the University Carrier; Another on the Same |
| *CB* | Commonplace Book |
| *CharLP* | Character of the Long Parliament |
| *Circum* | Upon the Circumcision |
| *CD* | De Doctrina Christiana |
| *CM* | *The Works of John Milton* (New York : Columbia University Press, 1931–1938). 18 vols. The so-called Columbia Milton. |
| *Colas* | Colasterion |
| *CivP* | A Treatise of Civil Power |
| *DDD* | The Doctrine and Discipline of Divorce |
| *1Def* | Pro Populo Anglicano Defensio |
| *2Def* | Defensio Secunda |
| *3Def* | Pro Se Defensio |
| *Educ* | Of Education |
| *Eff* | In Effigiei ejus Sculptorem |
| *Eikon* | Eikonoklastes |
| *El* | Elegia |
| *EpDam* | Epitaphium Damonis |
| *Epistol* | Epistolarum Familiarium |
| *EpWin* | Epitaph on the Marchioness of Winchester |
| *FInf* | On the Death of a Fair Infant |

| | |
|---|---|
| French, *Life Records* | J. Milton French. *The Life Records of John Milton* (New Brunswick, N.J.: Rutgers University Press, 1949–1958). 5 vols. |
| *Hire* | Considerations Touching the Likeliest Means to Remove Hirelings out of the Church |
| *Hor* | The Fifth Ode of Horace |
| *Idea* | De Idea Platonica |
| *IlP* | Il Penseroso |
| *L'Al* | L'Allegro |
| *Literae* | Literae Pseudo-Senatûs Anglicani Cromwellii |
| *Lyc* | Lycidas |
| *Logic* | Artis Logicae |
| *Mask* | A Mask (Comus) |
| Masson, *Life* | David Masson. *The Life of John Milton* (London, 1859–1880). 6 vols. plus Index. |
| *May* | Song: On May Morning |
| *Mosc* | A Brief History of Moscovia |
| *Nat* | On the Morning of Christ's Nativity |
| *Naturam* | Naturam non pati senium |
| *NewF* | On the New Forcers of Conscience |
| Parker, *Milton* | William Riley Parker. *Milton: A Biography* (Oxford: Clarendon Press, 1968). 2 vols. |
| *Peace* | Articles of Peace |
| *PL* | Paradise Lost |
| *PR* | Paradise Regained |
| *PrelE* | Of Prelatical Episcopacy |
| *PresM* | The Present Means |
| *Prol* | Prolusion |
| *Ps* | Psalm |
| *QNov* | In Quintum Novembris |
| *RCG* | Reason of Church Government |
| *Ref* | Of Reformation |
| *Rous* | Ad Ioannem Rousium |
| *SA* | Samson Agonistes |
| *Shak* | On Shakespeare |
| *SolMus* | At a Solemn Music |
| *Sonn* | Sonnet |
| *StateP* | State Papers |
| *Tenure* | The Tenure of Kings and Magistrates |
| *Tetra* | Tetrachordon |
| *Time* | Of Time |
| *TM* | Trinity Manuscript |
| *TR* | Of True Religion |
| *Vac* | At a Vacation Exercise |
| *Variorum Commentary* | *A Variorum Commentary on the Poems of John Milton.* 3 vols. to date (New York: Columbia University Press, 1970–    ). |
| *Way* | The Ready and Easy Way to Establish a Free Commonwealth |
| Yale *Prose* | *Complete Prose Works of John Milton.* 6 vols. to date. (New Haven, Conn.: Yale University Press, 1953–    ). |

# A MILTON ENCYCLOPEDIA

**LeBLANC, JEAN B.:** *see* Translations of Milton's works.

**LEARNING, MILTON'S.** Even in his lifetime Milton seems to have been noted for his learning, as Thomas Ellwood*, his pupil and friend, remarked : "a gentleman of great note for learning throughout the learned world." It was for this reason and his knowledge of languages that he became Secretary for Foreign Tongues* to the Council of State*. The extent of his reading and its use is observable from the references and quotations in his many prose works and poems, some exercising later scholars in their search for exact editions of works used, and from the numerous allusions that have been discovered in his poetry. His reading ranged, it seems, over the full breadth of Greek and Roman writing, Hebraic materials and of course scriptural commentaries, the Church Fathers, the church historians, rhetoricians, medieval and Renaissance authors, governmental and political thinkers and historians, theologians and philosophers, and creative literary artists (see the numerous entries for individual authors in this encyclopedia). He read these volumes in original languages*, for he knew Aramaic, Greek, Latin, French, Italian, German, Dutch, and apparently Spanish. Volumes that he owned and consulted (*see* Library, Milton's) can be compiled from extant books, personal statements, citations in his works, and *CB*. *CB* is nowhere near a good indication of his reading, however; it does record materials that he, from time to time, preserved for possible use in a kind of repository of prooftexts, and he did use

most of these materials at later dates. But it only begins to suggest the extent of his learning. What we know of his concepts of education and the actual practice to which he put those ideas amplifies its range and implies its depth (*see Educ* and Tutoring by Milton). Some of the projects that he devoted his time to (or that he is reported to have pursued) indicate his interest in education and his ability to pull together disparate materials, weigh them, and organize them for others' immediate use. We see this in the various texts discussed in *Educ*, in *Brit* (employed in the late seventeenth century and early eighteenth century as informational source and corrective), in *Mosc*, in *Accedence Commenc't Grammar*, in *Logic*, in *CD*, in the nonexistent Latin thesaurus, and in the reputed Greek thesaurus (*see* individual titles here and, for the last two, Canon). The compilation of reading that each of these items represents is separately impressive.

There has been some denigration of Milton's work in these compendia by those who have viewed *Accedence Commenc't Grammar* as only an amplification of William Lily's *Grammar,* which is cited for the majority of the illustrations of grammatical functions; *Logic* as only a pillaging of George Downham's* work on logic; and *CD* as a condensation of such authors as Johann Wollebius* and William Ames*. Each of these volumes is more than simply a derivation from someone else's work, and each has the aim of making the subject matter available comprehensively to a specific group of people. They illustrate a little differently what is evident from Milton's other prose: "Milton was simply not a profound or an original thinker. Intelligent and learned, yes; sincere and idealistic, yes; but profound and original, no" (Parker, *Milton,* 1:641). Criticism of these works does not detract from Milton's learning; it does point to Milton's function as an author.

Mention should also be made of Milton's alleged attack on learning in *PR* 4. 221–364. This section of the brief epic, being part of the second temptation and dealing as it does with acquisition for the sake of acquisition only, does not condemn learning: it argues that the Son* has all the wisdom, knowledge, and learning he needs for his present concerns through Scripture. To accept Satan's lure of intellectual prowess over other men would be to succumb to temptation. Such learning as the ancients offer is interpretation and amplification of God's basic truths; the poem itself and all else that Milton wrote is no more than that. The passage is not in conflict with his own learning to be more fit, a program and aim that he outlined in *Prol* 7 ("Learning is greater than ignorance") and referred to in *RCG.* [JTS]

**LEGAL INDEX:** *see* COLUMBIA MANUSCRIPT.

**LEIGH, RICHARD:** *see* ANTAGONISTS.

**LEIGHTON, ALEXANDER** (1568–1649), a Scottish Calvinist who strongly opposed Episcopacy early in the reign of Charles I*. He was arrested for his *Appeal to the Parliament; Or Sions Plea* (1628) and later tortured before his release in 1640. Milton refers to his book at the beginning of the *Postscript* to *Animad* (3:173). In the antiprelatical tracts Milton employs some images that are similar to those in Leighton's works, but the coincidences may indicate only a common verbal tradition in Puritan invective. [WBH]

**LEONORA, EPIGRAMS ON**. The three Latin epigrams that Milton wrote in honor of the Italian singer, Leonora Baroni*, appeared in both the 1645 and 1673 editions of his poems. He heard her sing during one or the other of his two visits to Rome in the winter of 1638–39 and probably wrote the poems shortly thereafter. They cannot be dated with greater precision than this because further information as to when and where he heard her is lacking. Althought they were not included, Milton may have written his poems for a volume of tributes to Leonora, *Applausi Poetici alle Glorie della Signora Leonora Baroni,* which appeared in 1639.

The object of these tributes was an enchanting young woman. Her mother and sister were accomplished musicians also, and to hear the three perform together was considered an especially memorable experience. Her charm and talent live most vividly in the description of a visiting Frenchman, André Maugars. With good reason have Miltonists from Thomas Warton* in the eighteenth century to John Arthos in the twentieth quoted it, for it aptly summarizes Leonora's appeal. Captivated not only by her musical expertise but by her appearance and manners as well, Maugars wrote: "She does not pretend to beauty, yet she is far from disagreeable, nor is she a coquet. She sings with an air of confident and liberal modesty, and with a pleasing gravity. Her voice reaches a large compass of notes, is just, clear, and melodious; and she softens or raises it without constraint or grimace. Her raptures and sighs are not too tender; her looks have nothing impudent, nor do her gestures betray anything beyond the reserve of a modest girl."

Milton's poems to Leonora are largely conventional. Ten, twelve, and eight lines long respectively, their brevity accords with their nature as epigrams; for the epigram was by definition a short poem attempting to capture the essence of a situation or action. Although its terseness and a tendency toward sententiousness made it especially suitable for satire, the epigram was occasionally used for other purposes as well; thus there is nothing surprising in Milton's employing it as the vehicle for his extravagant praise of Leonora. Neither is the praise surprising, however excessive it may seem to a modern reader. In the cultured circles with which Milton came in contact during his Italian journey, such extravagance of expression was *de rigueur*. Salzilli*, a Roman friend of Milton's, for example, wrote the young Englishman a poem that praised him as superior to Homer*, Virgil*, and Tasso*. Such statements tell us nothing about the personal relationships involved. With regard to Milton and Leonora, it is possible that he may never have spoken with her, even though he writes in the first epigram that the Holy Spirit speaks through her voice, in the second that her voice could have restored the insane poet Tasso to his senses, and in the third that she is "the liquid voiced Siren . . . Parthenope." From this, we can assume that her singing impressed him, but little more. [ERG]

## L'ESTRANGE, SIR ROGER (1616–1704), Tory pamphleteer.

A member of a Royalist family, L'Estrange fought with Charles I* and Prince Rupert against the Parliamentarian forces. He was apprehended in November 1644 in a plot to recapture Lynn Regis in Norfolk, and the royal commission that he held caused him to be imprisoned for more than three years under sentence of death. While still in prison he published in July 1646 a broadside setting forth his case, and in April 1647 a pamphlet, entitled *L'Estrange his Appeal from the Court Martial to the Parliament*. He escaped from Newgate in the spring of 1648, with the aid of authorities. From Holland in 1649 he published a defense of himself against criticism from both sides.

In 1659–60, with the changes in government being imminent, L'Estrange wrote a series of pamphlets attacking the army and republicans and urging a restoration of the king. A number of these tracts allude to Milton and one is directed against him. Allusions are found in *Be Merry and Wise, or, A Seasonable Word to the Nations*, p. 86; *Double Your Guards*, p. 3 (not certainly by L'Estrange); *Physician Cure Thy Self: or, An Answer to a Seditious Pamphlet, Entitled Eye-Salve*, p. 2; *A Plea for Limited Monarchy*, p. 3 (not certainly by L'Estrange; rptd., *Harleian Miscellany* [1744], 1 :14–18); *Treason Arraigned. In Answer to Plain English*, pp. 2–3, 5, 22 (error for 30); and *L'Estrange his Apology With a Short View, of Some Late and Remarkable Transactions, Leading to the Happy Settlement of These Nations*, which reprinted *Be Merry and Wise, Physician Cure Thyself*, and *Treason Arraigned*. In answer to Milton's *BN*, which criticized Matthew Griffith*, who had spoken of the imminence of the Restoration, L'Estrange wrote an abusive tract entitled *No Blinde Guides, in Answer to a Seditious Pamphlet of J. Milton's*; it was also reprinted in *L'Estrange his Apology*. He does not defend Griffith, but does firmly show the Royalist position concerning government and implies that the Restoration indeed is about to occur, as it did within a month with the action of General Monck*. In the ensuing years L'Estrange produced various other tracts against critics of the new government, particularly in connection with the church settlement and with licensing*. One of these, *Considerations and Proposals in order to the Regulation of the Press: Together with Diverse Instances of Treasonous, and Seditious Pamphlets, Proving the Necessity Thereof* (1663), p. 19, lists Milton's *Tenure* as still being unpunished by authority, and *Toleration Discuss'd* (1663), pp. 34, 45, 71, 85, 105, cites this same tract several times. (*Toleration Discuss'd* was rewritten in 1670 and the only references to Milton appear on pp. 64–65.) The continuing debate over censorship brought forth *A Seasonable Memorial in Some Historical Notes Upon the Liberties of the Press and Pulpit* in 1680, which shows awareness of Milton's position in *Areop*. The debate involved religious questions, and L'Estrange printed passages that he considered seditious in

*The Dissenters Sayings* (1681), in answer to the anonymous *L'Estrange's Sayings.* This evoked *The Assenters Sayings by an Indifferent Hand* (1681); in turn L'Estrange published *The Dissenters Sayings: Second Part* (1681), which reappears with the former as *The Dissenters Sayings, Two Parts in One* (1685). Milton is cited in the first on p. 31, in the second on pp. 47, 74–75, and in the combined version on pp. 25, 35, 38, and 53.

To reward his work for the royal cause, L'Estrange was appointed surveyor of the printing presses on August 15, 1663. He replaced his predecessor, Sir John Birkenhead's news sheet, *The Kingdom's Intelligencer,* with *The Intelligencer Published for the Satisfaction and Information of the People,* published on Mondays, and *The News,* published on Thursdays. *The Intelligencer* became *The Publick Intelligencer* on November 28, 1666. In his capacity as licenser, he approved Milton's *Epistol* in 1674, Edward Phillips' *Theatrum Poetarum* in 1675, and John Dryden's\* *The State of Innocence* in 1677, as well as Andrew Marvell's\* *The Rehearsal Transpros'd* in 1672. A pamphlet generally attributed to him contributed to the controversy and attack upon Marvell that followed the publication of the latter work: *A Commonplace-Book out of The Rehearsal Transpros'd* (1673), which refers to Milton's *Accedence Commenc't Grammar* on pp. 35–36.

The problem of the succession and the Popish plot also called forth various pamphlets from L'Estrange, who, as would be expected, took an accepted line arguing for the often shifting position favoring the king. At times he defends James and his alleged Roman Catholicism. *The Reformed Catholique, or, The True Protestant* (1679) refers to Milton on pp. 16–17; *A Further Discovery of the Plot: Dedicated to Dr. Titus Oates* (1680), on pp. 26–27; and *L'Estranges Narrative of the Plot* (1680), on pp. 6–7. In all these allusions L'Estrange shows his opposition to Milton's views and works and

shows no hesitation in accepting rumors about Milton's duplicity concerning his religious beliefs. He may have been associated with Thomas Flatman in the news sheet *Heraclitus Ridens, or a Discourse Between Jest and Earnest, Where many a true word is pleasantly spoken in opposition to Libellers against the Government* (1681–82; rptd. 1713 in 2 vols.). In no. 67 (May 9, 1682) Milton is called "that grand Whig," and no. 10 (April 4, 1681) discusses *LP.* His own periodical, *The Observator, In Question and Answer* (changed to *The Observator in Dialogue* on July 6, 1681, and to just *The Observator* on March 18, 1682) was issued three or four times a week, and posed a Tory against a Whig to rebut the latter's view of the political situation—the succession, censorship, Roman Catholicism, dissenters, and so on. Milton is alluded to eight times: nos. 133 (May 6, 1682), 190 (August 16), 208 (September 20), 283 (February 3, 1683), 292 (February 19), 317 (April 11), 382 (August 1), and 457 (December 17). The periodical was reissued in one volume in 1687, prefaced by "A Brief History of the Times," which dealt with the exposure of Oates's Popish plot. *The Observator* provoked a number of parodies.

L'Estrange continued his pamphleteering until the Revolution, siding with the Jacobite position. He was committed to prison on December 16, 1688, for his hostility to William of Orange, having been deprived of his licensing post shortly before. He was ridiculed by Thomas Brown for his political and religious positions in *Heraclitus Ridens Redivivus, or a Dialogue between Harry and Roger Concerning the Times* (1688). Prior to his fall, however, L'Estrange became one of the subscribers to the important fourth edition of *PL* in 1688. In later years he wrote or translated books on Aesop, Flavius Josephus, Seneca, Terence, Spanish literature, *Hudibras,* and others. Earlier he had also produced some verse, semi-fictional "letters," and other translations. [JTS]

## LETTER TO A FRIEND, CONCERNING THE RUPTURES OF THE COMMONWEALTH, A.

A letter (dated October 20, 1659) to an unknown friend obviously important in the government (most likely Sir Philip Meadows* or Sir Henry Vane*, but perhaps Bulstrode Whitelock* or Gualter Frost), this brief work deals with the recent dissolution of the Rump Parliament by John Lambert (October 13, 1659). Milton, afraid of Lambert's political ambitions, and fearing that England was falling into anarchy, expresses shock that the army that restored the Rump is now guilty of "backsliding." Instead, he states that both army and Parliament are needed; they should work "not to desert one another until death." The letter was first published in *A Complete Collection* (1698), 1 : 779–81, and is transcribed in the Columbia MS, pp. 21–23. [WM]

## LETTER TO AN UNKNOWN FRIEND, A.

In *TM,* pp. 6 and 7, are two drafts of a letter concerned with Milton's current lack of accomplishment and position in the public eye and defending his "studious retirement." The first draft includes a copy of *Sonn* 7, "How soon hath time." Of first importance is the date of the letter, for the unknown addressee, the occasion and context, and even the meaning may depend on its date. There are two datings offered : one, the more traditional and more usually cited, is somewhere around 1633; the other, apparently not generally accepted, is around September 1637.

Argument for ca. 1633 rests 1) on its position in *TM,* that is, after *Arc* and *SolMus* and before *Time* and *Circum;* 2) on the date of *Sonn* 7; and 3) on the suggested meaning and context. Since *L'Al* and *IlP* (dated 1631) do not appear in *TM* and *Arc* (before *Mask,* 1634) does, and since *Sonn* 7 is a transcription at some time after its composition (December 1632, or more traditionally 1631), the manuscript and thus the letter would seem to date ca. 1633. In addition it was written during the studious retirement

that began ca. July 1632. The recent dating of *Arc* in 1634 accordingly alters these dates to ca. 1634. The letter is addressed to an old friend and adviser who had rebuked Milton for his failure to enter the ministry for which he had been educated. This dating has led to the inference that a clerical career for Milton is still probable; no view of a different career, for example one in poetic writing, is seen. The circumstances, as summarized by Parker (*Milton*), would appear to involve Milton's meeting this friend, perhaps by chance, while visiting in London, returning to Hammersmith*, and writing the letter to justify his not having entered the ministry immediately and his attention to private study. The friend has been suggested as Thomas Young*, Milton's former tutor, or John Lawson, rector of All Hallows, Bread Street.

Argument for ca. September 1637 rests 1) on dating the first use of *TM* at this time; 2) on the possible interpretation of some phrases in the letter; and 3) on the suggested meaning and context. The basic transcription of *Mask* in *TM* employs the Italian *e* (*see* HANDWRITING, MILTON's) and *Arc* is a transcription; thus autumn 1637 is suggested for the first use of the manuscript and the presence of *Arc* (and other poems) does not require an earlier date. In the first draft Milton introduces the sonnet with the words, "some of my nightward thoughts," to which he added as an afterthought, "some while since." The second draft continues with the clause, "wch I told you of" (apparently the day before). Parker remarked that "it would have been most impertinent if Milton had sent him a sonnet written a long time before" (p. 786), yet "some while since"—an afterthought perhaps inserted because age is mentioned—is susceptible to an interpretation of more than only a few months, perhaps five years. Milton also wrote that his admonisher said that he has given himself up "to dreame away my yeares." The phrase seems preteritive in the letter rather than futural. In the first draft Milton wrote "to give you account . . . of my tardie moving" and in the second it became "to give you account . . . of this my tardie moving." "Moving" could imply that he was finally "moving" and the demonstrative "this" makes that interpretation even clearer. In 1633/34 he was not moving out of his studious retirement, but in the autumn of 1637 he was, as witness a well-known letter to Charles Diodati* in November. Thus the later date implies a different meaning and context for the letter. Along with his comment that he would "deale worse wth a whole congregation, & spoyle all the patience of a Parish," the date suggests that a clerical career has been rejected and that Milton has some purpose in his studious retirement beyond "meere love of learning"; otherwise, he says, it "could not have held out thus long against so strong opposition on the other side of every kind." "Thus long" does not seem like the year or so from his July 1632 graduation to sometime in 1633/34. That his end has become a poetic career is suggested first by the reference to the appropriateness of sending a sonnet, his nightward thoughts, which "come in fitly, made up in a Petrarchan stanza." (Draft two says : "because they com in not altogether unfitly made up in a Petrarchan stanza.") Second, Milton's noting the "desire of honour & repute & immortall fame . . . of every true scholar wch all make hast to by the readiest ways of publishing & divulging conceived merits as well those that shall as those that never shall obtaine it" implies an interest in writing. His lack of publishing to that date (only *Shak* in the Second Folio of 1632) is explained by the foregoing comment. Thomas Young* seems less likely as the recipient of the letter under this interpretation and date. In any case, this dating emphasizes Milton's "this my tardie moving" rather than a rebuttal of a rebuke for failure to enter the ministry.

In all, the date of the letter is an open question, and its meaning and context depend on its dating. It is a crucial question, however, for on its answer rests how one views Milton's life, career, and ambitions during the transitional period of 1632–1638.

The letter was first published in both drafts by Thomas Birch* in his biography of Milton appearing in volume 7 of *A General Dictionary, Historical and Critical: In which a New and Accurate Translation of That of the Celebrated Mr. Bayle, with the Corrections and Observations Printed in the Late Edition at Paris, Is Included* (London : James Bettenham, for G. Strahan et al., 1738), ed. John Peter Bernard, Thomas Birch, John Lockman, and other hands. See pp. 575–88, which also contain the first printing of the plans and subjects for a drama in *TM*. (Parker [*Milton*, p. 669], in error, refers to Richard Baron's revision of Birch's edition to the prose works in 1753 as the first printing.) [JTS]

**LETTERS, FAMILIAR:** *see* EPISTOLARUM FAMILIARIUM.

**LEUNCLAVIS, JOHANN** (1533–1593), German linguist and historian, author of *Ius Graeco-Romanum*. Milton quoted this work in *CB* from the Frankfurt 1596 edition on the subjects of "Marriage," "Divorce" (twice), and "King." In *Tetra* (4 :196), Milton quotes Matthaeus Monachus"—Matthew* Paris (d. 1259), author of *Chronica Maiora* and *Historia Anglorum*—from Leunclavis as an authority on how the Greeks understood the marriage* relationship. Indeed, any references to Matthew in Milton's writing probably derive from this secondary source. [WBH]

**LEVELLERS:** *see* HISTORY OF THE TIMES; LILBURNE, JOHN.

**LEVIATHAN.** In associating Leviathan and Satan in *PL* 1. 201, Milton used a commonplace symbol popular with biblical commentators such as Saint Gregory the Great. Commentators generally identified Leviathan with the whale, less frequently with the crocodile. The "Westminster Assembly's" *Annotations* in 1645 and 1651 said that because of its huge size, the creature must be multiple rather than single, and thus derived the term from Hebrew words for *couple* and *serpent*, or *dragon*—the sense used by Hobbes* for his *Leviathan*. More modern commentators say that the term derives from Hebrew or Arabic words for *wreath* or *twist*. In any case, the term was quite common in folklore and in Hebrew poetry, referring to an aquatic creature of enormous size, such as the one Sinbad the Sailor mistook for an island. This is the way Milton uses it in *PL* 7. 412, referring to the "Hugest of living Creatures" that "seems a moving Land." In *PL* 1. 201, however, he exploits connotations of evil acquired from Isaiah 27 : 1, "the piercing serpent . . . that crooked serpent," and of pride from Job 41 : 34, "he is a king over all the children of pride." [PMZ]

**LEWIS, C(LIVE) S(TAPLES)** (1898–1963), critic who, after earning his degree at Oxford University, taught there at Magdalene College until 1954, when he moved to Magdalene College at Cambridge. His important *Allegory of Love* (Oxford, 1936) is a standard study of courtly love as it existed in the literature of the Middle Ages and into the Renaissance. Not entirely successful is his *English Literature in the Sixteenth Century* (1954), one of the Oxford historical series. In the 1950s he published a number of children's books, but his largest group of readers bought and argued about his various discussions of the vitality of Christianity in the twentieth century, a cause in which he became one of its most notable lay apologists. His *Screwtape Letters* (1942) is his best-known work, fictional letters sent from a serious neophyte in evil to his master in hell. In Milton studies Lewis delivered an important series of lectures published as *A Preface to Paradise Lost* (1942), a temperate defense of the poem against its detractors that asserted Milton's essentially Christian orthodoxy. The book is especially important in that it places Milton's poem in a living twentieth-century religious context. [WBH]

**LEY, LADY MARGARET.** Daughter of James Ley, Earl of Marlborough, Lady Margaret became the wife of John Hobson on December 30, 1641. Edward Phillips mentions that Milton often visited the couple when they were his neighbors on Aldersgate Street (where they moved after their marriage) when the poet was "a single man again," and especially liked Lady Margaret, "a Woman of great Wit and Ingenuity, [who] had a particular Honour for him, and took much delight in his Company." The poet addressed *Sonn* 10 to her, praising both Lady Margaret and her father. The date is uncertain. Parker argues that for Milton to address her as "Lady" suggests a date before her marriage, but the poem's position in *TM* suggests a date sometime after November 1642; however, the poem was copied into the manuscript and not composed there. [WM]

**LIBERTY.** Milton's famous division of liberty into the three species of "ecclesiastical, domestic or private, and civil" (*2Def* 8 : 131) is in many respects misleading. The distinctions are not clear; they are incomplete even by 1654 and blurred chronologically, as Parker points out (*Milton*, 1 : 439). They do not adequately suggest either the breadth or complexity of Milton's thoughts on liberty, much less their refinements during his later years. Nonetheless, they reveal that in retrospect, at least, Milton saw his early works as a coherent defense of liberty, a defense he expanded during the 1650s, systematized in *CD*, and later dramatized in the three great poems.

The early attacks on temporal tyranny reflect at once Milton's hatred of spiritual thraldom, for in his scheme of things, "every bad man, according to his proportion, is a tyrant," a slave to vice who calls down upon his head a corresponding physical servitude (*2Def* 8 : 27). At the same time Milton understood that true liberty—which originates in virtue—cannot thrive under physical enslavement, nor can schemes for assuring liberation succeed where more modest tyrannies are permitted. It is to little purpose, he says, for a man "to make a noise about liberty in the legislative assemblies and in the courts of justice, who is in bondage to an inferior at home" (*2Def* 8 : 133). What the early tracts and pamphlets examine are precisely these kinds of "external" slaveries. Although there circulates in them what one commentator has called Milton's "supreme principle—namely, that real freedom could be found only within the bounds of moral law," even that principle "did not make him contend less strenuously for the inferior freedom which consists in liberation from arbitrary interferences with self-development" (William Morison, *Milton and Liberty* [1909], p. 64).

In the antiprelatical tracts of 1641–42 Milton assumes the role of liberator, his task being to "vindicate the spotlesse *Truth* from an ignominious bondage" (*Ref* 3 : 10). Custom and error have enslaved men for too long. The "Tyrannical crew" of prelates has hindered reformation by scorning reason, adopting licentiousness, and making the church a handmaid to civil affairs. Unable to discipline themselves, they have hypocritically enchained others by setting conformity at odds with conscience. In short, they have been "confiscating from us all the right we have to our owne bodies, goods and liberties" (3 : 57). By establishing a "Church-tyranny" (*RCG* 3 : 243) the prelates have also thwarted the end of liberty, which is devout worship of God. As Milton will argue later, "we are still enslaved, not indeed, as formerly, under the divine law, but, what is worst of all, under the law of man, or to speak more truly, under a barbarous tyranny" (*CD* 15 : 13). Prelacy is an "everlasting slavery," then, not only because it endeavors "to repeal and erase every line and clause of both our great charters" (*RCG* 3 : 270–71) but also because it spreads spiritual darkness. Here Milton strongly unites truth with liberty, falsehood with slavery, arguing that "The service of God who is Truth, her Liturgy confesses to be perfect freedom, but her works and her opinions declare that the service of Prelaty is perfect slavery, and by con-

sequence perfect falshood" (3 : 272). It is imperative, therefore, that truth be spoken : "For the property of Truth is, where she is publickly taught, to unyoke & set free the minds and spirits of a Nation first from the thraldom of sin and superstition, after which all honest and legal freedom of civil life cannot be long absent" (ibid.).

*Educ* and the divorce* tracts continue the attack on custom and error. Nothing militates against freedom more than domestic servitude, be it marital or academic. The educative method, particularly, is sterile, impractical, and aimless. Milton felt that education should in part fit a young man for all the offices of peace and war*, both private and public. This, at least, was one aim of "a compleat and generous Education" (*Educ* 4 : 280). The other was far more important: "to repair the ruines of our first Parents by regaining to know God aright, and out of that knowledge to love him, to imitate him, to be like him, as we may the neerest by possessing our souls of true vertue, which being united to the heavenly grace of faith makes up the highest perfection" (4 : 277). What Milton proposes is to free the student not simply from rigorous pedantry but from fear of knowledge itself. There is no excluding either the spiritual or secular planes of knowledge, the classical or Christian; all are brought together in his comprehensive scheme, the end of which is "the renewal of the unconstraining laws of virtue, and the achievement through obedience to them of both human dignity and Christian liberty" (Arthur E. Barker, *Milton and the Puritan Dilemma, 1641–1660* [1942], pp. 119–20). Remembering that "to form and increase virtue, the most excellent thing is liberty," it is clear that education cannot coexist with constraint (*2Def* 8 : 237). Also, it is itself a kind of liberty since it reforms man by teaching him temperance, justice, wisdom, bravery, and the like; to possess these virtues is to be free, "so, to be the opposite of these, is the same thing as to be a slave" (8 : 251).

In Milton's educative method the

student moves from nature to man, from assimilation to creation, from the outer to the inner. Similarly, without demeaning the physical part of marriage*, Milton turned to its other aspect. The aim of marriage, he felt, was not pro-creation, but "in Gods intention a meet and happy conversation" (*DDD* 3 : 391). Where unfitness, indisposition, or con-trariety of mind immutably bar such converse there is not, properly speaking, a "marriage" at all.

Milton's argument against "discon-solate household captivity" (*DDD* 3 : 381) speaks with irresistible reason. *Servility, bondage, unmerciful restraint, adamantine chains*—terms such as these define the cruelty of undesired wedlock. Marital tyranny also violates reason*, that spark which, even in fallen man, signifies his divine origin :

He who marries, intends as little to con-spire his own ruine, as he that swears Allegiance : and as a whole people is in proportion to an ill Government, so is one man to an ill mariage. If they against any authority, Covnant, or Statute, may by the soveraign edict of charity, save not only their lives, but honest liberties from un-worthy bondage, as well may he against any private Covnant, which hee never enter'd to his mischief, redeem himself from unsupportable disturbances to honest peace, and just contentment. (3:374)

It is unreasonable to make covenants permanent, since they are agreements subject to present affairs (a favorite Miltonic theme). Additionally, marital bondage demeans man by depressing his "high and Heaven-born spirit" (3 : 368), just as the prelates, by rigidly splitting clergy from laity, "have . . . made profane that nature which God hath not only cleans'd, but Christ also hath assum'd" (*RCG* 3 : 263). Whatever Adam's sin, man is still an image of God, his state one of natural freedom. Next, argues Milton, charity urges commiseration for the help-less. This does not mean condoning license and levity, but showing "some conscionable and tender pitty" for those "who have unwarily in a thing they never

practiz'd before, made themselves the bondmen of a luckles and helples mat-rimony" (*DDD* 3 : 385). As if realizing how little conscience prevails, Milton adds a final, prudential argument : even nature teaches that there can be no "fouler in-congruity . . . then to force a mixture of minds that cannot unite" (3 : 417). Mis-coupling, or *antipathia*, violates nature— the "sympathy or naturall order" of things (3.419)—and so must be broken. If it is not, if we endeavor "to stop every vent and cranny of permissive liberty," nature will assuredly rebel, "wanting those need-full pores, and breathing places which God hath not debar'd our weaknesse." The result then will likely be "some wide rupture of open vice, and frantick heresie" or else an inward, blasphemous festering "under an unreasonable and fruitless rigor of unwarranted law" (3 : 509–10; cf. p. 373).

To summarize briefly Milton's devel-oping thoughts on liberty : (a) without physical freedom man enjoys no higher, inner liberty, (b) that higher liberty is possible only for the virtuous, since a slave to vice holds himself in bondage, (c) liberty serves only truth, never custom or error, no matter what authority seeks to constrain it, (d) conscience and reason guide the virtuous man in exercising free choice, (e) liberty and human dignity are God-given, hence natural to man, (f) free-dom is essential to the progress of reformation, and (g) liberty is an expres-sion of Christian charity. In *Areop* these thoughts are set down again, but of particular concern here is Milton's demand for moral choice, especially in matters of knowledge. It is a development crucial to his mature concept of liberty.

The boundary between domestic and civil liberty is crossed at the beginning of *Areop* when Milton remarks : "this is not the liberty which wee can hope, that no grievance ever should arise in the Com-monwealth, that let no man in this World expect; but when complaints are freely heard, deeply consider'd, and speedily reform'd, then is the utmost bound of civill liberty attain'd, that wise men looke for" (*Areop* 4 : 293). Without the liberty of unlicensed printing, he adds, truth will be silenced, learning discouraged, and further discoveries "in religious and civill Wisdome" prevented (4 : 297). Milton's appeal, basically, is to allow unlicensed knowledge. A "free and knowing spirit" is by nature unconstrained (4 : 324); moreover, knowledge in itself does no harm "if the will and conscience be not defil'd" (4 : 308). From these assertions Milton moves easily to a synthesis of morality, free choice, and knowledge, arguing that virtue (which assures freedom) demands knowledge of vice, hence the liberty to read what one chooses. To be innocent in this world is one thing; to know evil* and still choose good is quite another : "He that can apprehend and consider vice with all her baits and seeming pleasures, and yet abstain, and yet distinguish, and yet prefer that which is truly better, he is the true wayfaring Christian. I cannot praise a fugitive and cloister'd vertue, unexercis'd & unbreath'd" (*Areop* 4 : 311). Since God trusts man with "the gift of reason to be his own chooser" (4 : 310) it follows that reasonable choice is possible for any man, an idea stated by Adam when he tells Eve that "God left free the Will, for what obeyes / Reason, is free, and Reason he made right" (*PL* 9. 351–52). Here Milton asserts a major premise of his religious* thinking—that man is a free agent, granted liberty by God and sufficient strength to choose a virtuous life. In *CD* Milton will insist that without liberty to choose, man is a shallow, conforming creature—orthodox, but not devout. In *Areop* he states the same point forthrightly : "A man may be a heretick in the truth; and if he beleeve things only because his Pastor sayes so, or the Assembly so determins, without knowing other reason, though his belief be true, yet the very truth he holds, becomes his heresie" (*Areop* 4 : 333). In the same way, government can regulate what people read, but this serves only to regiment manners. Unnecessary strictures force obedience and servility but do not make

us a whit more virtuous. "Banish all objects of lust," declares Milton, "shut up all youth into the severest discipline that can be exercis'd in any hermitage, ye cannot make them chaste, that came not thither so" (4 : 319). *See also* LICENSING.

At no time, however, did Milton advocate complete nondiscipline. From his earliest pronouncements on liberty he clearly understood the need for some regulation. *Ref* connects vice and servitude as follows : "when the people slacken, and fall to loosenes, and riot, then doe they as much as if they laid downe their necks for some wily Tyrant to get up and ride" (*Ref* 3 : 53). In *RCG* stricture is urged in another fashion : "there is not that thing in the world of more grave and urgent importance throughout the whole life of man, then is discipline" (*RCG* 3 : 184). In the divorce tracts Milton everywhere insists that freedom of divorce is thoroughly distinct from capricious abandonment. In other words, while Milton defended individual rights, he fully understood the temptation of individual anarchy. To understand liberty, then, he thought it imperative that man discern accurately its bounds, and neither shrink nor expand them.

> I will utter now a doctrine, if ever any other, though neglected or not understood, yet of great and powerfull importance to the governing of mankind. He who wisely would restrain the reasonable Soul of man within due bounds, must first himself know perfectly, how far the territory and dominion extends of just and honest liberty. As little must he offer to bind that which God hath loos'n'd, as to loos'n that which he hath bound. (*DDD* 3 : 373)

In the 1640s Milton still has faith that man can act freely and well, for "honest liberty is the greatest foe to dishonest licence" (*DDD* 3 : 370). As domestic and civil liberties give way in later years to more active political championing, that faith will largely fail Milton. On one point, however, he remained unshakable to the end : if bad men abuse honest liberty the answer is not to remove all freedom. There are always "bad causes would take licence by this pretext [specifically, divorce, but by implication any limited freedom], if that cannot be remedied, upon their conscience be it, who shall so doe" (*DDD* 3 : 493).

The subject of liberty and license takes us straight to the complexities of Milton's theory of liberty. History, for Milton, was largely definable in terms of human freedom : "the story of liberty began with Adam and its failure with the Fall of man" (George Williamson, *Modern Philology* 60 : 18). Adam failed to obey the command not to eat from the tree of knowledge, but then it was God, not some corrupt earthly ruler, who demanded obedience*. What does one do when conscience urges him to defy his king? If virtue (and therefore liberty) demands constraint, who fixes the limits? Is one authority higher than another; is conscience a dependable guide in ethical* decisions; given his fallen state is man's reason able to direct him? These and a score of similar questions force Milton's theory into the arena of practical application by emphasizing the conflict between individual or Christian liberty on the one hand and political obedience on the other.

Oddly enough, the subject of Christian liberty was neglected by Milton scholars until A. S. P. Woodhouse touched upon it in *University of Toronto Quarterly* 4 : 395–404, and developed it more fully in ibid., 4 : 483–513. Since then it has been treated by several Miltonists, notably Arthur E. Barker in *Modern Language Review* 35 : 153–61, and in *Milton and the Puritan Dilemma;* and William Haller in *Liberty and Reformation in the Puritan Revolution* (1955).

Woodhouse provides a good summary of the tenets of Christian liberty. The doctrine, largely grounded on St. Paul, became prominent in the Reformation revival of Pauline theology and was given its orthodox formulation by Luther* and Calvin*. At its center lay the idea that Christian liberty frees man from the condemnation of the Mosaic Law through faith* in Christ. "Under the Gospel," says Woodhouse, "believers are raised to

the status of sons, joint heirs with Christ, priests (as Luther asserts) and kings. Freed from the oppression of the law, they voluntarily obey the will of God, substituting an ideal of love, faith, and free activity for meticulous conformity to a complicated code, largely prohibitory in character—the spirit for the mere letter. Thus they enter into Christian liberty." At the simplest level this theory lent considerable force to Milton's defense of individual conscience and religious toleration. Since no man, he felt, can judge definitively the sense of Scripture to another, one cannot be forced to believe articles of faith contrary to his conscience. So far Milton's theory of liberty follows a natural course from hatred of prelatical authority to the defense of free knowledge to the setting right of terms such as *heresy* and *schism*. Because constant, open debate encourages contrary opinions, dissenting Protestant sects should not be persecuted for following sincere personal dictates, even though they err. (Roman Catholicism is rigidly excepted as no religion at all, but a "Roman principalitie" that has forfeited Christian liberty through "voluntarie servitude to mans law" [*CivP* 6 : 19]).

At a more complicated level, Christian liberty conflicts with political authority. Woodhouse has reminded us that for the seventeenth century as a whole, and for Milton in particular, "the two issues of religious and civil liberty are inextricably connected." *2Def* makes this connection abundantly clear. Real and substantial liberty—whether in the individual or the state—"is to be sought for not from without, but within" (*2Def* 8 : 131). As the truly free man is liberated through self-regulation and virtue, so the truly free state enjoys internal as well as external harmony :

> And as for you, citizens, it is of no small concern, what matter of men ye are whether to acquire, or to keep possession of your liberty. Unless your liberty be of that kind, which can neither be gotten, nor taken away by arms; and that alone is such, which, springing from piety, justice,

temperance, in fine, from real virtue, shall take deep and intimate root in your minds; you may be assured, there will not be wanting one, who . . . will speedily deprive you of what it is your boast to have gained by force of arms. . . . If, after putting an end to the war, you neglect the arts of peace . . . what you think liberty will prove to be your slavery. (8:239, 241)

Here is perhaps Milton's fundamental tenet of liberty : true freedom is internal and individual, the product of self-governing virtue. But problems clearly arise in the social realm, for few men, unfortunately, are "virtuous" in Milton's broad sense of the term. In fact, his strong Independency* during his later years led to the belief that only the regenerate are truly free, that only a small number of men choose the liberty that is available to all. Thus the regenerate constitute a virtuous minority that is not about to be enslaved by a sinful majority. Beginning with the premise that in virtue there is freedom, Milton made it "a consistent and fundamental part of [his] political philosophy that the more virtuous should govern the less virtuous" (Don M. Wolfe, *Studies in Philology* 33 : 266). Consequently, it was inevitable that he moved toward a providential and finally theocratic conception of the state. (See Ernest Sirluck, *Modern Philology* 61: 209–24, for an analysis of this movement.) So long as the regenerate found their aims consistent with those of the majority, "liberty" could easily be defended by right reason and nature's law. But as Woodhouse shows, Christian liberty spread beyond matters of individual conscience to embrace active rebellion, power through the rule of saints, and a revival of Antinomianism. It was inevitable that by 1660 the interests of the regenerate were no longer those of the general populace.

At its most complicated level, Christian liberty is expressed in the majestic paradoxes of Milton's three great poems. And it is here as well that Milton's theory of liberty is given perhaps its most coherent and persuasive utterance.

In *PL*, Satan's willful disobedience* is at once his surrender of freedom. God's "indulgent Laws" (*PL* 5.883) are a base servitude to him, and in his licentious eyes God's reign is an unjust "Tyranny of Heav'n" (*PL* 1.124). Thus Satan's rebellion is a mockery of lawful overthrow. What he seeks is not freedom but slavery, not true liberty but license. Throughout the poem Milton continues to weave a complicated pattern of inverted values : Satan sees good as evil, obedience as degradation, true liberty as servile captivity. At the same time the early scenes in hell develop an elaborate paradox involving internal and external liberty. Hell, Milton's symbol of imprisonment, is a "dungeon" complete with "Adamantine Chains" (*PL* 1.61, 48) that bind the fallen angels*. It is not they who break the bonds, however; God frees them so that, ironically, they may enslave themselves still further. Satan's "unconquerable Will" (*PL* 1.106) serves, therefore, to underscore his paradoxical situation : his is a will beyond virtue, reason, and obedience, hence his enthrallment, no matter what seemingly heroic feats he performs. So, too, his boast to Beelzebub —"Here at least / We shall be free" (*PL* 1.258–59)—furthers the irony of his plight. If "The mind is its own place, and in it self / Can make a Heav'n of Hell, a Hell of Heav'n" (*PL* 1.254–55), there is no escaping bondage to evil: "Which way I flie is Hell; my self am Hell" (*PL* 4.75). This is the point brought sharply into focus during the infernal debate. Moloch urges war (physical liberation); Belial counsels patient servitude (physical bondage); Mammon rejects "splendid vassalage" and "the easie yoke / Of servile Pomp" (*PL* 2.252, 256–57) in favor of "Hard liberty" (*PL* 2.256). Only Beelzebub and his prompter, Satan, understand how firmly God keeps "In strictest bondage . . . His captive multitude (*PL* 2.321, 323). Although the debate concerns liberty, the fallen angels are manifestly unable to comprehend the subject in other than physical terms. As they turn to higher thoughts "Of Providence, Foreknowledge, Will and Fate, / Fixt Fate, free will, foreknowledg absolute" (*PL* 2. 559–60) they find themselves "in wandring mazes lost" (*PL* 2. 561).

From the muddle of demonic debate Milton moves to heavenly discourse wherein God makes clear the nature of true liberty. It is a divine gift; an act of faith and love; an expression of free will*. Most important, it has certain bounds, which God fixes and the self-governing man obeys. In *PR* Milton makes it plain that self-restraint brings liberty to the social as well as individual man. A "true King," he who respects the rights of others, necessarily "reigns within himself, and rules / Passions, Desires, and Fears" (*PR* 2. 466–67). Such a man for Milton was Cromwell*, "A commander first over himself, the conqueror of himself, it was over himself he had learnt most to triumph" (*2Def* 8 : 215). But Milton was wary of power and so he cautions Cromwell to regard his spiritual liberty with care : "respect yourself," he says, "and suffer not that liberty, which you have gained with so many hardships, so many dangers, to be violated by yourself" (8 : 227). When passion prevails the true tyrant is born : "Subject himself to Anarchy within, / Or lawless passions in him which he serves" (*PR* 2. 471–72).

For Milton, human history began with the war between self-governance and self-anarchy. Possessed of reason, Adam was free to choose. Usurped by passion, he fell slave to Eve. Despite Raphael's advice on temperance and his admonition about "attributing overmuch to things / Less excellent" (*PL* 8. 565–66) Adam resolves to die with Eve, a sign that passion has overthrown reason. Fittingly, he finds himself in bondage to Eve, their natural order of authority reversed precisely as they have reversed their relationship to God. Together, they are "both in subjection now / To sensual Appetite, who from beneathe / Usurping over sovran Reason claim'd / Superior sway" (*PL* 9. 1128–31). In several respects this pattern is repeated in *SA*. The covenant between God and Samson is broken when the Nazarite, "O'recome with importunity and tears," allows Dalila to rule him

(*SA* 51). The extraordinary opening of *SA* with its emphasis on physical states —the pain, the blindness, the bondage at the mill—points paradoxically to Samson's more acute torment—the spiritual pain, the blindness both to Dalila's treachery and God's love, the bondage to a woman. It is more than fitting that Samson's punishment is the physical equivalent of his moral sin : "Put to the labour of a Beast, debas't / Lower then bondslave !" (*SA* 37–38). At the time he realizes himself that "true" slavery is not his yoke at Gaza but his choice of Dalila over God :

The base degree to which I now am fall'n,
These rags, this grinding, is not yet so base
As was my former servitude, ignoble,
Unmanly, ignominious, infamous,
True slavery, and that blindness worse then
    this,
That saw not how degeneratly I serv'd.
(*SA* 414–19)

Taken together, *PL* and *SA* dramatize Milton's theme that he who would rule others must first rule himself. As Israel's promised Deliverer, Samson's self-chosen bondage extends to his people : lacking self-governance, he enslaves a nation. Similarly, Adam's sin* bears upon his progeny, though here there is no second chance, no retemptation by Eve, no challenge from Satan's (or Dagon's) champion. What *PR* offers, then, is man's Deliverer—Christ, who restores liberty to man by supplanting Adam "and by vanquishing / Temptation" (*PR* 4. 607–8). This is the Christian liberty that Milton defends as man's right. Heaven-sent, the freely given gift of "one greater Man" (*PL* 1. 4), it was for Milton the very foundation of all liberties, the right of whoever believed and continued in the faith, the path to a virtuous life and a love of God. [DBC]

**LIBRARY, MILTON'S.** It is common knowledge that young John Milton's inbred love of learning and his thirst for knowledge were so great and his health so delicate that his parents had to ration his study time. Although no one knows the extent of his father's library, we may presume that the variety and scope of his home resources were relatively limited. Donald L. Clark has investigated the books available to Milton at St. Paul's School*. He certainly read even more widely when he moved to Cambridge. The polished rhetoric* of his *Prolusions* delivered there reflects a strong reading background in the Graeco-Roman and Judeo-Christian traditions and in the literary traditions of his native tongue. Following his formal education at Cambridge, Milton retired to the family home in Hammersmith* and then Horton* to read his way through a systematic program of independent study. In order to do this, he obviously had to have a plentiful supply of books. Fortunately he had an indulgent, rich father who could supply the leisure and the library; we may plausibly conjecture, in addition, that many books passed back and forth between sympathetic friends and neighbors and that he made occasional trips to nearby Oxford to acquire new reading material. In a letter to Charles Diodati*, dated November 23, 1637, he specifically asked Diodati to send him a copy of Bernardo Guistiniani's *De origine Urbis Venetiarum Rebusque ab Ipsa Gestis Historia*.

After his sojourn at Horton, Milton undertook a trip to the Continent, where he impressed nearly everyone with his charm, good looks, and sensible conversation laced with wit, his depth and breadth of learning, and his remarkable familiarity with the life and literature of his hosts. The aging Manso* in Naples presented him with gifts of books, probably autographed copies of his own works, possibly rare editions of their mutual idol, Tasso*. Nor did he neglect the opportunities to flesh out his library with book bargains readily available in Italy. In Venice, where volumes were especially plentiful because of the local printing industry, he packed up his purchases and shipped them home by sea while he returned by way of Geneva.

It seems reasonable to assume that while Milton could read for himself he continued to buy books as the spirit moved him. After his blindness*, however, he more than likely cut down on such expense, although we are told by various biographers* that he kept up with the world of books by having someone read to him regularly. Indeed, it was this onerous duty that grated most harshly on his daughters and allegedly caused their disaffection. Part of their unhappiness seems to have been rooted in money matters, for Elizabeth Fisher* testified during the probate of Milton's will* that they stole books from their blind father and sold them to the women of Dunghill. Perhaps Milton himself gave many of his books as mementoes to old friends and admirers who had paid their respects to him; perhaps he cautioned his widow to be chary of dealers and charlatans who would deprecate their value; indubitably he kept by his side well-thumbed old favorites to distract the mind when the miseries of the gout* became too acute or the tedium of eternal darkness grew oppressive. Had he had fewer books, he might have parceled them out individually to friends in his will, as did Ben Jonson* and John Donne; or, if his sight had continued, he might have left shelf lists, as did John Locke. Obviously, however, books were an important element in his life.

Of the estimated 1400-odd titles in Milton's library, sixteen have survived the ravages of time and the scrutiny of modern scholarship and are considered authentic Miltoniana. (*See* ASSOCIATION COPIES for a discussion of lost and questionable items.) Milton's Bible* (1612) is in the British Museum, as is his annotated edition of Aratus's* *Phaenomena* and *Diosemeia* (Paris, 1559). His copy of Euripides' *Tragoedia* (Geneva, 1602) is in the Bodleian Library. The Ely Cathedral Library has Chrysostom's* *Orationes LXXX* (Paris, 1604) and Sts. Polycarp and Ignatius's* *Epistolae* (Oxford, 1644). The New York Public Library has three works owned by Milton that were bound together sometime in the seventeenth century: Dante's* *L'Amoroso Convivio* (Venice, 1529), Giovanni Della Casa's* *Rime et Prose* (Venice, 1563), which is Milton's first known book purchase, and Benedetto Varchi's *I Sonetti* (Venice, 1555). The University of Illinois Library now owns Lycophron's *Alexandra* (Geneva, 1601) and Heraclides of Pontus's *Allegoriae* (Basel, 1544). John Creccelius's *Collectanea ex historijs* (Frankfurt, 1614) is in the Huntington Library; the Rosenbach Foundation Library of Philadelphia formerly had *De Bello Peloponnesiaco* of Thucydides (Basel, 1564). Harvard University owns two: Terence's *Comoediae sex* (Leyden,1635) and Jerome Commelin's* *Rerum Britannicarum . . . Scriptores Vetustiores* (Heidelberg, 1587). Two of Milton's books are privately owned: Ariosto's* *Orlando Furioso,* John Harrington's translation (1591), and Marc Antoine Muret's *Variarum Lectionum Libri XV* (Paris, 1586). All contain Milton's signature or holograph notes. [JCB]

**LICENSING.** The control of publication through official governmental approval is known as licensing. Various forms of licensing have been known in all ages, and Milton cites much of the history of such censorship in *Areop.* In England proclamations were made by Henry VIII in 1529 to reduce sedition and heresy, and in 1538 an act required licensing by the privy council or some other royal agency. Foreign books had been regulated previously in 1533. Further orders were passed in the sixteenth century, but the most important events were the granting of a charter to the Stationers' Company in 1557 and the Star Chamber ordinance in 1586, which Archbishop Whitgift promoted. The ordinance, backed up by the appointment of twelve licensers in 1588, required that all publications have an official licence, that no presses be allowed except those in London and at the Universities of Oxford and Cambridge, and that the number of presses be reduced.

*A Decree of Starre-Chamber, Concerning Printing,* passed on July 11, 1637, through the influence of Archbishop Laud*, proposed penalties for offenders and approved only certain presses, although printers* like Augustine Mathewes, who printed *Mask,* continued operations in defiance of the act. Orders from the House of Commons on January 29, 1642, known as the "Signature Order," on August 26, 1642, and on March 9, 1643, were temporary moves to reenforce licensing while a new act was being prepared. The first of these was often erroneously treated as requiring that only the signature of the printer or the author of a work be attached to a publication. Milton so viewed it in *Areop.* The new act was passed on June 14, 1643, and provided that each work be officially licensed and registered at Stationers' Hall, and that search and seizure, arrest, and punishment be pressed for offenders. It was reasserted on September 30, 1647, March 13, 1648, September 20, 1649 (to run for two years), January 7, 1653, and August 28, 1655. It was the act of 1643 that Milton was arguing against in *Areop* in November 1644. Milton opposed licensing, that is, prepublication censorship; he did not object to registration of the printer's and author's names or to punishing and suppressing mischievous or libelous authors and books after publication. That is, books should be freely published, but author and printer should be held accountable. Frequently *Areop* has been misinterpreted to mean that Milton was in favor of total liberty in matters concerning publication. Actually the restatement of the 1643 act on September 20, 1649, agreed with Milton's position, differing significantly from the earlier act. John Bradshaw's* Press Act, as it is called, ordered censorship of all newsletters only by demanding the name of the printer or author; but the order did not appoint a licenser. In effect licensing was now not required by law, although it continued. This was Milton's position, for the most part, in *Areop,* and it is possible that Milton had some influence on Bradshaw's thinking. Milton summarized the act as described above to Samuel Hartlib*, who recorded it in his diary. However, this interpretation was apparently not common, and the popular interpretation that all works were still to be licensed brought Milton afoul of the Council of State* a few years later. As *Areop* adequately proves, books were published without license, without the author's name, and without the printer's name during all the periods when licensing was supposedly in force.

There are a few allusions to *Areop* before 1679, but the only significant influence seems to have been on Gilbert Mabbott, where resignation as licenser in May 1649 reflects, without acknowledgment, Milton's arguments against licensing, and John Hall in *An Humble Motion to the Parliament of England Concerning the Advancement of Learning and Reformation of the Universities* (1649).

Milton functioned as licenser for the government from at least December 16, 1649, when he approved *Histoire entière & véritable du Procèz de Charles Stuart*. The fact that this book was in French may account for Milton's entry into licensing. He also licensed *Mercurius Politicus*, a semi-official governmental organ, from March 17, 1651 (no. 33), through January 22, 1652 (no. 85); he substituted for John Rushworth in licensing *The Perfect Diurnal,* another semi-official newsletter, on or before October 6, 1651. But he seems to have been removed from his position in 1652 as a result of having approved the Racovian Catechism*, around the end of 1651.

When the monarchy was returned a new licensing act had to be enacted. In 1662 the law forbade publication of material contrary to the doctrine and discipline of the Church of England or scandalous of Church or government. In 1663 Sir Roger L'Estrange* was appointed surveyor of printing presses, thus regulating the conduct of the book trade, as well as licenser. Milton's works published after the Restoration were licensed, and Jacob Tonson* reported in a letter written around 1732 that the only reason that the manuscript of the first book of *PL* was preserved was the license appearing on the front page. It was signed by Richard Royston, Warden of the Stationers' Company, and George Tokefield, the company's clerk, sometime before April 27, 1667. However, Brabazon Aylmer* was unable to publish the state papers in 1674 because they were not approved. The act of 1662 was in force for two years and then extended to 1679.

Not until 1685 was the act revived; it was extended then until 1694. At this time Parliament refused to renew licensing and it came to an end as an official function. In the last years of licensing various arguments were raised for or against it, and in three instances *Areop* figures in the discussions. In 1679 Charles Blount* published *A Just Vindication of Learning; or, An Humble Address to the High Court of Parliament in Behalf of the Liberty of the Press,* which is an eighteen-page adaptation of Milton's tract. In 1681 William Denton entered the controversy with *Jus Caesaris et Ecclesiae vere dictae. Or a Treatise of Independency, Presbytery, the Power of Kings, and of the Church,* which has a nine-page addendum entitled "An Apology for the Liberty of the Press," another adaptation of Milton's argument. And in 1693 Blount reused the work in *Reasons Humbly Offered for the Liberty of Unlicens'd Printing.* The former pamphlet reappears in *The Miscellaneous Works of Charles Blount, Esq.* (1695). The case against licensing in 1694 was prepared by John Locke on the basis that it had not achieved its purpose, it had not set up penalties for infractions, the licensers were often biased, and the problem of seditious publications and the like could be handled under common law. During the eighteenth century *Areop* was again significant in arguments concerning copyright law, then being devised; see, for example, Catharine Macauley [Graham], *A Modest Plea for the Property of Copy Right* (Bath, 1774). [JTS]

**LIGHT;** *see* PSYCHOLOGY, MILTON AND; METAPHYSICS

**LILBURNE, JOHN** (1614–1657), pamphleteer and political firebrand. An older brother was Robert (1613–1665), army officer and regicide, whose name appears in some of the correspondence addressed to Milton. Not a university man, John became active in disseminating Puritan tracts in the 1630s, for which he was publicly whipped and pilloried. He fought in the Civil Wars, gradually moving from the Calvinist* position to one of Independency*. His attacks upon his erstwhile allies, the Presbyterians*, led to his being jailed by Parliament, but he was freed in 1647 and now turned to a distrust of the Army and of Cromwell*, leading to another jail term after Pride's Purge. His political movement was steadily toward populism and "leveling"—toward an implied classless society. Thus he became a pamphleteer for the redressing of various economic grievances, activities for which he was banished to Holland in 1652. Upon the dissolution of the Rump in 1653 he returned (without permission) and was arrested, but in June he was acquitted, to great popular acclaim. In the last few years of his life he became a Quaker* and lived quietly in Kent. His importance then and now is his constant appeal to law and justice, the foundation of the various defense pleas forced upon him. Something of this attitude enters Milton's appeals to law and to justice in his pamphlets, especially those of the 1640s. Milton never mentions him, but he certainly was aware of his existence. The Council of State* ordered Milton to "make some observations" upon Lilburne's tract, *England's New Chains Discovered* (1649), but no printed response has been identified. In 1652 Lilburne quoted *1Def* in his *As You Were,* praising its "excellent and faithfull" advice to the Commonwealth. [WBH]

**LILY, WILLIAM:** *see* ACCEDENCE COMMENC'T GRAMMAR.

**LINGUAE ROMANAE DICTIONARIUM LUCULENTUM:** *see* CANON.

**LITERAE NOMINE SENATUS ANGLICANNI, CROMWELLII RICHARDIQUE:** *see* LITERAE PSEUDO-SENATUS ANGLICANI, CROMWELLII.

**LITERAE PSEUDO-SENATUS ANGLICANI, CROMWELLII.** Two editions of 136 state papers produced by Milton appeared in 1676. The first is identifiable by the device of a *cul-de-lampe aux fruits suspendus* on its title page ("basket of fruit" edition). This was printed by Peter and John Blaeu in Amsterdam, from a manuscript that seems to have come through Moses Pitt*, a London printer and bookseller. The manuscript may have been that prepared at the urging of the Danish Resident in London (reported by Thomas Birch* in 1738), and this may be the manuscript that Milton had planned to publish with *Epistol* before governmental intervention blocked publication. The second edition in the same year is identifiable by the advice of a *tête de Méduse* on its title page ("face" edition). This attempted to duplicate the first edition, but variations exist throughout the text. It seems to have been printed by E. H. Fricx in Brussels. The state papers included in these editions are accepted as Milton's, but additional ones have been discovered in various sources, as well as original manuscript copies or contemporary manuscript and printed copies of some of these printed papers. *See* PAPERS, STATE for a full discussion of canon, sources, and dates.

*Literae* seems to have been the source for an edition in Germany in 1690, entitled *Literae nomine Senatus Anglicani, Cromwellii Richardique,* printed by Christian Banckmann for Jo. Caspar Mayer, in Leipzig and Frankfurt. It was edited by Jo. Georg Pritius, who included an eight-page preface. Three translations into English also seem to derive from *Literae*: a loose, only approximate "translation" appeared in 1682 as *Milton's Republican-Letters,* apparently from a foreign press; Edward Phillips's version in *Letters of State* (1694) omits three items; and *Oliver Cromwell's Letters to Foreign Princes and States,* printed in London by John Nutt in 1700, offers nineteen letters in Phillips's translation, with an appendix discussing Milton's function as Secretary for Foreign Tongues* and the value of his work on the letters. On the other hand, *Literae* was not the source for certain other printings of the state letters. Gregorio Leti's *Historia, e Memorie recondite sopra alla vita di Oliviero Cromvele,* vol. 2, printed in Amsterdam by Peter and John Blaeu, gives the Latin texts of forty-nine-letters, sometimes with different dates that are both demonstrably wrong and demonstrably correct and sometimes with slightly different or more complete salutations and complimentary closes. Leti's *Life of Cromwell* was frequently printed during the seventeenth and eighteenth centuries in Italian, French, Dutch, and German, sometimes with all letters given, sometimes with only some, sometimes with the letters in Latin, sometimes in translation, and sometimes in two versions. Leti's printing seems to be the source for various incidental reprintings of a few letters, for example, in John Oldmixon's *The History of England, During the Reigns of the Royal House of Stuart* (1730). Nor was *Literae* the source for 115 state letters given in Jo. Christian Lünig's *Literae Procerum Europae* (Leipzig, 1712), three volumes, which likewise yields additional passages for some letters and variations in texts and dates. The existence of these printings of the state papers makes clear that a number of manuscripts were available, some seemingly more complete or accurate in some details than that which was published as *Literae* and construed as being derived directly from Milton's copies. [JTS]

**LITERARY CRITIC, MILTON AS.** As the term is usually understood, Milton left no formal literary criticism. His most extensive statement that might be so viewed, the Preface to *SA,* is more an explanation of the literary backgrounds

of his own play than criticism. And yet in his imitations of others and his passing references to them, a good deal of criticism is implied in many of his works.

Perhaps Milton's most famous critical or aesthetic statement is that in *Educ* (4 : 286), which holds that poetry is "more simple, sensuous, and passionate" than rhetoric*; but the comparative nature of this evaluation must not be forgotten even as Milton is clearly recognizing the emotive response that literature may elicit. The same judgment informs his only slightly less famous delineation of "the cool element of prose" (*RCG* 3 : 235), even though he produced (in *CM*) sixteen volumes in the cooler medium as compared with only two in the more passionate one. But his natural bent was toward the poetic : in prose he had "the use, as I may account it, but of my left hand" (ibid.).

One general principle seems to run through most of his critical evaluations: that literary judgments cannot be divorced from one's ethics* or religion*. Milton certainly brought such evaluations, extraneous for many modern critics, to his literary appraisals. He tried to do for his country what the classical writers had done for theirs—"with this over and above being a Christian" (*RCG* 3 : 236). His changing religious views seem to be reflected in his changing critical judgments. Thus the young Anglican praised masques in *L'Al* and *IlP* (and considered writing a major piece on Arthurian* subjects; see also his reading of romances reported in *Apol*), whereas the older Independent* decried both in *PL*; his dislike for romances appears even earlier in *Eikon* (5 : 87, 89). The Countess of Derby is praised as Queen of the Arcadians in *Arc,* but by the time of *Eikon* Sidney's *Arcadia* is judged to be "a Book . . . full of worth and witt, but among religious thoughts, and duties not worthy to be nam'd, nor to be read at any time without good caution" (5 : 86). Like others, he found models of various kinds of literature in the Scriptures : Job as a brief epic, Revelation as a tragedy*, the Psalms as lyrics (*RCG* 3 : 237f. and *PR* 4. 331ff.).

Much of Milton's criticism consists of undetailed praise of other writers—of Dante* and Petrarch* as the best writers of Italy (*Apol* 3 : 303), of Manso* as "not the least glory" of Naples (*EpDam*), of "sweet-tongued Marini*" and of the "mighty name" of Tasso* in *Mansus*, of Pindar and Callimachus in *RCG*. In his younger days he seems to have liked at least the romance elements in Chaucer*, for he invokes the spirit of the author of the *Squires Tale* in *IlP*. In *CB* he cites the *Physicians Tale* as support for the moral judgment that such activities as "feasts, and revells and daunces . . . maken children for to be too soon ripe" (18 : 154). Milton's praise of Spenser*, both direct and in imitation, is well-known, and his widow reported his high regard for Cowley*. On the other hand, he attacked Hall's* satires as "freshmens tales, and in a straine as pittifull" (*Apol* 3 : 329), adding that Hall had not originated the form in English and tracing it back to "Pierce Plowman" and earlier.

Shakespeare* is an especially interesting name in Milton's criticism. Probably echoing Jonson*, who would have known the truth at first hand, he comments on the dramatist's ease of composition : "Thy easy numbers flow" (*Shakes*). He also saw a profound aspect to Shakespeare, whose works bereave the reader of fancy, making him think instead, indeed making him "marble with too much conceiving." The comedies, on the other hand, are considered the products of "fancy's child," especially in contrast with the learning displayed in Jonson's (*L'Al*). But the tragedies praised in *IlP* are all classical; Milton returns explicitly to Shakespeare only once more, in *Eikon* (5 : 84) and then to draw a moral illustration : the tyrant Richard III can mouth pious words. Critics have found numerous echoes of individual lines in Milton's writing, though few can be assigned with absolute assurance.

Although he must have been deeply concerned with the theoretical aspects of poetry—his experiments prove as much—Milton makes disappointingly few observations upon them. In the *Marginalia* (18 : 284f.). there is a collection of passages illustrating the figure of metonymy. That he was concerned with cacaphony the list of rough Scottish names in *Sonn* 11 proves; his sensitivity to vowel sounds leads to his express preference for the Italian pronunciation of Latin in *Educ* (4 : 281). Rhythm is important : the sonnet to Lawes underlines this fact, as does the Note on the Verse of *PL,* which simultaneously observes that rime is not essential to poetry. In plays he clearly recognized that ideas argued by a character cannot be assigned to his author (*1Def* 7 : 307ff.), a fact sometimes forgotten by interpreters of *SA*.

Despite the existence of *PL* to prove his interest, Milton does not develop any theories about the epic*. Rather, he centers his comments about classical forms upon tragedy, as Aristotle* had done. Clearly the source for his thinking here was the *Poetics*, which he considers as the source of literary rules as opposed to "nature" in *RCG*, a traditional dichotomy and one that was to exist for centuries longer. Like Aristotle he saw tragedy—the ancient form at least—as a major literary medium and modeled *SA* upon it. The Preface to it develops from the Aristotelian analysis of the psychological effects of tragedy; agreeing that it concerns "Men in highest dignity"—not the average man—Milton at the same time emphasizes the un-Aristotelian idea that it is also a major vehicle for religious expression, a view that led him to read with Paraeus* the biblical Revelation as tragedy. Otherwise his understanding of the form is traditional; he adapts it to closet drama as his play is conceived, implying comparison with Aeschylus, Sophocles, and Euripides as "the three tragic Poets unequal'd yet by any," with no qualification from the great London theaters of his youth. One must remain disappointed of any reference by Milton to *King Lear.* [WBH]

**LIVINGSTON, WILLIAM:** *see* IN-
FLUENCE IN AMERICA, MILTON'S.

**LIVY, TITUS LIVIUS** (59 B.C.–A.D. 17),
a member of the Augustan literary circle
that included Virgil* and Horace*, apparently spent most of his adult life composing a history of Rome. He began with
the earliest legends and completed it down
to 9 B.C. in 142 books. Of these only
thirty-five and some fragments remain.
Many were recovered during the Renaissance when Livy was greatly admired and
when concerted efforts were made to
discover a complete manuscript. There
were classical epitomes of most of the
missing books, however, and these were
frequently printed in Renaissance editions
of Livy. More than fifty European editions,
including an English one (STC 16612)
and Holland's English translation (STC
16613), were printed before the time of
Milton's death.

Livy is a gifted narrator who vividly
re-creates events of the past. A versatile
stylist, he is a master of Latin prose.
Although Milton preferred Sallust* above
all the Latin historians, the scope and
purpose of Livy's history is comparable
to that of Milton's *Brit*. Each work is
motivated by the patriotic impulse of
presenting an interesting, continuous
narrative of the historical sweep of its
respective national heritage. Each depends
on other written sources without much
original investigation and customarily
questions these sources only when their
testimony conflicts. In spite of the fact
that Milton doubts the validity or usefulness of speculation about legendary
national origins in his *Brit* (10 : 1–2), he
proceeds to devote his first book to an
account of those origins, appropriately
justifying himself by the examples of
other historians, including Livy (10 :3),
whose first book treats the legendary
establishment of Rome. [PBR]

**LOCKWOOD, LAURA E(MMA)** (1863–
1927) scholar who earned her doctorate
at Yale with a dissertation later expanded
as *Lexicon to the English Poetical Works*
*of John Milton* (1907). Aside from some
brief notes, she also contributed a popular
school text, *Of Education, Areopagitica,*
*and the Commonwealth* (1911), which includes generous quotations of material
from the early biographies as well as
well-annotated texts. Her entire professional career was spent at Wellesley.
[WBH]

**LOGIC AND RHETORIC.** Logic occupied an important place in the intellectual
and literary tradition that formed John
Milton. This is certified in his own case
not only by evidence from his poetry and
prose generally but also by publication
in 1672 of his own *Artis logicae plenior*
*institutio ad methodum Petri Rami con-*
*cinnata (A Fuller Course in the Art of*
*Logic Conformed to the Method of*
*Peter Ramus)*.

In Milton's time, the centuries-old
rhetorical age, out of which logic had
grown, was coming to an end. Man's
originally oral culture was hundreds of
thousands of years old at the time of the
invention of writing about 3500 B.C. In
oral culture noetic activity was structured
largely around oratory. After writing or
script had been developed, oratory not
only continued to be predominant but was
even strengthened by being codified in
works such as Aristotle's* *Art of Rhetoric*.
As civilization matured in the ancient
world, rhetoric* became an academic
institution associated with grammar and
logic. Both of these arts had, in fact, grown
out of rhetoric, and with it were known
to the Middle Ages as the "trivium." The
art of rhetoric, and with it oratory, remained central to Western culture from
antiquity through Milton's time and up
to the Romantic age.

As the art of persuasion, rhetoric is a
practical and pervasive subject, concerned
with decision-making and action. Since
action has often to be taken even when
all the reasons pro and con cannot be
entirely articulated, rhetoric thus has to
do not only with explicitly conceptualized
and verbalized statement but also with
more or less inarticulate motives, or

"emotional appeal," as these are often rather inadequately styled. Aristotle says that the rhetorical equivalent of the logical syllogism is the enthymeme, by which he means argumentation from probable premises to a probable conclusion.

Unlike rhetoric, logic restricts itself to what is fully conceptualized and articulate. Formal logic grew out of rhetoric, that is, out of attempts to deal in full explicitness with the question, How or how far does what I say refute what you say? Logic concerns the connections between formally explicit statements. As a movement to the fully explicit or articulate, the movement from rhetoric to logic proceeds from the less fully conscious to the more fully conscious. It is a movement that is both an advance and a loss, for to achieve its formal clarity, logic leaves out of account the very real, necessary, and often quite reliable subconscious elements in any real human thinking.

Logic developed out of rhetoric by an antithetical movement, and from the beginning the relationship of logic and rhetoric has been as uneasy as it has been ineradicable. In the Ramist tradition, where Milton's logic stands, the relationship is crucial, for Peter Ramus* attempted to settle the relationship between logic and rhetoric once and for all, and in imperiously simple fashion.

Formal logic was developed for the first time in the history of mankind among the ancient Greeks, and was indeed discovered by Aristotle (384–322 B.C.). It languished somewhat after Boethius (A.D. 480?–524?). The scholastic philosophers revived it in the twelfth century and, starting in the latter half of the same century, constructed a new logic unknown to antiquity. This logic was metalogically formulated and employed an extremely sophisticated semiotics (Latin-based, of course). The Renaissance marked a temporary regression in the interior development of logic, but by no means total disappearance of interest in the subject, for the medieval curricular emphasis that had made logic

central to the entire educational enterprise continued through the Renaissance to a great extent unimpaired. Despite humanist protests against logical formalism, logic remained with a very few exceptions absolutely integral to the curriculum, although it shrank to a residual logic so that there are no great Renaissance logicians comparable to those of the Middle Ages. The Renaissance even produced the first histories of logic, the earliest of them by Peter Ramus. They were not very good histories, but they showed that even at the center of humanism* logic could not be ruled out of the intellectual tradition. Indeed, humanist rhetoric, which was calculated to dislodge logic, in many ways preserved it : compared to rhetoric as this is taught today, humanist rhetoric is quite close to formal logic in its attention to formal thought structures and in its identification and formal classification of the hundreds of figures of thought and speech that we still use today, more or less unawares.

Milton's understanding and use of logic grows out of the entrenched but uneventful humanist logic tradition. He is untouched by modern logic, or "mathematical logic" (also called symbolic logic or logistic), which had its indecisive beginnings toward the end of Milton's lifetime with Leibnitz (1646–1716). This logic, in fact, takes its effective rise only with the work of George Boole starting in 1847, branching out first from the object-language of ancient logic supplemented by its own rich use of variables, and after 1930 picking up again the medieval interest in semiotics, which the humanists had indignantly discarded as too remote from the human life-world to warrant attention. The features that relate medieval logic closely to modern logic are missing in Milton, as in humanist logic generally.

In the main current of learning and teaching as this flowed into the Renaissance on the Continent and later in England, rhetoric and logic appeared to overlap each other. The pattern inherited from Cicero* and widely adopted by Renaissance humanists presented rhetoric as made up of five "parts," which Cicero had suggested might well be called separate arts and which in fact derived from ancient Greek educational procedures rather than from anything like philosophical analysis of the subject. The five parts were : (1) invention (*inventio*), or the discovery of "arguments" to prove what one had to prove (today we would think of "invention" rather as "use of the imagination," but in the highly oral disputatious climate of antiquity, all statement was more or less presumed to be a statement-against-opposition and thus to require "proof"); (2) disposition or arrangement (*dispositio*) sometimes called also "judgment" (*iudicium*) of the material one had discovered, corresponding to what we would today call "composition" of an oration or bit of writing; (3) style (*elocutio*), or the investing of "naked reasons" with variously effective trappings by means of rhythmic pattern, balance, antithesis, metaphor, synechdoche, or other figures or tropes; (4) memory (*memoria*) or mnemonic control of the entire speech (normally never verbatim memorization, but mnemonic arrangement of themes and formulas); and (5) oral delivery proper (*pronuntiatio*). These last two parts of rhetoric, memory and delivery, commonly retained through Milton's day, make it clear that the art of rhetoric in principle concerned oral, not written communication. Even as late as Milton's day, although some unacknowledged adjustments were made to the demands of writing or print, rhetoric remains in effect a basically oral art; even the Ramist readjustment, which dropped memory, retained delivery.

In the tradition where rhetoric was commonly assigned its five parts, dialectic or logic was commonly thought of as consisting also of "parts," which were two : (1) invention (*inventio*) and judgment (*iudicium*). The coincidence of these two parts with the first two parts of rhetoric reflected the common origins and concerns of rhetoric and logic, but the

coincidence was not the result of any articulate theory : it was simply a historical fact, to which theories of course could be tied.

Ramus, whom Milton followed, decided to remove all this confusion. Insistently and repeatedly Ramus decreed the separation of dialectic (or, synonymously, logic) as an art from rhetoric as an art. Dialectic was the art of discoursing well (*ars bene disserendi*) and rhetoric the art of speaking well (*ars bene dicendi*). Invention and judgment were assigned to logic alone as its constituents: style and delivery alone constituted rhetoric. Memory was dropped. The alleged reason for dropping memory was that if one observed the "order of nature" (in actuality, this meant the order in which a subject was presented in Ramist textbooks) in accordance with Ramist "method," things followed one another in the mind readily and correctly without any particular attention to memorization. The real but unacknowledged (and probably unnoticed) reasons for dropping memory were two : (1) the entire Ramist arrangement of an art in accordance with "method" was nothing more than an elaborate recall system, and (2) the greater and greater exploitation of writing and print for knowledge storage and retrieval was making memorization less needed, though there was little if any explicit awareness of this fact in Ramus's or Milton's milieu.

The parts Ramus left to rhetoric make it clear that he managed to disentangle rhetoric and logic only at the cost of construing rhetoric as an art of ornamentation that added beauties to the naked reasons of logic and thus was always liable to charge of meretriciousness. Treating rhetoric as an art of ornamentation was not at all new: Boethius, for example, had so treated it, and so had the Englishman Alcuin (735–804) and many others, but no one had been so programmatic about the matter as Ramus and his collaborator Omer Talon (Audomarus Talaeus, ca. 1510–1562), under whose name the Ramist *Rhetorica* appeared.

Many of Ramus's Puritan followers, who typically cultivated the "plain style," a basically chirographic, nonoratorical, non-ornamental style, were in effect rejecting or at least minimizing rhetoric because they felt, under Ramist influence, that it was indeed nothing but superficial ornament. But Milton himself appears to have been little affected by the Ramist concept of rhetoric. This was doubtless in great part because his massive reading and learning kept him in intimate contact with the roots of Western culture, where rhetoric had a richness and reality that Ramist views of rhetoric could not deal with. Nevertheless, in opting for Ramist logic, Milton did implicitly endorse Ramist views of rhetoric, for Ramist logic and Ramist rhetoric were designed to complement one another.

Ramist logic eliminated all logics of probability. Many earlier theoreticians had distinguished the logic of "necessity" or strictly formal logic from the logics of probability, such as dialectic (understood as the art of debate*, dealing with the more probable of two sides), or rhetoric (the art of persuasion—to action, which often cannot wait for total certitude but must base itself on the probable) or poetic (where connections were not by strict logical structure but by "verisimilitude"). For Ramus, such logics of probability were outlawed so that one logic ruled all, operating with equal rigor in mathematics and poetry, although in poetry it was "thinner" than in mathematics. Besides probable logics, Ramus also discarded much else in the traditional logic course: the highly technical *Summulae logicales* of Peter of Spain, Porphyry's *Isagoge* or *Introduction* to Aristotle, and much of Aristotle's *Organon*.

Ramist logic, which could be presented in a small duodecimo volume of less than 100 printed pages, was simple both in its interior economy and in the way it applied to everything in the human consciousness and life-world. Inevitably of course, such "simplicity" generated commentaries, of which the first was by Talon and one of the last by Milton.

Despite Milton's title, which minimizes his direct dependence on Ramus, Milton's *Logic* does not deviate in any major way from Ramus's *Dialectic*. Milton's preference for the term *logica* over Ramus's *dialectica* means little, for Ramus himself had stated that the terms were synonymous. However, Milton's definition of logic as "the art of reasoning well" (*ars bene ratiocinandi*) rather than as "the art of discoursing well" (*ars bene disserendi*—Ramus's definition, following Cicero), shows that Milton, even more than Ramus, tends to assign thought not so much to a world of discourse as to the Cartesian monologic or solipsistic universe: "reasoning," unlike discoursing, can be presumed to go on in one's own consciousness independently of overt communication.

The two parts of Ramus's and Milton's logic, invention and arrangement, are systematically organized, the material in each being presented in further binary divisions and subdivisions and subsubdivisions constituting the well-known Ramist branching dichotomies, which many editions of Ramus's *Logic,* though not Milton's, chart in tabular outlines virtually identical with the binary flow charts worked up in computer programming today. Invention (*inventio*) consists of an operation whereby a person faced with a question, Is A B?, can locate a middle term (called by Ramus and Milton an "argument") that will either join or separate the two terms A and B. Discovery of such a term was achieved by running through certain headings, as we would today style them. Such headings, from antiquity through the seventeenth century, were commonly called *topoi* or *loci,* that is "places" (commonplaces, *loci communes,* if they provided arguments for all subjects in common). But Ramus and Milton do not use any of these terms, speaking instead simply of "arguments" collectively. Such arguments (or places) in Milton's Ramist listing include efficient cause, material cause (or matter, that out of which a thing is made), formal cause (or form, which constitutes a thing what it is), final cause (or purpose, end), effect, subject, related things, etcetera. Thus, faced with the question, Is Peter a human being? and running through these arguments, one can note that among the efficient causes listed and explained in dichotomized sequence are "procreant causes," such as father and mother. If one knows that Peter had a human father (and/or mother), that is, a human procreant cause, one can argue that he is a human being, since, as Ramus and Milton explain, when a being acts as a procreant cause it produces an effect of the same nature as itself. Or, noting that Peter's father (and/or mother) was a rabbit, one can argue that Peter is not a human being at all.

Although the first part of Ramist logic is styled invention or discovery, it says nothing about the process of discovery as such other than to intimate that one should run through the list of arguments to find which ones fit the case. The part of logic called invention is in fact not a treatment of process but a classificatory description of all the arguments that invention can discover and an explanation of the qualities of each one. This shows how each one can be used "logically." Thus, not all efficient causes argue the same nature in effect as in cause, though procreant efficient causes do, and so on. Explanations of this sort of course are far from simply formal logic. They verge on metaphysics*, a subject that Ramus had ridiculed.

The second part of Ramus's and Milton's logic, *dispositio* or arrangement, treats of how to arrange arguments, that is to say, how to construct, first, propositions and then syllogisms, and finally the longer assemblages of discourse—treatises or half-hour orations, for example. These longer discourses are governed by what Ramus and Milton call "method."

Ramist logic adds nothing to the interior development of the subject—the syllogisms with singular terms once attributed to Ramus as an innovation are to be found over two centuries earlier in Ockham—but his "method" is of major

cultural significance. The term method (*methodus*) is first given currency in the 1540s in dialectic textbooks by Johann Sturm, Philip Melanchthon, Ioannes Caesarias, and Ramus himself. All these authors had found in rhetoric a concern about the way to organize larger units of discourse and, for pedagogical rather than speculative reasons, grafted this concern from rhetoric onto dialectic or logic (where Descartes would later find it lodged). Ramus's prescription for organizing discourse was the simplest of all: he prescribed that all procedure be from the more general to the more particular. This procedure was Ramist "method." It can be seen in full operation in Ramus's organization of any "art," including his *Dialectic* or *Logic*. Here one starts with the general notion or definition of logic and proceeds to consider its two parts, then the subparts of these parts, the sub-subparts of the subparts, and so on until the matter in hand is exhausted in full particularity. Such method was to govern not only the classroom presentation of an art but in fact any and all discourse, from mathematics to poetry, with some allowance for occasional "cryptic method" (that is, reverse method, from particular to general) demanded by the ignorance, lethargy, or recalcitrance of a particular audience. By "logical analysis" of texts, Ramus could prove to the satisfaction of thousands of Ramists, if not to their thousands of opponents, that all effective discourse worked by his "method," from Virgil's *Georgics* through Cicero's orations. His chief source of resentment against Aristotle was that Aristotle did not present his material this way.

Ramus was in fact reacting with his logical method to what had become an impossible situation, for from classical antiquity until his time virtually the only mode for organizing discourse ever formally taught in the academic world was the oration (to which even letters were assimilated), with its various assigned parts, running from the basic two (statement of position and proofs) to seven or more. In his logical "method" Ramus substitutes a logical structure of great simplicity but uneven applicability for the rhetorical (oratorical) structure. Without being aware of the fact, he advanced his "method" because oral culture was wearing away after centuries of writing now abetted by print, and the oration simply was no longer so effective or essential a means of storing and retrieving knowledge. Ramist method is well adapted to writing. It more or less governs, for example, most of today's encyclopedia articles.

Up to roughly the Romantic age, both logic and rhetoric had a direct effect on literature that it is hard for those living after the advent of romanticism to imagine, and even harder for many of them to condone. Shakespeare achieves some of his finest effects through the superb and often inspired use of skills demonstrably learned in rhetoric classes at school—"To be or not to be" is exactly the kind of theme schoolboys often wrote on—and the great outburst of literary achievement in the sixteenth and seventeenth centuries is the work of writers who were trained in the trivium subjects with a rigor that earlier and later generations seldom could boast.

At St. Paul's School* Milton received the usual rigorous education in grammar (Latin and Greek), rhetoric (Ciceronian), which included study of Latin and Greek poetry, and doubtless some "petty logic" (the minimal acquaintance with logic that rhetoric demanded, comparable to the logic in some freshman English textbooks in today's United States). Whether this initial acquaintance with logic was Ramist we do not know. At Cambridge he continued work in rhetoric and studied logic more comprehensively, though how far he was at this time subject to Ramist views of logic is hard to say.

Milton's training in rhetoric and logic is reflected in the prolusions or academic exercises that he did at Cambridge in the later 1620s and published in 1674 with his personal letters. These prolusions (in Latin as all academic work normally was) develop subjects in the typical disputatious fashion that both rhetoric and dialectic or logic encouraged : "Whether Day or Night Is the More Excellent," "An Attack on the Scholastic Philosophy," "There Are No Partial Forms in an Animal in Addition to the Whole." Milton's early poems are full of similar disputatious logic and rhetoric : the paired *L'Al* and *IlP* are only the most obvious examples. Even his less openly disputatious poems, such as *Nat,* turn on hinges of "for's" and "but's" that show the argumentative movement of thought. And so, more or less obviously, on through *PL.* The greatest of Milton's poems announces its own argumentative purpose, "to justifie the wayes of God to men," and it achieves some of its finest effects in the carefully nuanced argumentation of its characters, for example, in the dialogue of Adam and Eve before and after the Fall in Book 9, where the occasional carefully managed defects in the reasoning are as telling as its correctness in other places. Milton, moreover, was certainly familiar with works such as those of Johann Wolleb* and William Ames* and Zacharias Ursinus, who analyze the causes of man's first sin in "logical" terms such as external cause, internal cause, principal cause, assisting cause, immediate and proximate cause, instrumental cause, and so on. In his later prose as well as in his poetry, Milton at times makes his use of logic explicit by conspicuously employing terms from Ramist logic : cause, effect, definition, etcetera. And his use of Ramist method for organizing some works, notably his *CD,* is unmistakable.

In practice Milton's use of logic was closely allied to his use of rhetoric. This accorded not only with the practical exigencies of real discourse but also with Ramist theory, which kept these arts utterly separate in themselves or in theoretical presentation but advocated uniting them in practice. For Milton and his age generally, logic went particularly well with rhetoric, for, like rhetoric, it was taken to be a combative instrument rather than merely an instrument for uncommitted analysis.

Milton's often contrived use of logic and rhetoric does not appeal to our romantic sensibility, particularly in poetry. But it worked remarkably well. Habits of casting up issues in logical form, seeking out logical arguments, and using consciously identified or identifiable oratorical devices were deeply ingrained in writers generally by the training common at the time and could be used imaginatively. On the other hand, knowledge of logic and rhetoric did not automatically fire the imagination and produce good poetry or prose. Such knowledge was an asset, but only in the hands of an imaginative artist.

However, even when Milton's procedures are traceable to patterns mentioned in Ramist logic, this does not always mean that Milton's use of logic was distinctively Ramist. Ramist logic was distinguished by some of the things it dropped from traditional Aristotelian logic. But in its positive content, there was little distinctively Ramist beyond the order or "method" in which it presented its material. Often, of course, Milton's precise understanding of terms such as efficient cause or procreant cause or oppositives or contraries and of other elements in logic was mediated and perhaps nuanced by Ramism, probably from his Cambridge days or even earlier, and certainly from the 1640s. But his reading was also so massive that Ramist influence was mingled with many other competing influences. Milton did not share Ramus's intense dislike of "Aristotelians," though he did share the fashionable aversion to "scholastic" thinking and the general total ignorance of the massive medieval developments in formal logic. Like that of other declared adherents of Ramus, Milton's position here is complicated by the fact that in its penchant for classification Ramism is a kind of scholasticism run wild.

In his use of rhetoric, as suggested above, Milton shows no particular interest in Ramist teaching on this art. He was trained in the much richer, more complex if less tidy Ciceronian or Ciceronian-and-Senecan tradition, with its insistence on *copia* (flow, fulsomeness), its sophisticated techniques of praise and blame, and its sense of the intellectual and infra-intellectual complexity of issues and of life. Again, Milton had done massive reading in ancient and patristic sources, and these are monuments of the old Ciceronian rhetoric. Ramist rhetoric seemed poor by comparison. Although he was a Puritan in at least some sense of that term, Milton hardly wrote prose or poetry in the "plain style." [WJO]

**LONG, THOMAS:** *see* ADAPTATIONS.

**LONGINUS.** Formerly regarded as the work of Dionysius Cassius Longinus (3d century A.D.), *Peri Hypsous* (*On the Sublime*) appears to be the composition of an earlier and unidentified author. A tentative date for the discussion is A.D. 80. Both the Greek text and several Latin translations were available to Milton.

Milton's single reference to "Longinus" in *Educ*—as one of several classical authorities on "a graceful and ornate rhetoric*" rather than on the "sublime art" of poetry—provides little evidence for his knowledge of or indebtedness to *Peri Hypsous*. Analogies between this treatise and Milton's own works involve commonplaces that he could easily have encountered in other classical rhetoricians or their Renaissance successors. Observing that Milton "seems not to have felt Longinus's charm," Samuel Monk in *The Sublime: A Study of Critical Theory in XVIII-Century England* (1960) notes the "strange paradox that the most sublime of English poets should not have caught from Longinus the suggestion of the sublime as the expression of ultimate values in art, beyond the reach of rhetoric and her handmaidens, the rules. . . ." There are, however, insufficient grounds for either a negative or a positive appraisal. The treatise had attracted critical attention in England before Milton, and had received high praise from scholars like Isaac Casaubon* and Francis

Junius*. The fact that Milton includes it in his ideal academic curriculum constitutes a strong argument that he had read it, but how deeply it may have influenced either his prose or his poetry must remain a matter of conjecture.

*Peri Hypsous* is significant for Milton scholarship less for its possible (but uncertain) influence on the poet himself than for its impact on his critics. Many of them had been stimulated by Longinus's "praise of an erring and irregular genius as opposed to a mediocrity that attains correctness by merely following rules" and by his "recognition of sublimity in nature" (Monk), and many of them applied his arguments for Homer's* sublimity to Milton. Marvell* extolled the latter's verse and theme as alike sublime. Dryden* ascribed Homer's loftiness of thought as well as Virgil's* majesty to Milton. Through the influence of Addison*, Dennis* (satirized as "Sir Tremendous Longinus"), Welsted, and other critics, Milton became, in eighteenth-century eyes, the supreme English exemplar of the sublime. [JMS]

**LOVE.** Milton's treatment of divine and human love follows the Christian tradition of John's assertion that "God is love" (1 John 4 : 8 and 16). Many Renaissance writers reflected a Platonic* bias that explained love as a sympathy of affinities and kindred souls, a harmony of spirits and natural feelings, and a reconciliation of opposites or *concordia discors*. What distinguishes Milton from his predecessors (such as Dante* and Tasso*) and contemporaries (such as Donne and Herrick) is his insistence on the identity of love and reason*. The consequences of this identity sustain nothing less than the personal, social, and cosmic order.

For Milton, the love of God for man is expressed through Christ; for it is "the Son of God, / In whom the fulness dwells of love divine" (*PL* 3. 224–25). Milton preserves, in fact, a distinction between an Old Testament God of wrath and justice and a New Testament Christ, through whose love the mercy, pity, and grace* of God are manifested (*PL* 3. 400–411). Milton proclaims Christ's offer to save man—"to die / For mans offence"—an "unexampl'd love," wholly divine (*PL* 3. 410-411), and otherwise described as "immortal love" (3. 267), "Heav'nly love" (3. 298), and love in excess of glory (3. 312). Such love is entirely the gift of God to man, a form of *agape* in no way deserved by fallen man.

Man's love of God is a matter of obedience*, and for Adam and Eve in prelapsarian Eden the sole injunction was not to eat of the forbidden fruit, their obedience being a "pledge" of their love. Among Milton's scriptural authorities was the Gospel text : "For this is the love of God, that we keep his commandments" (1 John 5. 3). The angel Raphael, after encouraging Adam and Eve to "be strong, live happy, and love" each other, admonishes them "first of all" to love God, "whom to love is to obey, and keep / His great command . . ." (*PL* 8. 633–35). Adam and Eve fail to keep this commandment, and as Michael explains to Adam after the Fall, Christ (the second Adam) will fulfill "that which thou didst want, / Obedience to the Law of God" and will do so "Both by obedience and by love, though love / Alone fulfil the Law" (*PL* 12. 396–404). "Love is the fulfilling of the law" (Romans 13 : 10). In *Leviathan*, Milton's contemporary Thomas Hobbes* likewise expressed the conventional Christian wisdom : "obedience is sometimes called by the names of *charity* and *love,* because they imply a will to obey; and our Saviour himself maketh our love to God, and to one another, a fulfilling of the whole law." More simply, Jeremy Taylor said : "Love is obedience" (*Holy Living,* 7th ed. [1663], p. 202).

Angels* are also bound by the divine command to obey, for as Raphael explains, it is "in our will / To love or not; In this we stand or fall"; "freely we serve, / Because we freely love . . ." (*PL* 5. 538–40). The divine equation between love and obedience is thus applicable alike to the Son of God*, the angels, and man, in short to all forms of being that have will. Furthermore, as a consequence of their obedience, Raphael tells Adam and Eve that

> . . . perhaps
> Your bodies may at last turn all to Spirit,
> Improv'd by tract of time, and wing'd ascend
> Ethereal, as we, or may at choice
> Here or in Heav'nly Paradise dwell;
> If ye be found obedient, and retain
> Unalterably firm his love entire
> Whose progenie you are. . . .
> (PL 5. 496–503)

Adam understands this to mean that "In contemplation of created things / By steps we may ascend to God" (PL 5. 511–12), and in the conclusion of Ref Milton envisions the faithful being rewarded with angelic titles. St. Augustine* had said that had man not fallen he would eventually have progressed to the same spiritual level as angels (Civ. Dei 14. 10). St. Augustine owed intellectual debts to Plotinus*, whose Neoplatonism* inspired numerous writers to imagine the means of the soul's liberation from the body, essentially through "contemplation" and spiritual love (Enneads 1. 1. 7; 3. 7. 7). Whereas Plotinus and St. Augustine distinguish between body and soul and imply a difference in kind, Milton implies that because body may "up to spirit work" (PL 5. 478) the difference is one of degree, and progression from one to the other is a matter of spiritual discipline, chiefly the love of God through obedience.

Among Protestants and Catholics alike, human love was thought to be a sign and symbol of divine love. Milton characterized it as "the love of God" and "as a fire sent from Heaven to be ever kept alive upon the altar of our hearts" (RCG 3 : 260). Adam and Eve practiced, moreover, "the Rites / Mysterious of connubial Love" (PL 4. 742–43), wedded love being a "mysterious law" (4. 750). Milton's scriptural authority was both St. Paul's description of coitus as a "mysterious" symbol of the "one flesh" that signified the relations between Christ and the Church (Eph. 5) and the Song of Songs. But Milton differs from St. Paul in recognizing that physical love is not a mere remedy for passionate desire but a means of binding lovers in mind, heart, and soul (PL 8. 604). Some readers (most notably C. S. Lewis) have objected to Milton's insistence on physical love in prelapsarian Eden (PL 4.488ff.; 8.484ff.), but both Augustine (Civ. Dei 16.26) and Aquinas* (Sum. Th. Q98, Art. 2) allowed the possibility, and no Protestant commentator ever denied that Adam and Eve knew each other before the Fall.

The love between Adam and Eve was not, however, love between equals (nor, in Milton's view, was it to be different for the men and women to follow), for man's is "the perfeter sex" (DDD 4 : 76), a view shared by the vast majority of Milton's contemporaries, dogmatized by St. Paul (1 Cor. 11 : 7), and going back at least to Aristotle*, who thought the female an imperfectly formed male (De generatione animalium 775a10). But whereas Adam is created "for God only" and Eve "for God in him" (PL 7.529–30), Milton recognizes that Eve is instrumental to Adam's self-knowledge (8. 359–66) and to the "harmonie or true delight" (8. 384) that is generated by their love. Adam's prelapsarian love for Eve is a desire for perfection, order, and being (8. 415–26), and the effect of Milton's celebration of their union is to elevate romantic love into an image of God, whereby in the union of male and female Adam approaches the sufficiency of God and repairs the "unity defective" of man alone without woman. [PEB]

**LUCRETIUS, TITUS** (ca. 94–ca. 55 B.C.), Roman poet and author of a single surviving but incomplete work, De rerum natura (On the Nature of Things). This long poem, sometimes classified as an epic*, expounds in hexameters the moral philosophy of Epicurus. In order to abolish superstitious fears propagated by religions and to argue instead a universe governed by mechanical laws, Lucretius considers cosmology in detail. Everything in the universe, he argues, can be understood in terms of sheer materiality, ultimately reducible to individual atoms (indivisible bits of various shapes), which fall eternally through an infinite space. The gods indeed exist, but they dwell in an Epicurean paradise where they have no concern for man's welfare: his problems would mar their pleasure.

Milton certainly knew Lucretius well. Despite the antireligious argument of *De rerum* . . . , Milton made it part of his educational curriculum (*Educ* 4 : 284), a fact that was to scandalize Dr. Johnson*. In *Areop* Lucretius's untraditional views are recognized as part of the argument that Romans did not censor unpopular ideas. But the most interesting influence of the Roman poet is that which *PL* reveals. Because *De rerum* . . . is the major poetic model in Western civilization for a "scientific" description of the material universe, the descriptions of Chaos in Book 2 and of the creation in Book 7 owe many of their details directly to this work. Examples are Milton's description of the "embryon atoms" of Chaos (2. 900) with their various shapes, the "vast vacuity" in which they exist (2.932), the fact that it is "illimitable . . . without bound" (2. 892), and its noise (2. 921). Milton also adopts some of the imagery of the Latin poem: the description of the dawn, for instance (5. 2; cf. *Drn* 2 : 211) or of voices in the night air (4. 681ff.; cf. *Drn* 2 : 586ff.).

In some ways his most interesting employment of a Lucretian detail appears in the description of Urania* at the beginning of Book 7. Lucretius had invoked the goddess Venus in the first lines of his poem as the creative power in the universe; she alone is the "guide into the nature of things." As Milton approaches the difficult subject of the creation of the universe, he implores the help of Urania. Whatever else he may have had in mind when he invoked this perplexing figure, he must have thought of the Heavenly Venus—Uranian Aphrodite—the creative being in Spenser's* *Fowre Hymnes,* ultimately descended from Plato's*

Aphrodite (*Symposium* 180D) through Lucretius. It can hardly be accidental that this aspect of Venus is invoked in similar circumstances in the two poetic descriptions of the universe, the one the eternal activity of Lucretius's goddess, the other the creativity of the same goddess now to be interpreted in Christian terms. [WBH]

**LUDLOW, EDMUND (pseudonym):** *see* ADAPTATIONS; EIKON BASILIKE.

**LUTHER, MARTIN** (1483 – 1546), founder of the Reformation in Germany. A private revelation convinced Luther of the doctrine of justification by faith alone, a view that led him to deny the mediatorial role of the Roman Catholic Church in individual salvation. From about 1520 until the end of his life he developed a body of religious, philosophical, and political opinions, many of which were the common inheritance of seventeenth-century England.

Although Milton does not appear to have been directly influenced by Luther, his own doctrine accords with the reformer's views upon the primacy of Scripture (as opposed to traditions), the priesthood of all believers, and the importance of preaching. Likewise the two men shared a minority belief in mortalism*, guardian angels*, and polygamy*.

Milton, however, did not agree with Luther's position upon faith as prior to works, holding the more nearly Arminian* view that works must accompany faith. Second, he differs on free will*, regarding man as free to choose in the question of his own salvation, whereas Luther limited man's free will to obeying moral and state laws. Third, Milton, unlike Luther, has a high regard for human reason*. Fourth, Milton demands "freedom of the individual conscience from human ordinances" (Barker), whereas Luther would set limitations upon it. Fifth, Milton believed in political freedom, against Luther's conviction that Christian magistrates should enforce "the one right discipline" (Barker).

Milton mentions Luther infrequently but with respect as an "eminent doctor" of the Church (*1Def*), "a singular instrument of God" (*Bucer*), and along with Calvin* and Hus a founder of the Reformation (*Areop*). He claims Luther's authority for divorce* upon grounds of mental as well as "corporal" lack of "benevolence" (*Tetra*), and, more important for the lawfulness of deposing tyrants (*1Def, Tenure*), confining to his private *CB* a notation that Luther opposed the spreading of faith by uprisings. Milton defends his own use of acrimony in controversy by citing Luther's example (*Apol*), again committing only to the *CB* his opinion that Luther's jests and "bitter remarks" were sometimes in bad taste. [EFD]

**LYCIDAS.** The basic texts of *Lyc* are to be found in *TM*\*, in *Justa Edovardo King*\* (1638), and in the 1645 and 1673 editions of the Poems. Though the text of *Lyc* is considerably revised in the manuscript, Grierson* is of the opinion that it may not have been Milton's first draft. The verso of the last sheet of *Mask,* known familiarly as the "trial-sheet," contains four drafts (one struck out) of three portions of the poem.

The passages worked over most heavily in *TM* are the "Orpheus" passage, which is revised in the main text, rewritten in the margin, and rewritten again in the trial-sheet, and the "flower" passage, which is drafted, struck out, and rewritten in the trial-sheet, with the main text providing a marginal direction for its insertion. The Orpheus* passage is expanded from four to seven lines; the menacing line "downe the swift Hebrus to the Lesbian Shore" is added to the marginal revision; its effect is intensified by the addition of "When by the rout that made the hideous roare" in the trial-sheet; and the avalanche of horror is given further momentum as Orpheus's "divine head" becomes his "goarie visage." In the flower passages the number of lines is reduced from twelve to ten; a certain amount of exposition is discarded; and the passage takes on the quality of a procession, with each flower given a distinct and vividly focused presence. The movement in one case is toward angry elementality; in the other it is toward conventionality, the pastoral* mood wrought to the height of its beauty. More than one view can be taken of these changes, which are examined in detail by J. B. Leishman (*Milton's Minor Poems* [1969], pp. 295–310). One possible view is that Milton recognized that the movement of his poem was shaped by certain basic oppositions and wished by his revisions to intensify rather than diminish those oppositions. Such a view would be borne out by the crucial replacement of "and crop yor young" by "shatter" in line 5, by the replacement of "sad thoughts" by "frail thoughts" in line 153, and by the restoration in 1645 of "nothing" which is replaced by "little" in the manuscript text of line 129. Later changes in the same direction are the restoration of "smite" in line 131 (1645; the 1638 version has "smites") and the replacement of "humming" by "whelming" in line 157, by Milton's hand in two copies of the 1638 text.

The King memorial volume consists of two parts, the first containing twenty Latin and three Greek poems and the second thirteen poems in English. Each part has a separate title page and is separately paginated. The book is rare, Parker* recording no more than 31 copies, of which the one owned by the Elizabethan Club of Yale University bears Izaak Walton's autograph. There is a facsimile edited by Ernest C. Mossner (1939). Milton's is the longest, last, and most elaborate of the English poems. The author is identified only by his initials. M. Lloyd in *Notes and Queries*, 5 : 432–34, suggests that the volume is designed as a unity and that *Lyc* is a summary and interpretation of themes already stated. The tone of the English poems is predominantly metaphysical and the verse predominantly in couplets, so that *Lyc* is set apart not merely by its excellences. Nevertheless references such as those in

Isaac Olivier's poem to Arethusa and to St. Peter's treading of the waves are not without their bearing on Milton's poem.

The 1638 text, set throughout in italics, is not arranged with care. Milton's paragraphing in the manuscript is only partially followed, with paragraphs beginning at lines 15, 37, 132, 165, and 186. In line 9 "Young *Lycidas*" is put in parenthesis for the first and only time and an exclamation mark is added. Typical misprints are "lord" for "lov'd" in line 51 and "stridly" for "strictly" in line 66. The recollection of "don" in line 67 leads to the printing of "do" instead of "use" later in the same line. "Hid in" for "Or with" in line 69 is a celebrated variant. The manuscript has "Hid in" struck out and replaced in the margin by the familiar reading. The most striking misprint is the omission of line 177. In the Cambridge University and British Museum copies the line is marginally inserted in Milton's hand. The misprints in lines 51 and 67 are corrected in the same hand, "humming" is changed to "whelming" in line 157, and "he knew" in line 10 becomes "he well knew" as it is in *TM*. The texts of 1645 and 1673 both have "he knew." It is not clear whether Milton changed his mind or abandoned hope.

The 1645 and 1673 versions give us the text of the poem substantially as we know it. Patrides described 1673 as "merely a reproduction of the 1645 text with a few misprints" (*Milton's "Lycidas": the Tradition and the Poem*, ed. C. A. Patrides [1961], p. 233). One of these misprints is "To end" instead of "To tend" in line 65. For fuller apparatus see Patrides, *CM*, the editions of Milton's poetry by Helen Darbishire (1952), H. F. Fletcher (1943), and John T. Shawcross (1963), and for a study of the text, Shawcross, *Publications of the Bibliographical Society of America* 56:317-31.

The two-handed engine was merely at the door in 1638 but by 1645 Milton was able to enter in the manuscript and to reproduce in print his vindication of the poet's gift of prophecy: "In this Monody the Author bewails a learned Friend, un-fortunately drown'd in his passage from *Chester* on the *Irish* Seas, 1637. And by occasion foretells the ruine of our corrupted clergie then in their height." Apart from the foretelling, the characterization of the poem as a monody is important. The important early poems are all suitably characterized. *Comus* is a "Mask," *Arc* is "Part of an Entertainment," and *Nat* is described in the text as both an "ode" and a "Hymn."

Both in 1645 and in 1673, *Lyc* is printed immediately after *Arc* and the juxtaposition cannot be accidental. The implied movement from Arcadia to anguish is gently underlined by the setting of both poems within the pastoral frame. Both make use of the story of Alpheus with its implication of rebirth in another country; but the "renowned flood" of *Arc* 29, remembered in *Lyc* as the "honour'd floud" develops characteristically into the "perilous flood" (85, 185). The "Genius of the Wood" provides the principal statement in *Arc*. In *Lyc* 183 the dead shepherd becomes the "Genius of the Shore," on the far side of the "perilous flood." The plants in *Arc* (53) are preserved from the worm and the canker, which in *Lyc* 45-46 are the initial symbols of those destructive energies which the poem is forced to pass through. Even more instructively, the celestial sirens in *Arc* (61ff.) sing to those that "hold the vital shears / And turn the adamantine spindle round." The "sweet compulsion" of music keeps "unsteady Nature" to its law and ensures that the "low world" moves in concert to the "heavenly tune." In *Lyc* the shears are "abhorred" rather than "vital," the power that wields them is "blind," and Nature, far from moving in "measur'd motion," is radically challenged by the forces of chaos. Yet despite the depth of questioning in *Lyc,* the resolution is still able to bring us back to some of the images of the earlier poem. In *Arc* (96–101) the Nymphs and Shepherds are called on to "dance no more" so that they can be welcomed on "A better soil." In *Lyc* the shepherds are invited to "weep no more" since Lycidas is alive amidst "Other groves and other streams" (165, 174). The tune that the "gross unpurged" ears of morals are incapable of hearing (*Arc* 72–73) is reborn in *Lyc* as the "unexpressive nuptial Song." The pastoral world is restored in a Christian context.

Edward King*, whom Milton's poem mourns, was born at Boyle in the county of Connaught, Ireland, in 1612. He was admitted to Christ's College*, Cambridge in 1626, received his B.A. in 1630 and his M.A. in 1633. In 1630 he was awarded a vacant fellowship by royal mandate. King's feeling for his college is evident in his will of 1637. "First all my debts to be payd. And what remains entirely to be left to the use of Christe Coll." Nine days later King was drowned en route to Ireland. According to the Latin paragraph prefacing the commemorative volume, "the ship in which he was having struck a rock not far from the British shore and being ruptured by the shock, he, while the other passengers were fruitlessly busy about their mortal lives, having fallen forward on his knees, and breathing a life which was immortal, in the act of prayer going down with the vessel, rendered up his soul to God, Aug. 10, 1637, aged 25" [Masson's translation]. Milton did not mention the incident, notwithstanding what his nephew, Edward Phillips, terms his "particular Friendship and Intimacy" with King. *Lyc* 96–99 may reflect the knowledge that it was not a storm that was responsible for King's death, but Henry King, Edward's brother, refers in his memorial poem to an "unluckie storm" and to the "treacherous waves and carelesse wind."

The commemorative preface mentions King's piety and erudition but says nothing about his poetic talent. However, Henry King claims immoderately that his brother's tempestuous eloquence was capable of Christianizing India! King wrote several poems on what Le Comte terms obstetric occasions while Milton, according to Northrop Frye, had been practising on corpses ever since the death of the fair infant. Ben Jonson's* death in the same month as King's and the death of Milton's mother in April of the same year may have wrought Milton's involvement in the shipwreck to the intensity of which *Lyc* is the witness. But when Diodati* died in the year following (the month being once again August) the greater grief provoked the lesser poem.

Hanford's* classic article on the tradition behind *Lyc* (*Publications of the Modern Language Association* 25 : 403–47) remains required reading after more than sixty years. Theocritus* and in particular his first Idyll (to which Milton refers twice in *EpDam*) constitute the "source" of the tradition and furnish precedents or beginnings for conventions such as a procession of mourners, the grief of nature at the death of the shepherd, and a reproach to the nymphs for not being present at the scene of the catastrophe. Bion's* *Lament for Adonis,* which follows, is "one of the great classical models of the pastoral elegy," but its erotic and decadent tone, according to Hanford, was rejected by Milton's "sober and classic genius." *The Lament for Bion* (also referred to in *EpDam*) is a further milestone marking "the full development of the pastoral lament as an independent type." One of the more important conventions it establishes is the mourning of an actual person, a poet-colleague of the maker of the lament.

Virgil* brings the lofty rhyme into the pastoral (notably in the fourth eclogue). Since his concern is with the use of pastoral machinery rather than with rendering the immediacies of Sicilian life, he both establishes the pastoral as a style and opens out the style's possibilities, giving us a poetry that can be oblique as well as direct. In Puttenham's words it is sought "vnder the vaile of homely persons and in rude speeches to insinuate and glaunce at greater matters, and such as perchance had not bene safe to have beene disclosed in any other sort, which may be perceived by the *Eglogues* of Virgill" (Scott Elledge, ed., *Milton's "Lycidas"* [1966], p. 113). Hanford sees the fifth and tenth eclogues as particularly

relevant to Milton's poem. More specifically, the tenth eclogue has an invocation
at the beginning, but no mention of the
shepherd singer till the end; a procession
of mourners; and an eight-line close
referring to the end of day and the departure of the shepherd. The fifth eclogue
establishes the convention of the apotheosis. Though Christianity gives the consolation in *Lyc* a different coloring, it is
hard to believe, according to Hanford
(Patrides, pp. 39–40), that Milton would
have made his reference to the "Genius
of the Shore" had not the idea held "an
important place in this eclogue of Virgil."
Milton's allusiveness is of course considerably more sophisticated than parallels
like these might in themselves suggest.
The multiple evocations of the Latin
poetry are a fit preparation for the kind
of literary performance that is called for
by the pastoral elegy in its later stages.
It is a world of poetry rather than individual poems that is summoned into
being around the performance.

Virgil's fourth or Messianic Eclogue
is easily seen as the obscure rehearsal of
a Christian truth to come. John 9 : 39–41
and 10 : 1–28, which Milton draws on in
his denunciation of the clergy, are two
among many biblical passages that en-
courage the conflation of the Christian
and the pastoral. In Petrarch's* sixth and
seventh eclogues ecclesiastical satire is
introduced, opening the way for Mantuan, Marot, and Spenser*. "It is to the
latter poet," says Hanford, "to whom we
naturally look as the predecessor in this
respect of Milton" (Patrides, p. 44). The
May, July, and September Eclogues con-
tan ecclesiastical satire, and May 38ff.,
according to Hanford, "bears a marked
resemblance to the invective in *Lycidas*"
(p. 51). In *Animad*, Milton quotes 103–31
of the May Eclogue. Such satire is expressive of the didactic strain initiated by
Petrarch and Boccaccio* and even more
strongly by Mantuan in his ten eclogues.
What Don Cameron Allen* calls the "inherited right" of the pastoral poet "to be
both satirist and allegorist" is confirmed
and elaborated. "These Eglogues came

after," Puttenham comments, "to containe
and enforme morale discipline for the
amendment of man's behauoir as be those
of *Mantuan* and other moderne Poets"
(Elledge, p. 113). Thus the introduction
of alien material into the pastoral—personal, philosophic, or didactic—is legit-
imized. The digressions in *Lyc,* though
without parallel, are not without precedent. It is also apparent that Johnson's*
complaint that Milton mingles "the most
awful and sacred truths" with the "trifling fictions" of the pastoral and that
these "irreverent combinations" are "in-
decent" and "at least approach to impiety"
censures a Renaissance practice rather
than Milton's alone. However, it is not
enough to reply as Warton* does that
Milton sins in company. The "combinations" must be shown to be demanded by
the logic and momentum of the poem.

Two Latin elegies of the Renaissance
cited as bearing upon *Lyc* are Castiglione's* *Alcon* and Sannazaro's first pis-
catory eclogue. The flower passage in
*Alcon* is one of many that Milton may
have remembered. Spenser's April Eclogue (136ff.) is often cited, Virgil's fourth
and fifth eclogues have flower passages,
though far less elaborate than Milton's,
and *Winter's Tale* 4. 4. 113–32, is, according to H. H. Adams (*Modern Language
Notes* 65 :468–72), a source that Milton
obscured in his revisions. James H. Sims
(*Shakespeare Quarterly* 22 :87–90) sees
a parallel between *Winter's Tale* and *Lyc*
in terms of the progression and not simply
the inventory. Apart from his flower
passage, Castiglione's description of the
friendship between the dead shepherd and
the singer of the lament reminds us of
*Lyc* but perhaps no more than other such
descriptions. Sannazaro's singer is Lycidas,
his eclogue mentions Panope (a rare name
among nymphs but used by Virgil in
*Aeneid* 5. 240), and lines in his poem may
have suggested *Lyc* 183–85, and the
arresting image of 158. The flower
passage in Sannazaro is unusual in occurring in the apotheosis. Sir J. E. Sandys
(*Transactions of the Royal Society of
Literature* [1914], pp. 233–64) considers

Amalteo's First Eclogue, which is entitled *Lyc,* a possible source. Dante's* influence, while not lying within the "tradition" narrowly conceived, should not be discounted. Irene Samuel (*Dante and Milton* [1966], pp. 36–37), finds Dante's impress "throughout the entire pattern" of *Lyc.* The "inner movement" of Milton's elegy asks the "great question" of the *Commedia* and reaches a similar understanding.

The pastoral lament in England was amplified by the several poems mourning the death of Sidney* in 1586. William Browne's elegy on Thomas Manwood (the fourth eclogue in the collection entitled *The Shepherd's Pipe*) has been cited as a possible influence upon *Lyc.* W. B. Austin (*Studies in Philology* 44 : 41–55) detects similarities between passages in *Lyc* and two Latin elegies by Giles Fletcher, the Elder, on Clere and Walter Haddon. Phineas Fletcher's* *Piscatorie Eclogues* published four years before *Lyc* may not have been out of Milton's mind. In general what Hanford terms "the vast and multifarious pastoral literature" written in England between *The Shepheardes Calendar* (1579) and *Lyc* can be accepted as a background that would have made a contemporary audience fully familiar with the gestures of Milton's poem.

Puttenham tells us that "Poeticall mournings in verse" were called "*Epicedia* if they were sung by many, and *Monodia* if they were uttered by one alone." Such lamentations had social status, since they were "vsed at the enterment of Princes and others of great accompt" (Elledge, p. 114). Scaliger* (Elledge, pp. 107–11) divides the epicedium into the praise, the narration, the lamentation, the consolation, and the exhortation. The praise can be preceded by a calm proem "suitable for those who are sorrowful and even dazed with grief." The succeeding part must praise not only the man but also the manner of his death. The narration should describe the loss calmly and then with increasing excitement, as the amplification of the theme increases the longing for the lost person. The lamentation

follows naturally as the agitation of the narration reaches its climax. The consolation then begins—the death of a king, for example, can be alleviated by the virtues of his successor, whose qualities can be set forth in "an ardent and brief account." Finally comes the exhortation: the dead are to be emulated rather than mourned and to mourn them unduly would be to disparage their survivors.

It is apparent that Milton does not follow these requirements closely. The manner of King's death could have been but is not commended. It is on the meaning (or lack of meaning) of that death that the forces of the poem converge. The praise passes into the pastoral claim of kinship. Similarly, the narration blends with the lamentation and the movement from calm to excitement occurs not once but thrice in the ebb and flow of the poem. The consolation is in terms considerably less mundane than those envisaged by Scaliger. The exhortation (to which the closing *ottava rima* corresponds) does not exhort but presents the event as over in the sense that it is assimilated into the experience of the mourner. Milton's adherence to this structure is indeed so free that it may be wondered whether he is following it at all. Certainly the three-part structure (see below) provides a far more instructive understanding of the organizing movement of the poem.

King was a "learned friend" and is mourned appropriately in a learned elegy. Milton's uses of the past in creating the literary present of the poem are apparent even in such details as the choice of the name Lycidas. Lycidas is a shepherd in Theocritus's seventh Idyll, faces death by drowning in Lucan (*Pharsalia* 3. 638–39), complains against social injustice in Virgil's ninth eclogue, is a Protestant pastor in Bathurst's translation of Spenser's May Eclogue (see E. A. Straithwaite, *Modern Language Notes* 52 : 398–400) and brings gifts to Mary and her child in Sannazaro's *De Partu Virginis* (3. 185–93). All these roles are relevant to Milton's poem. Yet an inventory of the past cannot pretend to provide an account of *Lyc*. The expectations that the tradition sets up are challenged as well as fulfilled. The inherited joins hands in the poem with the invented, but both the unattempted and that which is sung once more are stamped with the work's profound originality. "Where were ye nymphs" is a cry as old as Theocritus. The place names that follow take us into the world of Spenser and Drayton while preparing the way for that more majestic naming that surrounds the "great vision of the guarded mount." Milton's capacity to convey the elemental in the local is used here with a higher aim than virtuosity. The pastoral gesture is invested with momentousness and we are made receptive to the dramatic change of voice and proclamation of affinities as the Welsh landscape gives way to the Thracian, the Druid spells to the enchantments of Orpheus, and the spreading Dee is overwhelmed by the swift Hebrus. The "sudden blaze" into "Had ye bin there—for what could that have don?" (a question not asked by the pastoral tradition) is clearly called for by the forces of the poem. Similarly in line 99 ("Sleek *Panope* with all her sisters play'd") the name may not be Milton's but the characterization subtly bears his signature. The word *sleek,* fitted with fastidiousness into the pastoral diction, defines and vivifies the tactile quality of the line itself. Finally it suggests with deftness the comprehensive calm that prevailed, the multiple assurances of safety as the unruffled nymph played on the unruffled waters. The stock word *perfidious* gains in strength as we become aware of the dimensions of betrayal. We can even note that the question "Where were ye nymphs" has been answered in a manner that gives additional force to "what could that have don?" It is thus not simply in the higher mood that Milton is securely himself, and while competitive overgoing may take place (looking forward to the tactics of *PL*) the strings are not simply swept with greater brilliance. Modulation as well as surpassing, counterpoint as well as assertion, are part of the solemn music of *Lyc*.

Explorations such as those conducted above must be representative rather than exhaustive; but they should serve to indicate how fully *Lyc* exemplifies Eliot's* conception of tradition and the individual talent. The poem makes us aware of the presence of the past rather than of its pastness. It holds and shapes the literature of Europe from Theocritus to Milton's day, in an order that is simultaneous rather than chronological. The ideal order that a tradition constitutes is changed by its creative extension into a work of art that is "really new" in Eliot's sense. The individual talent in its turn is excited into distinctiveness by the felt presence of literary history.

Despite its recondite attachment to its genre, *Lyc* remains a poem in a contemporary setting. That contemporaneity is not a matter of the identity of "Old Damoetas," who is in fact young in Theocritus 6 and Virgil's third eclogue, though he is a dying man in the second eclogue and a clown in Sidney's *Arcadia*. Chappell*, Milton's tutor, and Joseph Mead*, a popular Fellow of Christ's, are long-standing suggestions. Fletcher (*Journal of English and Germanic Philology* 60 : 260–67) adds Michael Honeywood, a Fellow of Christ's from 1618, and Abraham Wheelock*, first Professor of Arabic. Others feel that the question cannot or need not be settled. More important is the status of *Lyc* in the wars of truth. Haller considers (*The Rise of Puritanism* [1957], p. 317) that on the ideal plane "*Comus* and *Lycidas* are as authentic expressions of the Puritan spirit on the eve of revolution as anything that came from the hand of Prynne." The reference to the ideal plane is necessary. Corruption endures beyond a particular establishment, and revolutions, as Milton learned, are made to be betrayed. Finally there is the question of how *Lyc* expresses what might loosely be termed the literary spirit of its time. Roy Daniells (*Milton, Mannerism and Baroque* [1963], p. 45) considers the poem mannerist* in its restlessness and in its "refusal to propagate a resounding resolution." For Wylie

Sypher (*Four Stages of Renaissance Style* [1955], pp. 74–76) *Lyc* is "perhaps the greatest mannerist poem" marked by its "intervals and discontinuities," its "constantly shifted level of statement," and its "very personal, willful" use of the traditional elegy. For Lowry Nelson, on the other hand (*Baroque Lyric Poetry* [1961], pp. 64–76, 138–52), *Lyc* is "one of the most nearly complete fulfilments of peculiarly baroque* tendencies in style," with the shifts in tense between the narrative past and the historic present enhancing one's impression of the poem as performance. Rosemond Tuve's cautions in "Baroque and Mannerist Milton" (*Journal of English and Germanic Philology* 60:209–25) need to be perused at this stage. Nevertheless it can be observed that what characterizes *Lyc* is not only the strong sense of literary performance but the eloquent involvement of the poet in the performance. Because the singer is caught in his song, not simply in its virtuosity but on the fundamental questions that it poses, his declamation can be successful only if it is also authentic as self-discovery. Given their distinct and powerful individualities, Milton at this point is not very distant from Donne.

With two books devoted entirely to *Lyc* and some hundreds of articles including over fifty on a single crux, the reader of Milton's pastoral does not lack advice on how to approach the poem or what to look for in it. Indeed, the problem of how to read the poem may soon become a subject apart from the poem. In the interpretation of interpretations five types of *Lyc* criticism have already been distinguished. With considerable simplification these can be classified as the approach via the genre; the poem as the expression of personality or of profoundly meaningful concerns, stated with the force of personal involvement; the poem as an escape from personality into the anonymity of the language-performance; the poem as archetype; and the poem as a pattern of imagery in which its fundamental meanings are located. Meyer Abrams, who is responsible for distinguishing these five

approaches, adds a sixth of his own, which is to read the poem with "dogged literalness, except when there is clear evidence that some part of it is to be read allegorically or symbolically" (Patrides, p. 221). The result of this exemplary caution is a reading in which the poem is approached through the interplay and development of its dramatic voices.

Of the "types" listed above, the approach via the genre has already been discussed. The poem as a declaration of personality goes back, though the practitioners of the approach may not realize this fully, to one of Johnson's more seminal intimidations : "Passion plucks no berries from the myrtle and ivy, nor calls upon Arethuse and Mincius, nor tells of rough *satyrs* and *fauns with cloven heel*. Where there is leisure for fiction there can be little grief." To those disturbed by this accusation or even to those who believe that conventional art is validated by something behind the convention, the natural reply is to suggest that the "real subject" of *Lyc* is not these pastoral gestures but the fundamental concerns that give meaning to the gestures. Thus for Tillyard (Patrides, pp. 59–60) the real subject is Milton himself and, more specifically, Milton's resolving of his fears of premature death "into an exalted state of mental calm." For Daiches (Patrides, p. 104) the subject is not "simply Milton himself" but "man in his creative capacity, as Christian humanist poet-priest." For Lawry (Arthur Barker, ed., *Milton: Modern Essays in Criticism* [1965], p. 114), *Lyc* is about "poetry and the poet, generally conceived, and of the conditions impelled by existence upon the poet and his works." Such distinctions anticipate the not-always-useful distinctions between conscious and unconscious meanings in *PL*. They also minimize the extent to which conventions themselves are the embodiments of universal and enduring concerns. There is a difference, of course, between embodiment and petrification, but Milton was clearly on the right side of this difference. The third approach, namely, to the poem as ritual performance, is open to the objection that ritual performances differ from each other by something more than the skill exhibited in the performance. It is also more than a verbal quibble to suggest that a poem can be impersonal without being anonymous. The archetypal approach begins at the other extreme, since its initial concern is not with the finished language-object, but with those basic rhythms and relationships through which experience is aesthetically received. The objection, however, is parallel to the one urged against the poem as performance. It is that archetypal statements in poetry differ from each other by something more than the authenticity with which the archetype is proclaimed. The poem found in its imagery may result, as Abrams not altogether frivolously suggests, in the conclusion that *Lyc* is really about water. At best it seeks the identity of the poem through only one of the poem's resources. We can argue that this identity should be declared in the imagery at least as clearly and probably more specifically than it is in the poem's other deployments. But the argument becomes less forceful when we admit that a poem's special cohesiveness may be found not in anything that the poem does, but in the way it puts together everything that it does.

It is apparent that these approaches do not exclude each other and that few critics are fastidious enough or obstinate enough to live wholly within the purity of any single approach. The temptation "to combine all these critical modes into a single criticism" is therefore strong, but Abrams warns us that it will yield "not an integral poem but a ragout." To provide a coherent reading, he urges, "a critical procedure must itself be coherent; it cannot be divided against itself in its first principles." The warning would be irresistible were it not for one fact. *Lyc* is a poem divided against itself and the strength of its achievement may be built on that division. It is therefore possible to think of yet another type of *Lyc* criticism, which would examine the multifarious oppositions in the poem, the structure within which these oppositions are engaged, the style of engagement and of reconciliation, and the manner in which the poem's resources are brought together by its pattern and movement. Such an approach would not be contradictory in its assumptions; but it would seek to bring together understandings that are contrary because they build their houses on divisions established for the poem's purposes within the poem itself. Douglas Bush (*John Milton* [1964], p. 62) describes *Lyc* as "at once an agonized personal cry and a formal exercise, a search for order and a made object, an affirmation of faith in Providence and an exploitation of pastoral and archetypal myth." It is reasonable to approach the poem's wholeness through the manner in which these differing aspects of its existence are intensified and eventually reconciled.

Little is new under the sun of Milton criticism and the view of *Lyc* suggested above has already been urged. It originates perhaps in what are popularly known as the "digressions" in *Lyc,* which Warton apologized for (Elledge, p. 231) as the "gothic combinations of an uneducated age." Modern criticism begins with the conviction that the digressions have a profound propriety. In other words they do not digress at all and the justification for them goes considerably deeper than literary precedent. It is apparent of course that the digressions grow out of authorized pastoral concerns—untimely death and institutional corruption versus Arcadian innocence. But the change in literary manners from stylized lament to passionate vehemence confronts us with a conflict that we cannot evade and that we respond to as "belonging" in the poem. This awareness encourages the suggestion that the digressions are the heart of *Lyc* and that the poem best declares itself when it divests itself of its embroidered cloak. But if we are to avoid further distinctions between the poem's real and nominal subjects, or suggestions that the poem has run away with the poet (anticipating one school of *PL* critics), it would be best to regard the heart of the poem as lying in the relationship between the two literary manners and what they are made to embody. The musical metaphor implicit in the interplay between first and second subject is brought out in Barker's description of the poem as "three successive and perfectly controlled crescendos."

> The first movement laments Lycidas the poet-shepherd; its problem, the possible frustration of disciplined poetic ambition by early death, is resolved by the assurance, "Of so much fame in heaven expect thy meed." The second laments Lycidas as priest-shepherd; its problem, the frustration of a sincere shepherd in a corrupt church, is resolved by St. Peter's reference to the "two-handed engine" of divine retribution. The third concludes with the apotheosis, a convention introduced by Virgil in *Eclogue* V but significantly handled by Milton. He sees the poet-priest-shepherd worshipping the Lamb with those saints "in solemn troops" who sing the "unexpressive nuptial song" of the fourteenth chapter of Revelation. The apotheosis thus not only provides the final reassurance but unites the themes of the preceding movements in the ultimate reward of the true poet-priest. (*Milton. Modern Judgements,* ed. Alan Rudrum [1968], p. 48).

This account of the poem's three-part structure is widely accepted. It will be noted that omitting the "sonnet" opening and the *ottava rima* close, the three parts consist of 70, 47, and 54 lines. It is familiar Miltonic practice that one part in a three-part structure should be carefully disproportionate. Indeed *Nat* draws attention (line 239) to the undue length of its third part. In *PR* and in *SA* the second temptation is considerably longer than the other two. The effect of irregularity within overall regularity is significant in *Lyc* for better reasons than the avoiding of boredom. It testifies to a vital quality of the poem itself and of the recognition it accommodates.

If we look more closely at the three parts we find that part one owes its length to its consisting of not one, but two crescendos—the Orpheus passage and

the passage on fame. With the underlying rhythm of questioning established, the second part can have the impact of brevity and the apocalyptic consolation, in particular, gains in force from not being further developed. The third part, unlike the first two, has only a threatened digression, but its consolation-cum-apotheosis of twenty-one lines is by far the longest, as befits its finality. These variations might be sufficient to undermine the sense of symmetry if the three movements were not parallel in their development. Each begins with a traditional pastoral passage—the recollection of idyllic days spent in the fields, the procession of mourners, and the strewing of flowers. The assault of experience on the convention then develops, and the movement from decorum to disturbance gathers force until the restoration of an equilibrium that permits the pastoral mood to be resumed. The final "resumption" is of such a nature as to preclude the possibility of any further disturbance. To quote Woodhouse (*Essays in Honour of Gilbert Norwood* [1952], p. 273) the first two parts culminate in passages that "shatter the pastoral tone, while the third does not shatter but rather transcends it."

The repeated establishing of a decorum that is then repeatedly violated is apparent not only from the text as it stands, but from its evolution, as previously discussed. In particular, the alteration in line 5 indicates not only the vehemence of grief and the reluctance of a poet to write before his "season," but also suggests the manner in which the poem is to attack its own conventions. The importance that Milton attached to this dominant characteristic of his three movements is also apparent when we notice that each of these movements is prefaced by a statement that the pastoral convention has been or is about to be violated. Two of these statements at lines 85–87 and 132–33 have been noted (J. Milton French, *Studies in Philology* 50 : 486, 489; Abrams, in Patrides, pp. 227ff.). The significance of the third at line 17 has been obscured because of the reminiscence of Virgil's fourth eclogue. But we have already been told of Lycidas's capacity to build the lofty rhyme (this in turn is a reminiscence of Spenser's October eclogue) and the invocation considered within the context of the poem puts us on notice that the pastoral convention is to be strained and surpassed. The lofty rhyme will give way, in a later poem, to the poetry that soars above the Aonian mount (*PL* 1. 15) and one can even suggest that the Christian apotheosis of *Lyc* leads into the later invocation of a Christian muse that surpasses its classical counterpart.

It can therefore be said that there is involved in *Lyc* an assault upon the poem's own assumptions, which the poem in the act of making itself recognizes and progressively strengthens. The assault can be found to begin in the poem's play of language, in the contrast between stylized declamation and vehement, anguished questioning. It is also to be found in the larger tactical maneuver of the pastoral spectacle thrice set up to be undermined. The total attack, both formal and linguistic, can be thought of as the stylistic correlative to the deeper assault of experience upon the sense of order; and the restoration of equilibrium in convention and language corresponds to, validates, and intensifies the deeper restoration of a sense of design in reality. The poem, to quote Isabel MacCaffrey, involves "a growth simultaneously of the speaker's understanding and of the pastoral form itself," and Milton through the concluding vision "confirms the metamorphosis of his genre" (*"Samson Agonistes" and the Shorter Poems of Milton,* ed. MacCaffrey [1966], pp. xxviii-xxix).

It will be apparent that one of the crucial functions of the three movements is to engage repeatedly, and thereby assert with mounting force, the terms of a dialectic that is first tentatively and then enduringly resolved. Varying descriptions of this dialectic are offered. For Brooks and Hardy (Patrides, pp. 136–52) the conflict is between Christian and pagan attitudes and the synthesis "finally accomplished" is a "typically baroque mingling" of both. It is an engagement exemplified in the imagery and particularly in the dual connotations of the word *Shepherd.* For Woodhouse (*Norwood,* pp. 261–78) the contrast is between the Arcadian world of the pastoral and the real world of extra-aesthetic life. Lloyd (*Essays in Criticism* 11 : 390–402), sees a contrast between the self-absorbed world and the world of the good shepherd with the pastoral imagery unifying the examination of both. Brett (*Milton's Lycidas* [1960], pp. 39–50) finds Renaissance humanism carried by the pastoral strain, in conflict with the Protestant convictions brought out by the digressions. Lawry (Barker, pp. 112–23) describes the "seeming opposites" as "pastoral *vs* local engagement, timeless poetry *vs* experience, art *vs* actuality." These produce a "reconstituted possibility of poetry which in part grows out of the formerly opposed modes, *both* of which have seemed, whether by impotence or by antagonistic assault to signal the defeat of poetry." Finally Marjorie Nicolson (*John Milton: A Reader's Guide to His Poetry* [1963], pp. 87–111) sees the conflict emblematized in the contest between the myrtle standing for mourning and the laurel standing for the triumph of the victor, whether living or dead.

Some of *Lyc* can be found between any of these contraries, but it is doubtful if the poem is any of these oppositions alone or even any of them fully. The varying descriptions might rather be seen as testifying to the richness of the poem's life and the range of issues that it is able to bring together in creative confrontation. The result is to draw the reader's mind into the poem more fully and to make him more deeply responsive to its intensity of questioning and its power of reconciling. The "perception of identity and contrariety," the "ever varying balance of images, notions, or feelings, conceived as in opposition to each other" that Coleridge* finds the shaping principle of *Lyc* (*The Romantics on Milton,* ed. Joseph A. Wittreich [1970], p. 179) may not be, as he claims, "the condition of all consciousness," but it does extend considerably the field of force of the poem. The principle that Coleridge invokes is not without foundation in seventeenth-century aesthetics. See H. V. S. Ogden, *Journal of the History of Ideas* 10: 159–82.

The two great classical myths the poem uses—that of Orpheus and that of Arethusa—can be seen as another manifestation of the poem's dialectic. Orpheus, born of Calliope, the muse of heroic poetry, represents the higher mood and the account of his death is in fact the poem's first ascent to that mood. Virgil's fourth eclogue, it might be added, specifically associates the loftier strain with Orpheus. Arethusa is the muse of pastoral poetry invoked, for example, in the tenth eclogue. Orpheus was interpreted as a type of Christ (Caroline Mayerson, *Publications of the Modern Language Association* 64 : 189–207). In Fulgentius's allegorizing of the Alpheus-Arethusa myth (D. C. Allen, *Modern Language Notes* 71 : 172–73), Arethusa represents the nobility of justice and Alpheus the light of truth. Alpheus's waters, by passing unpolluted through the ocean, demonstrate that truth is incorruptible. Carey and Fowler note (p. 246) that a similar view is taken by Sandys. It is significant that Arethusa is called upon after a reference to the purity and perfection of Jove's justice, while Alpheus is called upon after the two-handed engine delivers from a hostile world the shrinking stream of those who pursue the ideal. A slightly different interpretation is proposed by Peck (Elledge, pp. 297–99), according to whom the "mythologists suggest that as Alpheus (imperfection) follows Arethusa (virtue), so matter desires form as its proper good." Hughes* cites Conti to similar effect. It might be added that the truth (Osiris, formerly Alpheus) suffers in *Areop* (4: 337–38) a fate similar to that of Orpheus, and the "empty dream" of the muse who could not protect Orpheus is abandoned in *PL* (7. 1–39) for the heavenly guidance of Urania. Taken together, the two myths

embody the complementary recognitions of *Lyc* that man's fate is to be destroyed and to survive, to keep alive what is eternal in his identity, to pursue the harmony that has fled the world with what is lastingly creative in the self, to endure frustration and yet to find fulfillment. The upward metamorphosis already explored in *Mask*, the underground journey with its Christian overtones, and the reconciliation with the ideal in an order that transforms the terms of our reality are intertwined in a manner that once again bears witness to the integrative power of the poem.

The apotheosis in *Lyc* is a mingling of the Christian and the classical. It is reached, according to Abrams (Patrides, pp. 226–27), by "a gradual shift from the natural, pastoral, and pagan viewpoint to the viewpoint of Christian revelation." Nicolson, on the other hand (*Reader's Guide*, p. 96n.), considers the answers from above to be uniformly Christian. It is possible to regard the three consolations as built up by the three-part structure to provide an understanding that is cumulative and also progressive. Each part discloses a different face of God or, more precisely, a different form of man's recognition of God's nature. The God who calms the first wave of doubts is the God of justice, and emphasis is consequently laid on His impartiality, His "perfect witness," and on the "all-judging" power that weighs all things fully and impartially in its balance. The God of the second part is the apocalyptic God of retribution, whose single blow is sufficient to crush the armies of the godless. "Respiration to the just / And vengeance to the wicked" (*PL* 12. 540–41) are the complementary consolations offered and the complementarity extends to the nuances of tone. The first consolation stills the malignant, monosyllabic march as the blind fury slits the thin-spun life, replacing it by the heartbeat of reassurance. Milton arranges the transition in mid-line with significant delicacy. The rhythm of awareness has different consequences when it is set in a different perspective. The movement is tranquil, as calm of mind must be in stilling the mind's outbursts. In contrast, the second consolation is unassailable in its finality, terminating a torrent of corruption that would otherwise rage unchecked. The "But" of line 130 suggests that in the nature of the case there can be no other termination, and the poem's pounding eloquence itself embodies the momentum of the force that is paralyzed. To make understanding doubly clear, Milton defines the specific quality of each reassurance immediately after the reassurance has been offered. Significantly, these definitions occur in those two crucial passages which admit the violation of the pastoral decorum. We return to normality from the "higher mood" of justice; we return to it again from the "dread voice" of retribution.

The third recognition of God is the one recognition that can truly answer man's questioning. It is the consciousness not of justice, but of the power beyond justice, not the might of him who wields the two-handed engine but instead "the dear might of him that walks the waves." The angel who guards England is invited to "melt with ruth." The dolphins "waft" a Lycidas whose bones only a few lines previously were being "hurl'd" beyond the "stormy Hebrides." As a creature both in and out of its element, the dolphin seems fitted to bear the questioning mind to a higher order, to the "blest kingdoms meek of joy and love." The language of the consolation, compassionate and jubilant, is once again found in an accurately felt relationship to the previous consolations it both completes and supersedes. To quote *PL* (3. 212) it is the "rigid satisfaction, death for death" that has dominated the first two "resolutions" in *Lyc*. The third resolution transcends the law and so reminds us that there are energies in the poem that even the law cannot silence. If peace is to be won, it can be won only through the higher satisfaction of redemptive love. Justice and Wrath—the quiet reassurance and the resounding intervention—must be seen within a larger context if they are to be seen properly as part of the providence of God.

The development of the poem can also be treated as relating and eventually integrating two different perspectives. The ground-level, existential progress toward understanding is associated with the decorum of the pastoral order and its increasingly inadequate consolations. The higher mood, representing a more inclusive understanding, enters the poem at its moments of crisis, guiding the protagonist to a comprehension that is demanded by his intensity of questioning but that is not available within the terms of his world. These entries are managed with characteristic care. In a reminiscence of Virgil's sixth eclogue, the higher mood *descends,* touching the trembling ears of what we can imagine as an averted face. The two-handed engine stands at the door. If justice is from above, retribution is from without. Both point to another realm of principles and forces from which what Reesing (*Milton's Poetic Art* [1968], pp. 123–25) calls the "divine rescue" of the protagonist must be effected.

The "great vision of the guarded mount" needs to be considered in this context. As "vision," it is made to stand apart from the pastoral world it is called on to redeem. The assurance it offers is guarded against those sounding seas of doubt that have raged through the poem with increasing ferocity. The mount itself is evocative of Paradise. The geographical sweep of the proper names suggests the widening horizon of understanding and the attainment of a perspective not possible at the level of this world or within the blindness to which that level consigns us. As we look out on the seas on which the Armada met its fate, the perilous flood comes to mean deliverance as well as destruction. The hill on which the angel stands takes its place in relation to the hill of virtue at the end of *Mask,* the hill of truth in *Sonn* 9, the hill on which Adam stands in the final books of *PL,* and the hill on which Christ stands in *PR.* Above them is the hill (*PL* 3. 56–59) on which God is seated "high thron'd above all highth." This is the infinite vision that human comprehension approaches through the limited vision offered by lesser hills. The collisions of decorum and language in *Lyc* thus provide the means for the higher mood to take over and reaffirm the pastoral convention that it initially challenges and eventually redeems.

The much-discussed water imagery of *Lyc* (see below) further defines some of the poem's characteristic collisions. The Dee contrasts with the Hebrus, the "honoured flood" of the "smooth-sliding Mincius" with the "perilous flood" over which Lycidas comes to preside, and the "level brine" on which Panope plays with her sisters with those "sounding seas" that are stilled by the "great vision." Energy versus containment is the opposition immediately suggested, and if the forces of questioning rage with sufficient vehemence (as they undoubtedly do in this poem), they must undermine the possibility of meaning itself. The three movements confront us with the threatening likelihood that existence may be subject to no design except at best the design of malignancy. As Peck (Elledge, p. 273) and Nicolson in our time (*Reader's Guide,* p. 95) have noted, the Furies are not blind, and it is the Fates, not the Furies, who cut the thread of life. Milton's singular alliance is forged to suggest to us that persecution will be both arbitrary and relentless and that to stand apart is to invite being struck down. The second exposure of meaninglessness complements the first. If dedication is mocked, desecration must be rewarded. A corrupt priesthood is capable of higher irresponsibilities than the pastoral indulgence of sporting with Amaryllis, but the way of the world is inexorably "to good malignant, to bad men benigne" (*PL* 12. 538). Injustice flourishes until it is "smitten" by a power beyond the world. The phrase looks forward to *PR* 4. 561–62 and *SA* 1643–45. In this context the "monstrous world" of the third movement in which Lycidas's bones are "hurl'd" with familiar but intensified violence beyond the outer

limits of the known becomes the objectification of the poem's rampant forces of disorder. As Reesing observes (*Milton's Poetic Art,* p. 22), we are swept to the conclusion that "the world is governed, not blindly, but not at all; that reality is, not merely irrational or deliberately malevolent, but totally mindless." The depths of the abyss must be seen more starkly than ever, before the turn takes place into the poem's peace and the affirmation of peace is validated by the chaos through which it has been repeatedly made to struggle.

The turning point of the poem can be a matter of dispute. D. C. Allen, contrasting the imagery of the flower passage with previous flower imagery (e.g., 45–48), finds the turning point in the flower passage. Others remembering the "false surmise" of line 152 and the menacing lines that follow would prefer to locate the turn at lines 159–64. The function of this image to which Eliot concedes unsurpassed "grandeur of sound" but is apparently prepared to concede little else (*On Poetry and Poets,* pp. 163–64) has already been partially discussed. The angel Michael is imagined as looking southwards to Bayona, a Spanish stronghold about fifty miles south of Cape Finisterre, near which stand the mountains of Namancos. All these places, Hughes notes, "are picturesquely prominent on Ortelius's maps." Apart from standing guard for England against her traditional enemies, the angel is also, Hughes observes, the patron of mariners "in Jewish and often in Christian tradition." Milton's emendation of Corineus to Bellerus in *TM* moves the poem into the mythological distance without divesting it of its political evocations. The legendary and the contemporary unite in the protective strength that is to surround the final understanding; the "guarded mount," with its intimations of Paradise, suggests the restoration not only of Lycidas but of the pattern of order in the scheme of things; and the "great vision" prepares us for the concluding vision of the apotheosis.

In literary history and in legend,

others beside Lycidas have been wafted ashore by dolphins. Arion, a Greek poet credited with inventing the dithyramb, saved himself from a crew of hostile sailors determined to kill him for his wealth by leaping into the sea and being carried ashore by a dolphin. Line 164 has usually been taken as alluding to Arion. Significantly Arion was born on Lesbos, where Orpheus was killed by frenzied Bacchantes (lines 58–63). However, Richardson* and Newton*, followed by Mabbott (*Explicator* 5, no. 26) and others, take it as alluding to Palaemon, who was drowned near Corinth and later honored as the protector of sailors in a temple built at the spot where a dolphin supposedly carried his body ashore. Michael Lloyd (*Essays in Criticism* [1961], 397–98) notes that in "Servius's version of the myth, Phoebus Apollo himself in the guise of a dolphin rescued his drowning son Icarius and carried him to Mount Parnassus." Perhaps this is the account that best fits the pattern of *Lyc,* but it is not inconceivable that Milton meant us to think of the tradition as a whole—a tradition of which Yeats's *Byzantium* can be regarded as the modern sequel—rather than of any specific "rescue." A feature of the deliverance that the language calls to our attention is its gentleness, a serenity that is in significant contrast to the stormy cycles of the poem's questioning.

D. C. Allen (*The Harmonious Vision,* pp. 41–50) has investigated the manner in which the pagan paramythia (the transformation of the man into the legend) becomes the Christian consolation. Apart from Virgil's fifth eclogue (see above) and Spenser's November eclogue with its deification of Dido, key texts in this progress are the concluding sections of Seneca's *Ad Marcian,* the funeral orations of Gregory Nazianzen, and Jerome's* epistle to Heliodorus on the death of Nepolitan. This *"contaminatio* of pagan and Christian topoi" lies not behind *Lyc* alone, but behind all of Milton's elegies. While the tradition goes satisfyingly back, the texts from Revelation that the apotheosis invokes (7 : 17; 14 : 1–5; 19 : 6–9; 21 : 4; 22 : 2) carry the poem not only beyond time but into contemporaneity, since Revelation was so frequently used to expound the eschatological meaning of current events. Milton returns to allied texts from Revelation in the climax of *EpDam* and the nature of the "unexpressive nuptial song" is significantly glossed in a passage in *Apol* (3 : 306–7). We can also remember as we read lines 178–79 that in the battle in heaven in *PL* the loyal angels are repeatedly called saints and that the word in Puritan understanding signified the entire community of the elect. Everlasting blessedness in a kingdom that is at hand for all faithful herdsmen is an implication that may be strengthened if, as Madsen argues (*Studies in English Literature* 3 : 2–6), the speaker of the consolation is Michael. The general view, however, is that "the uncouth Swain" is the speaker.

Whatever its affiliations or whoever utters it, there can be no doubt of the security of the final affirmation. That security is also evident from the manner in which the closing lines detach the apotheosis from the persona whose dramatized search for meaning it has climaxed. The opening quasi-sonnet and the closing *ottava rima* frame that can now be seen as the creative turbulence of the poem also define the advance to "eager thought" from the passion-driven shattering of the leaves. The shift from first to third person has been discreetly prepared for by the shift from second to third person in reporting that the shepherds no longer weep (165, 182). At this point Lycidas becomes the audience of the poem rather than its subject; the next step is to objectify him as the genius of the shore; the shepherds, too, are other people as much as the singer's colleagues; and the stage is now set for the singer himself to step out of his own experience. The "uncouth swain" is clearly not one of those whom John Donne dismisses as having "sucked on country pleasures, childishly." Instead, the heroic, in Landor's words (Wittreich, p. 35), has "burst forth from the pastoral" and bucolic innocence has been found capable of taking in all of experience. Notable also is the manner in which the swain begins his song at daybreak (recalling 25–26) and ends it as twilight falls (recalling 29–31). Apart from the artful reminder of the poem as *mimesis,* we are advised that the day of the song is a day in the life of a shepherd, to be left behind as other days have been, including those days of companionship with Lycidas that were earlier mourned as gone never to return. The rhythm of things calls for progress as well as recurrence. If the evening star (30) shone over the close of one day, the morning star (171) "flames" over the meaning of another. The "Doric lay" has induced what Aristotle* (*Pol.* 8. 5) calls a "moderate and settled temper," putting the affections "in right tune" by its music. As in *SA,* the catharsis is one of understanding as well as of emotion, though the end here is not "passion spent" but vigorous expectancy. As the sun stretches out the hills, the "eager thought" of the singer seems to survey a widening horizon. The sun drops and the curtain falls. The singer in front of it twitches his mantle, the blue of which signifies hope and, to some, the Presbyterian* Covenanters. The fresh woods and new pastures advise us that a writer's covenant with his reader is that he shall not cease from exploration.

The "sources" of the "digressions" remain to be examined. Neaera's hair has entangled more than one commentator. Tibullus, Horace*, Joannes Secundus, and Buchanan* are among the poets who have referred to the subject. The poignant sensuality of the line is Milton's alone. For line 70 Todd* cites Spenser's *Tears of the Muses,* line 404 ("Due praise that is the spur of doing well"). Bush calls the thought a commonplace going back at least to Ovid, *Ex Ponto* 4. 2. 36. The following line is referred by Newton to Tacitus, *Hist* 4. 6 ("Even with wise men the desire for glory is last cut off") and by Bush to Boethius (*Consolatio Phil-*

*osophiae* 11. 7). In connection with Phoebus's consolation, Hanford* cites Spenser's October Eclogue, lines 13ff., where Cuddie is told that the praise is better than the price and the glory greater than the gain. As has already been noted, Apollo in Virgil's sixth eclogue touches the poet's ear and warns him against ambition. Fame was everywhere the spur in the Renaissance, but as Allen points out (p. 66), Milton had well before *Lyc* "found a higher definition of the word." This definition is in *Prol* 7 (12 : 279). *Lyc* at this point looks not only backward but forward to Christ's dismissal of glory in *PR* (3. 25–144). Apart from what it puts together, the passage is remarkable for the manner in which the movement of the verse reflects the true voice of feeling. The buoyant consonants lend their sprightliness to sporting with Amaryllis; the conflagration of line 74 is assisted by the positioning of "blaze" and the alliterative link with "burst"; a second link, this time with "blind," undercuts the excitement of ambition by its delusiveness; and the stealthy progress of the monosyllables in line 75 seems to join calculation mordantly to blindness. At the same time the steps taken up the ladder —the loss of sensual happiness, the clearing of the spirit from the lower distraction, the dedication to a higher infirmity recognized and yet intensely coveted, the total frustration on the edge of achievement, make evident in their entanglement the nature of that purity which must attend the final reckoning. There is, we are made to understand, a difference between "pure" and "clear" as well as between "pure" and "blind"; and the obvious difference between "clear" and "blind" is less decisive that it seems at the first reading.

The Pilot of the Galilean Lake is usually taken to be St. Peter; Hone (*Studies in Philology* 56 : 55–61) argues that he is Christ. In 1 Peter 2 : 25 Christ is described as the Shepherd and Bishop of a straying flock. In John 6 : 15–21 and elsewhere he saves a boat carrying his disciples from shipwreck. In Revelation

1:18 he carries the keys of hell and death. The keys given to St. Peter (Matt. 16:19) seem to fit better into Milton's text. The denunciation of false teachers follows from 2 Peter 2 and decorum is less strained than it would be by Christ's presence in the procession. Two keys are allowed St. Peter by various poets; the golden and the iron clearly anticipate *PL* 2.327–28, and 5.886–87, and Psalm 2:9 may be invoked.

Apart from biblical origins, notably John 10:1–28 and Ezekiel 34, Bernard of Morlais's handling of the John parable in his *De Contemptu Mundi* is cited (G. R. Coffman, *ELH: A Journal of English Literary History* 3:101–13), and *Paradiso* 29.103–26, and 27.19–66, may have been in Milton's mind. Other possible allusions to Dante are listed by Irene Samuel (pp. 285–86). J. M. Steadman (*Notes and Queries,* n.s. 5:141–42) thinks that Milton may have been drawing upon a scene between St. Peter and the condemned clergy in *La rappresentazione del di del guidizio.* Line 115 may echo line 126 of Spenser's May Eclogue but *PL* 4.192–93 and 12.507ff. are anticipated. Those who dislike Ruskin's celebrated interpretation of "Blind mouths" (Elledge, p. 239), in which blindness and rapacity invert the pastoral functions of seeing and nourishing, can turn to Strabo* (4.1.8), who applies the phrase to the choked estuary of a river. Shallowness and obstruction are the failing implied. Hunter (*Modern Language Notes* 65:544) considers that "rot inwardly" (127) comes from Aristotle's *Parts of Animals* 672 a–b, or a Renaissance adaptation thereof. Le Comte (69:403–4) argues that lines 125–27 are closely modeled on a passage in Petrarch's ninth eclogue where Petrarch is recalling the Black Death. The "grim wolf" (128) is usually read as the Roman Catholic Church. Le Comte (*Studies in Philology* 47:606) notes that the arms of the founder of the Jesuits, St. Ignatius Loyola, included two gray wolves. The forward-looking reader will think of *PL* 4.182–92 and 12.507–14. Apart from indicating

the range of Milton's reading, references to such details as the niceties of sheep-rot make clear the determination with which Milton keeps within the boundaries of the pastoral. The higher mood is established not by any change in the imagery or any deviation from the permitted topics, but by the vehement intensity of the utterance.

At this point the two-handed engine must be considered. Fortunately the prevailing interpretations are well summed up by Patrides (p. 240).

Research has yielded parallels in the writings of such diverse figures as Gregory the Great, Dante, John of Salisbury, Savonarola, Du Bartas, Jehan Gerard, Phineas Fletcher, Donne, Thomas Adams and Robert Burton; while the riddle itself has been variously interpreted as the two Houses of Parliament, or liberty as wielded by them; the temporal and Spiritual authority of the Court of High Commission; the destructive power of the imminent civil war; "Puritan Zeal" in general; the combined forces of England and Scotland, or of France and Spain; the Catholic Church; the pastoral staff; the keys of Heaven and Hell given to St. Peter; the lock on St. Peter's door; St. Peter's sword (Matt. 2051, John 18:10); the "Sharp two edged Sword" of the Johannine vision (Rev. 1:16, 2:12); the Sword of Divine Justice (Ezekiel 21:9–17), particularly as wielded by Michael "with huge two-handed sway" (*Paradise Lost* VI, 251); the axe in general, or, specifically, the axe that was "laid unto the root of the trees" (Matt. 3:10, Luke 3:9); the rod of Christ's anger; the Word of God; the Son of God; the scythe of Time; Man "in his dual capacity of labour and prayer"; the Sheep-hook; the iron flail of Talus (*Faerie Queen* V, i, 12; etc.); the temple of Janus; and so on and so forth.

Since Patrides wrote this note, commentary has been added by Thompson (*Studies in Philology* 59:184–200), Rhodes (*Notes and Queries,* n.s. 13:24), Stempel (*English Language Notes* 3:259–63), Tuveson (*Journal of the History of Ideas* 27:447–58) and Reesing (*Milton's Poetic Art,* pp. 31–49). The "sword" class of interpretations is most popular and Reesing (p. 173n.) lists sixteen scholars who find the engine a sword in "one sense or another." Reesing himself argues for the engine as the rod of Christ's wrath, "which is the archetypal reality behind every bishop's staff." It would be no tragedy if the crux were not resolved; some element of mystery is necessary for the apocalyptic effect. Meanwhile the imminence of the deliverance, the power that is deployed in it, its swiftness, and its decisiveness are all made evident by the words on the page.

"Flowerets and Sounding Seas," the title of Wayne Shumaker's study of the affective imagery of *Lyc* (Patrides, pp. 125–35), may at first strike one as yet another formulation of the poem's dialectic. But Shumaker is concerned less with the contrasts between the two classes of imagery than with the contrasts within each class. It is the use of these contrasts that enables *Lyc* to proceed from lamentation to triumph without shifting the terms of poetic discourse. The basic imagery remains consistent throughout, but its potentialities are used in different ways. Josephine Miles's examination of the primary language of *Lyc* (Patrides, pp. 95–100) discovers the integrity of the poem in its vocabulary, showing how the "essential motion from low to high, paralleled by that from past to future, takes place through the primary characteristic words of the poem." Apart from inherited pastoral diction, Milton brings certain words into strong use for the first time. Words such as "*fresh, new, pure, sacred, green, watry, flood, leaf, morn, hill, shade, shore, stream, star, wind, fame, ask, touch*" refer to the natural world "in more specific and sensory terms than were usual before Milton's time," but also transfigure that world through value-giving adjectives. Milton's language is strongly characterized by its "richness in adjectival quality." G. C. Taylor (*Notes and Queries* 178 : 56–57) finds the language less innovative. Of the 1,500 words in *Lyc,* only 46 entered the language after 1500. The Virgilian music is intriguingly achieved with a vocabulary that is 80

percent Anglo-Saxon* in derivation. Carey and Fowler (p. 234) note that Milton's coinages include "inwrought" (105), "freaked" (144), and "scrannel" (124), that "rathe" (142) is used in the *Calendar,* that "daffadillies" (150) suggests the *Calendar's* "daffadowndillies," and that "Guerdon," which Milton uses in *Lyc* for the first and only time, is found no less than twenty-three times in Spenser.

Noting that "Grief is eloquent, but not formal," Newton found a "natural and agreeable wildness and irregularity" in *Lyc.* Hurd attributed the "very original air" of the poem to "the looseness and variety of the meter." Keightley observed that Milton adopted from Tasso and Guarini the "practice of mingling three-foot lines with the regular verses of five feet" (Elledge, pp. 227–28, 236). More categorically, W. P. Ker has advised us that *"Lycidas, the Ode to Anne Killigrew, Alexander's Feast,* the *Odes* of Gray and Keats and before them all, Spenser's *Prothalamion* and *Epithalamion* all belong to the order of the Italian canzone" (*Form and Style in Poetry,* p. 162). In his study of the Italian influence on the versification of *Lyc,* Prince (Patrides, p. 161) notes that two "technical experiments—the attempt to evolve a poetic diction equivalent to that of Virgil, and the attempt to combine the tradition of the *canzone* with that of the classical eclogue—marked Italian pastoral verse in the sixteenth century." Both these endeavors bear their fruit in *Lyc.* Prince shows how the key rhyme (*chiave*) that links the two sections of a *canzone* enables the rhyme schemes of *Lyc* to look both backward and forward, how six-syllable lines are placed "so as to give a sense of expectation," and how the couplet is used to achieve arrest : "the only true couplets in *Lycidas* are those which conclude verse-paragraphs." The result is a verse form that is "closely controlled" and yet not only allows but facilitates "freedom of improvisation." Milton's creative use of previous rhyme schemes is not exhausted by his adaptation of the *canzone.* Oras (*Modern Philology* 52 : 12–22) finds precedents for *Lyc* in the madrigal, and Finney (*Huntington Library Quarterly* 15: 325–50) in the *dramma per musica*.

Prince's remark that Milton had "sufficient Renaissance authority" for the unrhymed lines of *Lyc* should stand next to Ransom's view (*Patrides,* p. 68) that the lines "technically do not belong in . . . any stanza, nor in the poem" and represent an intrusion of individuality in a poem that is only "nearly anonymous." The rhymeless lines register the "ravage" of Milton's "modernity," and no other poem of the time is "so wilful and illegal in form as this one." Critics from Newton onward have been more receptive to what has been accepted as the poem's irregularity, but a recent article by Joseph Wittreich (*Publications of the Modern Language Association* 84 : 60–70) persuasively argues that the irregularities are designed to play against a "single, enveloping rhyme scheme" of remarkable complexity, within which the irregular is eventually regularized. *PL* 5. 618–24 may well serve as an epigraph to Wittreich's article. Considered paragraph by paragraph, *Lyc* has ten unrhymed lines. Considered within the overall scheme, the ten lines reduce to three, "one in each of the *three* thematic units and always in the verse paragraph immediately preceding the consolation for that movement." The rhymes proceed through the alphabet and then repeat the process, with the final consolation coming, with numerological aptness, in the tenth paragraph and taking us precisely ten rhymes into a third alphabet. The "chief control for the poem's pattern is the English madrigal," and the pattern itself is "built of a series of circles, inscribed by the rhyme, suggested and supported by the imagery."

The history of *Lyc* criticism has been intermittently dealt with in this article. Johnson's strictures, which dominate that history, have been contested from the beginning and can now be thought of as annulled. The nineteenth century is not prominent in bringing about this annul-ment. Criticism of *Lyc* by the Romantic poets as assembled by Wittreich is not very extensive and Stevens in the *Reference Guide to Milton* (19930) lists only nine items on the poem from 1800 to 1899. Ruskin's remarks (Elledge, pp. 237–44) stand apart and remain of much more than historical importance. Mark Pattison in *Milton* anticipates some future criticism when he finds the "fanaticism of the covenanter and the sad grace of Petrarch" meeting in Milton's monody. These opposites, "instead of neutralising each other, are blended into one harmonious whole." Of early twentieth-century appreciations, Bailey's (*Milton* [1915] pp. 123–31) is among the more perceptive.

Despite relics of Johnson's objection, such as the view that *Lyc* is a poem strangled by art (Robert Graves) or that it is no more than a collection of magnificent fragments (G. Wilson Knight), it has been the privilege of criticism of the last half-century to fully meet the accusations of empty conventionality and uncalled-for juxtapositions. In the process a detailed consensus has developed testifying to the intricate unity of the poem, the profound pertinence of its alleged digressions, the force of experience that the genre is made to accommodate, and the highly charged meaningfulness of a creative performance that possesses the past in order to speak to all times. [BR]

**MACAULAY, THOMAS BABINGTON:** *see* INFLUENCE ON THE LITERATURE OF NINETEETH-CENTURY ENGLAND, MILTON'S.

**MACHIAVELLI, MILTON AND.** *CB* provides the proof that Milton studied the works of Niccolo Machiavelli (1469–1527). Of eighty-one authors cited in it, Machiavelli ranks fifth in the number of subject sections in which he is cited. He is the seventh most frequently cited author over all. Of the seventeen citations only two (made in 1640–1642) are taken from Machiavelli's *Dell' Arte Della Guerra;* the rest are from his *Discorsi sopra la*

*Prima Deca di Tito Livio* (entered apparently by Edward and John Phillips, 1651–1652). Since the citations to the *Dell' Arte* are accompanied by page numbers from the *Tutte Opere* of 1550, it is assumed that Milton also used that edition for his readings in the *Discorsi*. These notes have less to do with war* than with general observations on the nature and administration of the state.

Milton noted most of the *Discorsi* citations for support of his faith in republican government or his distrust of monarchy in the early 1650s. Cited are Machiavelli's contempt for inherited power (p. 195) and his argument that a republic chooses minor officials more carefully and is generally more responsible to the people than a monarchy (p. 198). Thus Machiavelli may have supplied some of the republican ideas in such prose tracts as *1Def* and *Way*.

Beyond such general observations, it is difficult to assess Machiavelli's influence on Milton's published works. Where one would expect to find a definite borrowing of ideas there is none, or the ideas themselves are Renaissance commonplaces. In one passage from *CB* under the heading "Of Civil War," Milton notes an argument justifying rebellion (p. 246) and supports it with a quotation from the *Discorso*. And under "The Tyrant" Machiavelli appears as one of the eleven authors cited who justified the destruction of an unjust monarch : "To cure the ills of the people, words suffice, and against those of the prince the sword is necessary" (p. 185). However, none of the antityrannical citations from Machiavelli seem to represent readings that might have played a clearly recognizable role in *Tenure*. In *Eikon* 18, there is an obvious reference to the passage from *Il Principe* that describes the political necessity to avoid traps like a fox and to frighten wolves like a lion. But the Machiavellian lion-fox emblem was a commonplace of Renaissance political imagery. The same may be said of the battle scenes in *PL*. The war in Heaven* contains principles of military strategy found in many sources

available to Milton other than the *Dell' Arte* and the *Discorsi*.

A few passages bear a slightly more certain relationship to Machiavelli. Lines 7–9 of *Sonn* 17 "To Sir Henry Vane" (1652) would seem to be a more direct use of a passage from the *Discorsi* noted twice in *CB*. Yet even here war's "two main nerves, Iron and Gold" could be as much a commonplace usage as a conscious borrowing from Machiavelli's discussion of an army's best strength (cf. pp. 148 and 193). In *PL* 1. 347–56, Milton's description of the multitude of fallen angels* gathering on the plain in hell* recalls the opening pages of Machiavelli's *Istorie Fiorentine,* which describes similarly the multitude of vandals who were to destroy Rome. These borrowings, however, represent a poet's response to an image or turn of phrase. They are not peculiarly Machiavellian passages.

Machiavelli's influence on Milton has been overestimated by some, and at least one critic has called Milton a Machiavellian in a pejorative sense. There are only two explicit references to Machiavelli in all of Milton's works written for publication—one in *Apol* (1642), the other in *DDD* (1644) 14. Both references are highly uncomplimentary, reflecting the earlier, Elizabethan view of the Machiavel. Certainly Milton read and was impressed by Machiavelli, but the influence in the prose and poetry is often more apparent than real, and he was hardly a Machiavellian in any sense. *See also* CABINET COUNCIL. [FBY]

**MACOCK, JOHN:** *see* PRINTERS.

**MACROBIUS, AMBROSIUS THEODOSIUS,** who flourished at the end of the fourth century A.D., was not a native of Italy, but other facts about his career are lacking, and his identification with an official of the same name mentioned in the Theodosian Code remains doubtful, as does his religious belief, whether Christian or pagan. Macrobius is the author of two important extant works : a *Commentary* on the *Dream of Scipio* by

Cicero* (the last portion of *De re publica*), and *Saturnalia,* a miscellany of pagan lore and antiquarianism in the form of a series of dialogues modeled on those of Plato* and Aulus Gellius. The *Commentary* of Macrobius had an important influence in the development of medieval thought, chiefly through its presentation of Neoplatonic* concepts, and there are numerous references to it in Chaucer*. The *Saturnalia,* in seven books, became interesting to Renaissance scholars for its melange of information on points of philology, history, and mythology; it also served the needs of Renaissance critical theory in pointing out parallels between Homer* and Virgil*, and in giving instances of Virgil's borrowing from earlier Latin writers such as Ennius. It was included in a list of assigned works for students at Cambridge in Milton's day. That Milton was familiar with *Saturnalia* is shown by his alluding to it for purposes of invective in *Animad* and in *2Def*; there are also two citations on grammatical points in the Columbia MS, but these are probably not Milton's. [PS]

**MAGALOTTI, COUNT LORENZO:** *see* TRANSLATIONS OF MILTON'S WORKS.

**MAGNANIMITY.** Milton says in *CD* that "magnanimity is shown, when in the seeking or avoiding, the acceptance or refusal of riches, advantages, or honors, we are actuated by a regard to our own dignity, rightly understood" (17 : 241). He refers to magnanimity and magnanimous men and actions many times throughout his poetry and prose, and seems to use the words to describe an ideal that originated in Plato* and Aristotle*, whose views were subsequently modified by many Christian writers. Two general senses of the word and the ideal it signifies appear in Milton's works. One is political and the other philosophical or religious, although the two are rarely separable.

In his political prose, Milton says that the actions of various groups and individuals display magnanimity—the parliamentary forces that called for the execution of Charles I* (*Tenure* 5 : 41); the English people who with "greatness of soul . . . conquered their own king, . . . and put him to death" (*1Def* 7 : 65, 553); Cromwell*; and such Romans as Cassibelan, Togadumnus, Venusius, and Caractacus, all men who heroically resisted tyrants. These men, who act out of a "magnanimity peculiar to heroes" in the defense of liberty*, show justice and temperance and the "highest courage to subdue what conquers the rest of the nations of men—faction, avarice, the temptation of riches, and the corruptions that wait upon prosperity" (*1Def* 7 : 65, 553). The magnanimous political man is thus one whose actions incorporate the classical virtues of temperance, courage, wisdom, and justice. Aristotle had likewise described magnanimity as "a sort of crown of the virtues; for it makes them greater, and it is not found without them" (*Nicomachean Ethics* 1123b–24b).

Aristotle's magnanimous man is very much like Milton's. He is a man who claims honor according to his deserts and "thinks himself worthy of great things, being worth of them." The Greek ideal, like Milton's political magnanimity, was closely tied to the rewards of this world, and was characterized by a refusal to tolerate injustices (*Posterior Analytics* 97b) and by an indifference to the vicissitudes of good and bad fortune. Only men of strong ethical character can manifest the ideal, and it is akin to Plato's "magnificence of mind" as described in the *Republic* (486a–b) and the common virtue that runs through all the other virtues as it is described in the *Meno* (74b).

Early Christian writers altered the classical concept in several important ways, adding to it a religious meaning it did not possess in ancient Greece. Milton's prose writings seem curiously indifferent to these Christianized meanings, whereas his poetry appears to embrace them. The Christian writers associated with magnanimity the themes of knowledge*, sacrifice, humility, and the rule of reason*. Clement of Alexandria* said that magnanimity was the intuitive knowledge that lifts us above events of this world (*Strom,* 2. 78–79). Origen* said that it expressed the Christian doctrine of renunciation and sacrifice, as shown in the example of Jesus (*Contra Celsum* 4. 42, 46). Augustine* combines both views when he says that magnanimity is that virtue which most scorns the things of the world (*De quantitate animae* 17), whereas Aquinas* reverts to Aristotle and declares magnanimity to be great honor achieved by great acts of virtue, wherein magnanimity regulates our desire for greatness by following the rule of reason (*Summa Theologica* 2. 2. 129. 3–4). All these meanings are shown in the character of Milton's Jesus, especially as seen in *PR,* as well as in that of Samson in *SA.* It is possible to say, in fact, that the trials of any Christian hero are a test of his magnanimity, when the ideal is understood as the "greatness of soul" that infolds all the classical virtues and seeks to glorify God. [PEB]

**MALATESTI, ANTONIO** (d. 1672), a member of the intellectual elite of Florence during Milton's two visits to that city in 1638–39. He acquired a reputation primarily as a witty poet but also as a mathematician and a painter. He and other Florentine savants, like Carlo Dati*, his close friend, befriended Milton in Florence and entertained him at the academies. Sometime while Milton was in Florence, Malatesti presented him with a manuscript of fifty sonnets, entitled *La Tina,* which had been written in the autumn of 1637 at Malatesti's villa in Taiano. The sonnets, which perhaps had been circulated among Malatesti's friends, were addressed to a rustic mistress, maybe imaginary, and their racy humor was derived from the use of equivocal expressions. The manuscript, which was shipped to England or transported by Milton himself, is not mentioned until eighty years after Milton's death. About 1750 Thomas Brand discovered in a London bookstall the manuscript that Malatesti presented to Milton and gave

it to Thomas Hollis, his friend. In 1757 an edition of *La Tina* was published in London, presumably from this manuscript or a copy. A few years later (ca. 1759) another edition of *La Tina* was published in Italy, probably from the original manuscript or a copy presented to Giovanni Marsili of the University of Padua, while he was visiting London in 1757. However, the manuscript presented to Milton by Malatesti has disappeared. [ACL]

**MAVVEZZI, VIRGILIO:** *see* MARGINALIA.

**MAMMON.** "The God of wealth," frequently associated with Plutus, *Mammon* is a "word signifying in the Syriak tongue riches, or wealth, and is derived from the Hebrew word *Hamon* . . . [meaning] plenty" (Edward Phillips, *The New World of English Words* [1658], sig. Aa iv^v). Behind Phillips's remark is one by Augustine* : "Riches are said to be called '*mammon*' among the Hebrews, and in the Punic the word has a corresponding meaning, for in that language the word '*mammon*" signifies profit. Therefore, whoever serves mammon is the servant of him who—in retribution for his perversity—has been placed over the things of this world, and is therefore designated by the Lord as 'the prince of this world' " (*Commentary on the Sermon on the Mount,* trans. Denis J. Kavanagh [1951], p. 155).

Mammon's name is seldom used in Scripture (Matt. 6 : 24, Luke 16 : 9, 11, 13); and when it appears in phrases like "the mammon of unrighteousness," the name seems to be used as an abstract noun rather than as a proper name. However, in the warning, "Ye cannot serve God and Mammon," the name is construed (by Gregory of Nyssa* and others) as yet another name for Satan. The tendency to identify Mammon with Satan is manifested first in apocryphal* writings, then in scholastic philosophy; and later it finds literary expression in Spenser's* *Faerie Queene.* Here "Mammon takes the place of Archimago, representing Satan in another form" (Edwin Greenlaw, ed., *Works of Edmund Spenser* 2 : 428). This interpretive tradition makes it clear that "when Milton speaks of Mammon as one of the fallen angels in hell, we have . . . not so much the flight of the poet's imagination as an indication of his familiarity with apocryphal lore" and an indication of his indebtedness to both the Church Fathers and to Spenser (see *Encyclopedia of Religion and Ethics*, ed. James Hastings et al., 8 : 375).

Milton's conception of Mammon, deriving from scriptural, exegetical, and literary traditions, preserves the occult notion that Mammon is prince of the tempters. "The Tempters and Ensnarers," says Agrippa, have the last place, one of which is present with everyman . . . their prince is *Mammon,* which is interpreted covetousness" (*Three Books of Occult Philosophy*, trans. J. F. [1651], p. 399). References to Mammon in Milton's prose works identify him as the god of the prelates, the father of Antichrist (*Ref* 2 : 42, 54; also *Tenure* 5 : 45), the spreader of "*Balaams* disease . . . *Mammon*'s Praestriction" (*Animad* 3 : 137). If Mammon is like Milton's Belial in his use of fraud and deception, he is like Milton's Moloch in his association with idolatry: "covetousness" says Milton, "which is worse then heresie, is idolatry" (*Tenure* 5 : 45). As Alexander Ross* explains, "The covetous man worshippeth his god *Plutus,* or *Mammon,* with as great devotion as any Idolater doth his idol" (*Pansebeia* [1672], p. 64). Besides equating idolatry and avarice, Milton preserves the connection between Plutus and Mammon (*Animad* 3 : 161–62) and, in a famous passage, writes :

> I cannot praise a fugitive and cloister'd vertue, unexercis'd & unbreath'd. . . . That vertue therefore which is but a youngling in the contemplation of evill, and knows not the utmost that vice promises to her followers . . . is but a blank vertue, not a pure . . . ; Which was the reason why our sage and serious Poet *Spencer* . . . describing true temperance under the person of *Guion,* brings him in with his palmer through the cave of Mammon, and

the bour of earthly blisse that he might see and know, and yet abstain. (*Areop* 4 : 311)

As Ernest Sirluck observes, "This is one of Milton's most interesting errors. . . . It is evidence not merely that Milton thought he knew the poem too well to check the incident, but also that he missed the exact point of Spenser's psychology in a rather important matter" (see Yale *Prose* 2 : 516n, and *Modern Philology* 48 : 90–96).

"The most Abject, Base, and Vile" of the devils (the phrase is Patrick Hume's*), Mammon is the architect of Pandemonium* and the first to rifle "the bowels of . . . mother Earth" (*PL* 1. 687). In him we contemplate "the passions of the infernals, envy and revenge in all their native deformity, without any rhetorical decorations" (*Poetical Works,* ed. Henry John Todd [1809], 1 : 268). "The least erected Spirit that fell / From heav'n" (*PL* 1. 679–80), Mammon leads the three multitudes who built Pandemonium—an "ascending pile" that dwarfs the greatest monuments and the most magnificent kingdoms of the world. Called Mulciber "in ancient *Greece;* and in *Ausonian* land" (but see Donald C. Baker, *Notes and Queries* 4 : 122–13), Mammon, in his adoration of "Heav'ns pavement," contrasts strikingly with "the astral contemplative of Seneca's *Naturales Quastiones,* whose soul, having attained the heights of Heaven, laughs at the pavements of the rich" (John M. Steadman, *N & Q,* n.s. 7 : 220).

Lacking the grandeur of the previous speakers in hell, but not their depravity, Mammon asks Moloch, "what place can be for us / Within Heav'ns bound, unless Heav'ns Lord supream / We overpower?" (*PL* 2. 235–37); and to Belial he says, "what joy can be found in awaiting new subjection" that will require from the devils "warbl'd Hymns, and Forc't Halleluiah's" (2. 242–43). Preferring "Hard liberty" to "the easie yoke / Of servile Pomp" (2. 256–57), Mammon contends that the devils can "create," they can "imitate," they can build a rival kingdom. Mammon's speech, recalling the tradition that sees "Satan" as "Gods ape," invites identification between himself and the archfiend (see Alexander Ross, *Mystagogus Poeticus* [1672], p. 104), and Lucas Debes, *Foeooe, and Foeroa Reserata* [1676], p. 404). As a creator, however, Mammon is "rigidly limited," his activity being "reduced to the circle of hell" (Arnold Stein, *Answerable Style* [1953], p. 43). Creating a hell that apes the City of God, Mammon "represents evil . . . as a parody of good" (Northrop Frye, *The Return of Eden* [1965], p. 77). Mammon's speech also recalls that of Juno in Virgil's* *Aeneid* but, unlike Juno's speech, quiets rather than inflames the assembly. What Juno says is compared to a rising wind, but what Mammon says is likened to the falling of the wind after a tempest (see *Poetical Works*, ed. Thomas Newton [1751], 1 : 104).

Owing considerably to Spenser's portrait, Milton's Mammon embodies covetousness or avarice, represented in carefully defined stages resembling those that Guyon confronts in the three temptations of *The Faerie Queene;* but Milton's characterization shows equally close connections with Pleonectes in Fletcher's* *Purple Island,* where "the three stages of avarice . . . merge almost imperceptibly into each other." It also illustrates the Ciceronian doctrine that avarice causes men to commit acts of injustice and recalls St. Paul's contention that money is the source of all evil. "No static symbol," Mammon is a "dynamic figure in whose soul avarice develops and expands until he eventually progresses beyond the limits of the original vice to embrace the more comprehensive vice of injustice" (Robert C. Fox, *Review of English Studies,* n.s. 13 : 30–39).

Though Merritt Hughes objects that any treatment of the devils as "deliberately patterned examples or embodiments of the Seven Deadly Sins, or of any other traditional abtraction of theology is to violate their essence as individuals" (*Studies in Honor of DeWitt T. Starnes,* ed. Thomas P. Harrison et al. [1967], p. 250), Milton's own symbolic scheme

seems to equate Mammon with the second master-category of sin (avarice)—a view that is given credence by the realization that the various devils tend to blur together and then merge imperceptibly into the figure of Satan. By virtue of the idolatry implied by his covetousness, Mammon resembles Moloch; and by virtue of his identity with things of this world, he resembles Belial. These connections with the other devils in the infernal council blur the singularity of Mammon's character suggested at the literal level of Milton's poem; they pave the way for his identification with Satan at the symbolic level, where, with Belial and Moloch, Mammon becomes one of the three faces of Satan. *See* BEELZEBUB. [JAW]

**MANNERISM, MILTON AND.** Though many art historians question the validity of the term *mannerism*—and still disagree as to its meaning and chronological limits and its relation to Renaissance and baroque* styles—those who accept this term usually apply it to a particular phase in the development of modern Western art, intermediate between the "classical" art of the High Renaissance and "baroque" art. Some regard it as an early and temporarily victorious rival of early baroque trends. Some distinguish two markedly different stages of mannerism. Some regard it as a constant in the history of Western art and literature, occurring both in antiquity and in medieval culture; and some have detected mannerist phases in the visual and verbal arts of other civilizations.

Wölfflin evolved a fivefold schema for analyzing the development from the style of High Renaissance art (characterized by an emphasis on line, plane, closed form, multiplicity, and absolute clarity) to the baroque (characterized by "painterly" qualities, recession, open form, unity, and relative clarity), but he did not include a specifically "mannerist" period. Nevertheless, in 1914—a year prior to the publication of Wölfflin's *Principles of Art History*—Walter Friedländer had delivered an important address on the origins of mannerism. While recognizing (with qualifications) the influence of Michelangelo on the development of mannerism, Friedländer credited three figures —Pontormo, Rosso, and Parmigianino— with the primary responsibility for developing this new style, which deliberately "cast off the classic, and against the Renaissance pattern of canonical balance, set up a subjective rhythmic figuration and an unreal space formation. . . ." This style was already fully formed between 1520 and 1523, and the "sack of Rome in 1527 scattered the seeds of the new tendency far and wide. . . ." This period was "not a mere transition, not merely a conjunction between Renaissance and Baroque, but an independent age of style, autonomous and most meaningful."

Differentiating this early phase of mannerism from a second and later phase (which began, in his opinion, around 1550), Friedländer argued that an "anti-mannerist style" of the late sixteenth century arose in opposition to this second phase of mannerist," but not at all to the same degree, nor in antithesis to the so-called High Renaissance." This anti-mannerist style can be termed "early, or rather pre-Baroque," but it is also in fact "a neo-classical or neo-Renaissance period . . ." See Walter Friedländer, *Mannerism and Anti-Mannerism in Italian Painting* (1965). In an introduction to this edition Donald Posner observes that seventeenth-century writers had applied the term *maniera* to "the art of the later sixteenth century because of its dependence on artificial and derivative representational formulae that depart from natural appearances." Posner briefly surveys the studies by Weisbach, Dvorák, Craig Hugh Smith, Shearman, Benesch, Pevsner, and Zeri on mannerist art.

Erwin Panofsky's *Idea: A Concept in Art Theory,* trans. Joseph J. S. Peake (1968) was first published in German in 1924. In Italian mannerist painting of the second half of the sixteenth century he recognized an attempt to "outdo the classic style . . . by modifying the regrouping of plastic forms as such."

Rebelling against "all rigid rules, especially mathematical ones," mannerist art "distorted and twisted the balanced and universally valid form of the classic style in order to achieve a more intense expressivity" and "abandoned the classic style's . . . clear rendering of space . . . in favor of that . . . manner of composition that pressed shapes into a single, often 'unbearably crowded' plane. . . . " The most characteristic quality of this art is "an internal dualism, an inner tension." It rejected "both the flowing freedom of baroque space and the lawful order and stability of Renaissance space," creating severer restraints "by means of planarity." While insisting on the freedom of the artist, it paradoxically affirmed that artistic creativity "could be systematized."

Emphasizing the Neoplatonic* element in mannerist art theory, Panofsky credits the latter with first achieving a "basic clarification" of the "subject-object" problem." For mannerist theory, the artist's primary loyalty is not to the external object but to the inner design or idea in his own mind, and this is of supra-terrestrial origin. The primary distinction between Renaissance and mannerist attitudes toward art lies in the mannerist "conviction that the visible world is only a 'likeness' of invisible, 'spiritual' entities and that the contradiction between 'subject' and 'object' which had now become apparent to the intellect could be solved only by an appeal to God." Subsequently, in *Meaning in the Visual Arts* (1955), Panofsky reexamined the question of a mannerist phase in the development of architecture. Though the historical view, "current until about 1920," which emphasized the "continuous development of the 'Classic' Renaissance into the Baroque" and regarded mannerism as merely a "side line or by-product" must be revised in "respect to the representational arts," it may still hold true in the case of architectural style. Though mannerism is "the rule in Central Italian painting," it "remains the exception in Central Italian architecture,' which did, on the whole, develop "rather continuously and consistently . . . from the 'Classic' High Renaissance into the Early Baroque." When mannerist architecture "did invade the territories of Florence and Rome, the buildings in question were not designed by professional architects, but by such artists as were at home in the representational or decorative arts," and this style actually "represented a rebellion of the non-architects. . . ."

Sir Anthony Blunt characterizes mannerism as an emotional, irrational, and unnaturalistic art. Frequently unworldly, often bordering on mysticism, and preferring subjects that permitted the painter to emphasize "theological or supernatural aspects," it was a reaction against the ideals and methods of humanistic painting, abandoning "Renaissance ideals of convincing space and normal proportions" and making "almost as free use as a medieval artist of arbitrary construction and deliberate elongation." Both in technique and in subject matter the mannerists are sometimes closer to medieval than to Renaissance painters. This art is the reflection of a "worldly, emotional, anti-intellectual kind of religion," and Blunt associates certain of its features with the Counter-Reformation. He also distinguishes between the earlier mannerists —"aristocratic and emotional"—and the "academic and eclectic" mannerism associated with the figures of Federico Zuccaro and G. B. Armenini in Rome and of Lomazzo in Milan (*Artistic Theory in Italy, 1450–1600* [1940]).

Like *baroque, mannerism* has entered the technical vocabulary of literary scholars. Curtius regards it as a "constant in European literature," as the "complementary phenomenon of the Classicism of all periods," observing that "much of what we shall call Mannerism is today set down as 'Baroque.'" Emphasizing its indebtedness to rhetoric* for devices like hyperbaton, circumlocution, annominatio, and mannered metaphor, he detects parallels between ancient, medieval, and Renaissance "mannerism." He traces "seven leading varieties of formal Mannerism" from antiquity to the Renaissance, at the same time emphasizing the close association of mannerism with the epigram and the "pointed style." He condemns the attempt to "separate seventeenth-century Mannerism from its two thousand years of prehistory and . . . to call it a spontaneous product of (Spanish or German) Baroque. . . ." See Ernst Robert Curtius, *European Literature and the Latin Middle Ages,* trans. Willard R. Trask (1963), pp. 273–301.

In *Mannerism: The Crisis of the Renaissance and the Origin of Modern Art,* trans. Eric Mosbacher, (1965), Arnold Hauser interprets mannerist art and literature as an expression of the "alienation" of Renaissance man under the impact of the new science and new religious movements, the economic and social revolution, and Machiavellian* politics. He associates mannerism with the birth of modern tragedy and the discovery of humor, but detects a "latent mannerism" as well as baroque trends in the art of the High Renaissance. He distinguishes several phases in the development of mannerism both within and outside Italy. Emphasizing the function of metaphor and conceit in mannerist literature, he associates Marino*, Tasso*, and the Italian Petrarchists with mannerism, a quality that he also sees in Gongora and Cervantes, Montaigne and Ronsard, Marlowe and Shakespeare*, and the English metaphysical poets*. He explores the complex relationships between mannerism, baroque, and classicism. In his opinion, both mannerist and baroque trends were "anti-classical" and "the product of the same spiritual crisis," expressing the "open split between the spiritual and physical values on the harmony between which the survival of the Renaissance principally depended." Nevertheless, the baroque "returned to the Renaissance naturalism and rationalism that mannerism dropped," and in contrast to the "more superficial points of contact between mannerism and the Renaissance, the baroque and the Renaissance share a whole series of common characteristics that are of more basic importance."

Hauser argues that "only in the later phases of its development" did the baroque "deliberately and systematically" turn against mannerism. The "complete and final breach with mannerism and its heritage was first made by classicism, partially within the baroque but mostly rather as a reaction against it."

The problem of Milton's alleged mannerism depends partly on the distinctions the critic draws between mannerism, baroque, and metaphysical styles, as well as on the similarities or differences that he perceives between the styles of Milton's own poems or between the poetry of Milton and his near-contemporaries. Metaphysical poetry has been classified both as mannerist and as a subspecies of the baroque. Tasso has been called a mannerist as well as a baroque writer. In accordance with these variable definitions and comparisons, Milton's early verse has been alternatively labeled mannerist and baroque.

For Wylie Sypher, mannerism was a reflection of contemporary malaise and distrust and represented the "formal dissolution" of an earlier artistic style based on "proportion and harmony and unity." In the mannerist period "renaissance optimism is shaken, . . . proportion breaks down and experiment takes the form of morbid ingenuity or scalding wit. . . ." Mannerism has "two modes, technical and psychological," and behind the "technical ingenuities of mannerist style there usually is a personal unrest, a complex psychology that agitates the form and the phrase." Mannerist art "holds everything in a state of dissonance, dissociation, and doubt. . . ." Its principal characteristics are "disproportion, disturbed balance, ambiguity, and clashing impulses," not only in the arts of design but in metaphysical poetry, "Jacobean drama, and all the witticisms of Cultism, Marinism, Gongorism, and emblematic verse." In Sypher's opinion, "mannerism in style accompanies mannerism in thought and feeling." Troubled and obscure, if not "illogical," it "treats its themes from unexpected points of view and eccentric angles, some-

times hidden." Its "images and metaphors seem perverse and equivocal," and its statements "intense and highly 'expressive' " (*Four Stages of Renaissance Style* [1955]).

Sypher finds the "dissonances" of mannerism "still audible" in *Lyc,* and Roy Daniells regards this poem as well as *Mask* as a mannerist work. "If the concept of Mannerism did not exist," Daniells suggests, "we should by now be compelled to invent it." Viewed in the context of mannerist tradition, the style of the English metaphysicals no longer seems a splendid aberration but "rather . . . the logical development from Spenserian or Sidneyan smoothness" and the necessary bridge to the baroque style of Milton's larger works. Like several art historians, Daniells stresses the mannerist deformation of classical conventions. It "unexpectedly combines" the elements of a "fixed traditional pattern" in order to "achieve effects of dissonance, dislocation, and surprise. . . ." Examining *Mask* in the context of mannerist conventions," Daniells notes the "firm reliance upon traditional stylistic elements" combined with "old discrepancies, sheerings off at an angle, changes of direction, failures to fulfil normal expectations. Familiar elements are reconstituted, familiar effects rearranged." The dislocations of this poem "reveal the efforts of an idealizing mind to find assurance," but the poet fails to push the mannerist approach "far enough or with sufficient vigour." In *Lyc* Daniells finds analogies with mannerism in the heavy dependence on tradition, the manipulations of space, the "pace and manner of shifting the scene," the versification, and the "self-conscious concern with a completed formal task. . . ." As "the most effective lyric utterance in the English language," *Lyc* "has relied heavily upon its Mannerist method." See his *Milton, Mannerism and Baroque* (1963).

In *Milton Studies in Honor of Harris Francis Fletcher* (1961), pp. 209–25, Rosemond Tuve challenges Curtius's and Sypher's criteria for defining mannerism and questions the reliability of *mannerism* and *baroque* as categories applicable to Milton's poetry and that of his contemporaries.

Though these art-historical categories may serve as convenient labels for differentiating variations in Milton's style, their utility is often compromised by their uncertain denotation. The same poems that one critic regards as clearly mannerist, another classifies as baroque or (to employ Hatzfeld's term) "baroquist." If these labels possessed a fixed denotation and if they could be disassociated from the controversial sociohistorical stereotypes they often evoke, they might be more effective as instruments of practical criticism. While these art-historical categories have enriched our technical vocabulary—most notably through the concept of *Spannung* or "tension"—they have also confused it; and we should regard them with cautious gratitude. [JMS]

**MANOA.** Though Manoa's role in *SA* and his characterization are largely Milton's own invention, they have nevertheless been partly suggested by the account of Manoah in the biblical narrative. The Book of Judges mentions Samson's father only at the beginning and the end of the history of Samson's life —*before* the hero's birth and *after* his death—and once in relation to the woman of Timnath. Here the spelling of the Authorized Version for biblical characters and places is retained, while Milton's spelling for the same persons and localities is reserved in a dramatic context. As James Thorpe has demonstrated ("On the Pronunciation of Names in *Samson Agonistes*," *Huntington Library Quarterly* 31 : 65–74), Manoa's name must be pronounced once as with three syllables, and elsewhere as two syllables; but stress in either case should fall on the *first* syllable.

The Manoah of Judges 13 and the Geneva Bible glosses to it is chiefly defined by his religious conception of the offices of a father, by his concern for the nurture (or education) of his son in obedience to the divine will, and by his limited knowledge of the divine intent. The biblical Manoah mistakes the identity of the angelic messenger just as the dramatic Manoa will mistake the divine intent underlying Samson's marriages with infidels. As biblical character and as *dramatis* persona, he is inclined to fear the worst and to misinterpret divine signs. In the drama he will exhibit the same parental care, the same oscillation between hope and dread, the same devotion to the will of God, and the same uncertainty as to the divine intent—but they will be complicated by his son's violation of his Nazarite discipline and by his apparent dereliction. In his marriage choices Samson has not, in fact, abstained from "any uncleane thing"; Manoa cannot understand the divine purpose that has granted Samson dispensation from things "forbidden by the Law," nor does he perceive that Samson's trial through suffering is itself a divinely ordained method of nurture—a means of perfecting him as a Nazarite, separating him from the world and rededicating him to the service of God. (See Ann Gossman, *Journal of English and Germanic Philology* 61: 528–41). The isolation of the hero, from friends and enemies alike in the course of the drama, is itself a mode of spiritual education and purification; but (like the marriage to the woman of Timnath) this is the "secret work" of God. Milton counterpoints divine and human care in the "nurture" of the heroic Nazarite, just as he counterpoints Manoa's scheme to deliver Samson with God's scheme to deliver Israel through Samson. Like the conception of the hero, his act of heroic deliverance must be accomplished by divine rather than by human power. Manoa's endeavors to ransom his son are as futile as his efforts to remove his wife's barrenness; and their futility points the same moral as the Geneva glosses on the barren wife.

In the drama, as in Judges, Manoa is perplexed by divine signs. Samson's miserable plight and sense of heaven's desertion seem to point to the loss of divine favor; on the other hand, the miraculous gift of strength seems to argue the contrary. Manoa correctly interprets the latter as evidence of God's favor, but misconstrues it as a sign that God will renew the hero's eyesight. The care he hopes to bestow on his blind son stands in striking opposition to the nurture he had given the Nazarite as a boy—the inglorious ease and enforced idleness of a defeated champion in contrast to severely disciplined education for a future heroic life. In the end Manoa's faith in the divine promise is miraculously confirmed, as it had previously been confirmed by the fire divinely sent from heaven "to consume their sacrifice"—and the poet significantly links the two passages together by the imagery of flame. But Manoa will receive, and understand, this second and conclusive confirmation of faith only at the very end of the drama.

The motif of God's honor, in turn, as distinguished from the honor of His servants, recurs throughout the drama. Samson's former pride in his own strength; Manoa's concern for the fame and honor of his son and his house —these must be fully subordinated to the zeal for God's honor before the elect champion can triumph through his own disgrace.

On the second occasion, when Samson demands the woman of Timnath as a bride, Manoah and his wife protest (Judges 14:1–4): "Is there never a woman among the daughters of thy brethren, or among all my people, that thou goest to take a wife of the uncircumcised Philistines?" For they "knew not that it was of the Lord, that he sought an occasion against the Philistines. . . ." The Geneva gloss on this passage comments that "Though his parents did justly reprove him, yet it appeareth that this was the secret worke of the Lord"; Samson is seeking an occasion to "fight against [the Philistines] for the deliverance of Israel." On this occasion, as in his reaction to the angelic prophecy concerning Samson's birth and nurture, Manoah is characterized primarily in terms of parental *pietas*—his concern to fulfill the

proper offices of a father—but the biblical account especially stresses his ignorance of the divine intent. The drama retains and accentuates both of these points; Manoa not only rebukes his son for his marriage choices (which appear foolish in themselves and particularly unseemly for a Nazarite) but explicitly questions their allegedly divine inspiration. He does not realize that Samson's first marriage and the Dagonalia itself (which seems to be the worst and most shameful of all the evils resulting from his second marriage) are both the "secret work" of Providence* and that the latter (like the former) will provide the occasion for an act of deliverance. Parental prudence, in the drama as in the biblical narrative, thus stands in striking opposition to the wisdom of God and to Samson's apparent folly. Just as Milton contrasts the power of God with the strength of human arms and armaments, he counterpoints the wisdom of God (which seems to be folly in human eyes) with the merely human prudence of Samson's father. This antithesis accentuates the opposition between the paternal and the divine roles in the education of a Nazarite hero.

The final reference to Manoah occurs after Samson's death : "Then his brethren and all the house of his father came down, and took him, and brought him up, and buried him between Zorah and Eshtaol in the buryingplace of Manoah his father" (Judges 16:31). The biblical text gives no indication that Manoah was still alive at the time; and the Geneva reading ("in the sepulchre of Manoah his father") might seem to suggest that Manoah was already dead. In Verity's* opinion, however, it is "quite likely" that Manoah was still living "at the time of Samson's death," since the reference to his burying place "may only signify the place of sepulture belonging to the family, without any implication that Manoa himself lay there"; see A. W. Verity, ed. *Milton's Samson Agonistes* (1932), p. lvii.

Though Milton utilizes all three of these passages in his drama, he does not consistently exploit them in direct relation to Manoa. The allusion to *"Eshtaol and Zora's* fruitful Vale" (the site of the camp of Dan [Judges 13 : 25]) is assigned to the Chorus of Samson's friends and neighbors, in its first address to the fallen hero. Samson himself recalls the angelic predictions of Judges 13 in his initial monologue; they are among the "restless thoughts" that torment him with the contrast between his former condition and his present state, and with the apparent frustration of the "Divine Prediction" concerning his deliverance of Israel. Manoa himself cites the events of Judges 13 only briefly: he had once "thought barrenness / In wedlock a reproach"; he alludes to the "pomp" with which God had granted his request, the visits of the angel, and the ordinance concerning Samson's holy nurture. The question of Samson's divine inspiration in espousing the woman of Timna in spite of his parents' opposition to this match (Judges 14) had been raised and answered in Samson's first exchange with the Chorus; but his father subsequently raises the subject again (lines 420–23). The third passage (Judges 16 : 13) provides the nucleus for the last lines (1728–44) of the old man's final speech. Manoa "Will send for all my kindred, all my friends" to bear Samson's body "Home to his Fathers house. . . ."

These are the only passages that Milton has utilized from the biblical account of Samson's father. The literary contexts in which he places them and the dramatic significance with which he invests them are, like the characterization of Manoa and his role in the action, the products of the poet's own creative imagination and his sensitivity to the demands of the plot. Like his son, Manoa initially alludes to the events of Judges 13 to question "heavenly disposition." These events illustrate and confirm his argument that God's gifts, earnestly prayed for, often prove our woe and bane. Subsequently, he refers to the "Divine impulsion" that had prompted the hero to wed an infidel —seeking an "occasion to infest our Foes" (Judges 14 : 4) only to discredit Samson's

alleged inspiration by emphasizing its diametrically contrary results:

> I state not that; this I am sure; our Foes
> Found soon occasion thereby to make thee
> Thir Captive. . . .

The third allusion (Judges 16 : 31) is transformed and magnified into the posthumous honors conferred on Samson's body and his tomb. In adapting these three passages to his drama, Milton has emphasized several of the leading motifs in the tragedy: first, the crisis of faith in Manoa's doubt of the justice and providence of God, and the questionable value of His gifts and promises; second, the "Divine impulsion" and the "occasion" that will ultimately lead to the hero's greatest victory over his foes; and finally, the meed of heroic glory.

Like the Chorus, Manoa endeavors to comfort Samson (see "The Argument"), but produces the opposite effect. His visit heightens the hero's "inward grief," and in this respect it recalls analogous failures in consolation in Greek tragedy and in the biblical story of Job. In Sophocles' *Oedipus Rex,* the messenger who comes "to gladden Oedipus and to remove his fears as to his mother" actually exposes the dreadful "secret of his birth" (see Aristotle*, *The Art of Poetry,* trans. Ingram Bywater, chap. 11). Similarly, the three friends who visit Job in order "to mourn with him and to comfort him" (Job 2 : 11) in his affliction increase and exacerbate his anguish. In the dramatic action of *SA,* Manoa is the principal agent in the abortive subplot "to procure his [son's] liberty by ransom." The old man's alternate doubts and high expectations intensify the tragic irony inherent in the contrast between providential and human vision; and his oscillations between hope and fear, joy and grief, heighten the passionate or affective element in the drama. The "passions well imitated" belong to Manoa (and to the chorus of Danites) as well as to Samson; and the purgation of emotion, the final "peace and consolation," and the ultimate "calm of mind, all passion spent" pertain to the old man who finds "Nothing . . . here for tears" and grounds for quiet "in a death so noble," as well as to the Chorus and to ourselves.

Manoa's visit stands in striking contrast to the visitations of the Philistines. The healing words of friends and the timely care of a father are ineffective. Samson cannot respond to consolatory efforts; Manoa's reproaches, calling forth a confession of sin and a positive hope in Jehovah's imminent victory over Dagon, are more effective than his hopes for the hero's deliverance. Samson is to be tried and perfected by adversity; the insults of his enemies accomplish what the consolations of friends had failed to achieve. At the end of Manoa's visit Samson is close to despair, a moral invalid who laments his inner griefs in the imagery of disease. At the end of the first visit of the Public Officer, immediately before the advent of the "rousing spirits," he has demonstrated his moral recovery, his inner fortitude and strength of mind, and he can speak confidently of his conscience* and internal peace. The external agents in this moral transformation have been the Philistines themselves. The Public Officer leaves behind him a very different Samson—in the eyes of the Chorus and the audience—from the dejected champion his father had left.

From this general survey of the context of Manoa's role let us turn to a more detailed examination of his character and his dramatic function.

Manoa does not recognize his son immediately; and Samson's identity must be pointed out by the Chorus. Like the first reaction of the Chorus, his initial response is amazement and grief at the sudden and complete reversal in Samson's condition—the "miserable change" that has reduced the "dread of *Israel's* foes" to impotence. He then proceeds, as Samson had done, to reflect on the limitations of "mortal strength," to challenge the value of the divine gifts, and to complain of the excessive severity of his son's punishment. He is shocked by the "foul indignities" heaped on Samson and God's

apparent disregard of him, for this is not merited by his former deeds. Manoa's next speech emphasizes another, and greater, indignity that he has brought upon himself and his father's house; he is responsible for the festival honoring Dagon and "disglorifying" the true God. Both of these speeches stir Samson to a confession of his own guilt and a defense of the Deity. In the first instance he defends the justice of his punishment; he himself is "Sole Author" and "sole cause" of the evils that have befallen him. In the second instance he expresses his hope that God Himself will discomfit Dagon and his worshipers—a hope that Manoa receives as a prophecy.

Manoa's remaining speeches in this episode are devoted to his scheme to free his son from "this miserable loathsome plight," countering Samson's objections with exhortations to self-preservation or submission to "high disposal," arguments to accept the "offer'd means" that God perhaps has "set before us" to return him home to his country and God's "sacred house," and suggestions that God may ultimately restore his eyesight.

The multiple ironies in this dialogue are lost on the speakers themselves; but the audience, familiar with the story, is aware that they all point forward to the events of the Dagonalia—that the feast that appears to be Samson's most shameful "reproach" and the heaviest of all his "sufferings" will be the occasion of his most signal triumph. Samson's "only hope" is only partially prophetic; God will "assert" His name over the rival deity, but Samson himself will be His chosen and consecrated instrument. His own role in the theomachy is not yet over, as he believes; and his hope "that the strife / With mee hath end" is true only in a sense that he does not surmise. The "high disposal" to which Manoa appeals will run counter to "self-preservation," The "offer'd means" that will bring Samson home to his own country are not the proposed ransom (as Manoa thinks); they are the pillars in the Philistine theater. Manoa will indeed bring his son home

—but not in the condition he expects. Samson will destroy the Philistines in the livery of a public servant, paradoxically annoying them by serving them "with that gift / Which was expressly giv'n thee to annoy them. . . ." Manoa's prediction that God will restore his son's sight is true only of the inner vision whereby he will "serve him better than thou hast. . . ." The prediction that Samson's miraculous strength must still serve a divine purpose and that "His might continues in thee not for naught" will likewise be fulfilled, though not in a way that either character can surmise.

Manoa departs on his mission, vainly counselling his son to be calm and heed the "healing words" of his friends. His father's visit has intensified the hero's inward grief instead of consoling him; and immediately after Manoa's departure Samson utters the fullest and deepest expression of his torments : "faintings, swoonings of despair, / And sense of Heav'n's desertion." The old man does not return until after his son's astonishing recovery, his successive moral victories over the three Philistine visitors, and his departure for the Dagonalia. The end of the play is within sight; at this point, subplot and main plot intermesh, and both will be concluded by the same catastrophe. Until the advent of the Messenger, Manoa is alone with the Chorus. Previously he had shared the stage with his tragic son; but on this occasion he himself is the central figure, and the emotional impact of the scene lies primarily in his personal reactions to the events occurring off-stage. These oscillate between hope and dread. After communicating his hopes for Samson's deliverance and the restoration of his eyesight, he fears that the Philistines have slain his son; and he rejects as "a joy presumptuous to be thought" the Chorus's suggestion that Samson's eyesight had been miraculously restored. He counters the Chorus's appeal to God's miracles in the past with cautious skepticism :

He can, I know, but doubt to think he will;
Yet Hope would fain subscribe, and tempts Belief.

The Messenger's report of the "sad event" first brings him close to joy, then dashes his hopes with the news of Samson's death, and finally mitigates his grief with pride in Samson's heroic death.

Though Manoah (or Manue) appears as a character in several Renaissance dramas on Samson—Zieglerus's *Samson,* Roselli's *Rappresentatione di Sansone,* and the Sieur de Ville Toustain's *Tragédie nouvelle de Samson le fort* (see Kirkconnell, pp. 3–5, 158, 170)—there has been no full-scale comparative study of his role in medieval and Renaissance prose and poetry and in Milton's drama. In portraying him, Milton had to consider Renaissance ideas of decorum. According to Aristotle, the characters in tragedy should be good, appropriate, "like the reality," and "consistent and the same throughout" (see Bywater, chap. 15). The poet must depict Manoa's "moral purpose," the appropriate behavior of an Old Testament Hebrew and of an aged and solicitous father, and individual characteristics of Manoa as the Book of Judges had portrayed them—and he must make the old man's words and actions seem consistent with his character throughout the tragedy. On the simplest level, Manoa exemplified what Milton's contemporaries would have called "the character of a good father"—loyal to his disgraced (and in his own eyes, disobedient) son and solicitous for his welfare; anxious for the good name of his family, his nation, and his religion—a characteristic representative of family *pietas.* He is, par excellence, the faithful father, as Dalila is the unfaithful wife. Though both, in fact, are far more than this, the more complex shadings of thought and character and passion are confined (on the whole) within these bolder, and comparatively simple, outlines. Milton had inherited an ethical tradition that stressed the offices and duties proper to the major categories of natural and social relationships, along with a literary tradition that defined the attributes of persons according to formal categories : age, nationality, religion, sex, *studium,* etc. Against this background it was logical, and virtually inevitable, that the poet should characterize Manoa primarily in terms of his paternal relationship to Samson, his view of Samson's relation to God (and God's relation to Samson), and his advanced age. Milton is able, in fact, to play these traits against one another, heightening his image of Manoa's paternal solicitude by stressing its incompatibility with his old age. The indecorum of the old man intensifies the decorum of the father:

But wherefore comes *Old Manoa* in such hast
With youthful steps? Much livlier than e'er
   while
He seems: supposing here to find his Son,
Or of him bringing to us some glad news?

. . . . . . . . . . . .

Fathers are wont to lay up for their Sons,
Thou for thy Son art bent to lay out all;
Sons wont to nurse thir Parents in old age,
Thou in old age car'st how to nurse thy Son,
Made older then thy age through eyesight lost.

In Manoa's relationship with his maimed son, the captive deliverer—as in Dalila's relationship with her betrayed husband, her espoused enemy—there are inherent paradoxes that Milton exploits as a source of dramatic irony as well as of emotional and dramatic tension. The kind of "love and care" and "nursing diligence" that Dalila promises as the "glad office" of a wife; the kind of paternal care and nursing that Manoa promises as the voluntary expression of a father's duty and love—both derive much of their dramatic effectiveness from their equivocal nature, and from their paradoxical observance and violation of ethical and dramatic decorum. In both instances, behavior that seems, on the surface, to represent a fulfillment of natural duties and social offices also involves a grotesque reversal of a natural relationship. The husband must be subservient to his wife; the adult son must be nursed by his senile father. In the context of Samson's sin and fallen condition, these and other human relationships have become ambiguous, accentuating the paradox of the

captive deliverer, the oxymoron of an impotent heroism and helpless strength. Both stand in striking contrast to the kind of care and love that (as we discover at the end of the drama) have been exercised all along by Providence—a solicitude and nurture that perfect and strengthen heroic virtue through trial instead of softening it through leisure and ease. [JMS]

**MANSO, GIOVANNI - BAPTISTA** (1561–1645), a wealthy and influential aristocrat of Naples who achieved renown as a patron of literature and the arts. Tasso*, Marini*, and numerous other Italian poets enjoyed his patronage, which they celebrated in their poetry. Tasso dedicated a treatise on friendship to Manso, who in turn wrote a biography of Tasso first published in 1619 at Naples. Manso's desire to foster learning and culture was manifested in his support of the Academy of the *Oziosi,* or "the Idlers," a group of savants who met to discuss literature and the arts at his Neapolitan villa. Furthermore, he founded the *Collegio Dei Nobili* for the education of the young Neapolitan nobility, which he maintained after his death with a generous bequest.

In recounting his itinerary throughout Italy, Milton mentions in *2Def* that he traveled, probably late in November of 1638, from Rome to Naples in the company of a certain eremite, not further identified, who introduced him to Manso (8 : 122–23). Milton toured Naples, including the palace of the viceroy, with Manso, who sometimes visited the young Englishman at his lodging. Certainly flattered by Manso's esteem for him, Milton explains in *2Def* that Manso would have been more attentive if Milton had been less outspoken on religion (8 : 124–25). Not only in Naples but throughout Italy, even in Rome, Milton asserted his Protestantism as he expressed his antipapist sentiments. Manso's affection for Milton, as it was moderated because of the young man's advocacy of Protestantism and his theological contentiousness, is reflected in a Latin epigram that he presented to Milton: "If your piety matched your intellect, your figure, your grace and charm, your bearing, your manners, you would be, not an *Angle,* but, in very deed and truth, an *Angel.*" Manso also gave Milton two cups (*"pocula"*) with intricate designs, which are described in *EpDam* 181–97. But these "cups" seem actually to have been two of Manso's own books (perhaps the *Erocallia,* his dialogues on love, and the *Poesie Nomiche,* a volume of his poetry), and the designs may not be ornamentation on cups but, rather, topics treated in the books. In short, Milton, like Pindar in the seventh Olympian ode, may be referring to an author's writings as a cup or bowl containing an inviting draught to be consumed.

To express his gratitude for Manso's friendship, Milton, at his lodging in Naples, composed the poem *Mansus,* an epistle in Latin hexameters addressed to Manso at his villa. In the poem Manso is depicted as the ideal patron; and Milton, while characterizing himself as a prospective epic poet who might celebrate the deeds of Arthur and his knights, expresses the wish that a patron like Manso would maintain him. [ACL]

**MANSUS.** A 100-line Latin poem that appeared in both the 1645 and 1673 editions of Milton's works, *Mansus* is addressed to Giovanni Battista Manso*, Marquis of Villa (1561–1647?), an Italian nobleman whom Milton met while visiting Naples during his journey of 1639. Milton gives us a few details of their friendship in *2Def* and in the headnote that he appended to the poem itself. There Milton tells us that "Manso attended him with unbounded goodwill, and bestowed upon him many kindly services, born of his true humanity. To him, therefore, the sojourner, before he left the city, sent this poem, that he might show himself not ungrateful." This comment enables us to date the poem with a fair degree of accuracy, since we know that Milton was in Naples in December 1638 and returned to Rome early the next year.

The poem, as Ralph W. Condee has shown, has many of the *topoi* of the Renaissance panegyric, although Milton handles them with characteristic independence (*Studies in the Renaissance* 15:174–92). He generously praises his subject for his service to the republic of letters, but there is nothing servile in his attitude. Indeed, the last twenty-two lines emphasize Milton's worthiness to have such a friend as Manso. These lines interestingly reveal that he is already considering an epic poem, although the subject that he has in mind at this point is not the Fall of Man but "the kings of [his] native land, and Arthur, who set wars in train even 'neath the earth. . . ."

Latinists like Dr. Johnson* and Walter Savage Landor have given *Mansus* high marks as poetry, and indeed, in the opinion of E. M. W. Tillyard*, "its sustained sweetness and dignity, rising at times to positive grandeur, make it the best of all Milton's Latin poems (the *Epitaphium Damonis* included) and the one which as a whole can seriously compete with, say, *L'Allegro* or *Arcades"* (*Milton* [1946], p. 90). [ERG]

**MANUSCRIPTS.** Holograph manuscripts by Milton are few, and they are described under separate entries: *see* CANON for *CarEl* and "Mane citus lectum"; *CB; Epistol;* and *TM.* These last three entries also record items in the hands of various amanuenses*. Manuscript materials written down by scribes or others include: *BrM** of *Mask;* two versions of Songs for *Mask,* for which *see* LAWES, HENRY, and below; *CD;* the Columbia Manuscript*, which includes some prose works and state papers; a copy of *EpWin;* various copies of the Hobson poems, for which see canon and below; *PL* Book 1; the original of *Rous;* copies of state papers*, single or in collections (three letters have holograph corrections); the Skinner Manuscript* of state papers; and a copy of *Time.* In addition, poems and prose were transcribed from editions (e.g., William Sancroft's copies of *Ps* 136 and *Nat* in Bodleian, Tanner MS 466, pp. 34–35,

60–66; and *Eikon* in British Museum, Stowe MS 305, ff. 89v–137v). These have no other importance than to indicate the "popularity" and spread of some of the works. See also *CharLP* for discussion of the manuscript version, called "The Digression."

The Lawes songs (words and music for five songs in *Mask*) are found in British Museum, Additional MS 52723 ("the Lawes MS"), nos. 74–78, and Additional MS 11518, ff. 1–2v (scribal hand). There are differences in both words and music. "On the University Carrier" is transcribed in Folger Shakespeare Library, MS 1. 21, ff. 79v–80. "Another on the same" appears in Bodleian, Corpus Christi College MS E. 309, f. 48; Bodleian, Malone MS 21, f. 69v; Huntington Library MS H.M. 116, pp. 100–101; St. John's College Library, Cambridge, MS S. 32, ff. 18v–19. "Hobson's Epitaph" (attributed) is found in Bodleian, Corpus Christi College MS E. 309, f. 48v; Bodleian, English Poetical MS f. 10, f. 101v; Bodleian, Rawlinson Poetical MS 26, f. 64; Bodleian, Rawlinson Poetical MS 117, ff. 105v–106; Bodleian, Tanner MS 465, pp. 235–36; British Museum, Additional MS 5807, f. 2v; BM, Additional MS 6400, f. 67v; BM, Additional MS 15227, f. 74; BM, Additional MS 30982, f. 65–65v; BM, Harleian MS 791, f. 45; BM, Harleian MS 6057, f. 15 (lines 1–2 only); BM, Harleian MS 6931, f. 24v; BM, Sloane MS 542, f. 52; Folger Shakespeare Library, MS 1. 27, f. 68v; Folger, MS 452. 1, p. 50; Folger, MS E. a. 6, f. 4–4v; Harvard University Library, English MS 686, f. 78; Huntington Library, MS H. M. 116, p. 103; John Rylands Library, English MS 410, ff. 31v–32; James H. Osborn Collection, Yale University, Commonplace Book, Box 12, no. 5, pp. 225–26; Rosenbach Collection, Philadelphia, MS 239–27, pp. 359–60; St. John's College Library, Cambridge, MS S. 32, f. 18v.

It is interesting to remark the works for which no manuscript material exists: none of the prose works (except for one prolusion, *CB, CD,* and some familiar or

state letters); none of the foreign language poems (except *CarEl* and *Rous*); none of the translations; none of the original English poems dated 1628–1631 (except for miscellany copies of the Hobson poems and *EpWin*); none of the three major poems (except *PL* 1, preserved because of the inclusion of the license for publication). As new drafts were made, replaced drafts were probably destroyed, and as a work was printed, its final manuscript copy received the same fate. Among manuscripts that may have been preserved until Milton's death but that have now disappeared (other than inedited and unknown pieces) are notebooks similar to *TM* for other poems (although it may have been the lack of publication of *Sonn* 15, 16, and 22 that caused that document to escape destruction), the *Index Theologicus\**, and the Latin and Greek thesauri. *See* CANON. [JTS]

**MAREUIL, ABBE, LE P. DE:** *see* TRANSLATIONS OF MILTON'S WORKS.

**MARGINALIA, MILTON'S.** Frequently volumes have been referred to as containing notes written by Milton, but many times this has proved untrue or the volumes have disappeared for further examination. Included below are volumes containing Milton's authentic signature and/or authentic notes, and, separately, a few volumes that it seems possible may contain notes in Milton's hand and that may eventually reappear to allow careful consideration.

Dante\*, *L'Amoroso Convivio* (Venice, 1529); Giovanni della Casa\*, *Rime e Prose* Venice, 1563); and Benedetto Varchi, *I Sonetti* (Venice, 1555), three volumes now bound together, with note of purchase, 1629, and signature on title page of della Casa, a sonnet added at the end of the della Casa (by John Phillips), and markings and textual corrections in all three; the copied letter in Varchi, p. 278, is not in Milton's hand; in New York Public Library.

Aratus\*, *Phaenomena* (Paris, 1559), note of purchase, 1631, and thirty-six marginalia, dated 1631–1638 (chiefly 1631–32) and

1639–1642 (chiefly 1641–42); in British Museum.

John Creccelius, *Collectanea* (Frankfurt, 1614), note of purchase, 1633, and signature; in Huntington Library.

Lycophron, *Alexandra* (Geneva, 1601), note of purchase, 1634, and marginalia; in University of Illinois Library.

Euripides, *Tragoediae* (Geneva, 1602), note of purchase, 1634, and numerous marginalia, some dated 1634–1637, others dated after 1637; about 167 others are not in Milton's hand; in Bodleian Library.

Dio Chrysostom, *Logoi [Orationes LXXX]* (Lutetiae [Paris], 1604), note of purchase, 1636, signature, and four corrections of Greek (pp. 177, 312, 321, 322); in Ely Cathedral Library.

Heraclides Ponticus, *Allegoriae in Homeri fabulis de dijs* (Basel, 1544), signature and note of purchase, 1637; in University of Illinois Library.

Terence, *Comoediae* (Leyden, 1635), signature and a few markings; in Harvard University Library.

Sir John Harington's translation of Ariosto's* *Orlando Furioso* (1591), p. 405, marginal note of date of reading, September 21, 1642; other marginalia are not Milton's; owned by Miss M. K. Surridge (New York).

Polycarp and Ignatius*, *Epistolae* (Oxford, 1644), note of purchase and five annotations (pp. iv, xi [2], xxvii, lxxxix); in Ely Cathedral Library.

Bible*, 1645(?)–1652(?), birth records, notational marks throughout, and marginal notes alongside 2 Kings 5:6, Nehemiah 13:31, 1 Cor. 13:12; British Museum, Additional MS 32310.

Three volumes that have disappeared but that may have Milton's holograph in them are : Theodore Beza*, "book of portraits of reformers" (Geneva, 1580), signature and inscription; Mary Milton's Bible, four notes in English and one in Latin, which are known through Thomas Birch's* transcription (British Museum, Additional MS 4244, ff. 52–53); Thucydides, *De Bello Peloponnesiaco Libri Octo,* translated by Laurentius Valla (Basel, 1564), bound with Francis Irenicus, *Germaniae Exgesso* (Basel, 1564), signature and two notes (p. 322), formerly in Rosenbach Collection, Philadelphia; and Marc Antoine Muret's *Variarum (Lectionum Libri XV* [Paris, 1586], signature, owned (still?) by Arthur Swann of New York).

Other volumes that are often cited as evidencing Milton's hand but that do not are :

Paul Best, *Mysteries Discovered* (1647); in Bodleian Library.

Bible belonging to Elizabeth Minshull Milton, acquisition dated 1654, signature may be a scribe's; in University of Texas Library.

William Browne, *Britannia's Pastorals* (1613–16); owned by Mrs. Josephine H. Fisher (Detroit).

Thomas Cooper, *Thesaurus Linguae Romanae et Britannicae* (1573); in New York Public Library.

Thomas Farnaby, *Systema Grammaticum* (1641); in Harvard University Library.

Virgilio Malvezzi, *Discourses upon Cornelius Tacitus,* translated by Sir Richard Baker 1642); last owned by Thomas O. Mabbott (New York).

Pindar, *Pindari Olympia, Pythia, Nemea, Isthmia* (Saumir, 1620); in Harvard University Library.

John Sleidan*, *De Statu Religious et Reipublica* (Strassburg, 1555); in New York Public Library.

For other volumes that have not been proved to contain holographs but that have been associated with Milton, *see* ASSOCIATION COPIES and LIBRARY, MILTON'S. [JTS]

**MARINO, MILTON AND.** The Neapolitan poet Giambattista Marino (or Marini) was the leading literary personality of his time in Europe. With the publication of his *Rime* (later known as *La Lira,* 1602–1614), Marino established his claim to being the successor to Tasso* as a lyricist in the Petrarchan* tradition and the forger of a new style characterized by sensuous detail, witty imagery and thought, and an abundance of rhetorical figuration, often treating frankly sensual subjects. His turbulent life, magnified by legend, took him to the leading courts of Italy, where he sought the protection and patronage of the nobility he flattered in countless panegyrics. Invited to Paris in 1615, he ingratiated himself with his colorful personality and a series of works he published there that increased his influence among native poets as well as contemporary writers of England, Spain, Germany, and his own Italy. These included : the *Epitalami* (1616); *La Galeria* (1619), a collection of iconic poems dealing with real or imaginary works of art; *La Sampogna* (1620), collection of pastoral* and mythological* poems or idylls containing his best poetry; and his nominal masterpiece, *L'Adone* (1623), a poem of epic length that tells the myth of Venus and Adonis swelled out to twenty cantos and over 40,000 lines of *ottava rima* by a host of digressions and padding devices, including borrowings from most of the known genres and from many ancient and modern writers. Quarrels over its claims to be an epic or some new kind of poem, and about its borrowings and style, were to erupt shortly and continue for decades after the poet's death.

Marino returned to Italy in 1623, amidst tumultuous applause and growing controversy over the propriety and literary worth of his masterpiece. The last work he completed before his death, *La Strage degl'Innocenti,* was published in 1632, posthumously, and with the rumored endorsement of the poet, who was alleged to have asserted that this was his real masterpiece. In the *Strage* Marino retells the incident of the Slaughter of the Innocents in four books of over 400 *ottave,* and in a style that parallels treatments of the same subject in Baroque art.

Marino's influence in England may be divided into imitation of his secular love poetry, which appealed to such poets as Drummond, Carew, Marvell*, and Stanley, and imitation of his religious lyrics and *La Strage*, especially by Crashaw, who translated the first book of the posthumous poem in the English Baroque* style first introduced in England by Southwell. Milton's knowledge of and interest in Marino seem limited to his awareness of the Italian poet's controversial reputation as successor to Tasso, and to *La Strage* as precedent for biblical epic. Marino is highly praised by Milton in *Mansus,* which is dedicated to Giambattista Manso*, Marquis of Villa Lago, and famed as a patron of both Tasso and Marino. Milton, as he tells us in the *2Def,* had visited Manso and discussed epic poetry with him. It was thus probably from Manso rather than careful reading of Marino's works that Milton gained the impression of the latter's greatness that we find in *Mansus*. It does seem clear, however, that Milton read *La Strage,* since verbal echoes (e.g., *Strage,* 1. 31, and *PL* 1.54) are obvious, whereas the imitations that have been alleged from time to time by scholars of lines from the *Rime* and the *Adone* in Milton's epics and other works are not definitive. [JVM]

## MARRIAGE AND DIVORCE. Milton's ideas on marriage and divorce* may be found chiefly in the four divorce pamphlets—*DDD, Bucer, Tetra,* and *Colas*—and in *PL*. Works such as *Mask* and *SA* touch upon similar matters, but it is necessary to distinguish Milton's praise of the Platonic* virtue of chastity* from praise of sexual abstinence and to avoid seeing Dalila as the aging and embittered Milton's ill-tempered condemnation of the treacherous wife. Milton's ethic stressed the chastity of the married state and not only did not recognize sexual abstinence in itself as a virtue but condemned its overvaluation as a perversion of the doctrine that "marriage is honorable in all." And Milton's representation of Dalila is so finely objective that it is entirely possible (although by no means necessary) to read her conscious resolutions as high-minded and generous. It would, of course, have been base for Samson to have yielded to her again, his progressive consciousness of his role being as strong as it is in the play. But in herself, far from being a temptress of diabolical calculation, she seems merely a victim of unregenerated reason, making on the basis of a limited moral and spiritual context a judgment otherwise righteous and sound. She has nothing to gain in leading the blind Samson from the mill except a husband to whom she can give comfort; the danger of her offer as a temptation lies in its implications as an act of Samson's will and not necessarily in her intention. Although she is represented in matrimonial literature as a type of perfidy, Milton's drama takes up her history after the notorious act of treachery

has occurred, and she seems, at least, a somewhat complex, tentative, and ambiguous figure. Hence both her attractiveness and the danger she presents to Samson.

Milton started writing the divorce tracts in 1643, shortly after the desertion of Mary Powell Milton, his first wife. Whether through family pressure or her own distaste for a soberly academic, Puritan, and republican household, Mary, who had left London for a visit to her family in Oxfordshire, did not answer his request to return. Milton claimed that he had been interested in questions of divorce and matrimony long before writing the tracts and that they were a natural consequence of his zeal for a more complete Reformation in England. Both the entries of *CB* and the meeting of the Westminster Assembly* at this time bear out the assertion, as does the idealism of the tracts themselves, which seems ingrained, a part of Milton's very habit of regarding marriage, and not the accidental result of a sudden pressure to argue his cause. But the claim seems partial, nonetheless, and it is equally true that Mary's desertion was an immediate precipitant of the argument.

The literary effect, however, is not easily understood in terms of biographical cause. Analogies with the circumstances of *Areop* are instructive. In its crudest form, the argument runs that one of Milton's pamphlets—in fact one of the divorce tracts—had been condemned and was in danger of continued censorship, that Milton wanted his works published legally and therefore wrote *Areop*; analogously, that Milton's wife deserted him, that he wanted to divorce her, and therefore wrote the divorce tracts. (Of course, neither labor was successful: Parliament perpetuated the custom of licensing* and did not until 1670 alter the procedures or grounds of divorce inflicted by canonical heritage upon it.) While such *post hoc* arguments, rooting Milton's convictions in a narrow egoism, myopically reduce the latitude of his tolerance in *Areop*, they produce actual distortions of the

meaning and intention of the divorce tracts. Milton may have had his own divorce in mind when he wrote them, but then, curiously enough, they in no way bear directly on his case. Milton's argument, not only in the 1643 *DDD*, but also in the tracts published a year later, when the ill success of the first tract had been made only too clear to him, rests firmly on the principle that marriage is founded on spiritual union and that incompatibility of temperament, by all the laws of God, nature, and man, should be the primary cause of divorce.

Milton's first tract on divorce was written hurriedly, and to some extent uncharacteristically, without resort to "authorities" or to the history of the debates on divorce that had led to revisions of the law in other Protestant countries and to the proposals of revision in England. In fact, Milton did not learn of Martin Bucer's* anticipation of his opinions until after he had written the first tract, when he assumed that his own position was, strangely, without precedent. The argument of *DDD* is based on a theory of marriage available, Milton believed, to every Christian who read the Bible. The reader can easily discern the structure of the argument by reading the epitomes that preface each chapter in the 1644 version. The principles that underlie and allow for elaboration of these arguments are probably more important for an understanding of Milton's position than the argument themselves. They are chiefly (1) that marriage was instituted by God for man in Paradise, to satisfy the demands of his soul as well as body; (2) that woman was made to be man's companion; (3) that the final cause of marriage is human society; that procreation, while a necessity, is not its primary end; and the remedy of lust as an end of marriage is an accident of the Fall*; (4) that the formal cause of marriage is love; (5) that a marriage in which the clash of temperaments continually thwarts love (or renders it impossible) is no marriage and must be dissolved; (6) that marriage is properly a contract between individuals and that the partners to the contract rather than the Church or the State have the right of jurisdiction over it; the State can only legitimately determine the equity of the conditions of the separation.

In *DDD,* no less than in *Tetra,* Milton deals with three biblical statements on divorce and one on marriage. The very title *Tetrachordon* is a metaphor for the harmony that Milton believed was created by statements that on the surface suggested contradictory values and ethical positions. Moses had allowed divorce for cases in which the wife should "find no favor in [her husband's] eyes, because he hath found some uncleannesse in her" and permitted the remarriage of both parties (Deut. 24 : 1–2). Christ, on the other hand, had apparently placed limitations on at least one aspect of Moses' law in allowing divorce and remarriage only in cases of adultery (Matt. 19 : 3–9). Saint Paul had restricted the use of divorce between believers and unbelievers only to those cases where the faith of the partner constituted a temptation to the Christian (1 Cor. 7 : 10–16). It was possible, then, to identify the cause of incompatibility with Moses, of adultery with Christ, and of idolatry with Saint Paul, and the most difficult feature of Milton's task in *DDD* is to reconcile the apparently permissive attitude of Moses with the apparently repressive attitude of Christ. Milton's strategy is to acknowledge the difficulty, to define the ends of matrimony in order to interpret the problem, and to give emphasis to the first statement about marriage in the Bible as the chief source of our knowledge of those ends : "And the Lord God said, let us make man an help meet for him . . ." (Gen. 2 : 18). Thus Milton can define marriage as a "meet and happy conversation" that fulfills the intention of God himself. He interprets the "uncleannesse" of the passage in Deuteronomy as those expositors familiar with Hebrew had, referring it to some defect of body or mind that renders the woman unfit for marriage; this quality he identifies with temperamental incompatibility. The passage, then, upholds the idea

of marriage as a union of souls as well as bodies and allows for grounds of divorce consonant with the nature of the institution. But Milton refutes the "common expositor" on the interpretation of the statements of Christ and Saint Paul, arguing in both cases from either "moral law," the "law of nature," or some precedent "rule" by which their meaning can be soundly understood. This "rule," of course, is characteristically identified with the nature of marriage as defined by the passage in Genesis.

Milton's *Bucer,* a translation of parts of the second edition of Martin Bucer's *De Regno Christi* (1577), is merely an argument from authority in support of the theories already expounded in *DDD* of 1643 and 1644. Bucer confirms conclusions that Milton had reached earlier —that ecclesiastical control of divorce was inappropriate, and that the narrow interpretation of Christ's prohibition of divorce misconstrued his meaning. But Bucer also gave to the latter view valuable support from the Fathers of the Church and from Roman law.

*Tetra* gave Milton an opportunity to undertake what he had not done in the first tract on divorce—to search out "authorities" and to integrate the debate on divorce with his own forms of proof. The tract adds nothing to the substance of his ideas on marriage or divorce but it is an impressive piece of biblical exegesis, and in it Milton alters a significant detail of the strategy of *DDD.* He offers an interpretation of Christ's reply to the Pharisees that does not limit the application of the phrase "hardnesse of heart" to them and therefore extends the Mosaic law on divorce to all men. Instead of characterizing the Pharisees' licentious and obdurate natures, the phrase now refers to the general imperfection of man since the Fall.

*Colas,* the last of the divorce tracts, is a vituperative, grainy, and spirited attack on the critics of Milton's position. Like *Tetra,* it adds nothing essential to his case, but it demonstrates his willingness to trade jest for jest with his opponents and his talent for the satiric* modes of argument.

Divorce in the tracts becomes an example of the failure of mankind to take advantage of the privileges allowed to his fallen condition. In *PL* Milton can expatiate more freely upon the nature of both ideal and fallen marriage (and, by implication, upon the different contexts of nature's primary and secondary laws). Neither marriage nor nature is wholly corrupted after the Fall, since God through the forms of grace restores to man some of the liberty* and power destroyed by it. But Milton shows the corruption too and, by pointed reference to the fallen matrimony of Adam and Eve and their heirs, Milton can delineate in sum the breakdown of forms of internal, domestic, and social order.

It is as an expression of order and of a fully harmonious human nature that prelapsarian marriage in the Garden of Eden invariably appears. Marriage is not only a reflection of the cosmos in the domestic hierarchy of Adam and Eve, but also a completion of the scheme of universal and individual nature. Eve completes the work of creation and the marriage of Adam and Eve is the epitome and convergence of its various forms of order. These forms of order, in turn, depend on the continued consonance of right reason* and will. Eve's willing and submissive acknowledgment of Adam's closer approximation to the nature of divinity renders him her superior by consent as well as by design. Eve at the pool, at first more attracted by her own beauty, which is of a smoother and more graceful kind than Adam's, quickly recognizes in Adam's appearance, with its signs of aspiring intellect, a sublimity superior to her beauty, and she is attracted to what is more "truly fair" in him. Adam, of course, is not only immediately impressed by Eve's beauty but expresses to Raphael his gradually keener sense of Eve's kindliness, her responsiveness, and her affection, all of which demonstrate their natural affinity.

Milton's representation of marriage in *PL* is not without acknowledgments of hazard. Carnality as such does not yet exist, but Adam's affection for Eve is capable of clouding his judgment, and Eve's posture of inferiority is not always easy to maintain. However, the potential deformities of marriage and love* are symbolically represented in the figures of Satan, Sin, and Death, whose mutual attractions and repulsions parody not only the relationship of the Trinity but natural relationships of the human family. Satan's lust for Eve in the temptation of the dream and later, when he has assumed his serpent form, introduces into the Garden of Eden that courtly praise of women which, while proceeding from lust, makes idols of them and hence subverts the distinction between the human and the divine—in fact creates divinity out of frailty. But the true perversion of love in marriage occurs at the time of and just after the Fall—when Eve feigns love for Adam to persuade him to repeat her act of disobedience* and when, their reason and will deranged by their act of defiance, Adam and Eve take solace in their passion for one another. In their new awareness of purely carnal passion, the mysteries of love become acts of mutual defilement, and the psychological consequences of the Fall are first measured in their frenzy of abandonment.

These corruptions of love are to be repeated throughout human history, and Milton does not hesitate to catalogue the accident of mismating among the ills that succeed the Fall. But marriage, like everything else affected by the Fall, does not lose all its value even in a world from which natural virtue has disappeared. In the aftermath of the Fall, Eve leads Adam toward reconciliation and repentance. Her sympathy and submissiveness, renewed after the experience of sin, become the means by which the will of Adam can be moved toward rectification through grace*. And when Adam and Eve are expelled from Paradise, the affinity that had been imaged by their first appearance in the poem, "hand in hand," is mirrored in their last, as "They hand in hand with wand'ring steps and slow, / Through *Eden* took their solitary way."

The influences upon Milton's concepts of marriage and divorce were as many-sided as the Renaissance itself, but in general terms these concepts represent a characteristic fusion of Puritanism and humanism*. Although no longer a sacrament to the Puritans, marriage was a recommended means by which men and women achieved sanctification, and the conduct of husband and wife, as well as family observances generally, played a large role in their popular ethical literature. For the humanist, earthly love could still be a legitimate means to heavenly love, since earthly forms incorporated and made manifest the radiance of divinity. Neoplatonic* theories of love as the principle of emanation, creation, sympathy, and sublimation find their way into the divorce tracts as well as into *PL.* But to say that the Puritans encouraged the idea of marriage as a mutual spiritual effort is not to say that they proposed a specifically Puritan theory of marriage different in kind from that of Anglicans or Catholics, or that Milton owes his greatest debt to them. Milton's language tends, especially in *PL,* to owe rather more to the poets and humanists who focused his ideals in the terms of Plato rather than of Calvin*.

What is most noteworthy about the spirit of Milton's ideas of marriage and divorce is the extent to which man is made the measure of truth and the source of the active principles governing the institution. The idea that marriage was created primarily for man and is directly dependent on his nature rather than for God, for the Church, or for the State, places a fairly wide distance between Milton's position and that of those who might accept the principles of his argument but draw specific sanctions and prohibitions from the traditions surrounding marriage. Milton carries the spirit of Protestant anti-institutionalism as far as it will go in this case; he upholds the Protestant and humanistic principle of illuminated Reason as interpreter and

resolver of all conflict; and no precedent, rule, or custom, even those sanctioned by biblical texts, goes unexamined. [JGH]

**MARRIAGES, MILTON'S.** Milton was married three times: to Mary Powell, to Katherine Woodcock, and to Elizabeth Minshull. Specific records are missing for the first marriage, but it probably took place in June 1642. Four children were born of this union: Anne (1646), Mary (1648), John (1651 and who died a year later), and Deborah (1652). Milton's marriage to Mary has been the source of various fictions largely because she returned to her parental family soon after the marriage for three years. The reading of Milton's personality and the differences in the couple's ages, backgrounds, and religious and political persuasions have supplied some of the substance of these fictions, but no adequate psychological investigation of the marriage has been undertaken. Perhaps a bill of divorcement was considered during the separation and remarriage proposed, but there is no hard evidence. With Mary's return the marriage seems to have been on strong foundation, to be terminated only by Mary's death in childbirth in 1652. Milton's interest in divorce preceded his marriage, and the quips connecting publication of *DDD* with his separation from Mary seem to be unfounded.

Milton's second marriage four and a half years after the death of Mary lasted only a year and a half, for Katherine died in 1658 as a result of illness connected with the birth of their daughter Katherine, who died six weeks after her mother. Milton's third marriage—an apparently happy one despite some stepmother-daughter antagonisms—took place five years later. Elizabeth survived her much older husband and inherited the bulk of his estate.

For Milton's attitudes toward marriage, *see* MARRIAGE AND DIVORCE, MILTON'S VIEWS ON. The fact that all three wives were much younger than he and that he was already thirty-four when he was first married may be significant in understanding the nature of those marriages. At least his household position would appear to have tended more easily to dominant figure and even to father figure than would have been usual in other seventeenth-century unions. [AA]

**MARSHALL, STEPHEN.** A noted Puritan preacher and one of the Smectymnuus* group (his italics supplying the first two letters), Marshall (1594?–1655) later became a member of the Westminster Assembly* and one of its commissioners to Scotland. Any direct connection with Milton is unknown, but see the antiprelatical tracts. [WM]

**MARTIN, JOHN:** *see* ILLUSTRATIONS.

**MARVELL, ANDREW** (1621–1678). No one knows the exact circumstances that brought Marvell and Milton together, but their names have been linked from the early days of the Commonwealth period. Rumor, no longer entirely dismissed, implied that Marvell assisted Milton with preparation of *Eikon* (1649). Marvell's chief literary biographer, Pierre Leguois, insists that the connection is spurious, based entirely on the irresponsible word of gossipy Mrs. Anne Sadleir*, Cyriack Skinner's* aunt (*Andrew Marvell: Poet, Puritan, Patriot* [1968], p. 93). Leguois suggests that Marvell, being inclined at that moment to the Royalist cause, would have been an unlikely helper in the regicide pamphlet. In 1649, his commendatory poem appeared with the arch-Royalist Richard Lovelace's *Lucasta*; and as late as 1650, Marvell wrote "Tom May's Death," a poem highly uncomplimentary to the Parliamentarians. On the other hand, as the treatment of Charles's execution in "An Horatian Ode upon Cromwell's Return from Ireland" indicates, Marvell was capable of immense poise, which might well have embraced admiration of Charles's conduct, and disgust for certain Parliamentarians, without any firm Royalist convictions. In any event, W. R. Parker leaves the issue of Marvell's involvement (as distinct from

collaboration) with *Eikon* open : the story, recorded in 1653, might well be based on common knowledge within the Marvell family, with whose members the Skinners were well acquainted. And in 1649 Marvell definitely was in London (*Milton*, p. 964).

Marvell was the most important literary figure with whom Milton had close personal acquaintance, and their friendship touched two of the most important interests in their lives : poetry and politics. In 1653, Milton put Marvell's name forward to John Bradshaw*, then President of the Council of State*, for a post assisting in the Secretaryship for Foreign Tongues*, describing him as a man fully capable of serving the government in Dutch, French, Spanish, and Italian, as well as in the classical languages. Although Milton's strong recommendation did not lead to Marvell's immediate employment, the younger poet was soon brought into service as tutor to Oliver Cromwell's ward, William Dutton, with whom he went to live (in the household of John Oxenbridge) at Eton. Within a year, Milton sent him a copy of *2Def*, which Marvell praised in a letter to his "most honoured Freind John Milton Esquire, Secretarye for the forrain affairs" (*The Poems & Letters of Andrew Marvell*, ed. H. M. Margoliouth [1952], 2 : 292–93). But it was not until 1657 that Marvell finally joined Milton as his colleague (serving directly under John Thurloe* [see Margoliouth, 2 : 350–52]) in the Latin Secretaryship. About this time Marvell's active interest in politics was showing itself; he was elected to Parliament as a member for Hull in Yorkshire, wrote what is perhaps the most fervently eloquent Republican poem of the period, "The First Anniversary of the Government Under O. C.," and, later, when the cause was lost, resisted all efforts after the Restoration to recruit him into the King's court.

Marvell survived the Restoration as an MP for Hull (see John M. Wallace, *Destiny his Choice: The Loyalism of Andrew Marvell* [1968]), and evidence indicates that he used what slender influence he had to help Milton, during what was for the blind poet a time of great danger. Milton was, as Marvell was not, a public defender of the regicides; contemporary accounts, including that of Milton's nephew, Edward Phillips, indicate that Marvell was active in protecting Milton from reprisals; even after the Act of Oblivion, when Milton was free of all political charges, Marvell found occasion to render aid. On December 17, 1660, Milton was in prison, held because of a large sum required by the Sergeant-at-Arms, after all formal charges against him had been dropped. Marvell rose in the House of Commons to protest the unfairness of the sum; soon afterwards, the amount was reduced and Milton was freed.

After the Restoration, Marvell enjoyed increasing success as a political satirist, a success that earned him (and certain of his friends, including Milton) the animosity of Bishop Samuel Parker*, whom Marvell had lampooned as "Bayes" in *The Rehearsal Transpros'd* (1672). Parker responded quickly with *A Reproof to the Rehearsal Transprosed* (1673), assailing (along with Marvell) John Milton, whom he accused as the co-author of the satire. In a rejoinder to which Parker never replied, Marvell came back with a scathing rebuttal, placing special emphasis on the Bishop of Oxford's ungenerous remarks about Milton: "why," he asks toward the end of *The Rehearsal Transpros'd: The Second Part,* "should any other mans reputation suffer in a contest betwixt you and me" (p. 377)? As for Parker's main accusation, Marvell flatly denies any collaboration, claiming that he had avoided Milton's company in order to spare him from precisely this kind of political embarrassment:

> For by chance I had not seen him of two years before; but after I undertook writing, I did more carefully avoid either visiting or sending to him, least I should any way involve him in my consequences. (p. 377)

Further, Marvell suggests that had Milton (rather than he) taken Parker in hand he would "not [have] escap'd so easily," but would have had authentic cause "to repent the occasion" (p. 377). As the situation stood, however, Parker's treatment of Milton had no rational motive:

> But he never having in the least provoked you, for you to insult thus over his old age, to traduce him by your *Scaramuccios,* and in your own person, as a School-Master, who was born and hath lived much more ingenuously and Liberally then your self; to have done all this, and lay at last my simple book to his charge, . . . it is inhumanely and inhospitably done." (pp. 379–80)

Having saved his most withering shot for last, Marvell reminds Parker that at one time he had been a favored recipient of Milton's hospitality, that he had, though Milton generously refused publicly to recall it, "frequented *J. M.* incessantly and haunted his house day by day." Marvell points out that, like Milton, Parker, too, had been a Republican, and that his vaunted Royalism had burgeoned with the Restoration:

> At His Majesties happy Return, *J. M.* did partake, even as you your self did for all your huffing, of his Regal Clemency and has ever since expiated himself in a retired silence. (p. 379)

Milton's dignified silence, indicative of an unswerving political and moral integrity, provides a devastating contrast to Parker's expedience. But Marvell is unwilling to characterize Parker's mentality in terms of political expedience, which, in such a revolutionary period, might be excused. He sees Parker's offense as one of personal betrayal: "It was nothing less than a warning to all men: . . . to avoid (I will not say such a *Judas,*) but a man that creeps into all companies, to jeer, trepan, and betray them" (p. 380).

The most notable literary link between the two poets appeared with the publication of the second edition of *PL* (1674). Marvell's "On Mr. Milton's *Paradise Lost*" was one of its two commendatory poems. Written in heroic couplets, the poem praises the form and scope of the first major attempt in nondramatic poetry at the use of blank verse*. The poem demonstrates Marvell's critical sense; his admiration is explicitly couched in a sophisticated awareness of the technical and cultural problems Milton had assumed in writing the poem:

When I beheld the Poet blind, yet bold,
In slender Book his vast Design unfold,
*Messiah* Crown'd, *Gods* Reconcil'd Decree,
Rebelling *Angels,* the Forbidden Tree,
Heav'n, Hell, Earth, Chaos, All; the Argument
Held me a while misdoubting his Intent,
That he would ruine (for I saw him strong)
The sacred Truths to Fable and old Song,
(So *Sampson* groap'd the Temples Posts in
    spight)
The World o'erwhelming to revenge his Sight.

As for the technical innovation of blank verse, Marvell expresses unqualified approbation at his own and Dryden's* expense. The story is a familiar one: Dryden had asked Milton's permission to render *PL* in dramatic form, as an opera. In so doing, he would be expected to follow his own prescriptions, as laid down in the *Essay on Dramatic Poesy* (1668), turning the poem from blank verse into rhyme. According to Aubrey*, Milton replied laconically, giving Dryden leave to "tag" his verses (*The State of Innocence* was published in 1677). Harking back again to the figure of "Bayes" in Buckingham's *The Rehearsal,* but shifting from Parker to Dryden, Marvell parodies him as the foolish advocate of rhyme at the expense of meaning:

    Well mightst thou scorn thy Readers to
      allure
With tinkling Rhime, of thy own Sense
    secure;
While the *Town-Bays* writes all the while and
    spells,
And like a Pack-Horse tires without his Bells.
Their Fancies like our bushy Points appear,
The Poets tag them; we for fashion wear.
I too transported by the *Mode* offend,
And while I meant to *Praise* thee, must
    Commend.
Thy verse created like thy *Theme* sublime,
In Number, Weight, and Measure, needs not
    *rhime.*

                   (45–54)

By drawing attention to his own poetic limitations, Marvell's poet stresses the constructing impact of 'fashion," implying that Milton's achievement, both metrically and thematically, is justified on grounds of divine inspiration. The *"Mode"* offends as it restrains; whereas Milton's chosen blank verse and "his vast Design" are, alike, free of social norms. In effect, the objections that the speaker himself once felt, being expressions of *"Mode,"* become evidence of Milton's sublime poetic gifts; theme and form were "created," but not by Milton alone. In suggesting that his (and Dryden's) verses offend in their rhyme, the poet imputes divinity to Milton's metrical system as well as to his subject. Since he is forced to "Commend" when he would *"Praise,"* Marvell's speaker presents the poem as an example of those limits that *PL* transcends: those of rhyme, to be sure, but those also of satire, of mundane, topical interests, in general. [SSt]

**MASENIO, JACOBO:** *see* LAUDER, WILLIAM.

**MASK, A.** Milton wrote his second dramatic entertainment for the Earl of Bridgewater and the Egerton family*. Although the Earl had been made President of the Council of Wales in June 1631, and Lord Lieutenant of Wales and the Counties on the Welsh border in July 1631, he did not formally begin his duties until the fall of 1634. On Michaelmas Night, September 29, 1634, Milton's celebratory work was "presented" at the Earl's official residence, Ludlow Castle. The poem was recited, sung, and danced by the Earl's daughter, Alice Egerton, aged fifteen, who played the Lady; the Earl's two sons, John, aged eleven, and Thomas, aged nine, who played the Brothers; and the children's music master, Henry Lawes*, who played the Attendant Spirit-Thyrsis, composed the music*, staged the work, and had it anonymously published in 1637 as *A Maske Presented at Ludlow Castle, 1634.*

    In his dedicatory letter to the elder

son, John, Lord Viscount Brackley, Lawes explains that the poem "although not openly acknowledged by the author" is, nevertheless, " a legitimate offspring, so lovely, and so much desired, that the often Copying of it hath tired my Pen to give my several friends satisfaction, and brought me to a necessity of producing it to the public view." There is, however, some uncertainty as to what Lawes "copied" to produce the text of 1637, and even more debate over what he copied or had copied for his friends, and, especially, for the Bridgewater family.

The two extant manuscripts of the poem differ considerably. *TM* (Milton's working copy) is not, as John Diekhoff has shown, in any of its forms the original draft of *Mask*, but a later transcript subjected to considerable revision before and after the 1634 production and the 1637 edition. It contains, among its many alterations and transpositions, a canceled version of the Epilogue as well as the full Epilogue with its references to Venus, Adonis, Cupid, and Psyche. *BrM* was once thought to be in Lawes's hand, but has been definitively identified as the work of a professional scribe. However, many commentators have accepted this manuscript as the version of the masque Lawes staged for the Egerton family in 1634, although the proof for this notion is entirely circumstantial. The *BrM* is shorter (908 lines) than the published versions (1023 lines) and the cuts seem to have been made primarily to accommodate the speeches as Milton originally wrote them to the acting capacities and memories of the Earl's children, to insure that no one in the first audience would be offended by extended discussions of the Lady's chastity* and to provide Lawes with an opening song instead of an inductive speech.

For those who date *BrM*'s transcription around 1634 it provides a neat, evolutionary link between the early version of the poem (obscured behind the deletions and corrections in *TM*) and the printed version of the poem (revised *TM*). However, John Shawcross has chal-lenged *BrM*'s date. He argues that it was probably not transcribed until 1637–38, that it "was transcribed from a copy of the *Trinity MS* during its development into the version which survives," and that "the 1637 Edition was set from this same intermediate copy, revised by corrections and additions from the *Trinity MS*." He contends, therefore, that "the form of the mask which we know today as *Comus* could not possibly have been the form of the mask presented at Ludlow Castle." The debate is still open, although recently, Carey in his edition and Parker in his biography have accepted Shawcross's view. However, whether or not *BrM* is *the* Ludlow version of *Mask*, it is still a valuable reminder that Milton's work was a theatrical, familial enterprise as well as an intricately structured poem.

The later publishing history of *Mask* is less tortured than the state of its manuscripts. There is general agreement that the text for the 1645 edition of the poem, Milton's first printed acknowledgment of it, is based on the 1637 text with corrections, most of which are found in *TM*, and that the 1673 text is based, with slight changes, on the text of 1645. In the collected edition of his poems, 1645, Milton gave *Mask* the place of honor. It was, in Masson's phrase, "still in respect of length and merit his chief poetical achievement." It came last, with a separate title page, and was attended by Lawes's 1637 dedication as well as a letter from Sir Henry Wotton* in high praise of the "dainty peece of entertainment's" "Dorique delicacy." By the time of Milton's second collected edition, *Mask* had lost its premier ranking and Milton printed it without the endorsements of Lawes and Wotton.

Although Lawes was responsible for the first publication of *Mask*, he most probably worked with Milton in establishing the text for 1637 and he almost certainly elicited from Milton the introductory motto from Virgil: *"Eheu quid volui misero mihi! floribus austrum / Perditus—"* ("Alas what harm did I mean to my wretched self when I let the south wind blow upon my flowers?"). The question remained entirely rhetorical during Milton's lifetime. The poem was highly regarded and, apparently, gave no trouble. However, early in the next century, *Mask* suffered the distinction of becoming the only poem Milton wrote that was retitled by his critics. When John Dalton* "adapted" Milton's poem for a benefit performance in 1738 he called it (following Toland's* biography) *Comus*, and revised it by deleting some passages and including others from several of Milton's shorter poems. Although he undoubtedly changed the title for theatrical convenience (as Masson* said, approvingly, "it was really inconvenient that such a poem should be without a briefer and more specific name"), Dalton's liberties with the title and the text are, in an important sense, major acts of criticism. His arbitrary new title powerfully suggests the difference between the 1634 performance and all other performances of the poem, and it also suggests the transient history of the genre in which Milton chose to project his entertainment.

The original title conveys, as no other title could, the local insularity of the form as well as the particular pleasures it must have given when it was first produced, pleasures that can now be felt, at best, at two removes from their source. Despite its allusive range and serious treatment of serious themes, Milton's poem was a libretto written for specific actors, a specific audience, and a specific place. The titular change from *A Maske Presented at Ludlow Castle* to *Comus* critically acknowledges the conversion of the unique performance of 1634 into a performable literary text, a process that had effectively begun with the edition of 1637. There is no evidence to indicate precisely how the Ludlow performance was managed, but it was certainly different from all subsequent performances of the poem in three crucial details: in the 1634 version, the actors (except for the performers, never identified, who played Comus and Sabrina) played themselves before an audience consisting of their family and friends on a stage in the Great Hall of their new home. Lawes's dedicatory letter makes obvious reference to the masque's ceremonial linking of the imaginary and the real when he concludes, "Live sweet Lord to be the honour of your Name, and receive this as your own, from the hands of him, who hath by many favours been long oblig'd to your most honour'd Parents, and as in this representation your attendant *Thyrsis*, so now in all reall expression your faithfull, and most humble Servant *H. Lawes*."

Neither Milton nor Lawes left any record as to how the poem was mounted, how much music accompanied it (five songs by Lawes survive in manuscript), or how long it was danced, but its mingling of the real and fictive characters of its "presenters," its celebratory notes, its combination of verse, music, dancing, and spectacle clearly align it with other works of the period granted without argument the generic status of "masque." Milton's poem is certainly less open to spectacular effects than many masques of the period, but this is partly accounted for by the size of Ludlow's Great Hall (30 by 60 feet), and by the relatively domestic character of his audience and the subject of his celebration. Nevertheless, the poem has been turned into an aesthetic orphan, a work without a genre. It has been called among other things, a "dramatised debate" (Welsford), a "dramatic masque" (Haun), "an elaborated university disputation" (Tillyard), "a lyric poem in the form of a play" (Macaulay), "a musical drama" (Finney), "a pastoral drama" (Brooks and Hardy), "a dramatic composition" (Greg), " drama in the epick style" (Johnson), "a didactic poem or a dialogue in verse" (Hazlitt), "a Platonic dialogue in the guise of a masque" (Wright), "a Platonic pastoral drama" (Carey), "a debate in semidramatic form" (Muir), "a semi-dramatic poetical debate on a moral theme" (Leishman), "a philosophical ballet" (Charles Williams), and "a suite of speeches," "an epic drama," "a poem," or "a series of lines" (Thomas

Warton). However, the absence of any single, defining, theoretical model of a masque, and the existence of many different, critically certifiable masques makes the task of those who would deny *Mask* its generic place (and its original title) very difficult. *See* MASQUES.

By the time Milton took up the form it had radically grown from simple "disguisings" into elaborate pageants (almost always conveying a moral theme through simple, contrasting, frequently allegorical* types) ending with a formal dance of considerable duration. In addition, both the City Masques and the Court Masques were inevitably complimentary in nature. The poet's main task was to create an exciting "device" or "invention" by which the compliment could be grandly made in a mythological* manner, while the designer's and director's job was to construct an ingenious "hinge" that would turn the "device" by completing the plot and releasing the masquers so that the formal dances could begin. Although the details obviously vary with individual masques, the key to the genre's "device" and "hinge" is a moment of striking transformation leading to dance.

The "entertainment" the masque provided derived in large measure from the wit and power of the "device"—in short, in the way the audience was drawn to the action and, ultimately, into it, and concomitantly, in the way the central masquers were concealed and then revealed. A masque is distinguishable from a play, then, not merely in its formal combination of diverse elements, but, more important, in the integration of the actors and the audience, the recognition of the audience (which does not want to remain and is not allowed to remain anonymous), and the incremental extension of the audience's participation as this is made possible by the form itself. There were no prescriptive proportions of music to dance to verse to spectacle, and no exact relationships of the serious to the comic or the ludicrous demanded of the poet. What seems to bother most critics of Milton who do not want to call the

work a masque is that it is demonstrably better than any other masque, or as Leishman says, it is easier to "derive specifically literary pleasure" from it than from the others.

Milton's poem is unquestionably less spectacular than many other masques of the period (including Carew's and Lawes's *Coelum Britannicum,* in which the Earl's sons had recently participated), but it was not, perhaps, quite so spare as some of its critics suggest. Part of the problem here lies in the fact that when Jonson* sought to save his masques for the future, he printed with his texts elaborate descriptions of the scenery, the changes of scene, the costumes, the *effects* of the transformations, and any other details he thought might help convert the transient into the perpetual. In Milton's "literary text" (Tuve, Broadbent) the descriptions of scene and costume are held to a minimum, but there are clear enough indications that in the costuming and in the atmospheric effects, and, possibly, in the movements of the Attendant Spirit and Sabrina, Lawes was attempting the typically gorgeous and striking effects of the more opulent masques.

In brief, those who think the work is a masque and like it try to show (often with a polemical edge) how it succeeds where all the others fail; those who think it is not a masque and does not succeed try to show that it is too ambitious to be a masque but not ambitious enough to be a fully developed drama; and those who think it is not a masque and does succeed, try to show either that it is *sui generis* or that its successes lie in its themes rather than in its structure. Recently, B. Rajan set the dispute over *Mask's* generic status into the larger perspective of all Milton's poems when he observed that "the moral surely is that it is Milton's habit to strain at the form, to oblige it to surpass its own dimensions; yet the impression given is not of violation but of a highly individual fulfilment, of something latent being raised into imaginative actuality."

Among those critics who consider the

work sufficiently masquelike to discuss its structure in the context of the masque's decorum, the most serious divergences occur in the analysis of its "hinge," which has been variously named "a myth," "an act," "an emblem," and "an appearance," and in the identification of the principal masquers. There are some commentators who think there are no masquers in the conventional sense in the poem, some who think the children may be construed as masquers from the poem's beginning, and still others who consider the children as the principal masquers, but only in the last scene (when they do not speak). There has been more agreement about the wit of the "device." Milton's plot and the selection of the Earl's children as the principal actors have been attached, since Oldys, to a story (probably apocryphal) that the children "had been on a visit at a house of their relations, the Egerton family in Hertfordshire; and in passing through Haywood forest were benighted, and the Lady Alice was even lost for a short time." And very recently, Barbara Breasted has restated evidence of deep scandal in a branch of the Bridgewater family that gives special point to the masque as a "cleansing family ritual" for that first audience "seeing Lady Alice Egerton act out her resistance to sexual temptation." However, independent of tale and scandal, the strength of the "device" lies essentially in its formalizing of the voyage of the Earl's children on their way to congratulate their father, a compliment increased by the fact that the children "present" themselves in elaborate and engaging poetry. (And Milton was probably not present at the original performance to claim immediate credit for his "invention" and spoil the illusion of the children's skills.)

The power of the "device" is evident as well in Milton's use of his "sources." Despite the Attendant Spirit's boast, "I will tell you now / What never yet was heard in Tale or Song / From old, or modern Bard in Hall, or Bowr," most critics of the poem have found an ample supply of "sources" related to the poem's structure and its putative themes.

One of the most recently discussed sources is a letter by a brother-in-law of Lady Alice, Robert Napier, who describes the fears of the Countess of Bridgewater that her daughter Alice had been bewitched. More distant but more literary bewitchments occur in most of "those lofty fables and romances" to which (in Apol) Milton says he "betook" himself. The defense of chastity dramatically rendered in the conflict between feminine virtue and malevolent magicians recalls Spenser* while Ariosto* and Tasso* hover a bit more in the background. A frequently cited source for the poem is Peele's Old Wive's Tale (1595), in which two brothers seek their sister who has been enslaved by a magician. By a "commodious vicus of recirculation" most of the Renaissance versions of enchantment recall Circe's bewitchments in the Odyssey (10, 12) where the protective herb moly (unlike Milton's "haemony"*) is of sufficient power to neutralize Circe's transforming poison. Rosemond Tuve has shown at great length how out of the "known connoted meanings" of the Circe-Comus myth "the pervading imagery of light and darkness springs quite naturally," and how "this is elaborated with the greatest originality by Milton, with conceptual refinements and extensions impossible to a lesser genius." Many other commentators on Milton have traced the permutations of the Circe myth through Ovid* (Metamorphoses 14), Tasso's Armida episode (Jerusalem Delivered 14), Spenser's Acrasia (Fraerie Queene 2. xii), and especially Spenser's story of Amoret and Busyrane in which the lady is freed from a male enchanter by Britomart (Faerie Queene 3. xii).

There have also been studies of the possible influence of the pastoral* drama on Mask. At one time, the vogue was to cite Guarini's Il Pastor Fido and Tasso's Aminta as significant sources, but their places have been preempted by Fletcher's* The Faithful Sheperdess (ca. 1610), which has received very careful attention from Carey and Leishman, among others.

The paradigmatic conflict of vice and virtue at the center of most masques' "devices" makes it difficult to locate individual masques that might have had a particular influence on *Mask*. Of the masques of the period, Jonson's *Pleasure Reconcil'd to Virtue* is probably the closest in design and does have a Comus as one of its characters (although he is much more of an obscene caricature than Milton's), but it is primarily helpful for showing how successfully Milton could use the essential components of the masque form for his own purposes. Other analogous masques include Browne's *Inner Temple Masque*, Shirley's *The Triumph of Peace,* and Townshend's *Tempe Restored* (for which John Demaray has made an extended case).

In general, studies of the sources for *Mask*'s plot and structure have been less definitive and compelling than studies of the masque's verbal and mythographic echoes, since these have been traced to Shakespeare*, Sylvester*, Jonson, Virgil*, Horace*, and especially Spenser (with regard to the images of paradise) by the poem's many editors from Warton* and Todd* to Carey and Hughes*. And all of Milton's critics who have touched on the subject of sources have noted his imaginative liberties with the available material on the characters of Comus, who is, in the poem, a French and Italian import, not native to the Shropshire woods (out of Philostratus's *Imagines* and the Latin *Comus* of Hendrik van der Putten, 1608) and Sabrina (out of Geoffrey of Monmouth's* *History of the British Kings,* Warner's *Albion's England,* Drayton's *Polyolbion,* and Spenser's *Faerie Queene*).

*Mask*'s formal structure derives, however, not from any particular external source, but, rather, from two essential choices Milton made, one in keeping with the decorum of the masque, the other a variation on usual masque practice. Milton chose as his central figures lightly allegorical types—an Attentive Spiritual Messenger and Guide, an Unyielding, Virtuous Lady, two Brother-Heroes, a Vile, Sensual Enchanter, and a Restored, Virgin Sea-Goddess—and set them into a mildly plotted fable centered on loss,

disability, resolution, and heroic recovery. He made no effort to develop his characters fully because he recognized that such development would put too much pressure on the delicate fabric of his stylized entertainment (and, possibly, too much strain on the young presenters). He did, however, decide to establish from the beginning of his masque the conflict between the forces of order and virtue and the forces of disorder and sensuality instead of (more typically of the genre) waiting to engage the opposing virtues and vices in a single climactic scene. By introducing the allegorical adversaries at the beginning of *Mask,* Milton freed himself from the usual severe restrictions on dialogue in the masque, enlarged the dramatic potential of the antimasque (which was essentially a divertissement in Jonson), and invested the relationship between the songs and dances demanded by the form and the energetic details of his story with an unusual degree of necessity and probability.

Milton organized his device *spatially* by dividing the action into a complementary series of vertical and horizontal movements. In this way, he gracefully developed a sense of the integral relationship between natural and supernatural events. The masque begins with the descent of the Spirit from "before the starry threshold of *Joves* Court," continues with the wanderings through the "drear wood" of Comus, the Lady, the Brothers, and the Attendant Spirit as Thyrsis, climactically images the ascent of Sabrina from "under the glassie, cool, translucent wave," the Lady's ascent out of Comus's "marble venom'd seat," and the descent of Sabrina "to wait in *Amphitrite's* bowr," journeys with the Lady, the Brothers, and Thyrsis to the palace of the President of Wales for the songs and dances of victory and celebration, and concludes with the ascent of the Spirit to the domain "far above" of Cupid and Psyche or "to the corners of the Moon."

The poem's opening speech is a good illustration of Milton's commanding use of the forms and *ficelles* typical of the genre. An induction is a common feature of many masques of the period, but in *Mask* the Attendant Spirit is both a dramatic character in the masque and the traditional "presenter" of the "device."

Before the starry threshold of *Joves* Court
My mansion is, where those immortal shapes
Of bright aereal Spirits live insphear'd
In Regions milde of calm and serene Air,
Above the smoak and stirr of this dim spot,
Which men call Earth, . . .

. . . som there be that by due steps aspire
To lay their just hands on that Golden Key
That ope's the Palace of Eternity:
To such my errand is.

The Spirit describes his role in the forthcoming action, and also presents in a concentrated form the framework within which all the characters in the masque will be placed. His "mansion" serves as the heavenly coulisse for all the other places—benevolent and malevolent—in the masque's physical and moral geography. His image of the earth as a "pinfold" where men are "confin'd" and "pester'd" establishes the masque's concern with the varieties of confinement that mark the natural and supernatural world—confinements by which men and women are tested and from which they may rise. The gloriously circumscribed life of the platonically "insphear'd" Spirits and "enthron'd gods on Sainted seats" provides counter-images to the distorted and corrupted life in Comus's palace of pleasure and to Comus's paralyzing, magic chair. This opening cluster of images is characteristic of the masque's complex verbal design. Through it Milton explores the essential distinctions between virtuous stability and monstrous fixity, between restraint and license, between the pure and the impure. The phrase "this mortal change" rings the first modulation on the masque's further concern with the existential process and spiritual meaning of transformation, and in his reference to "due steps" the Spirit introduces an idea that will be dramatically and imagistically resolved only at

the end of the masque when the Lady's dance of freedom and the Spirit's vision of a stellar paradise finally set the wild and "tipsie" steps of the "solemn" dance of Comus and his rout of monsters into the clearest spiritual, psychological, and moral perspectives.

Many commentators on the masque have observed that the compliment is central to the form. As Northrop Frye says, "the masque is usually a compliment to the audience, or an important member of it, and leads up to an idealization of the society represented by the audience." In *Mask* Milton approached the conventional compliment with the same inventive boldness he approached the conventional prologue. The compliment to the President of Wales is preceded by the description of a world divided between Jove and Neptune. This is not a gratuitous mythological formulation. It narratively prepares for the dramatic moment when Neptune's surrogate, Sabrina, is raised by Jove's surrogate, the Attendant Spirit, in the masque's climactic scene. The Spirit's narration of Neptune's presentation of his domain to his "blu-hair'd deities" leads directly to the compliment:

And all this tract that fronts the falling Sun
A noble Peer of mickle trust, and power
Has in his charge, with temper'd awe to guide
An old, and haughty Nation proud in Arms:
Where his fair off-spring nurs't in Princely lore,
Are coming to attend their Fathers state.

Aside from its high praise for the attending Earl and his Welsh guests, the compliment sets the fable in motion, suggests the linear direction of the plot at its literal level, looks forward to the Brothers' philosophical debate, prepares for the introduction of Diana into the masque's categorical mythology, and describes a secular power that is virtuous because it is restrained. Furthermore, the Spirit's representation of a sacramental world in which the powers of good and evil are ranged against one another leads naturally to his discourse on Circe. She is described as the daughter of the sun, and the plot will engage her night-roving son, Comus, against the "sun-clad" chaste daughter of the secular regent of the land of the falling sun.

The final part of the Spirit's prologue establishes the masque's moral polarities in richer detail. The Spirit reinforces the radical disparity between Comus's dark domain and the "Regions milde of calm and serene Air" of the "bright aereal Spirits." This is an especially important comparison because Comus thinks of himself as an "imitator," yet his native haunts are, clearly, a grotesque distortion of those heavenly realms he seeks to imitate. In this poem only the court of the Earl of Bridgewater stands as an appropriate natural source of Jovian peace and harmony.

As the Spirit's narration ends and the dramatic action begins, the Spirit decides on a plan of attack. He will put off his "skie robes" "And take the Weeds and likeness of a Swain / That to the service of this house belongs / Who with his soft Pipe, and smooth dittied Song / Well knows to still the wilde winds when they roar, / And hush the waving Woods." This is Milton's gracious compliment to Lawes and the house he serves, but it is also the first of the active transformations anticipated in the first lines of the prologue. Moreover, it signals the beginning of a series of emphatic reminders of the power of song, helps integrate the masque's plot and dialogue with its music, and anticipates the raising of Sabrina, the masque's incarnation of pure harmony.

When Comus enters, the Spirit hears "the tread / Of hateful steps." Comus's movements contrast, for all his mimetic skills, with the movements of those "that by due steps aspire." Comus's position in the moral hierarchy of the masque is dramatically reinforced by the simultaneous appearance of the untempered anti-masquers: *"with him a rout of Monsters, headed like sundry sorts of wilde Beasts . . . they come in making a riotous and unruly noise."* Milton integrates the traditional masque dances into the overall movement of *Mask* in the same way that he makes the traditional songs structurally and thematically appropriate. Comus's first speech suggests that the movements in his world are imaginatively ordered, while the actual dances of his "rout" make it clear that in his world all movement is emphatically disordered. The rout's appearance destroys any illusion of dance as harmonic form that might be derived from Comus's description of the activities in his enchanted night-world. Despite his lilting language, Comus cannot conceal his true nature and the true nature of his rout. Despite his elaborately sustained images, the dramatic impression he makes is not of serene order but of frenzied disorder. His characteristic utterance mates a rhetorically gorgeous language to contradictory or paradoxical impulses. His images of fulfillment, containment, rest and recovery ("the gilded Car of Day, / His glowing Axle doth allay / In the steep *Atlantick* stream") are intercepted by the contrary rhythms of "midnight shout and revelry / Tipsie dance, and Jollity."

The self-expressive aspect of dance as gesture is heightened, conventionalized, and rendered morally significant by the masque. Anti-masquers have no choice: they must dance as a rout. Milton used the anti-masque as he inherited it from Jonson to reflect his themes formally. The appearance of the anti-masque is visual proof that life with Comus is a life of imprisonment. Despite their frenzied gestures, the anti-masquers are deeply constrained. They see increased beauty in their transformed heads but they constitute a herd. Although they appear to be physically free, they are morally paralyzed. Their dance is the dance of slaves. They dance only to Comus's lyric orchestrations.

Comus links himself with the monsters. After his invocation to the "Goddess of Nocturnal sport / Dark vail'd *Cotytto*" he "solemnly" declares his part in the anti-community of the woods: "Com, knit hands, and beat the ground. / In a light fantastick round." And they all dance "the Measure." But their revels are interrupted by "the different pace, / Of som chast footing near about this ground." The Lady's "chast footing" holds the moral middle between Comus's "tread of hateful steps" and the "due steps" of those who aspire to the Palace of Eternity, just as her later dances and the dances of her family will establish the proper earthly models of the starry round (as Comus's wavering motions cannot). Yet, although the Lady stops the rout she is in danger, not only because she is lost in a dark wood, but because she mistakes the source of the noises she hears:

This way the noise was, if mine ear be true,
My best guide now, me thought it was the
    sound
Of Riot, and ill manag'd Merriment,
Such as the jocond Flute, or gamesom Pipe
Stirs up among the loose unletter'd Hinds.

The Lady will have to confront a devotee of *Cotytto* rather than *Pan,* but before she does, and to keep her spirits up, she first invokes her guardians and then sings a lyric to *Sweet Echo.* The song is filled with color and delicacy. The innocent and virtuous Lady knows of worlds less "drear" than Comus's, and her song with its romantic mythology, aerial perspectives, and fresh, flowering landscapes frees the action for a moment from the constrained closeness of the "blind mazes of a tangl'd Wood." The lyric is a reminder that song can be ordered and harmonious, and a reminder, too, of the close connection between music and transformation: *"So maist thou be translated to the skies, / And give resounding grace to all Heav'ns Harmonies."*

The Lady's song, ironically, brings Comus (transformed into a "gentle Shepherd") out into the open and with him an oppression that will not be lifted until Sabrina is invoked through a song by the Attendant Spirit to save the paralyzed Lady. Between the Lady's song and Thyrsis's invocation, the world of the poem is bereft of music as the Lady is caught, trapped, and bound by an "imitator" of the starry quire. It is partly through song, then, that Milton estab-

lishes the children and court of the Earl as virtuous tribunes of harmonious order. Whether (as has been frequently debated) the presenters perform a Platonic or Christian vision of harmony, their music (and later their speeches and their dancing) range them clearly against the intrusive negative axis symbolized by Comus, Circe, Cotytto, and Hecate.

The contrasting chords of harmony and disorder struck in the opening scenes of the masque continue to sound as Comus and the Lady confront each other. Comus is affected by the Lady's song, and his response seems, at first, a momentary easing of the tension, but as he adds another singer and kind of song to the growing catalogue of singers and songs, he again demonstrates that he is the Lady's antitype:

I have oft heard
My Mother Circe with the Sirens three,
Amidst the flowry-kirtl'd *Naiades*
Culling their potent hearbs, and baleful drugs,
Who as they sung, would take the prison'd soul,
And lap it in Elysium.

As Comus leads the Lady off to his "low / But loyal cottage" the two Brothers make their first appearance in the masque. Although Johnson* and Greg, and, more recently Carey and Wilkinson (among others) have attacked this section of the poem, the speeches of the Brothers and their subsequent dialogue with Thyrsis serve as a commentary on the preceding scene between Comus and the Lady, imagistically forecast the Lady's career, and introduce "Divine Philosophy" into the masque. The Elder Brother, for example, introduces three new names into the masque's mythological register. First he puts the conflict between "Chastity" and "Vice" in terms of the story of Diana and Cupid, and then he thinks of Minerva:

What was that snaky-headed Gorgon sheild
That wise Minerva wore, unconquer'd Virgin,
Wherwith she freez'd her foes to congeal'd
    stone?
But rigid looks of Chast austerity,
And noble grace that dash't brute violence
With sudden adoration, and blank aw.

The Elder Brother's moral and spiritual reading of mythology dramatically sanctions a characteristic feature of masque mythography. He also verifies in an elegant way the Spirit's observation that he has been "nurs't in Princely lore." Yet Milton has also managed to wedge the speech into his fable. The Elder Brother does not know that he has ironically inverted the correct application of his "congeal'd stone" image. His sister is about to be tested by Comus and *congeal'd* and *rigid* are words that will better describe her condition than the condition of her enemy. It is Comus who (at least superficially) holds Minerva's power, not the Lady. However, the latter part of the Elder Brother's speech correctly prophesies the Lady's forthcoming response to Comus's blandishments, for she will be unmoved by the "unchast looks," the "loose gestures," and "foul talk" by which Comus hopes to "clot" and "imbrute" her soul.

After this philosophical dialogue, the Attendant Spirit as Thyrsis arrives and, in a pastoralized version of his earlier summary, alerts the brothers to their sister's predicament. Thyrsis's narrative substantiates the Second Brother's fears for his sister, but it also gives the Elder Brother another opportunity to expostulate on the defensive power of virtue as well as to declare his own heroic prowess. It is in answer to the brothers' declaration of heroic intent that the Attendant Spirit explains the affective powers of the "med'cinal" "*Haemony*," a restorative herb loosely related to but more powerful than the Odyssean "*Moly.*" And after the various options for freeing the Lady are explored, the masque moves directly to the climactic scene in which the Lady is twice transformed.

The change of scene incorporates the hinge of the masque : "*the Lady set in an inchanted Chair, to whom [Comus] offers his Glass, which she puts by, and goes about to rise.*" As he begins his temptation of the Lady, Comus intrudes into the masque's mythological world a new and far more serious equation than has yet

appeared. *Minerva, Diana,* and *Echo* are now threateningly replaced by the rigid *Daphne* :

Nay Lady sit; if I but wave this wand,
Your nerves are all chain'd up in Alablaster,
And you a statue, or as *Daphne* was
Rootbound, that fled *Apollo.*

In her reply, the Lady establishes the effective power of chastity :

Thou canst not touch the freedom of my minde
With all thy charms, although this corporal rinde
Thou haste immanacl'd, while Heav'n sees good

Comus then offers "refreshment," "ease," and "timely rest." The Lady counters with a description of the restorative quality of spiritual goods. She has, unlike the monster rout, a "well-govern'd" appetite. Comus, in turn, then appeals to nature. Using his well-tried rhetoric* of deceit, Comus tries to persuade the Lady with superficially splendid images, but his own material concerns are egregiously present in his speech. When he describes nature "strangl'd with her waste fertility," the principle of plenitude becomes a principle of license. He describes the "riches" of nature in such gross terms that his argument undercuts itself : "Beauty is natures coyn, must not be hoorded, / But must be currant." Furthermore, his explosive discussion of the nature, uses, and adversities of beauty takes place in the hostile context of the "grim-aspects" of his palace. The disjunction between the physical appearance of the palace and the grotesque configuration of its inhabitants (as the Lady very well perceives) is an emblematic reminder of the disparity between the richness of Comus's rhetorical display and the monstrous sense of his pronouncements. The Lady's response to Comus's set speech demonstrates her inviolate morality and her powers of analysis. Although some of Milton's critics consider the Lady's reply poetically inconsequential or philosophically evasive, she correctly identifies Comus's technique as "obtruding false rules pranckt in reasons garb," she does call for an "even proportion" of Nature's bounty, and she does establish a sense of context that makes her observations quietly exact :

> for swinish gluttony
> Ne'er looks to Heav'n amidst his gorgeous feast,
> But with besotted base ingratitude
> Cramms, and blasphemes his feeder.

And then she fully dismantles Comus's pretensions to participate in the starry choir :

> To him that dares
> Arm his profane tongue with contemptuous words
> Against the Sun-clad power of Chastity;
> Fain would I something say, yet to what end?
> Thou hast nor Ear, nor Soul to apprehend
> The sublime notion, and high mystery
> That must be utter'd to unfold the sage
> And serious doctrine of Virginity.

The power the Lady defines is stronger than the Elder Brother's "complete steel," and what she says proves dramatically true with Sabrina's appearance, for Sabrina's offensive weapons do not consist of material armament or logical argument, but the power and mystery of song.

The masque's "device" is now turning on its "hinge." After Comus is routed by the brothers, the Spirit enters but discovers that he cannot "free the Lady that sits here / In stony fetters fixt, and motionless." This is the emblematic climax of the masque. There is very little action in *Mask* before the turning of the device, but the masque remains vital and energetic in its first half precisely because Milton translates the *language* of the device in motion into the *actions* of the device turned.

In his opening speech, the Spirit described the conjunction of sea and sky power. This description is dramatically realized when Thyrsis, recognizing his own deficiencies in sympathetic magic, narrates the history of Sabrina. The story is brief. However, it fits naturally into the masque's design. Sabrina's "quick im-

mortal change" recalls all the changes, real and hypothetical, that have been established through the language and action of the masque. Each of these transformations provides perspective for, and is afforded perspective by, all the others. They include : the transformation experienced by those who after "this mortal change" are embraced by the "enthron'd gods" on "Sainted seats"; the transformation experienced by those who are foolish and weak enough to be tempted by Comus's words and who fall under the power of his julep or his wand; the transformation of *Echo;* the transformation of the Lady into a paralyzed mute; the transformation of Sabrina from a mortal into a surrogate of the gods; and the transformations of the Attendant Spirit into Thyrsis and Comus into a "harmless villager." And all these internal transformations are informed by the vehicular transformation effected by the masque itself as the audience—as a restored community complete in all its parts—is absorbed into the action through celebratory dance when the Lady and her two Brothers are presented to their parents by their Attending Spirit.

In the Sabrina episode, the relationship of song to the Lady's problem is finally made explicit : Sabrina can "unlock / The clasping charm" but she must be "right invok't in warbled song." As the Lady sang her song to *Echo* for help, so here the power of song is enlisted in her behalf. The combination of verse and song is abstractly pleasing, but the combination of *these* verses and songs is also necessary and probable, given the dramatic situation as it has progressed to the climactic scene. The Spirit sings :

> *Sabrina fair*
> *Listen where thou art sitting*
> *Under the glassie, cool, translucent wave,*
> *In twisted braids of Lillies knitting*
> *The loose train of thy amber-dropping hair,*
> *Listen for dear honours sake,*
> *Goddess of the silver lake,*
> *Listen and save.*

Sabrina is free. She has overcome the confinements of a negative force. She is the masque's mythological incarnation of freedom as well as a complimentary tutelary Welsh sea-spirit. She may, as some commentators have observed, represent the power of Grace*, but she certainly represents graceful power. The free-flowing beauty of her hair is *ordered* beautifully. Comus wanted his nymphs to knit their hair as a prelude to his exotic night life. Sabrina's hair is free but also restrained. The Spirit calls on Sabrina to "Rise, rise." She does. In answer to the Spirit's summons she appears first as song; and in her song she sings of a scene and an atmosphere that with its blues and greens serves as an effective contrast to the artificiality of Comus's palace. The Lady's song to *Echo* has finally been answered. The free-moving Sabrina and the paralyzed Lady face each other :

Brightest Lady look on me,
Thus I sprinkle on thy brest
Drops that from my fountain pure,
I have kept of pretious cure,
Thrice upon thy fingers tip,
Thrice upon thy rubied lip,
Next this marble venom'd seat
Smear'd with gumms of glutenous heat
I touch with chaste palms moist and cold,
Now the spell hath lost his hold;
And I must haste ere morning hour
To wait in *Amphitrite's* bowr.

The scene conveys a sense of power and serenity. "Sabrina *descends, and the Lady rises out of her seat*." The device has turned. In a sacramental world, processes are complementary and interchangeable, and in Comus's palace the activities of the Lady (in speech) and Sabrina (in song) symbolically complement each other. The exact nature of the exchange is mysterious, but the results of Sabrina's ministrations are direct. With Sabrina's support, the Lady undergoes a magical restoration. She has been touched by a mysterious feminine sea-power and can now proceed horizontally on her way home to her father's house, a seat of secular safety, the palace of the President of Wales.

With the change of scene to Ludlow town and the President's castle, the presentation of the children to their father,

family, and friends becomes the center of the dramatic action, as the masque draws away from spiritual and psychological allegory and moves closer to the literal and domestic fact of their return home.

First, a group of rude "shepherds" dances. This is the literal analogue to the supernatural anti-masque performed by Comus and his monster rout. The revelry of these harvesters is not grim. It does not involve a perverse imitation of the starry choir. It represents, rather, the motion and music the Lady originally *expected* to encounter when she found herself lost in the drear wood, and it can be dispelled easily by the lyrics of the song now sung by the music-master-Thyrsis : "back Shepherds, back, anough your play." There is no moral drama here because magic and energy are unnecessary. Milton incorporated the familiar technique for banishing the anti-masque (most anti-masquers are simply *told* to go away—and they do) into his dramatic fable to reemphasize the quality and degree of the magical dispensations that have freed the Lady from Comus's enchantments. The ease with which the Spirit dismisses the last group of anti-masquers (there is no need for either *Haemony* or Sabrina) introduces a note of seriousness into the several appearances and disappearances of the anti-masquers that is uncommon to the genre. The final anti-masquers can be disposed of through the power of song alone, and they will be replaced by the *"lighter toes, and such Court guise / As Mercury did first devise."*

The next song presents, with a "crown of deathless Praise," the three children who, having moved through *"hard assays,"* have *"so goodly grown."* The testing voyage is over and the dances that conclude it represent the *"triumph" "O're sensual Folly, and Intemperance."* The dance is ordered and restrained; it is the most overt gesture of the victory over sensual disorder. The conventions of the genre called for a final dance, but Milton so manipulated his device that a dance is *exactly* what we should expect from the Lady. After the threat of paralysis and then the temporary experience of paralysis, the Lady appreciates her physical freedom more fully, and the natural gesture of her appreciation is motion formally ordered and restrained but not constrained. The court dance fully corresponds to this formula. The Lady's dance is, then, the dramatic quotient of all the various stages of the masque's action and serves to integrate herself, her brothers, and her family, and it was at this moment, quite likely, that the audience joined the celebratory and ritualistic triumph initially staged by the Lady alone.

After the dances end, the masque concludes, as it had begun, with a serious speech by the Spirit. (In Lawes's production, however, the masque may have ended with a brief song rather than a long speech.) In his epilogue the Spirit recalls and reinforces all that has happened. He images a flight to the west and describes the Garden of Hesperus. He imaginatively soars above Comus's woods toward Paradise. Color returns with greater variety than ever before in the poem. The Spirit's autobiographical passage concludes with a visionary flight to complementary mythological pairs: Venus and Adonis (the forces of seasonal generation) and Cupid and Psyche. The paradisiac freedom of the wondering Psyche reinterprets and expands the significance of the wandering Lady's similar experience of freedom.

The masque ends with a final emphasis on restorative action: "Heav'n itself would stoop to [virtue]." The action of the poem has shown Heaven stooping in the form of a rising Sabrina. Through the movements of his device, Milton shows that heaven's bourne includes not only the "Spheary chime" but the land below the translucent wave as well. The domains of Jove and Neptune are both homes for those guardian spirits who come to the aid of distressed virtue.

As Milton composed Mask the thematic emphasis seems clear. The masque begins with the Spirit's description of the "crown that Vertue gives" and it ends (as the directions reverse) with the Spirit's

(sung or spoken) injunction: "Mortals that would follow me, / Love vertue, she alone is free, / She can teach ye how to clime / Higher than the Spheary chime." However, despite these guides, Mask has been subjected to an extraordinary variety of diagnostic allegorizations. The disputes over the poem's meaning frequently revert to the Lady's statement to Comus during their debate that she will not reveal to him the "sage and serious doctrine of Virginity." Many of Milton's critics suggest that even if the Lady retreats into silence the poem does not and that Milton revealed the doctrine symbolically rather than discursively. A distinct minority of contemporary critics is willing to let Mask off as a light allegorical invention. For the most part, the current reading of the poem's themes usually involves an elaborate exegesis centered on one or more of the following topics: the character of the Attendant Spirit, the speech of the Elder Brother on virtue, the description of Haemony, the debate between Comus and the Lady, the Sabrina episode, and, most especially, the relationship between the epilogue and the whole poem.

Three decades ago, A. S. P. Woodhouse* attempted to apply the schematic ground plan of nature and grace to the development of Mask's action. Woodhouse's central theorem is that "nothing less is symbolized in the Epilogue than life itself, as the Christian mind grounded in nature but illuminated by grace, alone can apprehend it." In the service of this proclamation, he tries to distinguish four different "virtues" in the Lady: temperance and continence (belonging to the order of nature), chastity (belonging to the orders of nature and grace), and virginity (belonging to the order of grace alone). He attempts to resolve what he sees as an apparent confusion in the poem between the doctrine of temperance and the doctrine of virginity by arguing that the epilogue is the dialectical resolution of the two principal thematic ideas operating in the poem up to its conclusion. Woodhouse's insistence on the central importance of the epilogue to the masque's themes is supported by Tillyard*, who argues on the basis of the revisions in *TM* that Milton changed the epilogue in order to suggest allegorically that the Lady should enjoy spiritual chastity in marriage rather than remain a virgin. The crucial change occurred, Tillyard argues, because Milton himself underwent a radical transformation of sensibility when he gave up the idea of a creative celibacy. A. E. Dyson dismisses the emphasis on the epilogue as "altogether exaggerated." He finds in it "a significance which only a scholar who knows the text, almost literally, backwards, is likely to consider convincing." He, therefore, makes a primary philosophical substitution. For him "the great 'debate' is not between Chastity and Incontinence, and still less between Virginity and Marriage, but between Reason and Passion as controlling factors in human conduct." In this reading the Lady is "Chastity (or Virtue) incarnate, and her purpose is to illustrate the immutable nature and wisdom of this virtue." For John Arthos, however, "Platonic* and Neo-Platonic* illustrations provide a self-consistent and comprehensive interpretation of the thought of the *Mask*." His major ally is Sears Jayne, who argues that "the subject of the Mask" is the four-step Platonic attainment of Virtue through passion (Comus), philosophy (Brothers), reason (Alice), to *Mens* (Sabrina). These views are put through the analytical wringer by Richard Neuse, who contends that to "read the poem as radical spiritual allegory of the Neoplatonic variety, does not seem to do justice to its particular mode of symbolization." Neuse strives to show that "the theme of *Mask* is close to 'pleasure reconciled to virtue' and involves the poet's traditional concern with the life of the senses rather than the exaltation of an ideal like virginity as a vehicle to the divine." In this reading the epilogue becomes "a great emblem of youth" that "stands in direct contrast to the make-believe world of seasonless 'waste fertility' into which Comus lures his followers." And whereas the Attendant Spirit—an early model of the Heavenly Messenger—generally resembles a guardian angel in the Christian dispensation for James Arnold, a typically Euripidean prologist for Welsford, a Platonic or Neoplatonic daemon for Arthos and Jayne (and is called, alternatively, a "daemon" in *BrM*), for Neuse he "comes to be seen as a representation, almost a definition of the functions and limits of poetry."

The most comprehensively balanced views of the masque's themes are those of Reesing, Demaray, and Rajan. Reesing observes that the two main categories of transformation (those determined by moral choice and those which involve the change into a beast or into a god) that underlie the anti-masque and masque sections may be identified as fundamental to an understanding of the poem. He sees these transformations as a fusion of Ovidian, Platonic, and Christian materials. He identifies the poem's theme as "the moral character of the timeless world of permanence and the moral conditions for membership in it." The masque is, therefore, "about the prospect of divinization open to all human beings who live virtuously." Reesing is one of the few modern critics of the poem who seem to be willing to accept the possibility that "it is sometimes hard to say where literal meaning ends and allegorical meaning begins." In this openness, he is close to Demaray, who writes that "if Milton, who was not generally disposed to allegorize, intended that the magic instruments and rituals in *Mask* have allegorical meanings, he did not make these meanings clear in the text." Demaray can find no common agreement on "what Milton's alleged allegory might have been," and thus concludes that "nothing in the text indicates that Comus's wand is meant to represent anything except a wand. The cup and potion of Comus also seem to be only magical objects. . . . The power of Sabrina is nowhere referred to in the text as anything except the power of a chaste, pagan Goddess of the Severn River." For Demaray, the masque's central theme is "the triumph of virtue, associated with rational restraint and order, over vice, associated with excessive passion and disorder." This view links him with Rajan, who thinks that Milton criticism tends to regard the Nature-Grace, Reason-Passion thematic axes as "exclusive of each other," whereas "in fact their amalgamation is likely to be a primary objective in any poet determined to consummate the classical in the Christian." Rajan accepts the idea of Platonic purification as a helpful gloss on the poem, but he can accommodate it to Christian as well as Platonic leanings: "The soul's seeking of its form, its dedication to what is noblest in itself, is the true index of chastity." Rajan suggests that although "Sabrina may be an agent of grace," she is also "a water-spirit, a force in nature." He further argues that in the epilogue "youth and joy are shown as the outcome of the restraint that Comus scorned when he taxed the lady with letting youth slip by," and in this generation we are to understand that "a lower reality is not annulled in the acceptance of the higher." Rajan meets the poem on its own linguistic terrain when he observes that "the world of the senses is included and not annulled by consecretation to the world of the spirit; discipline forms the basis for the liberation of creative energy rather than the means for its confinement."

Despite the variations, most of the critical allegorizers treat *Mask* seriously and as a thematic success. On the other side, writers such as Carey, Greg, and Wilkinson have attempted to demolish its pretensions to seriousness. Carey's is the most intensive attack : for him (following Muir), the poem is either ironic or hopelessly inadequate. Carey suggests that Milton actually wrote two poems in one masque. The outer shell of *Mask* gave the aristocratic Ludlow audience the opportunity to be self-congratulatory. The inner core of the masque allows for partial pleasures of a very different order : "There is no reason to suppose that [the Egerton children] would be sacrosanct to a high-minded middle-class intellectual.

The first audience was complacent enough for any implied criticism to pass over its heads. But without turning *Comus* into a warren of 'ironies,' it is possible to ask some simple questions about what is said and done, and end up with the conviction that if the watchers on Michaelmas night 1634 scanned one facet of Milton's purpose with eager approval, another went, for that reason, uninspected." However, by the time Carey is finished asking his "simple questions" he leaves the poem a shambles. Although he begins his essay by observing that Johnson's realist strictures are not appropriate for a genre like the masque, he nevertheless resorts consistently to Johnson's approach to show how the poem demonstrates the moral, spiritual, social, and intellectual faults of its principal characters. And while Wilkinson considers the debate between Comus and the Lady a failure on aesthetic grounds because the combatants do not "engage poetically," Carey considers the debate a failure on ethical grounds : "it is not so much a matter of allegory being an inadequate mode as of Milton's being an inadequate allegory —dangerously so, by fostering belief in tempters who untemptingly mishandle their advantages." Greg surrounds these criticisms with his own. For him, all the speeches in the poem introduced "with a directly moral and philosophical rather than a dramatic end must be pronounced artistic solecisms."

The middle ground between attack and praise is held by the Bulloughs, who identify the governing ideas in the poem as a mixture of Platonism and Christian asceticism, but who find a confusion between Milton's apprehension of purification through an ever-increasing spirituality (derived from Plato) leading to divine union and the worship of Temperance, "as if the act of self-denial were an end in itself and its result the Platonic vision of absolute joy." However, in their evaluative summation they become partisans : "the glow and ardour generated in the attempted union of Christian renunciation and Platonic sublimation suffuse the poem with a warmth and light and joy which Milton never recaptured." This is a view very close to Arthos's judgment that the masque "is everywhere written nobly, and the songs and the Epilogue, in their sense and above all in their music, communicate a kind of spiritual clarity that is the poem's most perfect achievement. This remains its final excellence, an accent and a music creating a clearer temper than we often imagine to be found in life."

The "accent" and "music," the strength and serenity of *Mask* derive, in part, from its style. Even Dr. Johnson (who had little else positive to say of the poem) recognized that in *Mask* Milton "formed very early that system of diction and mode of verse which his maturer judgement approved." The blank verse* poetic paragraph holds an important structural place in the masque as Milton alternates it with rhymed, four-stressed lines, heroic couplets, and the more free-flowing lyrics of his songs. The blank verse is of the declamatory sort although, as the Bulloughs point out, "Milton allowed himself considerable freedom in the placing of stresses and in the number of unstressed syllables." They have also noted that "a fair proportion (about 1 in 12) of lines have feminine endings," and that "most clauses and sentences finish at the end of a line, but there are frequent medial periods." Nevertheless, Milton did not attempt to make his blank verse carry the subtle weights, pressures, and irregularities of individual character in action.

Milton did, however, support the dramatic *logic* of the masque with stylistic variety. The poem begins with the Spirit's blank verse prologue, which is followed, in Comus's first speech, by four-stressed couplets occasionally interspersed with five-stressed lines. When Comus must break off his "conceal'd Solemnity," he speaks in blank verse to describe the Lady's "different pace." The Lady enters speaking blank verse but then moves into her echo-song. The customary echo in this conventional mode is not forthcoming. Rather, Comus responds to her "enchant-

ing ravishment" in a blank verse declamation that is quickly followed by the disjunctive *stichomythia.* When the Brothers enter they speak in blank verse, but Milton made some effort to distinguish them. The Elder Brother uses a more elaborately imagistic language than the Second Brother (although, as C. S. Lewis* notes, Milton, in the successive versions of the poem in *TM,* carefully toned down some of the Elder Brother's more excessive phrasing), while the Second Brother tends to use a vigorously alliterative diction that reinforces his sense of his sister's distress.

Each of the sublunary characters uses a considerable number of semi-personified abstractions. Comus welcomes Joy and Feast and scorns Rigour, Advice, Strict Age, and Sour Severity; the Lady perceives Conscience*, Faith*, Hope*, and Chastity; the Elder Brother meditates on Virtue, Wisdom, and Contemplation; while the Second Brother fears the fate of Beauty in the grasp of Bold Impertinence, Danger, and Opportunity. Milton's use of these figures has been observed by Broadbent, who also describes other working elements of the verse : its colloquial idiom, its "extravagant naturalistic metaphors" (which were highly praised by Warton as "wild and romantick imagery") and its "idealistic images checked by a sense of the concrete." But, as Broadbent says, "the verse as a whole does not reconcile these varieties or commit itself to any one of them. It wings from one to the other, displaying its own astonishing virtuosity. The variations in tone and tempo are remarkable." Broadbent argues that there is a discrepancy between the masque's themes and its style : "the action and ideology of the masque suggest, rather than realize, ideals of harmony and fruition. In the same way the verse lacks an assured norm that would draw and shape its virtuosity into a recognizable individual act." Certainly, by the stylistic standards of Milton's epics and *SA*, this is an accurate judgment. But, in a way, it brings up, once again, the problem of the poem's genre. It might be argued that, in a stylized entertainment like *Mask,* the verse functions best when it does not overwhelm the music, dancing, and spectacle, as it surely would if it were able to measure up to the evaluative norms Broadbent sets for it. This is not to say that Milton, in 1634, could have produced a more integrative style. It is rather to note that, as in his treatment of the other elements that, compositely, make a masque, Milton forged a style with imaginative boldness but still allowed for the delicacy of his chosen form. He was, after all, the only writer of a masque who was able to produce a serious entertainment in which a "barbarous dissonance" is dramatically modified and subdued by a verse that could "still the wild winds when they roar / And hush the waving woods" as it converts itself into music and, finally, dance. [RBW]

**MASON, WILLIAM:** *see* INFLUENCE ON SEVENTEENTH AND EIGHTEENTH CENTURY LITERATURE, MILTON'S.

**MASQUES.** Seventeenth-century court masques of the kind written by Ben Jonson* and his followers are staged theatrical productions—involving song, dialogue, dance, and scenic spectacle—in which disguised aristocrats "triumph" over figures of vice, perform in a ballet complimenting one or two seated nobles, and then engage with the audience in an evening of indoor social dancing. The works are characterized by a minor "hinge" or plot, pagan character-types and settings, elaborate costumes and scenery, and, when successful, a harmonious blending of the various theatrical arts. Masques were created to celebrate a hierarchical aristocratic establishment which, in the context of the works, is depicted as ruled under "Jove" by one or two honored nobles seated on chairs of state. Commoners played the roles of evil figures by singing, speaking, and dancing in a manner suggesting disorder; the featured aristocrats, representing figures of virtue, restored harmony to the theatrical world primarily through gesture and orderly dance. At the climax of the productions, the main masquers performed their ballets and were "presented" to the seated nobles representing the state. The main masquers then "took out" members of the audience by dancing with them and so beginning the formal masked ball.

In the late Renaissance, masques were performed in rectangular halls with the audience seated on "tiers" or "degrees" —wooden boards raised to differing heights—around three sides of the chamber. A stage space, usually with proscenium arch and curtain, was arranged at a narrow end of the hall. The chair of state was placed on a raised platform at the rear-center of the hall facing the stage area.

The initial action of masques took place in the stage area. There the main masquers, wearing vizors and glittering costumes, were "discovered" as music and song sounded and ingenious scenic devices "opened." They appeared suddenly from scenic mountains, temples, sea shells, groves, and woods; sometimes they floated down from scenic heavens on paper clouds illuminated from within. After overcoming or driving off the figures of vice, the performers stepped from the stage area into the center of the hall in order to engage in main masque dances, be presented to the state, and then participate in the masked ball. On occasion masques ended when, following the masked ball, the performers returned to the stage area where the scenic devices "closed" upon them as an epilogue was spoken or sung.

Under Kings James I* and Charles I*, court masques, produced at great expense with the aid of the Revels Office, were regularly mounted for Shrovetide or for state or religious holidays. Between 1603 and 1632, Ben Jonson, the most prolific English writer of masques, created twenty-five of the works, including *The Masque of Blackness* (1605), *Hymenaei* (1606), *The Masque of Beauty* (1608), *The Masque of Queens* (1609), *Oberon, the Faery Prince* (1611), *Pleasure Reconciled to Virtue* (1618), *News from the New World discover'd in the Moone* (1621), and

*Chloridia* (1631). Court architect Inigo Jones designed the costumes and stage settings for these productions, introducing figures and emblems that reappeared in masque after masque and gave continuity to the works. Court dancing masters Hierene Herne and Thomas Giles devised ballets so intricate that the main masquers sometimes rehearsed their steps for thirty days before performing in public. The Kings Music, court musicians among whom was Milton's friend Henry Lawes*, regularly sang in the masques in the roles of "airy spirits." The audiences were composed of court and government officials, foreign diplomats and dignitaries, and members of the nobility.

In the masque *Hymenaei* (1606), Ben Jonson established a structural pattern for English court masques that he and numerous other writers regularly followed. Disorderly dances introduced at the beginning of the presentation are balanced against a concluding, harmonious main masque ballet. At the opening of the work, eight male masquers representing the four Humours and the four Affections dance with abandon and disrupt preparations for a wedding being made by the figure Hymen. But eight goddesses descend on a cloud from Juno; the Humours and Affections submit to the goddesses; and the paired couples engage in a main masque ballet signifying wedded union. In *Hymenaei* there is a prologue, wild anti-masque dances, main masque speeches and *Deus ex Machina* spectacle, a main masque ballet, a "presentation" of main masquers to the state, and an epilogue. Jonson explained his method of setting unruly dances against a main masque ballet in the preface to *The Masque of Queens* (1609), and he adhered to this technique in twenty-one of his following works.

While having its origins in ancient pagan rituals celebrating the seasons and fertility, the formal Renaissance court masque developed in the fifteenth and sixteenth centuries from *balletto,* or figured dances, performed in Italy by vizored nobles during carnival season. In Florence, Verona, Rome, and other Italian cities, the aristocrats, often accompanied by torchbearers, appeared *in mascara* at balls to flirt and to dance in figures with the ladies. Carnival-season balls were sometimes given together with *Triomfi,* street processions that featured masquers who danced before a throne of state erected in an outdoor location. But as the masques and *Triomfi* grew ever more elaborate, the main theatrical events—the surprise appearance of the masquers and their presentation to and dances before the state—came to be performed indoors as part of a staged show. At Castello Sant' Angelo in Rome, such shows with climactic ballets were given before Pope Sextus IV. Roman cardinals and members of the clergy joined with aristocrats in dancing in an indoor court ballet at the Council of Trent. At the wedding of the Duke of Milan to Isabella of Aragon in 1489, a grand ballet was performed at a banquet held in Tortona, Italy.

Under the influence of the Italian musical dramas such as Politian's *Orfeo* (1471) and Nicola da Correggio's *Favola di Cefolo* (1489), the staged shows ending in masked balls were created to include songs, minor action, and dialogue. In France Baltasar de Beaujoyeulx (also known as Baltazarini de Belgiojoso), together with members of the French *Académie de poésie et de musique,* produced the famous *Circe* or *Balet Comique de la Royne* (1581) with the conscious intent of unifying all of the theatrical arts in a work culminating in a grand ballet and "presentation." Though somewhat episodic, the *Balet Comique* is given a basic structural coherence by a prologue spoken by a prisoner of Circe, main masque action centered upon Circe's magical control of virtuous figures, a main masque spectacle in which Jupiter, Pan, Minerva, and other deities free the enchantress's captives, and concluding figured dances before the chair of state. In England and most of Europe masques of this kind, having a relatively integrated form, superseded the more discursive *mascarade* and grand spectacle.

According to *Hall's Chronicle,* the first English masque took place in 1512 when Henry VIII and his courtiers made a surprise entry at a Whitehall ball. "On the daie of the Epiphanie at night," writes Hall, "the kyng with xi. other wer disguised, after the maner of Italie, called a maske, a thyng not seen afore in Englande . . . ; these Maskers came in, with six gentlemen disguised in silke bearying staffe torches, and desired the ladies to daunce. . . ." In the time of Henry VIII and Queen Elizabeth, masked entries of this kind became commonplace; and in 1594 a rather elaborate spectacle entitled *Proteus and the Adamantine Rock,* an anonymously written masque with a structure reflecting that of the *Balet Comique,* was presented at Gray's Inn. Among the masques performed in England in the following years that reveal the general influence of the *Balet Comique* are Samuel Daniel's *The Vision of the Twelve Goddesses* (1604), Thomas Campion's *Lord Hay's Masque* (1607), Francis Beaumont's *Inner Temple Masque* (1613), Thomas Middleton's *The Masque of Heroes* (1619), Aurelian Townshend's *Albion's Triumph* (1632) and *Tempe Restored* (1632), James Shirley's *The Triumph of Peace* (1634), Thomas Carew's *Coelum Britannicum* (1634), and William D'Avenant's *Britannia Triumphans* (1638) and *Salmacida Spolia* (1640).

The masque had a pervasive influence on the poetry of John Milton. In *L'Al* the movements of Mirth and her crew resemble those of dancers in a masque. Moreover, Milton asserts in the work that "mask, and antique Pageantry," are among those sights of which "youthful Poets dream / On Summer eves by haunted stream" (128–30). And there is firm evidence that the poet's *Mask* (or *Comus*), the work performed in 1634 at the installation of John Egerton* as Lord President of Wales, was written as a sequel to Aurelian Townshend's *Tempe Restored,* the latter masque being in its turn an imitation of the French *Balet Comique.* In Townshend's work a prisoner of Circe speaks in the prologue of the freedom of man's mind; the anti-masque includes a dance by beast-headed men presented before the palace and person of Circe; and in the main masque virtuous figures enter and force Circe to dissolve her enchantments. The musician Henry Lawes and two children of John Egerton had roles in Townshend's work; and two years later, as a result of a collaboration between Lawes and Milton, *Mask,* concerned with the enchantments of the son of Circe, was staged before John Egerton by a cast including three of his children and Henry Lawes.

In *PL* the palace Pandemonium, which rises from the ground of Hell as music plays (1.708–30), has been found to resemble the scenic palace that rises from the stage in William Davenant's *Britannia Triumphans.* And the angels that circle the throne of God in Milton's poem (5. 619–27) have been cited as reflecting main masquers dancing around an honored guest seated in a chair of state. [JGD]

**MASSON, DAVID** (1822–1907), biographer and editor of Milton. He was born in Aberdeen, Scotland, on December 2, 1822, and was educated in the Aberdeen Grammar School, Marischal College of Aberdeen University (M.A., 1839), and Edinburgh University, where he studied theology under Dr. Thomas Chalmers (1780–1847). Though his friendship with Chalmers lasted until the latter's death, he early abandoned his plan to enter the ministry, and returned to Aberdeen to serve for two years as editor of *The Banner,* a Free Church weekly. Acquainted with Thackeray and the Carlyles, and closely associated with De Quincy, he was drawn to a career in writing, and in Edinburgh, he became a frequent contributor to *Fraser's Magazine, Dublin University Magazine,* and other periodicals. In 1847 he removed to London, where he continued to write and began to teach. Five years later, he succeeded Arthur Hugh Clough as professor of English literature in University College, London. He founded *Macmillan's Mag-*

*azine* in 1858, and served as its editor until 1865. In that year he was appointed professor of rhetoric and English literature in the University of Edinburgh, where for thirty-five years he was an admired teacher. He continued to write for periodicals, to publish full-length biographical and critical studies, and to edit the works of important authors. His output was very large. Among his many important publications are: *Essays, Biographical and Critical* (1856), which includes "Milton's Youth"; *The Three Devils: Luther's, Milton's, and Goethe's* (1874); and *In the Footsteps of the Poets* (1893), which includes an essay on Milton. His *The Poetical Works of John Milton* (1874, 1890) is notable for its learned introductions and its copious notes. Masson's outstanding work is *The Life of John Milton, narrated in Connexion with the Political, Ecclesiastical, and Literary History of his Times*, 7 volumes, (1859–1894); revised edition, volumes 1–3, (1881–1896). It is a massive compendium of facts, compiled with extraordinary diligence and thoroughness. Though its historical interpretations and critical judgments have been questioned by competent authorities, it remains a reference work of exceptional importance. W. R. Parker in his *Milton* (1968) says (1 : vi), "I have perched like a pygmy on Masson's noble shoulders. . . ." Masson was twice honored by appointment to public office. In 1879 he was made Editor of the Register of the Scottish Privy Council; in 1893 he was named Historiographer Royal for Scotland. He died on October 6, 1907, and is commemorated by a portrait bust in Edinburgh University. [DAR]

**MATERIALISM:** *see* METAPHYSICS.

**MATHEMATICS:** *see* SCIENCE, MILTON AND.

**MATHER, COTTON:** *see* ADAPTATIONS.

**MATHEWES, AUGUSTINE:** *see* PRINTERS.

**MATTER.** Original matter, Milton explains in *CD*, "was a substance" derived from God, at first "confused and formless" but "afterwards adorned and digested into order by the hand of God" (15 : 23). It "proceeded incorruptible from God" and is therefore "intrinsically good" (15 : 23). Thus Milton avoided a Manichean pitfall, which held that matter and all embodied forms were corrupt.

Matter is also, Milton says in *Logic*, "divided into primary and secondary; the secondary into proximate and remote" (11 : 53). This division and subdivision of the classes of matter are largely determined by the analytic method Milton employs in *Logic*, a binary system that proceeds from general to specific by dividing each class into two. But aside from his logical* method, his classification of types of matter bears striking resemblances to Aristotle's* in the *Physics* (191A) and *Metaphysics* (1029A, 1070B). Within prime matter—"it is clear that there must be something to underlie the opposites" (*Physics* 191A)—appear the four qualities of hot, cold, wet, and dry, which inhere in the four elements of earth, water, fire, and air, from which are formed all corporeal things. Aristotle's prime matter is comparable to Milton's primary matter, a passive principle of incorporeality (unperceivable to the senses), which Milton describes as composed of "embryon Atoms" (*PL* 2. 900). These potential atoms are a pre-elemental material that contains Milton's "four Champions fierce" (*PL* 2. 898)—hot, cold, moist, and dry—at a later stage of development. *Logic* classifies this development as secondary remote matter, which is corporeal chaos governed by chance, a "wild Abyss, / The Womb of nature . . ." (*PL* 2. 910–11). Following the four qualities, subsequent stages in the development of matter would be the four elements and all other visible things (secondary proximate), if one extrapolates from the system outlined in *Logic*.

Milton's primary matter exists, as Raphael says (*PL* 7. 216ff.), before the creation* of heaven and earth, but is generated at a point in time* (15 : 19) and involves the exercise of the divine will. All things are, moreover, produced from the potency (or potentiality) of matter, *ex potentia materiae produci* (15 : 49).

A correct understanding of this potency of matter helps to explain much of the philosophical meaning of Milton's work. Like most reformed theologians, Milton appears to draw eclectically from both Augustine* and Aquinas*, with their respective loyalties to either Platonic* or Aristotelian* traditions. "Every *form,*" Milton says, ". . . is produced from the power of matter," by which he means that the passive, material element has a capacity for being formed into something, of becoming an entity. Milton's first matter is thus simple potentiality and may, under the agency of God's will, develop into more and more fully formed levels of existence, such that "body up to spirit work" (see Raphael's reply to Adam, *PL* 5. 469ff.). These features of Milton's ontology, which is neither philosophically precise nor systematically argued, accord well with Aristotle's and Aquinas's ideas of *potency* and *act*.

Milton's ideas also accord well with some aspects of Augustinian and Neoplatonic* thought. Both Plotinus* and Proclus* asserted that matter was a last emanation from the One or God. For Plotinus it was sheer potentiality (*Enneads* 2.4.3), entirely indeterminate, incorporeal, and "evil" because of the total absence of the Good (*Enneads* 2. 4. 12; 3. 2. 47; 1. 8. 51). Raphael tells Adam (*PL* 5. 469–70) that "All things proceed" from God and return to God unless they are "deprav'd from good" (*PL* 5. 460–72). This clearly reflects a Neoplatonic concept of emanation, but it should be pointed out that Milton never elaborates on the mystical theologies of such writers as Philo Judaeus*, Plotinus, or Proclus.

According to Augustine, following similar ideas found in Heraclitus, Anaxagoras, and the Stoics, God created all things, including matter, simultaneously—some actually and others potentially. These

potential forms of being were called "seminal reasons" (*rationes seminales*), implanted seeds that develop with God's active Providence*. When God's active will is absent, chance governs, as it does in Milton's corporeal chaos (*PL* 2. 910–11). Milton does not, however, mention Augustine's seminal reasons, although he does say that the Earth's "fertile Womb" brought forth "perfet forms . . . out of the ground" (*PL* 7. 450–56).

Unlike the Neoplatonic writers, Milton believes that the emanation of matter from God involves the exercise of the divine will and is not therefore a necessary and eternal process. Milton's God chooses to create matter out of His own nature (*creatio ex Deo*). As He tells the Son : "I am who fill / Infinitude, nor vacuous the space. / Though I uncircumscrib'd myself retire, / And put not forth my goodness, which is free / To act or not . . ." (*PL* 7. 168–72).

Besides the Neoplatonic ideas of emanation, one should not overlook the fact that the Neoplatonists were inspired by the teachings of Plato*, particularly by the *Parmenides* and *Timaeus,* and that Milton read Plato carefully. Plato's "nurse of becoming," which is the space or receptacle in which the Demiurge creates changing copies of the ideal Forms, is very like Milton's "womb of nature" (*PL* 2.911) and infinite space that is not "vacuous" (*PL* 7.168–72). Milton may well have remembered Plato's ontology and coupled it with ideas developed by Aristotle, the Neoplatonists, Augustine, and Aquinas to form his own understanding of an original matter created by God out of His own nature, capable of being formed into successive stages of higher development, always subject to divine Providence, and in essence good. *See also* METAPHYSICS. [PEB]

**MATTHEW OF WESTMINSTER,** supposed author of *Flores Historiarum,* a compilation of English history actually taken from the writings of Matthew Paris*. The book was popular and generally accepted as accurate in the seventeenth century. Archbishop Parker first printed it in 1557. Milton refers to it as an authority almost a hundred times in *Brit*. [WBH]

**MATTHEW PARIS** (d. 1259), author of an important English history, which he drew from the records of the monastery at St. Albans, the *Chronica Majora*. It was published in part by Archbishop Parker in 1571 and again by William Wats in 1640. Although in *Tenure* Milton terms its author "the best of our Historians" (*CM* 5 : 25), all of his citations are from Leunclavius's* *Ius Graeco-Romanum* (Frankfurt, 1596). They appear three times in *CB*, twice in *Tetra* (4 : 196, 217), and in *1Def* (7 :443). [WBH]

**MAURICE, PRINCE:** *see* RUPERT, PRINCE.

**MAY, THOMAS** (1595–1650), dramatist, historian, poet, and translator of some note. Thomas May became a littérateur because his "stumbling" tongue (Andrew Marvell's* term) deterred him from the practice of law in which he had been trained at Gray's Inn. In 1627 he published what has proved to be his most important work, a translation of Lucan's *Pharsalia*; three years later he extended this account of Roman history down to the death of Julius Caesar, dedicating the volume to King Charles. Commanded by the King, he next composed two narrative poems on the reigns of Henry the Second and Edward the Third (1633, 1635). But when he did not receive appointment as poet laureate or as chronologer of London—posts left vacant by the death of Ben Jonson* (who had commended his *Continuation* of the Pharsalia)—May then, according to the report of his contemporaries, shifted his allegiance to the Parliamentary cause.

In 1646 he became secretary to the House of Commons. In 1647 he published his *History of the [Long] Parliament*, an official apologetic work; this was followed in 1650 by his *Breviary*, which broke off the account of contemporary history "before" the death of "great Charles." It is this *History* upon which Milton drew in writing his *Eikon* (1649), though the extent of his reliance on it is debated by scholars. (See George W. Whiting, *Milton's Literary Milieu* [1939], and *Studies in Philology* 32 :74–102; see also Merritt Y. Hughes's edition of *Eikon* [Yale *Prose* 3 : 1962] for a reconsideration, together with an affirmation of Milton's stylistic independence.)

A tangential connection with May is perhaps to be found in Milton's unflattering allusion in *RCG* (3 : 224) to John Barclay's *Icon Animorum* (1614), the fourth part of a four-part satire against Catholicism by a writer who was later to become reconciled to that faith. In 1631 May had translated this fourth part as *The Mirrour of Minds or Barclay's Icon Animorum*; Milton could of course have known the work either in the original or in May's translation. In the *Life of Cowley* Dr. Johnson judged that May's "Latin performances" are better than those of either Cowley or Milton. [ESD]

**MAZZONI, IACOPO** (1548–1549), Italian philosopher, critic, and philologist. Gifted with legendary powers of memory, Mazzoni reputedly covered all the branches of literary and philosophical studies in his time. After his famous answer (*Discorso*, 1572) to the attack of one (probably pseudonymous) Castravilla on Dante* set in motion one of the most famous literary quarrels of the Cinquecento, he was elected to the Academy della Crusca, recently founded to promote the study and use of the vernacular. A very late heir of Ficino, whose hope was to unify the wisdom of the ancients and put it at the service of the faith, Mazzoni attempted to demonstrate that the principles underlying ancient philosophers were basically similar, publishing a treatise on this subject in 1576 and immediately following it with a prodigious list of 5,193 questions on the work, to which he invited public challenge. Although Mazzoni wrote extensively on grammatical and rhetorical subjects as well as philosophy, he remains best known for his defenses of the *Divine Comedy* against neo-Aristotelian attack. His *Della difesa della Comedia de Dante* is a vast compendium of classical materials that presents an elaborate and truly worthwhile theory of poetry. Conceived as a rebuttal to Bellisario Bulgarini's answer to his first defense of Dante in 1572, the work appeared in two parts, the first in 1587, the last only posthumously in 1688.

Although Milton names Mazzoni along with Tasso* and Castelvetro* in *Educ* (4 : 286) as an authority on the "sublime" art of poetry, one must be cautious in assuming that he agreed with Mazzoni's views any more than with, say, Castelvetro's*. There is little indication of direct influence on the English poet. Many passages would undoubtedly have interested Milton, however. As Mazzoni explicitly rejects Castelvetro's notion that poetry addresses itself to common audiences, Milton's attitude ("fit audience . . . though few" [*PL* 7. 31]) on this point, at least, is compatible, though Mazzoni also declared that the poet should labor to "satisfy" both the learned and the vulgar. But, fundamentally, Mazzoni's theory is traditionalist in its eclecticism, carefully leaving room for Dante's use of allegory* in terms suggestive of both Aquinas* and Plato*, whereas works like *PL* operate on the "literal," not the "spiritual" (or allegorical) plane that one finds in Dante or Spenser*, and Mazzoni's analysis of the *Divine Comedy* may have clarified for Milton how different his own endeavor would be. As for dramatic criticism, Mazzoni's elaborately Platonic definitions, of considerable originality, allow him to treat poetry not only in the usual Renaissance terms of ethical or political utility, but also as a recreative art designed for pleasure and as an aesthetic entity the end of which is to imitate well. Such schemes find little echo in Milton, though, for the Preface to *SA* and the passages in other works keep imitation and pleasure instrumental to or concomitant with the more common idea

of moral utility. As for catharsis*, their closest point of rapprochement, Mazzoni interprets purgation of the passions as a moderating, not an extirpative process, as does Milton. Mazzoni also agrees with Milton (and most Renaissance critics) that the arousal of pity and fear is desirable because it effects catharsis. Regarding the objects of catharsis, however, he wavers. Sometimes he adopts the position that pity and fear "purge" many other undesirable passions, and he cites with approval his predecessor Vincenzo Madius, whose view of catharsis Milton was careful to avoid; at other times, he merely suggests that catharsis purges the mind of ills and troubles. Because Milton specified the objects of catharsis as pity, fear, and "such like passions," he is much more definite on the matter, and if he meant not passions distinct from pity and fear as the objects of catharsis, but pitylike or fearlike emotions such as horror, terror, rue, commiseration, and the like, his view of catharsis would be entirely different from the Italian's. However, Mazzoni's fullest treatment of purgation was not printed until 1688, making it highly unlikely that Milton knew his position at firsthand. In any case, the two theorists differ fundamentally on so many essential points as to nearly preclude any basic philosophical agreement. [PRS]

**McCOLLEY, GRANT** (1896–1954), scholar. After completing his doctorate at Northwestern University, he held a variety of academic appointments in the Midwest and then directed the graduate English program at Smith College from 1935 to 1939. He returned briefly to Chicago, at the Illinois Institute of Technology, briefly held a consulting position with Inland Steel in 1942, and spent a year as chairman at Western Carolina Teachers College. Thereafter he left the academic world to serve in the Navy in Washington during World War II. He remained there for the rest of his life, holding a variety of appointments in the Civilian Production Administration and the Office of the Chief of Naval operations. His contributions to Milton scholarship were all made by 1940. While at Smith he had edited Francis Goodwin's *Man in the Moon* (1638). At the same time he was engaged in publishing a series of studies that laid the groundwork for *Paradise Lost: An Account of Its Growth and Major Origins* (1940). This important book establishes much of the religious* background underlying the poem, especially the hexameral tradition*, the astronomical theories argued in it, and the position of the epic in its author's development. [WBH]

**MEAD(E), JOSEPH** (1586–1638), Fellow of Christ's College during 1613–1638, an authority on Homer*, a much-praised teacher, and an Anglican divine. His influence on and relationship with Milton have not been demonstrated, although influence has been assumed. It has been suggested that Milton alludes to him as "old Damaetas" in *Lyc*. [JTS]

**MEADOWCOURT, RICHARD** (1695–1760), divine and author. A graduate of Merton College, Oxford (B.A., 1714; M.A. 1718), Meadowcourt was a fellow there and later held the living at several parishes. His sermons, some of which expressed his views on current religious controversies, were variously published. In 1732 he published *A Critique of Milton's Paradise Regain'd*, the first book devoted to one of Milton's poems. Only Addison's* *Spectator* papers on *PL* offered a prior full-length critical study. In comparison with *PL*, Meadowcourt wrote, "The Verse of *Paradise Regain'd* is more artless, and is less embellish'd with Flights of Imagination, and with Figures of Speech. But it supplies a much richer Fund of intellectual Pleasure; it conveys the most important Truths to the Understanding; it inspires the most large and liberal Notions, and every where dissipates vulgar Prejudices and popular Mistakes" (p. 15). For the most part, however, Meadowcourt employs extensive quotation from the poem worked together by only brief introductory comments. His critique was amplified in 1748 as *A Critical Dissertation with Notes on Milton's Paradise Regain'd,* with emendations and notes on pp. 43–49. Meadowcourt also supplied Bishop Newton* with manuscript notes, such as those on *Lyc* 160, 162, concerning *Bellerus* and *Namancos*. [JTS]

**MEADOWS, SIR PHILIP** (1626–1718). Appointed assistant to the Secretary for Foreign Tongues* in 1653 on John Thurloe's* recommendation (over Milton's for Andrew Marvell*), Meadows filled the position satisfactorily for three years. In 1656 he was appointed English envoy to Portugal, and later to Denmark and Sweden, for which service he was knighted in 1658. He is mentioned numerous times in *StateP* in his capacity as envoy. After the Restoration, he went into retirement, but again served in several governmental posts after 1688. [WM]

**MEDICINE:** *see* SCIENCE, MILTON AND.

**MEDINA, JOHN BAPTIST DE** (1659–1710). Milton's first illustrator*, Medina has been credited with the design of twelve engravings for the fourth edition of *PL* (1688). (Bernard Lens the Elder executed the design for Book 4, and those for Books 1, 2, 8, and 12 are unsigned. Medina probably did not design the illustrations for Books 2 and 12.) The engravers were "M. Burgess," (that is, Michael Burghers) and P. P. Bouche for Book 4. Medina studied in his native Brussels under François Duchatel, and became familiar with the conventions of continental history painting. He arrived in England in 1686, when there was no English school of history painting. In 1688 the Earl of Leven invited Medina to visit Scotland, and arranged portrait commissions for him with the Scottish nobility. He became a successful portrait painter, was knighted, and died in Edinburgh in 1710. Medina's portrait of the first Duke of Argyll and his two sons is at Wentworth Castle, and a self-portrait is in the Florentine Gallery.

The designs for *PL* may be Medina's only extant work other than his portraiture. Marcia Pointon speculates that Medina may have supplied the designs for the 1713 edition of *PR*, but Wittreich has pointed out that the 1713 designs were executed by Nicholas Pigné (*Calm of Mind* [1971], p. 310). C. H. Collins-Baker speculates that two designs engraved by Michael Burghers for a 1701 Oxford Bible may belong to Medina, since Burghers was the engraver for Medina's *PL* designs and there are stylistic similarities (*The Library,* 5th ser. 3 : 8n).

The importance of Medina's designs is discussed by Helen Gardner in *Essays and Studies,* n.s. 9 : 27–38. Medina establishes certain topics that later illustrators tend to follow (see Collins-Baker); he provides, in most cases, a literal reading of Milton that reveals the seventeenth-century understanding of the poem; and in several instances he handles the problems of composition and interpretation with some imagination and success.

In composition, Medina compromises between the single scene that presents a dramatic moment, and the series of episodes that carry a narrative line. Illustrations for the early books focus on the single scene; those for the later books are more episodic. The illustration for Book 12, which returns to a single scene ("The Expulsion from Paradise"), reflects conventional art on the subject rather than a reading of Milton, but this is the only case where Medina appears to ignore Milton completely. (For some problems in depicting this scene, see Merritt Y. Hughes, *Journal of English and Germanic Philology* 66 : 70–79.) Overall, Medina is uneven in his rendering of detail, but he uses the combined techniques of focus on one and several episodes in an apparent effort to confront the complexity of the poem's structure and scope. Further, as Gardner notes, Medina perceived the decline of Milton's Satan and attempted to portray it by rendering a gradual degeneration from Angel to Satyr.

Whether or not one agrees with the depiction, it helps show, as Gardner says, "that Medina was making a serious attempt to illustrate and not merely to decorate the poem, and that he had studied it with some care." [SW]

**MELA, POMPONIUS,** a Roman geographer of the first century, whose compendium was entitled *De Situ Orbis.* In *Educ* (4 : 283), Milton refers to Mela as one author for youth to study. In spite of some serious geographical errors, Mela was still regarded as an authority, particularly considering the early date at which he wrote. It is possible that Milton was first led to the geographer by his mention of a Roman expedition into Britain. Milton introduces Mela in three other passages, all in *Brit.* The first (10 : 4), in a passage where he has been speculating about the origin of the island's name, mentions the giant Albion who went from Britain to Gaul and "was there slain in fight." Mela is summoned for partial confirmation of the story : "And Mela the Geographer makes mention of a stonie shoar in *Langeudoc,* where by report such a Battel was fought." In another passage (10 : 49) Milton lists Mela in the margin as one of three authorities for the excellent fighting qualities of the Britons compared with the Romans. The third reference (10 : 50) concerns resources: "Yet Gemms and Pearles they had, saith *Mela,* in some Rivers." Just below, Mela is again listed in the margin as authority for Britons' "oft-time warring one with the other, which gave them up one by one an easie Conquest to the *Romans.*" [RRC]

**MERCURIUS POLITICUS,** a semi-official Parliamentarian newspaper, edited by Marchamont Needham*. It began publication on June 13, 1650, and suspended with Needham's removal by the Restoration government on April 9, 1660. Earlier arguments that Milton wrote or edited this newspaper have been disproved by J. Milton French in *Studies in Philology* 33 : 236–52. Only one sentence in no. 91, February 26–March 4, 1652, p. 1443, seems to French to be assignable to Milton : "First for *Kings,* give me leave to shew (what I once published upon another occasion) that tis no new thing for Kings to be deprived, or punish't with death for their crimes in government." Milton, as Secretary to the Council of State*, did license the paper, however, starting with no. 33, January 23, 1651, and continuing through no. 85, January 22, 1652. His name appears frequently in the Stationers' Register for one or multiple issues. Registry was irregular after no. 85, but Milton seems to have been relieved of this responsibility perhaps because of the problem over his licensing of the Racovian Catechism*. Licensing of the newspaper was required under the Press Act of September 20, 1649. Milton may have considered it a perfunctory job, and in any case he did not believe in forbidding publication.

The prospectus of the newspaper, dated June 8, 1650, stated that it would supply intelligence about affairs in the British Isles, defend the Commonwealth, and keep its people informed and undeceived. To accomplish this "it must bee written in a Jocular way, or else it will never bee cryed vp," but it will sail between scurrility and profaneness. Needham called it "Politicus" because the government is truly political since it is opposed to despotism. Among the notices in the paper are a dozen references to the Salmasian* controversy and *1Def,* advertisements for a number of Milton's works, letters from abroad that often cite Milton or his works, the erroneous announcement from Leyden on September 20/30, 1652, that Alexander More* was the author of *Regii Sanguinis Clamor ad Coelum, Adversus Parricidas Anglicanos,* and the errata for the first edition of *Way* in the issue of March 1–8, 1660. [JTS]

**MERIT.** Merit may be considered in relation to Christ and in relation to man. Quite apart from the controverted question of Milton's precise views on the Trinity*, it seems clear at least that the Son's* position in heaven is his by right; he is Son of God both by merit and by birthright; he reigns by right of merit; is worthiest to reign (*PL* 3. 309; 6. 43, 888). He is deserving of his role as head of the angels*, at the right hand of the Father*.

Christ's exaltation as man, as the *CD* (1 : 16) states unequivocally, is partly from his own merits, partly from the gift of the Father (15 : 313). *PL* 3. 311ff., echoing Philippians 2 : 6–11, sees his final exaltation as a reward of his humiliation; and Christ himself speaks, in *PR* 3. 196, of meriting his exaltation.

Men are justified by the application to them of Christ's merits. Statements to this effect abound, both in *CD* and *PL.* "It is evident therefore that justification, in so far as we are concerned, is gratuitous; in so far as Christ is concerned, not gratuitous; inasmuch as Christ paid the ransom of our sins, which he took upon himself by imputation, and thus of his own accord, and at his own cost, effected their expiation" (16 : 27–29; see also *PL* 11. 35–36; 12. 409–10).

The attitude toward man's own power to merit is less clear-cut. While it is stated categorically that no countenance can be given to the doctrine of human merit, "inasmuch as both faith itself and its works are the works of the Spirit, not our own" (16 : 41), and the Father is at pains to make clear that those who are saved are saved by grace*, not their own will (*PL* 3.174ff.), this doctrine is accompanied by a certain respect for man's part in the process, the view held by Arminians*. It is Christ's merits, not his own, which justify man; yet the faith* in those merits must be accompanied by some corresponding works on man's part. *CD* avoids the use of the term *merit* (which *Areop* does apply, somewhat loosely; see 4 : 319), but stresses the fact that good works must accompany faith and that they will be rewarded, a point made more than once by Michael in *PL* 11 : "By Faith and faithful works"

(64); "And one bad act with many deeds well done / Mayst cover" (256–57); Abel's faith will not lose its reward (458–59); Adam is shown "what reward / Awaits the good" (709–10). A purely passive justification through Christ's merits seemed to Milton incompatible with free will*: "Since therefore we are not merely sense-less stocks, some cause at least must be discovered in the nature of man himself, why divine grace is rejected by some and embraced by others" (14 : 129); if our personal religion were not in some degree dependent on ourselves, God could not properly enter into a covenant with us (15 : 215). His explanation turns on a distinction between man's natural and supernatural faculties: the power of willing and believing is a gift of God, but so far as it is inherent in man, it is from a natural faculty (14 : 139); it is always God who shows mercy, but one man may be less reluctant, less backward, less resisting than another (14 : 133).

The angels, too, seem to have power to merit, both in their initial test (God praises Abdiel for his fidelity) and per-haps in the attainment of a certain rank in the hierarchy; see *PL* 2. 18—21; 3. 305–11; 5. 588–94. An ironic inversion of angelic merit is seen in certain terms applied to the fallen angels: Satan is raised by merit to his eminence in hell (*PL* 2. 5–6); his followers have achieved merit in counsel and fight (2. 21); even Sin and Death "have amply merited" (10. 383–93).

To summarize: in Milton's thought, Christ as God has in some sense merited his position in heaven; as man, he has certainly merited his own exaltation and the justification of mankind. No man is able, strictly speaking, to merit his own justification, but there is a sense in which his cooperation merits further grace. The angels have at least a limited power of meriting. [MCP]

**MESSIAH:** *see* SON, THE.

**MESSIANIC HUMILIATION AND EXALTATION.** Messianic humiliation and exaltation describe the sacrifice Christ undertook and the glory Christ earned himself and man. Milton derived from terms of Christian doctrine a paradoxical simultaneity, one probably inspired by Paul's first letter to the Corinthians, which declares God's choice of the foolish, weak, lowly, and spiritual for defeat of the shrewd, mighty, proud, and worldly (1 : 27–28). Milton's definition of Christ's redemptive mediation in the fourteenth through the eighteenth chapters of the first book of *CD* is permeated with the feeling that Christ's exaltation in his resurrection and ascension to glory at God's right hand is inseparable from Christ's humiliation in the painful sacrifice of becoming mortal: the mediatorial office "includes the state of humiliation to which our Redeemer submitted, as well as his state of exaltation." (*See* ATONEMENT and MIN-ISTRY OF REDEMPTION.) For Milton the greatest sign of this concept was the incarnation* ("As Christ emptied himself in both his natures, so both participate in his exaltation; his Godhead, by its restora-tion and manifestation; his manhood, by an accession of glory"); another major signification is the title *Christ, Messiah, Anointed,* which refers dually to Christ's unction to sacrificial priesthood and to his coronation to kingship. (*See* KENOSIS).

In his prose, primarily in the anti-prelatical tracts of the 1640s but extending as well through the defenses of the Com-monwealth in the 1650s to the pre-Restoration tract *CivP,* Milton used Messianic exaltation within humiliation as an exemplum against the worldliness of Anglican bishops and against the arrogant abuse of power by public officials. The finest statement appears in an extended biblical mosaic in *RCG,* concluding in a nearly direct quotation from 1 Corinthians 1 : 27–28 : "For who is ther almost that measures wisdom by simplicity, strength by suffering, dignity by lowlinesse, who is there that counts it first, to be last, something to be nothing, and reckons himself of great command in that he is a servant? yet God when he meant to subdue the world and hell at once, part of that to salvation, and this wholy to perdition, made chois of no other weapons, or auxiliaries then these."

In the early poetry Milton associated with Messianic humiliation and exaltation not only the concomitant pairs of Christian meekness over pride and weakness over strength, but also concord out of discord, eternity out of time, light out of darkness, and rising out of falling, associated as well with other such sources as the Gospel according to John and the fortunate fall. Milton first used the verbal, imagistic, and allusive imagery in *FInf*, but he first fully exploited the patterns in *Nat*. The opening stanza of *Nat* modulates from jubilation over redemption to the immense sacrifice that redeems joy; the second stanza contrasts the Word's brilliance in the harmonious courts of heaven and his descent to discord in the dark tabernacle of the corrupted flesh of humanity, which earns his own reascent with that of mankind; together the stanzas involve shifts in verb tenses from past into present mixed with past, which establish a continual present in fallen time. As well as extending into the "Hymn" of *Nat,* the image clusters of Messianic humiliation and exaltation are represented in *Passion, Circum,* and the early Latin funeral elegies. All imply the glory of redemption in the quality of anguish exacted; the joy is as infinite as the sacrifice is profound.

The ideational and figurative clusters of terms within the paradox of Messianic humiliation and exaltation continue in *PL.* Though the sense of sacrifice involved is often overwhelmed by the sense of glory and achievement, it is never wholly absent, even in the most exalted jubilation; humiliation is necessary to and invariably precedes exaltation. In Book 3 God describes the Son's* humanizing descent through the unfathomable hiatus created by man's disobedience before he accepts the Son's offer of self-sacrifice and describes the Son's reward:

because in thee
Love hath abounded more then Glory abounds,
Therefore thy Humiliation shall exalt

With thee thy Manhood also to this Throne.
(311–14)

The definition is reenforced in the epic by mention of the humiliation along with each of the Son's acts and exaltations, by allusions to Christ's sacrificial life such as that to his prayer for glorification in Gethsemane before his arrest, when he hastens out to victory over the rebellious angels* in Book 6, by the repeated use of the traditional fortunate fall and Johannine light / dark imagery, and by the contrast of Satan's degrading imbrutement in a snake to Christ's incarnation in a baby.

Milton's climactic expression, as his first full formulation, of Messianic humiliation into exaltation, appeared in a celebration of the incarnation. The sense of the achievement of exaltation through the humiliation of incarnation, which earns man's redemption, forms the crux of *PR,* God himself establishes the rudimentary terms of the Son's victory over "Sin and Death the two grand foes,/ By Humiliation and strong Sufferance" during the temptation in the wilderness: "His weakness shall o'recome Satanic strength / And all the world, and mass of sinful flesh." As the extensive sacrificial trial continues, Jesus recognizes that he is to earn exaltation by suffering even more than before or now. The terms build to a climax in the final temptation on the tower. When Satan challenges the Son to demonstrate his godhead by standing on the precarious height, the Son's humiliation reverses to exaltation; he stands and Satan is struck down. The paradoxical symbolic structure in the discovery had already been established in Jesus' earlier warning to Satan that "My rising is thy fall, / And my promotion will be thy destruction." The ritualistic preparation imitates both Satan's rising to fall of *PL* and Christ's being raised on the cross for atonement and victory. After he stands and Satan falls, the Son is taken up into the light of heaven, where in a theological oxymoron the angelic choir "the Son of God our Saviour meek /

Sung Victor." As the Son regains the fairer paradise for men by vanquishing temptation, his humiliation in incarnation becomes an exaltation of himself and man; once again and always, he illuminates the dark tabernacle of humanity in the reflection of God:

> True Image of the Father, whether thron'd
> In the bosom of bliss, and light of light
> Conceiving, or remote from Heaven, enshrin'd
> In fleshly Tabernacle, and human form.
> (4. 596–99)

[IC]

## METAPHYSICAL POETS, MILTON AND THE.

There is no evidence that Milton ever read so much as a single verse by John Donne, the preeminent metaphysical poet of the seventeenth century, nor has investigation yielded one unmistakable echo of any of the other metaphysicals in all of Milton's poetry. On the other hand, Milton's widow is reported to have said that, among the English poets, he most favored Spenser*, Shakespeare*, and Cowley*. And Abraham Cowley, though no longer regarded as a major poet or even as a particularly representative metaphysical poet, enjoyed a solid reputation in Milton's time and was regarded as an heir of Donne. Furthermore, during the 1650s, Milton's political activities brought him into contact with Andrew Marvell*, who is now held to be one of the most important metaphysical poets, and who authored a handsome commendatory poem for the second edition of PL. Finally, as a young boy, Milton could have been acquainted with Donne himself, for he lived near St. Paul's, where Donne became Dean in 1621. At the very least, some of the eminent divine's sermons must have been heard by Milton during his attendance as St. Paul's School*, adjacent to the Cathedral.

Any consideration of Milton and the metaphysicals then is vexed by a persistent puzzle. It is likely that the younger Milton, an omnivorous student of modern as well as ancient literature, encountered the widely circulated poems of Donne and quite possibly those of his successors in "the line of wit"—George Herbert, Marvell, Henry Vaughan, and Richard Crashaw; but, given this likelihood, why does Milton's own poetry appear to be unaffected by what was evidently a major literary movement of his time? This question is complicated still further by another difficulty, which has been succinctly summarized by Douglas Bush:

> It would doubtless be a good thing if the term "metaphysical" had never become established, since it is in itself quite misleading, since it has been conveniently applied to a school or group of poets who were not a school or a group and who for the most part had little in common except that they wrote in the earlier seventeenth century, *and since it does in fact apply more or less to nearly all poets of the period. (English Literature in the Earlier Seventeenth Century* [1962], p. 132, emphasis added.)

The problem then is twofold: how to describe with some accuracy a mode of poetry whose practitioners were distinctive personalities with significantly diverse literary talents and techniques; and how to explain the apparent absence of a fruitful relationship between them and the seventeenth-century's greatest poet. It is a problem with which two scholars in particular have wrestled.

E. M. W. Tillyard* has claimed that certain of Milton's minor poems do exhibit traces of the metaphysical style, but suggests that this is due less to the imposition of Donne's "particular pattern of . . . mind" on Milton than to a temporary influence of Donne's rhetoric (*The Metaphysicals and Milton* [1956], p. 2). Tillyard sees Donne and Milton as ultimately taking different artistic directions, the former investing his emotional and intellectual energy into a "private" mode of poetry (amatory and religious lyrics), the latter choosing a more "public" mode for the expression of his passions and thoughts (poems on familiar persons, events, and themes, dramatic works, and epics). Tillyard finds in Milton's poetry a sense of "public or social obligation" that he does not observe in Donne's (p. 12). Therefore, Donne's was a "narrower, more personal talent"; Milton's was more "in harmony with the requirements of his age" (p. 74). Tillyard's conclusion, like his book, is highly argumentative. He is concerned with "restoring" Milton to the eminence he enjoyed prior to the enthusiasm for the metaphysicals that peaked during the 1930s. Furthermore, the question Tillyard raises as to whether Milton or Donne is the more representative seventeenth-century poet is too complex to be resolved by mere assertions, and it may in any case pose a false dilemma—a possibility that will be considered below.

William John Roscelli has outlined some of the differences between Milton and Donne with regard to image-construction, the treatment of ideas, and techniques of language and versification (see *Texas Studies in Language and Literature* 8 : 464–84). He has also examined the minor poems for what he takes to be the only firm evidence of Donnean influence—the presence of "metaphysical conceits," metaphors involving ingenious comparisons that point up "certain resemblances in function or essence between apparently dissimilar things" (p. 471). By this strict standard only seven poems *FInf, Passion, EpWin,* the two *Carrier* poems, *Shak,* and *Nat*—are held to approximate the metaphysical mode. (Helen Gardner seems to concur with Roscelli to the extent of including the first *Carrier* poem and *Shak* in the second edition of her collection, *The Metaphysical Poets* [1967]; but she adds *Time* and omits the five other poems classified as quasi-metaphysical by Roscelli.) *FInf,* and *EpWin* are rated failures by Roscelli due mainly to what he alleges to be Milton's inept handling of the metaphysical conceit, while *Nat* is characterized as the most "metaphysical" of Milton's poems. There is no evidence that the younger Milton was influenced by any one metaphysical poet, Roscelli concludes, and if there were, "the debt would have been slight and of short term" (p. 484).

Roscelli gives minimal attention to *Vac* and the *Carrier* poems, and because of his strict construction of the term *metaphysical,* he disregards the major poems. A broader view has been taken by Louis Martz, who believes that Donne and his followers may be more aptly described as writing "meditative" rather than "metaphysical" works. A "meditative poem" is "one that bears a close relation to the practice of religious meditation" during the Renaissance, a relationship that "is shown by the poem's own internal action, as the soul or mind engages in acts of interior dramatization" (*The Meditative Poem* [1963], p. xvii). Meditation, as a formal religious exercise, requires of its practitioner the vivid recreation of some momentous event in the theater of his imagination, a searching analysis of that event's implications, and a climactic emotional and spiritual resolution of the tensions generated by the experience. Similar intellectual and psychological processes can frequently be observed in metaphysical lyrics—as well as in such poems of Milton as *Sonn* 18, 19, and 23, *Time, Nat,* and *FInf.* The more "public" qualities of the other minor poems and the larger designs of the major poems, however, render them somewhat more resistant to analysis in terms of so "private" a mode as the meditation.

Another, broader approach to Milton's poetry that reveals some points of contact between him and the metaphysicals has been taken by Roy Daniells (*see Milton, Mannerism and Baroque* [1963]). Daniells has shown that both Milton and the metaphysicals display the "mannerist" tendency of taking traditional themes and materials and treating them in untraditional ways. *Lyc* is a case in point : it is a poem that neither accepts nor rejects all of the conventions of the pastoral elegy but rather accepts some, rings changes on others, and offers innovations of its own. Similarly, metaphysical poetry is regarded by Daniells, not as a reaction against the poetry of the late sixteenth century, "but rather as the logical development from Spenserian or Sidneyan smoothness and the necessary bridge from this island of stability to the Baroque terra firma on which the larger works of Milton are erected" (p. 12). Milton then comes to be seen as a transitional figure, in his earlier "mannerist*" works (*Mask, Lyc*), being allied—on his own terms—to the metaphysical sensibility, but in the major poems exhibiting an evolution from that sensibility to its successor, the "baroque*."

In the course of his discussion of "the baroque Milton," Daniells remarks that "Milton too is metaphysical but on a great scale, and his conceits are displayed on a stage of grand proportions" (p. 131). This statement suggests that Milton and the metaphysicals share the same *zeitgeist*; but it also takes cognizance of their different artistic visions and offers a viable resolution to the main problem posed in this discussion. For some time it has been evident that no other metaphysical poet was always "metaphysical" in the same ways in which Donne was, and it is now clear that Milton rarely was. In the interest of arriving at a fuller understanding of both Milton and the metaphysicals and of the relationship between them, it will be more profitable then to seek out possible resemblances than to dwell on obvious differences, to adopt the premise that, as seventeenth-century poets, they share some kind of common sensibility, and then to proceed to consider a few of the ways in which that sensibility is figured forth in their poems.

A reader coming to metaphysical poetry for the first time can hardly fail to be struck by its "dramatic"—even "theatrical"—qualities. In a theatergoing age, Donne had the reputation of being "a great frequenter of plays"; the same might well have been true of Milton, who had the opportunities for playgoing and, very likely, the inclination. And it was, after all, Milton rather than Donne who authored two important dramatic works and planned others, and who alluded in his writings to contemporary as well as classical dramatists. The theatricality of Donne's poems, however, is evocative of the more realistic or satiric scenes played upon the popular stages, whereas Milton's

dramatic sense takes more of its inspiration from university and court drama and from the classical stage. The typically Donnean "dialogue of one," with its illusion of private emotions in a private setting, generally gives way in Milton to the illusion of more public emotions in a more public setting. The "drama" of metaphysical poetry, in short, tends to be on a small scale and individualized, whereas Milton's is on a large scale and tends to become ritualistic.

Like the theater, the university and the church were key factors in the shaping of seventeenth-century sensibility. The university afforded undergraduates opportunities for experiencing the dramatic both in its curriculum and in its extracurricular life, the church in its ceremonies and myths. In addition, both provided a variety of opportunities for encountering poetry as well as philosophy, rhetoric as well as religion, dialectics as well as dogma. Thus, linked by history and tradition, the university and the church produced intellectuals and poets as well as pedants and priests. Donne at Oxford, Milton at Cambridge, both received the mandatory indoctrination into scholastic learning, but it was an indoctrination that Donne in the main accepted and Milton in the main resisted. This difference makes itself felt in their respective works, but both write poetry that is "intellectual" in the sense that it is permeated with ideas in conflict, with dialectic, with erudite learning and theology, and with wit and irony in varying degrees. Milton, the Puritan, and the Anglo-Catholic metaphysicals can all be viewed as intellectual and artistic Janus-figures, foreshadowing in their poetry future scientific, theological, and philosophical trends, yet at the same time being acutely responsive to the millennia of Judeo-Christian history that were their common heritage.

It is a commonplace of criticism that metaphysical poetry embodies an intense fusion of the intellectual and the emotional, but the effect of intensity is due in part to the metaphysicals' inclination toward the shorter poem. The younger

Milton, on the other hand, tested the possibilities of the poetics of expansion as well as those of the poetics of compression. Though the former would ultimately be preferred by the mature artist, the kind of fusion of dialectic and passion that marks the metaphysicals has its analogues in the more dramatic passages of *PL,* in the temptation scenes of *PR,* and in the confrontation sequences of *SA.* Milton's art seems different because his style is suited to the decorum of the longer poem rather than to that of the lyric. One need not seek very far to find examples of wit, irony, paradox, and other "metaphysical" qualities in the major poems; the difference is that they must indeed be sought for, whereas they are readily discernible landmarks in the topography of metaphysical lyrics.

The metaphysicals' tendency towards compression and Milton's toward expansion makes the formers' verse seem more spontaneous and self-expressive and Milton's more stylized and impersonal. Such differences can, however, be overstated. Donne's poetry, for example, may appear to be unusually immediate and intimate, but he is in fact a highly conscious manipulator of poetic techniques. His is an art that conceals art, whereas Milton's art tends to proclaim itself as such. Milton's persona is generally thought of as bardic and Donne's as molded very much in the image of the man himself, yet some of Milton's Latin and Italian lyrics, certain sonnets, and even *L'Al* and *IlP* strongly suggest the personality operating behind them : and when the invocations to Books 1, 3, and 7 of *PL* turn autobiographical, the effect is very close to that seeming reduction of distance between the poet and the poem which characterizes metaphysical verse.

It has been said that the metaphysicals are obliquely criticized by the young Milton in *Vac,* where he makes a reference to a currently popular type of poetic language—"new fangled toys, and trimming slight / Which takes our late fantastics with delight" (19–20). It is more likely, however, that this jibe is directed against erstwhile versifiers known to Milton at Cambridge, for *Vac* itself, with its Aristotelian* metaphysics and wordplay, exhibits the kind of mingling of the serious, the witty, and the ironic that is associated with the school of Donne. Furthermore, in the *Carrier* poems, also written during the Cambridge period, Milton comes close to playing the metaphysical poet himself. Both works utilize metaphors that approximate metaphysical conceits. In the first Milton transforms the familiar notion of life as a journey into a myth (a characteristic of his), and then out of the fabric of that myth he creates a touching miniature drama (a characteristic of Donne's), one that concludes with the quietly colloquial line of dialogue—"*Hobson* has supt, and's newly gone to bed."

Milton's second epitaph on the same subject is perhaps his most metaphysical poem. Utilizing the conventional scholastic wisdom that motion generates time, Milton pretends that so long as Hobson was on the move, driving his cart between Cambridge and London, he was immortal: stopping became the death of him. Wit, humor, paradox, pun, wordplay—all techniques associated with the metaphysicals— give this poem (and its companion piece) the effect of Donnean "game." Unlike some of Donne's "games," however, it is one that openly acknowledges itself as such, and one that keeps death—an admitted obsession of Donne's—at a safe aesthetic distance.

A seemingly more serious poem, but possibly one that, like some of Donne's, is more than anything else an exercise, is *Time.* Here, as in Donne's Holy Sonnets, control over a painful subject is achieved more through the invocation of dogma than through wit or erudition. The poem centers upon the Christian promise of a life beyond death and thus beyond time, a paradox that prepares the way for a concluding vision of a heaven where, "Attir'd with stars, we shall for ever sit, / Triumphing over Death, and Chance, and thee O Time." The thought is commonplace, but its manner of expression does call to mind Donne's "Death Be Not Proud."

In *Circum,* a poem of unquestioned seriousness if uncertain success, Milton comes closest to the style of Richard Crashaw. Crashaw, whose poetic technique was to stretch the metaphysical mode to its limits (and sometimes beyond), was addicted to the kind of spectacular effects with which *Circum* begins—all fire and angels and music. Crashaw likewise was fond of images of tears and sighs in passionate profusion like those in lines 6–9, and of ingenious sanguinary conceits such as Milton develops in lines 10–11. Milton, however, can not or will not prolong his rhetorical ecstasies as Crashaw does and, indeed, *Circum* ends on a sudden, understated, less frenetic note that is reminiscent of the poetic clotures of still another metaphysical, George Herbert.

Finally, there are moments in the major poems where seriousness, wit, and irony mingle, but on a much larger scale than in the typical metaphysical poem, for example, the confrontation between Satan and Sin and Death (*PL* 2); the Limbo of Vanities sequence (*PL* 2); the War in Heaven* (*PL* 6); and the exchange between Samson and Harapha (*SA*). Indeed, seriousness mingled with wit and irony could be said to pervade not only the textures but the very structures of the major poems—witness the well-known "ironic parallels" of *PL.*

By way of summary then, it could be said that if the metaphysicals were not "Miltonists," nor could they have been, Milton himself, their fellow seventeenth-century poet, *was* a "metaphysical"—at least in the very broadest sense of that elusive term. [RBR]

**METAPHYSICS.** A poet pursues metaphysics as a means; yet, because Milton seriously needed his for his religious determinations, his polemics, and his poetry, he made himself surprisingly competent for one who could grumble about its "quibbles" and "gargarisms." He

welded apparently disparate doctrines into a body of thought that approached the harmony of a system. For it he borrowed so widely that the following summary of his main positions must all but ignore his sources. Whatever he took from Plato* and derivative Platonism or from Aristotle* and the commentary of the schools he made distinctively his own by altering and augmenting at need.

Not so with Scripture. He used all his best knowledge and thought to understand his Bible in the letter of the text according to its original intention. Though we may not in our time feel his need to make all the canonical writers agree, objective scholarship has far more often than not confirmed his readings. In Scripture's unalterable *données* he found a Hebraic God who acts—to create, to govern, and to intervene in history. To explain the structure of reality close at hand he followed Aristotle in the main, but forsook him in supernal matters wherever Aristotle's way led to his static, aloof God. Here Plato offered an account partially acceptable in that creation* means cosmos drawn out of chaos* by form imposed upon matter*. But a creator working upon a matter of alien origin and incompatible nature set up a frank dualism in being inconsistent with the unity of Milton's Hebraic God, and obliged him to take what appears to be pretty much his own way. As a young man he proclaimed his devotion to Plato (3 : 305), and his mature works certify a close reading. We meet Platonism in his late work constantly, but most often in ethical* and political* teaching. In metaphysics narrowly defined he avoided Plato's doctrine of separated essences and expressly denied it. He appreciated it as a poet, "fabling," though it led to "smooth conceits" (*PR* 4. 295 cf.1 : 295 [38]); and in a youthful essay he ridiculed the literal-minded Aristotle for being unfair to it (1 : 266f.). He probably thought the ontological difference between Plato and Aristotle of small practical consequence, for he sometimes called both men to testify to the same point (11 : 59, 239–41; 3 : 464). He judiciously mixed appreciation and common sense in his academic exercise on the Pythagorean and Platonic "fable," the music of the spheres (12 : 149), a myth that he introduced time after time, most frequently in his youthful works. In the oratory of *Prol* 7 he sounded like a Platonist (e.g. 12 : 261 [17]; cf. 255 [17]), and in his most important poetry he personified universals, once or twice implying that they confer reality (e.g. 5, 292; denied 11 : 239 [5]f.). Writing, in the language of suasion, of aesthetic and ethical transcendentals like harmony, truth, justice, virtue, he probably intended no doctrine in ontology; yet this is the best evidence hitherto presented for a metaphysical debt to Plato. The debt is great, but not predominantly metaphysical.

So far as we can draw his comments on knowledge—its origins, validity, and limits—into the fragmentary outlines of an epistemology, it appears orthodox for his century and appropriate to one whom earlier times might have called a moderate realist. From his *Logic* (11. esp. pp. 471f.) we can gather some rudiments. The universal is in its nature prior to the particular, but it has no independent existence and is never immediately knowable. It invites the mind to rise. The scale of knowledge, following the scale of nature or being, begins with "low" knowledge of low objects, the physical things of sense (3 : 229 [10]). At the same time, sense reports of these appropriate objects afford the clearest cognition. True axioms provide the first real knowledge. Our judgment of their truth is intuitive and reliable. Drawing upon experience by way of memory, the mind arrives soon at the species, and by way of the species first recognizes and classifies fresh sense perceptions of the particular (11 : 475 [23]; 471 [5]). Because the rising (or broadening) genera progressively drop the exceptional, universals, once known, are more clearly known in proportion as they are remote from sense. Their clarity does not alter the fact that whatever in the mind we can call knowledge is founded on sense, as Milton assures us in *Educ* and elsewhere (4 : 277 [9]; *PL* 5. 104). Nowhere do we read that knowing is a process of remembering something innate, or that any knowledge is *a priori*. The nearest approximation is his and everybody's doctrine of nature's light. God implanted in Adam clear natural tendencies toward right choice in conduct, and they survive the Fall (15 : 209; 16 : 101). Thus we are born with some basic morality without precept (15 : 115–17), but with an innate power of reason and conscience, much like that by which we perceive the truth of axioms.

In commanding such powers the mind is no blank and passive receptor, to be sure. Knowing takes a middle way between a reality impinging on consciousness by way of sensation and a mind reaching to abstract from sense data its close approximation of reality. This active process does not make any part of the mind an *intellectus agens* in Aristotle's sense. Even the beasts, whose highest soul is sense, share it in some degree (12 : 283; *PL* 8. 374). Because being is intelligible and the human mind seeks a sufficient reason, cause is the continuing fount of knowledge while the understanding moves by causes to essences (11 : 31 [15]). It is by form that cognition comes to knowledge (11 : 61 [27]), and by form that essences participate in the genera (11. 239). Where causes and formal causes in particular, are imperfectly known, opinion replaces knowledge (11 : 308 [12–18]; 14 : 343 [17]). Some causes can be known, else all knowledge would be opinion, the untenable position of the skeptics (12 : 281 [14]). To begin with, the senses provide the mind with a reliable report. Christ's curt dismissal of the philosophers who have methodically "doubted all things, though plain sense" (*PR* 4. 296) can surely be read as Milton's own opinion that to question the senses is absurd skepticism. Any other would consist ill with the dignity and reality of matter in his ontology. To question the adequacy of man's entire cognitive apparatus may border on impiety. It would impugn God's justice, as we shall hear presently. Milton applies the argument to man in a fallen condition: "The *wisdome* of *God* created *understanding,* fit and proportionable to Truth the object" (3 : 33). But, to interject an analogy, just as a rifle may be accurate as far as it will carry, so man's mind is both adequate and finite. Even within its normal range, experience shows us certain exceptional limitations, accidental failures due to individual imbecility (8 : 251 [12]; *PL* 1.472), the mental inferiority of women (9 :483), or clouding by passion and interest (8 : 551f.; *PR* 2. 173). Every created mind, even angelic, must accept the limits imposed by finitude (15 : 107 [12]), and all men, like some angels*, are further limited by the Fall* (15 : 111 [3]). Like many before him, Milton observes that education is the means to restore some of man's lost information (4 : 277 [3] and the art of logic* some of his lost power (11 : 367 [3]). Despite his imperfections, each partial truth that he attains is true. That is to say, the only measure of truth is correspondence with reality, the thing itself (11 : 309). Each partial truth is in its own nature absolute, and each emancipated mind has a duty to go on matching truth to truth, never thereby expecting, before Christ returns, to fill out the whole body of truth (4 : 337[25]f.).

To this end we need good habits of mind, the dianoetic virtues that Milton encouraged as educator. Michael, teaching Adam (11. 334), improves his pupil in all, by either precept or example, beginning with the lowly practical virtues of well making and well doing, or art and prudence, and rising to the speculative virtues of *intellectus* (intuition), *scientia* (the knowledge of proximate causes), and *sapientia* (the knowledge of ultimate causes—in Michael's lessons, final causes chiefly). Even in innocence Adam has never had the almost exclusively intuitive intelligence of the angels. As one angel draws for him a distinction between "discourse," or reasoning by steps, and intuition (5. 488) :

<blockquote>
discourse
Is oftest yours, the latter most is ours,<br>
Differing but in degree, of kind the same.
</blockquote>

It appears that intelligence, like knowledge, goes by the scale of being, and that the angels can eclipse even that "sudden apprehension" by which Adam names the animals according to their natures. After his fall Adam's intuition is not what it once was (*PL* 11. 633), but improves steadily, along with his knowledge, under the angel's tutelage. As Milton explains intuition, the mind possesses natively the power to grasp certain axiomatic truths or a valid consequence (11. 367, 471). This sudden apprehension is simply a power, yet out of it springs the first and truest knowledge (11 : 323). When Milton simplified Aristotle's logic in his own textbook and called his book Ramistic, he gave intuition considerable work to do —more than Aristotle, though less than Ramus*. The mind can often be relied on to perceive truth and leap to it without climbing a tedious ladder of full syllogisms (11 : 395f.). But no matter how good the mind of man or angel, it must content itself with knowing that God has not made all knowledge available. Milton is able to collect from Scripture evidence of angelic ignorance. In particular, the Schoolmen were wrong to suppose that God permits the good angels to glimpse his bosom secrets (15 : 107). He does not permit even the Son* to know his hidden purposes (14 : 317 [26]).

Learning, that is, *scientia* or knowledge in the broad sense, is the search for proximate causes. Though in itself admirable, it is a virtue only so long as it is temperately bounded and profitably directed. It cannot be profitable unless it is possible, and the limitations of an intelligent essence, what the vessel can contain (*PL* 12. 559), set the permitted bounds. Before Uriel's unsuspecting eyes comes Satan disguised as a young cherub eager to learn more about natural science*, about astronomy and cosmography*. In a cherub the eagerness is altogether commendable as long as he pursues learning with the right motive, of giving God the more glory. No excess is possible as long as he bears in mind that he will not discover all the causes that God has hidden, for his is a created mind (3. 705). For a cherub with angelic mobility such knowledge is both relevant and fully profitable; for earthbound Adam it is not, and partly because it is not, Raphael counsels Adam to diminish his interest in celestial motions (8. 66f.). He would do better to think only what concerns him and his essence (174).

On that Socratic note Milton joins the chorus of humanists*. His standard jibes at astronomy uttered with intent to exalt self-knowledge, the highest earthly wisdom, are an ancient topos of their rhetoric. Self-knowledge begins with the prime (primary) wisdom : what lies before us in the daily life. Knowing for the sake of knowing—curiosity was once its pejorative name—does not serve man's good, his end as man, his ultimate final cause, true happiness. So far as it distracts, it is foolish "impertinence." What concerns man's essence can be learned and with profit; it is a study broad and high enough to embrace the best in human culture. By proceeding in it from proximate to ultimate causes man achieves wisdom; learning tangential to it may or may not be additional wisdom (PL 12. 575f.). Socrates, a pagan, commended the same study that Raphael commends, and properly, for Adam is a natural man. Except for God's sole command, he lives by reason alone. Raphael is right, then, to teach that self-knowledge is the highest wisdom. Socrates, ignorant of the Fall, was almost right.

His direction was right, as nothing more clearly shows in Milton's writing than a psychology* framed to teach the primacy of reason*. We may appropriately pause to consider it. Where the popular psychology of his contemporaries often gives the soul its two "wings" of reason* and will*, Milton's enthrones reason as queen in solitary preeminence.

About most of the mind's subordinate powers, its "many lesser faculties," he is as indefinite as anybody else. Each poetically has its appropriate "cell" (PL 5. 109), for Milton, like Spenser*, invites us to think of the mind's inner "wards and limits" (3 : 249). We know that the chief antagonists of reason are the passions that she holds in check, but their precise seat we can nowhere discover. Nor do we know more about the "many" faculties like memory (PL 5. 100–102). If we combine two passages that pretty well cover all we actually know (5. 97f.; 9. 343f.), we observe that reason, if right, is an instrument to transmute perception into knowledge and, by informing the will, thought into behavior. If we please, we may think of the path from sense to act as passing over a deep arc. The data given by the senses rise in cognition and descend by way of the will. On the upward journey the data may somehow reach the fancy and thence ultimately pass to reason's work of selection and arrangement. In sleep, fancy takes the same data for irrational combination in fantasies and dreams*. At the top of the curve of the mind's "severall vessels, and ventricles" (3 :49) reason, or else understanding, receives information and judges it to be true or false. Sometimes understanding seems to be a separate cognitive faculty to fashion our knowledge and opinion (3 :249). Again, she seems an exact synonym for reason, directing the will (PL 9.1127). Reason, herself both noetic (3 : 249) and practical, appears so by her associations—law (she is the "Law" of law) (5 : 121), judgment (PL 8. 636), conscience* (14 : 29), and logic (11. 11). So long as she is vigilant she is capable of penetrating the most specious falsehood (3 249f,; PL 9.359f.), and no injustice can be imputed to a God who created man able by reason to defend himself (15 : 47; 4. 319).

We meet her most often in her ethical capacity. She is man's immediate guardian of order within and without. When "upstart Passions catch the Government From Reason" (PL 12.88; 9 : 1123f.), the result is anarchy. It unfits the ruler (5: 128, 131, 177; 7 :445; *PR* 2. 466f.) and enslaves the subject, because God permits tyrants to rule those who permit passion and appetite to dethrone reason (*PL* 12. 87f.; *PR* 4. 144). So it is that reason and liberty go "twinn'd" (*PL* 12. 85). In defending man's moral responsibility Milton has much to say of the freedom of the will*. This perfectly acceptable manner of speaking is not psychologically descriptive, for reason, not the will, initiates choice (4 : 319[8]; *PL* 3. 108, 123). The will, informed, then translates the choice into act. The will itself is obliged to obey either appetite or reason, and only what obeys reason is free (*PL* 9. 352). Once reason loses control, both she and the will, components of "inward man" (6 : 20), are alike reduced to servitude. Reason's rule cannot be tyrannical, any more than God's. When man fell by disobeying both, he damaged his understanding and hence his freedom (15 : 203, 207); and when he returns to God by faith, submits himself and becomes a new creature, God restores to him in large measure his power both "to form right judgment, and to exercise free will" (15: 367). God has bestowed on man unique privileges and with them great perils; reason is his shield against danger (8 : 11 [17]). What Adam teaches Eve (*PL* 9. 350) is valid for any servant of God :

Against his will [man] can receave no harme.
But God left free the Will, for what obeyes
Reason is free, and Reason he made right,
But bid her well beware, and still erect,
Lest by some faire appeering good surpris'd
She dictate false, and misinforme the Will
To do what God expressly hath forbid.

In his quest for *sapientia* in a fallen world Milton enjoyed access to the express will of God, his written Word, and thus had the advantage of Socrates. Two of God's angels bring to Adam the gist of Scripture, together with generous exegetical commentary, and receive his gratitude for truth otherwise out of his reach (*PL* 7. 70f.; 12. 552f.). Angels of the sinful crew try philosophy without revelation

and lose themselves in the same persistent problems that bedevil the unassisted human intellect (2. 557f.). Here again, as in his depreciation of merely curious astronomy, Milton embellishes a commonplace of great vitality in his generation. Many proclaimed what nobody denied: unless it is judiciously subordinated to Scripture, pagan philosophy becomes, by St. Paul's estimate, "vain wisdom all and false Philosophie" (2. 565). If Milton could read in Aristotle's ethics of intellectual virtues*, he could read almost anywhere of intellectual sin*. It was divisible into two forms. Sinful or dubious curiosity was ordinarily a conservative's appraisal, looking forward, of some intellectual novelty or other. Vain philosophy was normally a liberal's estimate, looking backward, of some piece of surviving Scholasticism* or comparable overwisdom that blurred the clear light of Scripture with its obfuscations. In that he was traditional as a humanist and radical as a churchman, Milton was both conservative and liberal, and he completes his account of vain philosophy in *PR* (4. 285f.). For reasons that would carry us beyond the domain of epistemology, Christ denies that pagan learning, both its thought and its expression, is the necessary handmaid of divinity. This time the issue under debate is quite obviously not self-knowledge, which is scantly mentioned as a piece of evidence to a larger conclusion. It is not Christ's own store of learning and wisdom. He already possesses perfectly God's revealed will (4. 215f., 288–90). He almost surely possesses the very learning that is being proposed to him (286), for he replies to Satan with the authority of ripe scholarship. On both counts, then, he is knowledgeably prepared to reply "sagely" (285). On the other side of the argument, Satan concedes at the outset the primacy of Scripture; he asks for one concession: human learning is indispensable as well, as a postcript. For reasons irrelevant here, Christ upholds Scripture's absolute sufficiency. The arguments he uses against the pagans, all standard, can be reduced to three : learning (*scientia*) and art may be good without being Greek (331f.); wisdom (*sapientia*) begins in a disposition of the mind and is not necessarily improved by much reading (321f.); and —here lies his emphasis—pagan wisdom can in no event be the true sophía because it cannot reach to ultimate causes (309f.). By reading the philosophers man cannot firmly know whence he comes, what he is, or what he should strive toward. The pagan philosophers knew themselves imperfectly, though by nature's dim light they saw something of ethical truth (cf. *PL* 2. 566–69). They knew less of God and nothing of man's need for grace.

When Eve listens to Satan's sophistries (9. 679) she hears him address the deadly tree :

O Sacred, Wise, and Wisdom-giving Plant,
Mother of Science, Now I feel thy Power
Within me cleere, not onely to discerne
Things in thir Causes, but to trace the wayes
Of highest Agents, deemd however wise.

Satan's philosophy is more scrupulous than his use of it, for Milton gives him precise concepts and appropriate terms. He himself in other contexts uses the word *wisdom* with easy latitude. Sometimes it means prudence; sometimes it is a transcendental attribute of ordered being; sometimes it is the idea of that being in God's mind. But, to our purpose, in *CD* (17 : 31), formulating a studied antithesis between wisdom and folly, he carefully turns Satan's proffered wisdom to folly. There wisdom is both noetic and practical; he calls it knowing and doing the will of God. When we turn to *PL* (3. 445f.) we find that the notable fools consigned to limbo are all, from Empedocles forward, those guilty of superstition, that is, works of supererogatory religion beyond the service that God plainly tells us He requires. *PL* and *PR*, then, emphasize two different but complementary forms of wisdom for man perfect under nature and under grace*. In Milton's ontology a higher entity, by its very superiority, "virtually and eminently" contains the lower. If the principle thus technically expressed applies here, the higher wisdom, the

knowledge of God, implies all the capacities and capabilities of the lower, the knowledge of self. The whole knowledge of God's will means, of course, more than knowing intellectually what is written. The regenerate soul, truly spiritual and adopted in Christ, knows by his faith and by his life of faith what the Spirit intends, sometimes even when the text of the Word is obscure (16. 277 [29]f.). The act of knowing God by faith*, love*, and obedience* perfects then the knowledge of self. The filial fear of God is the beginning of wisdom, and in his will is our peace.

Our methodical, if pedestrian, way to approach Milton's ontology will be to collect some rudiments toward a textbook he might have written. We can gather them from his writings, particularly from his kindred textbook of logic, and in quantity sufficient to establish his predilection, in these rudiments, for Aristotle. Our hypothetical treatise begins with the principles of being, grounded in the notion of being. The notion inheres in the first law of thought, that of identity : That which is is, or, Being is being. Though called the first law for its position in the real order, both it and the third law (of excluded middle) are, in logic, the inescapable consequences of the second, the law of contradiction : Being is not nonbeing. This law Milton appeals to early and late (11 : 311 [12]; 14 : 313 [15]), once to prove that a person cannot be his own father. From such a beginning we arrive quickly at a corollary : Unity follows being, or, so to speak, Each being is its own. It is Milton's stubborn position against orthodox Trinitarians. His epistemology warrants our adding a further note of being, intelligibility. Nothing can be intelligible without a sufficient reason, being is intelligible by cause, and in many a philosophically responsible passage Milton assumes that cause belongs to reality( e.g., 14 : 179; 15 : 21). His *Logic* gives the fullest account of the causes (11 : 29f.). It allows all four of Aristotle's and takes his familiar path from efficiency to finality. Efficiency may flow from an agent outside a passive being, from within an animate being, or from potency to act in a changing being. It may be procreant or conserving, just as God creates and his Providence conserves (15. 3f., 55f.). Agent efficiency without discoverable direction is unintelligible (4 : 101). In one way or another a being "seeks" its perfection or "goodness," either real or apparent, drawn by the appetency of its form. Thus a being is affected by its end, its final cause (11 : 63). Marital experience shows that it sometimes fails to achieve the end sought (4 : 104 [18]). Causes both efficient and final may be either proximate or ultimate. In such generally accepted fashion Milton finds the first principles of being implied in the metaphysical notion of being.

The essence is an individuated segment of matter and form in combination (11: 59f.). Matter is ontologically prior. It is the passive potency, the principle of change; and on it efficiency operates, just as finality operates on form (11 : 51; 59[1]). These operations establish a close affinity between efficiency and matter and between form and finality. Where direction results from conscious rationality, as in an art (11 :13[20]) or in marriage* (15 :155), form and end approach identity. In the logical order, an essence may be captured in a "perfect" definition by its four causes—efficient and material, formal and final (11 : 263–65; 4 : 100 [26]). Genus and differentiae suffice for a succinct definition. Milton frequently needs to make a practical and dissimilar use of the words *essence* and *existence*. God's demonstrable existence, for example, is assuredly not the same as his unknowable essence (14 : 25 [14], 39 [9]). But because in Milton's this-wordly speculations the metaphysical act of to be plays no part, we may fairly call his working ontology an essentialism.

The simple substrate of the being that is bounded in distinct essences is substance, or *Stoff*, and in his habitual use of the terms *essence* and *substance* Milton is consistent. Substance is graded in "degrees" (15 : 21 [28], 23 [2]; *PL* 5. 473)

according to its "grossness." It bears its own form while excluding particular individuation and accidents. Unlike essence, it may be common to two or more beings and necessarily implies existence. Without his distinction of these two terms, Milton's ontology and important conclusions in his revealed theology become unintelligible. In *CD* the Latin everywhere distinguishes, but the standard English translation twice makes it appear that essence and substance mean the same thing. Milton misled the translator by using "hypostasis" (etymologically "substance") to mean essence, or more specifically, "perfect essence existing *per se*" (15 : 269 [22]; 14 : 43 [8], 222 [6]).

Other terms are less crucial. A person is an intelligent essence—a man, an angel, even, on appropriate occasion, a dove (14 : 43, 371 [1]). "Metaphysical trifling" aside, a subsistence is a substantial essence or the sum of its properties (14: 309; 15 : 269 [10]). Since an essence is chiefly determined by its form, Milton sometimes calls it simply a form or even, in mere English, a shape (e.g., 3 : 2 [14]). The nine younger brothers of Substance, the "sons" or predicaments of Ens, that he once wrote into a schoolboy skit, *Vac*, turn up more soberly here and there in his writings (e.g., 11 : 85f.), but of these Aristotelian accidents none is of particular interest at all except perhaps time*. It is the measure of motion (1 : 33 [7]; 15 : 35 [5], 241 [22]; *PL* 5. 580). For Milton here as for Aristotle, motion is change, actualization, and celestial motion is therefore not the only measure of time. In the sense of duration time can be predicated even of God in eternity* (11 :93 [24] f.; *PL* 5. 580f.). The practical result is that Milton and his Bible allow us—even when they do not quite enable us—to understand in a convenient chronology God's prehistoric decrees and emanations.

The doctrine of essence brings us to what is probably a question of terminology : is Milton a monist? The label began to be applied to him after 1920 as readers became aware of what for a while was called his Christian materialism. To understand why, we may need to review some facts not importantly in dispute. In his view matter and form in combination constitute all substances in created being from the gross at the bottom of the scale up to the "pure" or "ethereal." (The latter word is not to be taken to mean that he posits an aether or quintessence; his elements are four.) Air and fire can be preternaturally attenuated, but not to the exxclusion of their matter, which is explicitly declared to be the substrate of all created being (*PL* 5. 472). The living substance compounded of this tenuous matter is spirit. Its grosser mode is body. In neither the animate nor the inanimate series does Milton mention an altered ratio of form to matter. Inanimate substance rises from gross to pure, animate from body to spirit. God Himself is revealed to us as spirit (14 : 41 [22]), and for that very reason we may suspect that Milton's God is in some way corporeal. Assuredly God embraces some kind of "bodily power" (15 : 25 [25]), and informed opinion concludes that, for all his reticent caution in speaking of God's substance, Milton must mean that it involves some principle analogous to matter. It seems probable indeed. The universe, both form and matter, lay "substantially" in God's "virtue" (capability) before it was externalized. Grant as we must that the material principle in God's substance transcends our highest notions of purity, yet if Milton had thought His substance altogether immaterial, he would have insisted that it was so and explained the change that being underwent on its externalization. He would not, instead, have insisted that matter is in its own nature good enough to be worthy of God's substance (15 : 23). By being spirit, God *virtualiter et eminenter* contains a corporeal "faculty" (15 : 25 [15]). Again, matter in any mode implies a measure of potency. Contrariwise, potency implies matter, and Milton accepts a God of potency when he rejects a God of *actus purus*. What Aristotle and Aquinas* meant by the phrase is not to the purpose here. On this point Milton has been sometimes dubiously read in both Latin and English, but his argument against a God of pure act runs thus : "Sic enim agere nihil poterit, nisi quod agit; idque necessario; cum tamen omnipotens sit liberrimeque agat" (14 : 48 [5]f.). God, then, cannot be both omnipotent and free if He has exhausted all His possibilities and has, as we might say, nowhere left to go. In this we see, then, that Milton leaves for his pinnacle of being not, like Aristotle, the pure form and pure act that *are* God. Form and act inhere *in* God, but do not exhaust His being. Nor do matter and potency. They are not God but in God, virtually, to say the least, and eminently.

Treating of matter at the bottom of the scale, Milton in the *Logic* perfunctorily mentions Aristotle's prime matter as a common conception and changes the subject (11 : 53 [17]). While very young, and while jesting, he brings up this purely notional nonentity of Aristotle's (12 : 187), but in his mature account of reality probably never includes it. His order of created being begins in what he calls first matter. This original matter, first in time and in reality, is already "a substance"; it is extended and it is "confused" until by God's hand it is "digested into order" (15 : 23 [9]). If we find it hard to understand how a formless matter can be a substance, we may find it harder to understand formless substance as disorderly. Still, we ought to do as Milton bids us and think of this original substance as the ultimate real supposit, the ground of generation and corruption, formless in the sense that it is in no way individuated in essences or differentiated in degrees, as later it will be. After it is so "digested," we perceive Milton's departures from Aristotle : informed substances rise by matter's mode instead of its quantitative proportion; insubstantial prime matter is dropped from the beginning of the series; God, extended downward at the top of the series, admits matter in its perfect purity. For these adjustments we are asked to include Milton among the monists. Obviously, neither

Aristotle nor Milton is an Eleatic monist if Parmenides has been correctly interpreted. He reduced being ultimately to uniform sameness and explained apparent differences as the unreliable report of the senses. Plato countered with two principles, matter and form, to account for altitude and multitude, but in separating them set up an antagonism between them that in later Platonism was to lead to a Manichaean dualism. Aristotle compromised, advancing the hylomorphic theory that seemed generally sensible to Milton. In Aristotle it is not called monism: degrees of substance permit a scale of being; essences insure multiplicity; accidents afford variety. And at this point it will be convenient to leave monism for only a moment.

Let us examine some distinctive features of the scale of being as Milton conceives it. We cannot expect a plenum of forms, because his God must be left free to create at will. From Milton's repeated assurance that by an orderly contemplation of the creatures the mind can rise "by steps" to God (4:277; 12:255f.; *PL* 5.511) we might suppose the steps to be more numerous than we find them. Not that he should have tried the impossible feat of numbering God's creatures (*PL* 3.706), but he might have expressed a belief that they fall in, say, an orderly progression of kinds. If he thinks they do, he never quite says it. The four elements, with a scattering of their products, cover the entire inanimate scale. They are spatially disposed "from center to circumference" (5.510) and ontologically from gross to pure in a common sequence. At Creation, what is most adverse to life is forced lowest (7.237). Similarly, the whole animate series is ordered into four: the usual three Aristotelian grades by "soul"—vegetative ("vital"), sensitive ("animal"), and rational, with the last distributed in discursive (human) and intuitive (angelic). The angels fit into the progression, but on the far side of a gap in the scale so apparent that Milton sometimes peoples it in half-serious speculation. Plato's genius

or his daemon appears repeatedly in the early works (e.g., 1:43, 93; 12:265). The Attendant Spirit in *Mask* was at first a daemon; we notice that he comes not from Jove's court, but from its "starry threshold," and he returns no higher than "the corners of the moon" (1:85[1], 123[1016]). Again "middle Spirits" may inhabit the moon (*PL* 3.461). And a more particularized series may lie in potentiality. God may have in mind future inhabitants for planets created empty (7.622); Adam and his sons may move up ontologically by degrees (5.498). Possibly because extrascriptural guessing about angelic orders is curiosity in the bad sense, Milton never says that the good angels do anything of the sort, or even that they exist in various degrees of substance. He may have thought it likely. He must have known how Aquinas multiplied his wholly immaterial angels—vertically, one to a species. His own cannot be killed, lacking specific vital organs (6.347), and probably cannot be annihilated (1.117, 138), but almost certainly not because the chain of being cannot endure the hiatus. To be sure, the Son created the angels in their "bright degrees" (5.838); the defeated crew keep their rank even while God's prisoners of war. Good and bad differ in capacity and power. And in ontology the fallen angels sink as they sin (6.661; *PR* 1.378; 2.122f.).

Milton tells us, while he is arguing for a material cause or principle in God, that heavenly spirit contains "virtually and eminently" (by superiority is capable of) the "faculties" of growth and sense that reside in more corporeal substance (15:24[12]f.). We learn from the angel Raphael both the doctrine and what it implies about the materiality of spirit above man (*PL* 5.409f.). While the poet is disclaiming all metaphor (5.434), the angel eats human food with zest; he can digest it and return the residue to the air by transpiration. Transsexual at will (1.424), the otherwise masculine angels (10.890) couple in their superior way when they love (8.625f.). And though we are told no more, we observe that the stripling cherub is no novelty in Heaven. All now agree that Milton's angels, not grossly corporeal, must be corporeal in a higher fashion or they would not be spirits. This consensus supports the attribution of monism: from original matter up to, and probably into, the being of God, all things are of one material substance, differing but in degree, of kind the same. Calling Milton a materialist for this may easily require more cautious qualifying than the misleading term is worth. The difference between body and spirit is great and real, and the continuity carries no radical consequence for ethics. A little more remains to say on the subject.

Man's immortal soul as orthodoxy conceives it introduces a disruptive anomaly into the animate series of being. Milton's conception does something to bridge the interruption, though he too leaves a gulf of separation from the lower orders by reason of man's intellect and his ultimate immortality. Reason, man's distinguishing difference, determines his essence (*PL* 5. 487). All animate being has life, or life and sense, or life and sense and reason, according to its degree; and in the beginning God breathed one of the three kinds into all living things (15:53 [12]; cf. 52 [14]). But for man alone he first made an organic body that doubtless had originally its proper matter and form. The spirit that he breathed must have had its own, too, for, extensible, it filled every part of the material body and entered into indissoluble combination with it. This spirit became the body's form. We need not go on to think that subsequent bodies are similarly compounded of two combinations, for man became, on the first "intimate blending," a living soul, that is, material body in living, feeling, thinking form. The same manner of combination explains other degrees of life, differing in powers and capacities. The foregoing account is summarized from Milton's opinion carefully stated in *CD* (15:39f., 219, 227f.). There soul (a Hebraism for the whole living being) is a combination of body and spirit (a Latinism for what is "breath" in the Hebrew).

Hence spirit is primarily the life-giving principle and soul is any living thing (*PL* 7. 392; 15:43). Milton acknowledges that, for communication, other meanings must be allowed, as in the common phrase *body and soul* (15:41 [25]), and throughout his whole corpus he freely uses *soul* in its public religious and psychological significance. Or else either *soul* or *spirit* may suggest *psyché* as *spirit* may mean emotional attitude, lofty being, product of bodily humors, and whatever else the context and the reader may require. Such accommodation in use of words does not determine doctrine so clearly as formulated statement. Milton rejects both the preexistence and the special creation of the soul. Spirit is so intimately blended that man's natural means of propagating the body propagates both, by the passive potency of matter (*ex potentia materiae*) (15:43f., 49 [6]). In the same manner the death of the body entails the death, not the sleep but the real death, of the spirit as well. Confined to the grave, both body and spirit return to their natural elements (15:51 [2], 243 [9]) to await the conjoined resurrection of both that Scripture promises. As we leave this matter of man's ontology, and with it the evidence for Milton's monism, we observe that man is material in all his substance, like the rest of finite being.

Monism has become the normally accepted word for any philosophy that resolves being into one substance, and thereby an appropriate name for Milton's, so long as we do not permit the name to obscure his thought. Substance, or informed matter by his definition, is perhaps not his ultimate resolution if it is indeed a hylomorphic combination. Unless Aristotle is a monist, what Milton's monism must finally hang by is just one cryptic remark written in the warmth of an argument to prove the goodness, even the divinity, of matter: "Forms themselves are material" (15: 23 [24]). It goes without saying that any form without matter is meaningless, and include materiality within either form or the unexplained remark may be meant to essence as "within" a higher principle that "virtually" subsumes the lower. Where Aristotle thinks of form as physical shape, or where form (essence) becomes the matter of a higher essence, he can agree that form, too, is or can be material. But to say in any sense that forms are material is not to say that forms are matter. It would not occur to most readers that during the Six Days the Creator is occupied with inducing matter into matter. Until we are assured that Milton thought so, *monist* is a name that we might be wise to qualify. We do not do Aquinas the injustice to call him a dualist for teaching that in certain circumstances form may be separated from matter. But sometimes Milton is "emphatically" a monist for teaching that the two real principles are never, or probably never, separable. Matter is the principle of change. When God digested Chaos into order, surely he infused into the world of real being some principle of stability.

The vitality in Milton's world of nature can best be accounted for by the creative process, and in exploring that process we shall pause for cosmographic detail only so far as it will illustrate ontology and causality. A distinctive feature of the process is consistent with Milton's devotion to God's unity and lies near the center of his philosophy of being: creation *ex Deo* instead of *ex nihilo*. First, God produces matter out of his own substance. Then, by the proximate efficiency of the Son while he himself remains divinely immobile, he induces form into the matter. The doctrine seems to Milton scriptural, and, by dignifying matter, it admirably binds nature, man, and all spirit in one substance. Ae he understands, perhaps naively, the tenet of creation from nothing, it raises an obvious question: where can an infinite God turn to find a bit of nothing? Milton puts the difficulty (15: 27 [2]) more generally: can God, by creating *ex nihilo,* receive accession? God is already perfect, and yet not bound by His perfections. When Milton lists them he follows his Bible, but one he guards with special care—unity. Much of his care

for that attribute belongs to his Christology and revealed religion rather than his metaphysics, but its consequence, God's freedom, philosophy can claim. Unity excludes all division of ultimate godhead, all possibility of original not-God. And thence flows God's perfect freedom to act.

His surrogate in all external operation, including acts of creation, is his Son, and his earliest operation (internal in its inception) is to generate the Son out of his own substance. The distinction in essence between the Father and the Son (14:187) enlarges unusually the transcendent distinction between the ultimate Creator and His creation. By emanation God may produce without the Son, a circumstance that has seemed to some to narrow the degree of God's transcendence. Acts of creation account for Heaven, Hell, our world, and their inhabitants, man and the angels, all explicitly or necessarily the immediate work of the Son. By Scripture, nothing was made without Him. On the origin of the Holy Spirit* as a person, Milton and Scripture are silent (14:403), whether He was produced or created. Of other primitive entities we have etiological information sometimes considerable, sometimes scanty, from *CD* (for the next moments "the treatise") and from *PL* ("the poem"). They are four: the Deep, Old Night, first matter, and Chaos. The Deep belongs only to the poem. There it is called boundless and identified with absolute space. It is therefore infinite, and infinite specifically because God fills it, though not with His full and perfect essence. What, exactly, fills it from all eternity, before any emanations "in time," we are not told. As long as any solution to the problem must be a guess, the least inconvenient guess would be Old Night. Like light, she is "eternal" and "uncreated" and "unoriginal" (3.18; 2.150; 10.477) and twice she is the eldest of things (2.894, 962). If she is so, as Eve is the fairest of her daughters, Night is older than all things. No contradiction follows if we include her among what Milton calls those "back parts of God," which are not, "properly speaking, God;

though we nevertheless consider them to be eternal" (15 : 31 [10]). God clearly says that there is a portion of His being into which He does not extend His "goodness," which is generally identified with his creative light (3. 713; 7. 171; 15 : 29 [19]). If this is Old Night, she will satisfy Milton's note that the original darkness of Genesis was no mere negation, but a positive ens (15 : 19), and will exclude vacuity. In every other mode of priority light must be prior, for in the fullness of His being God has dwelt in light from eternity (*PL* 3. 5). Nowhere does Milton affirm that Night was created. To prove the real being of original darkness, the only text he can find is Isaiah 45 : 7 : "I [Jehovah] form the light, and create darkness." To explicate the text he must use the verb that he finds in it, but he explicates to prove that the darkness is an entity, not that it is a creature. If it is created, then by the text so is original light, contrary to Milton's conviction (3. 6). The Hebrew verb, he tells us elsewhere, will bear several senses. In some sense it is easy to think that God "creates" darkness by restraint. It is not easy to think how, when, or why the Son might have created Old Night in his known way.

Original matter, handled only in the treatise, must be an emanation. Milton does not use the word but chooses instead verbs like *to proceed, to be* (of), and *to derive* (from). But he discusses it in a division of his treatise appropriate to emanation, just before he comes to God's creative activity. The generation of the Son, the possible generation of the Holy Spirit, the "effluence" of eternal light, and the emanation of matter—all normal dogma except the last—are all the activities in this kind that Milton records of God. As we have earlier considered, matter as produced is already a substance capable of being "propagated, diffused, and extended . . . far." It is *indigesta* and *incomposita* (15 :23[9]). We are not told how far God is pleased to extend it, but if it is identifiable with the Chaos of the poem, it is called infinite. Just possibly, then, it is coincident with Old Night.

Only one considerable reason has been advanced why we should hesitate to identify this original matter (not in the poem) with Milton's half-Greek Chaos (not in the treatise) : Chaos of the poem seems somewhat further advanced ontologically. We shall return to it after noticing that some lines once adduced to distinguish Chaos from first matter actually tend to equate the two. The words are these (*PL* 3. 8–12) addressed to light :

> before the Sun,
> Before the Heavens thou wert, and at the voice
> Of God, as with a Mantle didst invest
> The rising world of waters dark and deep,
> Won from the void and formless infinite.

The passage has been understood to tell us that by God's *creative* light a finite Chaos ("waters") was won from an "infinite" first matter, "void and formless." This somewhat strained reading requires us to understand the key words metaphorically and then, from metaphor, to set literal bounds in physical space. To be sure, in some lines that follow, light becomes an obvious metaphor, and even in the lines quoted may by poetic ambiguity suggest God's original creative light. But that literal sense which is required for determining bounds in cosmographic space fits only the physical light of the First Day. It shone "at the voice of God" (15 : 7 [8]f.) three days before there was a sun and one day before the visible heavens (the plural excludes the highest Heaven). From its temporary cloud this created light shone on waters because on that day there was, in the "rising" or incipient world (cf. *PL* 7. 102) below it, nothing else to shine on. Instead of penetrating their surface like a creative beam, this light stopped and there rested like a "mantle." Occasionally elsewhere Chaos is called a sea, but Chaos is not the particular "waters" that these lines bound within an outer infinity of confusion. These waters are part of the "rising" cosmos, and the "void and formless infinite" surrounds that cosmos. On the evidence of these lines alone we should be urged to identify Chaos with the "confused and formless" first matter of the treatise.

After Satan plunges into Chaos—and even before—he is traversing the dark outskirts of God. A problem arises from a diversity of sorts between the two accounts of the repository where God finds "dark materials" *(PL* 2. 916) to create new worlds. In the treatise its substance, though formless, is *per se* good, so good, in fact, that the accession of forms adds fitness and nothing more (15 : 23[23]). Its confusion is mentioned without emphasis. Even so, where Milton deals with Chaos in generalities, poem and treatise consist pretty well, considering that in the treatise he has a polemic motive for insisting on the goodness of matter and in the poem a dramatic motive for insisting on the horrors of Chaos : he needs a real obstacle course for Satan's expedition. If we take Milton at his word, Chaos is an infinitely extended existence; it is potency rather than act so far as pictorial language can suggest potency. It is an "Illimitable Ocean" *(PL* 2.892), thus "void and formless infinite." It lacks ordered movement to measure time, and dimensions to measure space (2. 894). By ethical measure it is good so far as it is being, otherwise neither good nor bad. Because indifferent things and good things, too, can be ill used, Sin and Death can parody God by carpentering chaotic materials (10. 282f.), just as Satan's engineers can mine ordnance from Heaven's soil, which by different efficiency produces flowers (6. 474f.). Sin and Death encounter no enmity or resistance, and there neither does God. In its own right of being, Chaos resents cosmos, whether our own or Heaven's, or that nether cosmos of Hell (2. 1002f.), but only with submissive grumbling. In such a sense it is the "foe" of nature as it is the helpless foe of Hell. What by God's grand design has been "the Womb of nature" and may become her grave (2. 911) has in the interim no purpose but to go on existing *in statu quo,* hence the opportunistic and transient league with Satan : he will have revenge; Chaos will recover his preempted ter-

ritory (2. 987). Or Old Night's, for it is her standard that will rise again (2. 985, 1003). Apparently she has the prior claim as the elder possessor of the realm.

In the course of Satan's journey Milton raises no philosophical problem by telling what is appropriate to any matter, that Chaos is "pregnant" with potency to receive form in its four essential "causes," but only after it is ordered into degree and given finality. We know from the way God prepares to create by first separating the elements that, while they are "mixt Confus'dly" in their causes, Chaos is not ready for individuation in essences (2. 913). It is ill-prepared matter. What have puzzled some readers are the accidents that chaotic substance supports. They seem appropriate only to a substrate advanced beyond first matter. Its very confusion is locomotion. It is differentiated into vestigial elements or a least their properties (898), the embryon atoms have their qualities (900); we find relative distance (1007) and relative position (691). Is Old Night "eldest" because she is the nurse of forms, and has she transmitted vague forms of chaotic matter? Does Old Night, as Aristotle's prime matter, bear in her own substance (if we can think how that notion can be a substance or contain anything) Augustine's* *lógoi spermatikoí, rationes seminales,* seeds of forms that, springing up, yield secondary matter, or Chaos? Either hypothesis posits a significant demi-Creation between first matter and the First Day, on which Milton is silent, and which he would be at a loss to justify by either Scripture or philosophical necessity. We should need, too, to be told elsewhere in Milton of those "seeds." Otherwise, if Chaos itself is the result of any kind of creation by the induction of form into matter, the Son should be the proximate cause of some odd abortions. Further, it would seem that Milton would have discussed a matter of such importance along with God's other creative activities in his treatise—unless, indeed, we must discount the treatise entirely in interpreting the poem. If the poem must explain itself, we may as easily suppose that Milton borrows entities from Genesis and from familiar pagan analogues of Genesis to make Satan's audacious journey a lively story. Told in words, it must employ concepts drawn from human experience. All in all, it seems natural to understand Chaos as a dramatically heightened account of original matter.

As a preface to Creation, Milton's God utters these familiar words (7. 168f.):

Boundless the Deep, because I am who fill
Infinitude, nor vacuous the space,
Though I uncircumscrib'd my self retire,
And put not forth my goodness, which is free
To act or not, Necessitie and Chance
Approach not mee, and what I will is Fate.

In Genesis darkness is on the face of the Deep. If the Deep is boundless because God fills it, it should follow that God contains both the Deep and its coincident Night. The alternative would be two independently eternal entities—as objectionable, surely, and on the same ground, as coeternal matter. Milton dismisses that division of godhead as inconceivable (15 : 21[3]). It seems unnecessary to think that God must surround the Deep in order to contain it, that is to say, in order to establish within His own infinity a hyperbolically boundless space; for the lines seem to say clearly enough that God is in, not around, the space that is the Deep, and that the Deep itself is by God's virtue infinite. On the eve of Creation God exists as He has probably always existed, in two modes. In one he fills out the perfection of His goodness; in the other He extends himself spatially to infinity. We may imagine, if we please, a concentrated node of perfect deity surrounded by an infinity of incompletely actualized deity. In the past the potency has been twice educed into form in different times and places—in Heaven and in Hell, the one creation apparently much earlier than the other (15 : 29 [24]; PL 2. 1002). In these successive creations God relaxes only a little the posture of restraint that it pleases Him to hold. Neither in His early production of matter nor in His

later imposition of form is He pictured as retracting himself. God's process of creating by retraction as described in the Zohar is not found elsewhere in Milton; it must be in the passage quoted or nowhere. There it hardly consists with the phrase "put not forth my goodness." The context asks that we understand retire in the transitive sense (OED 5, vt) of "restrain" or "withhold." By his own volition God reins Himself in and puts not forth His creative virtue until he is ready. If the usually accepted punctuation is correct, the sense, or a part of it, goes on : "I am infinite, even though, being under no external compulsion whatever, I prefer not to be infinite in my full perfection. By withholding myself I grant some license to necessity and chance, even to fate; yet their triumph is illusory and cannot come near me, for they are my instruments" (cf. 14 : 27[11]). Elsewhere in the poem Chance is engaged as chief minister in Chaos, and in CD (14 : 27 [20]) is assigned a comparable post. In PR (4. 315) fortune and fate are erected by pagans into chill substitutes for God and His Providence*.

PL describes a creative process that is partly one of imposing forms and partly one of educing them, the former employed for inanimate being, the latter for living creatures. The details of either may be poetic metaphor, because the creative act is instantaneous (7. 154, 177). The angels apparently see it as a sequence, for Uriel (3. 708f.) and Raphael (7. 216f.) separately so report it. The two angels agree in the main as far as they both cover the same ground, and can be easily harmonized if, for Raphael's brooding Spirit of God, we allow Uriel's creative light. CD supports such a conception (15 : 29 [18]f.). Both angels begin with a preparation—quieting the Deep—then narrate the circumscription of a site, the Spirit brooding (or light shining into Chaos), and a segregation of the elements. This Raphael clearly means when he has like "conglob'd" with like. Uriel stops here, and Raphael continues alone with the story of the days. God forms inanimate things directly from matter, beginning with physical light, which he fashions from some unnamed substance fetched from the Deep (7. 243), some pure, ethereal quintessence. Possibly encouraged by the hint of a world egg in Genesis, Milton makes the creation of each form of life an analogy of hatching. The same hint may have suggested to Augustine his *rationes seminales*. No contradiction hinders those readers who like to speculate that just here, no earlier than the creation of the world, these *rationes* are implanted in the Abyss by the Spirit. But Milton explicitly tells us that the brooding Spirit infuses vital virtue and vital warmth, and details the process no further. This "virtue" is the efficiency requisite to educe living form from the passive potency of matter. Germination follows : the waters give birth to the land, the earth brings forth plants, the waters spawn, the coves hatch the eggs that hatch the brood, the clods calve (7. 276, 284, 417, 453, 463, 475). When God, through the eyes of the Son, inspects the finished work to assure himself that it answers his "great idea," he sees no mechanistic world but a great organism beautifully alive.

The universe has always lain "multi-form" and entire in God's "virtue" (15: 21 [26]), but once externalized it becomes properly "other" (25 [9]). It is not now usual for special students of Milton's ideas to speak of his pantheism. God's production of matter out of Himself is not, even in Milton's defense of the idea, that which causes its goodness, and its goodness is in no sense divinity. It should hardly be counted one of those "back parts" of God which "properly speaking" are not God. His perfectly orthodox om-nipresence is not an indwelling, and to overemphasize it, Milton fears, may dishonor God (14 : 47 [15]). He dwells in unapproachèd light, not in the creature. His revelations, His grace, and His Providence are as carefully mediated in Milton's theology as in another's. The creature is distinct and expressly distinguished from its Creator. Nothing in Creation or above it derives any part of its essence from God, not the Son, the Holy Spirit (14 : 379 [11]), Heaven (15: 31 [4]), or man's soul (15 : 39 [14]).

Milton once wished that the word *nature* could be reserved for God's creative command that set the organism in act, and that in other contexts the word Providence could be substituted (15 : 93 [23]f.). Ordinarily, of course, he is obliged to use both words as others use them. Nature holds its course by God's regular Providence. But the creatures are driven by no established routine and passive obedience. Vitalist as he is, Milton takes pleasure in thinking that they consciously and joyously obey the voice of God (*PL* 5. 153f.). In our visible world the sun is vicegerent to bless and, in some respects, to order. It sheds warmth and vital influence to nourish life and to transmute inorganic substance (3. 576f.); it fosters the growth of minerals in the earth, waters the ground, lends light to the moon and stars, and by magnetic beams holds the planets to their courses. To accomplish this and conserve resources it receives exhalations that it turns to rivers of potable gold. Cyclic, too, are the physical elements. They feed each its higher (5. 415f.) as they "in quaternion run Perpetual circle" to "mix and nourish all things" (181). Raphael's familiar lesson of the tree links this elemental cycle by analogy with the vital chain of animate being (479f.). The tree is both metaphor and example. Its parts—dark roots, lighter green stalk, airy leaves, and bright, spiritous flowers—correspond to the four physical elements from "center to circumference" to join the two series in a common kind of movement. Each part nourishes the next, all tending to a final cause, the fruit. That goes on to nourish man by being "sub-limed" to vital spirits appropriate to each stage of his tripartite soul. In all this there is no destruction. Milton questions that God is able, and declares that he is unwilling, to annihilate utterly any creature (15 : 27 [15]; cf. *PL* 2. 154). To do so would be to create nonbeing, an evil act. All being, and only being, is good—until vitiated. Hence (*PL* 5. 469)

one Almightie is, from whom
All things proceed, and up to him return,
If not deprav'd from good, created all
Such to perfection, one first matter all
Indu'd with various forms, various degrees
Of substance.

The first three lines have suggested the doctrine of *egressus* and *regressus* to be found in some Neoplatonism*, but where the topic is this-worldly nature, we should perhaps seek closer to home. By orthodox religion with its eschatology, all things proceed from God and all pure things ultimately return—heaven, nature, and man. All things are of one first matter, which need not be prime in order to be indued with forms and degrees. Nor does it, on its emanation, contain the seminal forms necessarily, active potencies that will come spontaneously to act. The words "indu'd with . . . forms" can as easily mean that matter has been indued at some time since its emanation as that it was already indued when produced.

Milton apparently thought that those Neoplatonists were right who taught that morality could alter ontology, and that man had thereby some control over his place in the scale of being. He may not have seriously held or long retained the doctrine in the extreme form that he gave it in *Mask* (453f.), though some of his Platonic contemporaries took it seriously: the body of the good man, the man both virtuous and spiritual, will "by degrees" turn to spirit. Milton fitted his eloquent lines into an emphatically ethical and Platonic allegory and never repeated the thought exactly. He may have expected the lines to be understood as hyperbole true only symbolically. Or they may be the overexcited conclusion of the optimistic Elder Brother. They may be simply his great aria, more lyrical than literal. For anything we know, Milton may have come to look on the described phenomenon, so contrary to experience, as "fabling" or a "smooth conceit," for in *Mask* the remarkable possibility is open to fallen man in the world of our experience. But for his ideal world before the Fall, Milton retains the doctrine. Obedience to the will of

God, "long tri'd," will purge unfallen man of his gross matter until, by degrees of merit, "body up to spirit work" (*PL* 5. 478, 493f.; 7. 159). Contrariwise, the sinning angels begin at once to "imbrute" (6. 661). Man's free will leaves his direction to his own choice, in our world as in Paradise; only the manner of his progress differs.

Metaphysics touches the question of fate and freedom at the point where Milton brings the unity of his God and the dignity of matter to bear upon man's moral responsibility. How does evil first enter a pure mind and win approval? To use Satan or any tempter to solve the problem is only to evade it, but Milton is ever more concerned to deal practically with man in a world already sinful than to account theoretically for the origin of sin. Satan, the proximate cause, has free will when he first sins, and confesses as much (4. 67), but does not reveal precisely how he deviated, by his very first motion, from the line of right (50). How does a self-tempted sinner enter upon that deviation which is sin (15 : 199 [16])? How does sin come into a universe that is exclusively God's, that contains nothing evil in its own nature, where even every action is in itself good (199 [15])? Milton left himself an insoluble problem—just as every speculative thinker leaves himself such a problem somewhere—by excluding both determinism and dualism.

In "natural and civil things" the dogma of absolute predestination* that Milton came to detest implies no sweeping determinism, but imposes a determinism in what most concerns, the matter of man's eternal salvation. Milton assures us (15 : 71–73) that God cannot be the cause of the evil in evil acts and cannot promise one thing and purpose another. If by his secret will He damns some men by name before their birth and any wrong done, leaves them in inherited and actual sin, and meanwhile shows them in Scripture what they can do to be saved, His secret will contradicts His revealed will. Revealed goodness covers concealed evil, and only this double nature in God can make possible the bondage of man to amoral fate. Milton finds it better to justify God by reinterpreting the predestinarian texts to eliminate the ethical dualism (14:91f., esp. 109; 15:213 [27]). As there is no Manichaean determinism in his ethics, so there is no Manichaean dualism in his ontology. Had he left himself an independent principle of evil to mar God's perfect unity, he would have had no conspicuous problem of evil. For Platonists and Manichaeans it was matter, a bait irresistible to the many. According to a Manichaean explanation recorded by Augustine (*Civ. Dei* 14.12), Adam and Eve were punished because they chose not an apple, but matter. This the very gravity of their punishment proves. Milton follows Augustine in convicting the culprits of a long list of the sins comprehended in one act of disobedience (15: 1818 [26]f.) In *PL* (9. 745–833; cf. 10. 16) he dramatizes such a list. The apple is indifferent, no more than a token of obedience to God's will. Man's wisdom, then, bids him avoid a false, apparent good, the fruit of the "Wisdom-giving Plant." Adam knows perfectly well his true good when he promises (7. 77) that he and Eve will

> his admonishment
> Receave with solemne purpose to observe
> Immutably his sovran will, the end
> Of what we are.

Nature obeys the voice of God with no difficulty. On earth man alone enjoys the perilous gift of free choice, the unique power to take a wrong direction and forsake "the end of what we are." Milton calls it man's free will, and believes in it with all his moral earnestness.

In the place or two where he comes close to grappling with the philosophic question Whence evil? he finds himself close to forgetting God's unity. He cannot entirely purge himself of dualism. Once, when his theory of the emanation of matter from God forces upon him the question of evil's origin, he answers with what is in effect another question (15: 24 [7]f.): Why cannot a good from God be drawn into sin, inasmuch as, after it

is made external to God, it falls under the power of otherness (*alterius*)? Another time Milton is no less interesting and no more helpful (14:79 [19]f.). Because man's free will precludes God's perfect foreknowledge, it follows, "as all confess," that the idea of certain events, like the Fall, are "suggested to God from some extraneous source (*aliunde*)." We cannot expect Milton more than another to harmonize man's free will with God's perfect unity and with all the rest of God's perfections. When he comes to the point where he must choose, man's moral responsibility comes first. [HS and JS]

**MICHAEL.** The angel* Michael appears in two roles in *PL*: in Book 6 as commander of God's host and victor over Satan in single combat, and in Books 11 and 12 as God's emissary to reveal the future to Adam and Eve and to remove them from Eden. Both roles are important to the epic, and the second gives Milton room to develop Michael as a character beyond the stern speeches that his stern duties require. Some modern critics, nevertheless, have held both roles ill-conceived or Michael ill-drawn. Thus R. J. Werblowsky thinks that Michael "plays . . . a St. George in a pseudo-Arthurian heaven" (*Lucifer and Prometheus* [1952], p. 10) and J. B. Broadbent that in the Garden he is so much the "plenipotentiary" that we lose sight of him as spiritual messenger (*Some Graver Subject* [1960], p. 270). John Peter thinks that he suffers "deflation" when God names the "unimpressive Gabriel" as next to him in prowess and that we are displeased with Michael when Adam attributes "misogynism" to him by bidding Eve retire at his coming. Peter acknowledges, though, that this supposed deflation and displeasure are only passing and that Michael is "comparatively easy to accept, for on the whole his presentation is much more integrated and coherent" than that of Gabriel or Raphael (*A Critique of Paradise Lost* [1960], p. 29).

The Hebrew of *Michael* seems to mean "who is as God" or "The Strength of

God." It is one of only two angel's names in the canonical books of the Bible. Daniel 10 says that Michael, "one of the chief princes," sponsored Daniel to the Persian king. Catholic commentators and many Protestant ones took the reference to be to the angel of Persia. The marginal gloss in the Geneva Bible, however, is that Michael here is Christ. In *CD* 1 : 9 Milton says firmly that Michael is "one who presides over the rest of the good angels"; Scripture uses the name so. Milton cites Revelation 12 : 7, 8 on "how Michael and his angels fought against the dragon" and Jude 9 on a contest between Michael and Satan for the body of Moses. *Michael* cannot mean Christ, Milton says, because Michael did not defeat the dragon, as Christ surely would have done, and because he "durst not bring . . . a railing accusation," a restriction not applicable to Christ.

Michael is very prominent in Jewish biblical commentary and in occult works, where he has a wide variety of often grotesque activities to his credit (see Gustav Davidson, *A Dictionary of Angels* [1967]), some of which orthodox Christian angelologists notice. Milton, however, touches this material on Michael hardly more than by the association that his common levy with it on Scripture makes unavoidable. From Zechariah 4 : 10 and Revelation 5 : 6, for instance, he accepts in *CD* that seven angels "in particular" serve God, and in *PL* 3. 650 adds the traditional idea that they stand before the Throne. He names only Uriel as of the seven, but angelological listings always name Michael too.

In spite of his biblical warrant as commander, Michael is not a dominating figure in the War in Heaven\*. He routs Satan personally but cannot end him, and his army gets hardly better than a draw. Whether or not we agree with G. Wilson Knight that the inconclusiveness of these efforts makes Michael cut a poor figure, the fact seems to be that the poem does not call for Michael or any other good angel to win by military feats honors that we are to think characteristic of God's host. As B. A. Wright notices, "Milton puts into Michael's mouth during his coaching of Adam one of his most powerful condemnations of the false idea of the soldier as hero" (*Milton's Paradise Lost* [1962], p. 197), and Joseph H. Summers explains that the good angels lose no face through their limitations in battle. They obey God's command in serene consciousness that "the larger context" of divine plan may include an act yet hidden from them and not their act. Thus, facing Satan, Michael hopes to end it, "but remembers that the end may rather be by "some more sudden vengeance wing'd from God" (6. 279; *The Muse's Method* [1968], pp. 127–28). Michael is certainly not so salient a character as Christ, for whose glory he stands aside, or Satan, deity's great adversary. But he does serve God with dignity and worth in the battle, and Milton's account of him there seems adequate.

Most critical attention to Michael has been to his part in Books 11 and 12. For Michael as instructor of Adam, Milton had no warrant in the Bible, and though the Cabala names an angelic instructor for Adam, it is Raziel, not Michael. In *PL*, Michael is, as Isabel Gamble MacCaffrey says, first chorus, then narrator, and sums up the wisdom Adam gains "in words that compass the whole of the poem's universe," though the "drama has shifted from the physical . . . to man's soul" (*Paradise Lost as "Myth"* [1959], p. 61). Michael has, Irene Samuels points out, like Virgil in Dante's\* *Purgatorio*, a "vast course of instruction to complete," and he imparts a sense of urgency. Like Virgil, too, though he does not treat his pupil as an equal, he is gentle with Adam's bewilderment, for his assignment is on balance a healing one : to leave Adam "renewed confidence that he can cope with his damaged world" (*Dante and Milton* [1966], p. 227). Michael's task is bound, says Dennis H. Burden, to Milton's problem of differentiating "the ways in which God's foreknowledge could make for either despondency or reassurance." Michael shows Adam the future to confirm his faith (*The Logical Epic* [1967], p. 27), and to this end, Kester Svendson* notes, Michael has limited foreknowledge, divine enlightenment (*Milton and Science* [1956], p. 160). The character is consistent, though perhaps too authoritarian for modern taste. [RHW]

**MILLAR, ANDREW:** *see* PUBLISHERS.

**MILLENNIALISM,** the active belief in the thousand-year reign of the saints on earth with Christ, foretold in the Apocalypse of St. John (20:1–3). The doctrine is a matter of faith in most churches but is generally conceived as a futuristic theological abstraction, a conventional element of traditional eschatology. Milton's definition of the millennium in *CD* (1.33) seems, for example, thoroughly neutral and devoid of immediacy. It is also fairly conventional, setting its beginning with Christ's Second Coming, identifying it with the Last Judgment, and describing its duration as extending until the eruption of a final renewal of universal war with Satan and his followers. With their downfall there would be a complete separation of the damned from the blessed, who would then enjoy the eternal life of perfect glorification.

But this kind of description is, in effect, merely a scenario for the faithful to transform imaginatively when the proper occasions arise. Then in its virulent form millennialism becomes a primitive but powerful ideology, lending authority and conviction to the efforts of fundamentally religious men to explain the meaning of contemporary crises in terms of prophecy, making the past and the immediate future conform to those forecasts of joyous hope and terrible doom that notably abound in Daniel and Ezekiel, but particularly in Revelation. In this active form the belief is also called millenarianism and chiliasm, or more generally, apocalypticism. Like its progenitor Jewish messianism, it is usually associated with periods of great communal stress or of singular cultural isolation in the midst of a contrasting society. In the latter form it often appears,

even to this day, among fundamentalist churches that tend to regard themselves as a spiritual remnant, and where the prophetic element in the Bible is regularly applied to historical interpretation.

Throughout the Protestant Reformation varying degrees of active millenialism affected all the Protestant churches, especially those of a characteristically sectarian nature, such as the notorious Anabaptists who tried in 1534 to set up a Kingdom of Heaven in Munster, an incident that long discredited the most active forms of the belief. However, a milder, more stable form became endemic in Protestant England from the time of Queen Mary's reign and was given some support by John Foxe's* *Book of Martyrs,* a work so revered that it was placed by Queen Elizabeth's order next to the Bible in English churches. The martyrology enshrined nationalistically a prophetic view of the history of the Church and of Reformation in England, encouraging the faithful to hope that in the English Reformation's fulfillment the Kingdom of Christ would somehow be realized, with England spiritually leading the way. The Puritans of the seventeenth century became the true heirs of this traditional view, associating it with their demand for further reformation, as well as with their harassment and persecution within and outside the Church of England, until out of hope and exasperation they had fashioned a potentially revolutionary myth with which to justify themselves. The story of this emergent ideology is nicely sketched in the full title of William Haller's study of Puritan propaganda, *The Rise of Puritanism, Or, The Way to the New Jerusalem, as Set Forth in Pulpit and Press* (1938).

With the onset of the Puritan revolution in 1640, the myth became a central feature of the many exuberantly millennial productions inspired by the cause of church reformation and the Parliamentary struggle with the King, including the best of Milton's antiprelatical prose. His first tract, *Ref,* concluded with the rhapsodic thanksgiving for England's transfiguration as a Kingdom of Christ and with a spectacular view of himself as her millennial poet, while in *Animad* he soared to a new apocalyptic height, exulting over the millennial outpouring of the Holy Spirit* on his countrymen, with himself again cast in a special role as poetic spokesman for their gratitude. Both occasions were deliberate indulgences in the kind of inspired, spontaneous effusions characteristic of extemporary prayers, but for that very reason they represent the truest picture of Milton's initial revolutionary hopes in their most uninhibited form, when it looked to him as if all obstacles to complete religious reformation would be, with God's help, miraculously dissolved. His millennial faith was perhaps more eloquent, certainly more personally conceived as a poetic self-apotheosis, than the millennialism of other Puritans in the early stages of their revolutionary enthusiasm, when rather less than more tended to be seen by them of the essential differences in their visions of reformation.

The Presbyterians* were quickest to moderate the intensity of their expectations, particularly as they were the more numerous and the first to propose a specific visible form for Christ's Kingdom in the shape of a clerically dominated, centralized national church. But their program met with ambiguous Parliamentary support and aroused resistance from Independents* and more radical sectarian groups, generating in them in turn a renewed and more special sense of crisis. The radicals' counterarguments also involved some abatement of immediate millennial expectations, but by way of compensation they developed more intensively the idea of a special spiritual outpouring of new divine revelations on their behalf. If the final kingdom was not immediately at hand, England was already experiencing the dispensations of the last ages before the millennium, when, as foretold, the saints would be greatly enlightened and nations made conformable to their interests. This sense of enlightenment steeled them to resist conforming to any centralized national church, Presbyterian or otherwise, while the priority of their own interests as saints led them to develop an aggressive attitude toward the drift of national policy. (*See* ECCLESIOLOGY, MILTON'S; POLITICS, MILTON'S.)

Milton's millennialism does not find expression in the period in which he wrote the divorce tracts, but to the extent that it reappeared in *Areop* it had considerable affinities with the sectarian sense that England's saints, in this age, were assuredly not to be spiritually repressed or made to conform to any dogmatic version of one partial truth, whether it was ecclesiastical or otherwise. England was the vanguard for the "reforming of Reformation it self," a nation to whom God had in precedence revealed himself, "as his manner is, first to his Englishmen." But this remarkable phrase is perhaps the last impulse of the millennialism of the antiprelatical tracts, for Milton's optimism was clearly blunted even as he wrote, and his vision seems to have been only rekindled to bring England's leaders back to a certain understanding of a basic truth, rather than to celebrate a triumphant expectation. In the years that followed, until the trial and execution of Charles I*, his enthusiasm apparently ebbed even further away until he came to believe that the one lasting religious reformation attainable was actually negative, the safeguarding by political means of the Christian liberty of all professing kindred forms of free (nonestablished) Protestantism. To this extent alone he sympathized with but did not fully share the radical sectarians' view, still suffused for them with millennial hopes, that the nation at large was to be made conformable to the interests of the saints.

By 1647 these interests were most militantly supported by the Independent Army, which on behalf of spiritual liberty (and its own interests) found itself opposing the Parliamentary majority as well as the King. During the period until 1649 when the struggle came to a head, millennialism was phenomenally renewed within the Army and its supporting base of

Congregational (Independent) and Baptist* churches. Indeed, the millenarians were a main part of the pressure on Oliver Cromwell* and the Army leadership to reduce Parliamentary opposition by force and bring the King to trial for his life. As an active and dedicated supporter of those revolutionary changes Milton, in *Tenure, Eikon,* and *1Def,* made use of millenarian-sounding theocratic arguments. He invoked, for example, the rights of the saints to execute justice upon the enemies of God, their rights as the most virtuous of England's citizens to defend their civil and religious liberty* against the majority; and, as did the millenarians, he affirmed as a vindication of their cause the special providences* of God in the Army's favor. However, there is little trace in Milton's writings of the extreme excitation typically animating the millenarians (or Fifth Monarchy men, as they were called by 1651), or of any renewal of his hopes for the realization of the Kingdom of Christ on earth in any proximate sense. He seemed rather to be exploiting the depth of revolutionary support in the Army and churches, assimilating to their ideology his own Christian humanistic bias toward an aristocratic republicanism with a theocratic Old Testament overtone, the political preference perhaps most congenial to his own sense of values.

When Cromwell broke with the Fifth Monarchists after the failure of their great political experiment, the Nominated or Barebones Parliament, Milton as a spokesman for the Protectorate regime broke with them also, criticizing them, albeit obliquely, in *2Def,* as dangerously ignorant and superstitious. The fact that Fifth Monarchist agitation contributed to the general political instability of the Protectorate, and to the near anarchy following Oliver Cromwell's death and the downfall of his son Richard Cromwell, was briefly but bitterly noted by Milton's attack on their pretensions to a rule of the saints in the first edition of *Way.* So died in Puritanism's downfall millennialism as a political force in England. For Milton the millennium itself apparently had long before reverted to its original nature as a futuristic article of faith, certainly not to be expected in his lifetime, but nevertheless still powerfully appealing to his poetic imagination as the context of his vision of ultimate beatitude. [MF]

**MILTON, ANNE.** Daughter of John Milton, scrivener, and Sara Jeffrey Milton, and sister of the poet, Anne was married to Edward Phillips (I) on November 22, 1623, by Rev. Thomas Myriell in St. Stephen's, Walbrook, bringing him "a considerable dowry" (Marriage Settlement, dated November 27, 1623). She bore him the following children: John (baptized January 12, 1625; buried March 15, 1629), Anne, the "Fair Infant" (baptized January 12, 1626; buried January 22, 1628), Elizabeth (baptized April 9, 1628; buried February 19, 1631), Edward (born August 1630; died 1696?), and John (born October 1631?; died 1706?). She survived Phillips, who died in late summer 1631, and was then married to Thomas Agar (possibly on January 5, 1632, in St. Dunstan in the East), bearing him two children: Mary, who "died very young," and Anne, who married David Moore, December 29, 1662. The exact dates and places of her birth and death are unknown. A deed dated January 18, 1628, and a deed dated December 29, 1639, both possessed by the Shrewsbury Public Library and Museum, contain her signature. [REH]

**MILTON, CHRISTOPHER,** and family. Born about November 24, 1615, Milton's brother Christopher was baptized on December 3 at All Hallows Church*. He also attended St. Paul's School* and Christ's College*, Cambridge, under the tutelage of Nathaniel Tovey*, as had his brother. He entered Christ's on February 15, 1631, but left the next year and was admitted to the Inner Temple on September 22, 1632. He was called to the bar on January 26, 1640. Prior to this time he had married, moved his family to his father's home at Horton*, and then apparently returned alone to London to complete his schooling.

Christopher's wife was Thomasin Webber, daughter of John and Isabel Webber of St. Clement's Churchyard, London. She was baptized at St. Clement Danes on October 18, 1618. Her father, a tailor, was well off by the time of his death; he was buried from the church on June 5, 1632. She had a brother William and three sisters, Anne, Isabel, and Katherine. The date of Christopher and Thomasin's marriage is unknown, but it probably occurred in early 1627 and at least later in the year Thomasin went to Horton to reside with the now widowed John Milton, her father-in-law. This seems likely because Christopher was "restored into commons" by the Inner Temple on November 26, 1637, and John Milton, her brother-in-law, was now able to contemplate a move to London and soon a trip to the Continent.

The family resided with the father until sometime around 1640 (after Christopher had been admitted to the bar), when they all moved to Reading where they stayed until the siege of April 1643. Thereafter, they were in London, John Milton, senior, going to live with his elder son, and they moving in with her mother. Christopher, now engaged in legal and governmental activities, was in Wells in 1644 and in Exeter in 1645 and 1646. Baptisms of two children, John in 1645 and Thomas in 1647 at St. Clement Danes, evidence the separation of the family, which may have required closer association of the poet and his wife with his sister-in-law. Mary Milton had stayed for a short time with Mrs. Webber and Thomasin Milton in 1645, when she returned to London and was awaiting Milton's move from Aldersgate Street into the larger house on the Barbican. Further evidence of the separation during 1644–1646 is seen in payments for keeping Christopher's children on July 1, 1644, December 16, 1644, and October 17, 1645. The records have disappeared, but it had been reported in the early nineteenth century that a "Mrs. Elijah Webster" was so paid; this would seem to be a misreading of "Mrs. Isabel Webber." Thomasin Milton died sometime after 1656, when she gave birth to her daughter Mary.

While he was residing at Reading, Christopher became a Royalist; he was in active service until April 1646 as a Royal Commissioner of Sequestrations for three counties under the Great Seal at Oxford. He was back in London by April 20, 1646, when he took the Covenant to the Parliamentarian government. On August 7 he petitioned for the return of his sequestered house called Cross Keys in St. Martin's parish, Ludgate, which he had inherited from his father. John Milton, senior, had acquired the house from the estate of Sir John Suckling (not the poet) in July 1629. He was fined £200, which was reduced to £80, paid in halves on September 24 and December 24. But in December 1649 and January 1652 the new government tried to collect the full amount of the fine. Attempts were made to sequester any estate in Reading, but Christopher owned none there. The Ludgate property was sold in February 1654. By 1652 the Miltons were residents of St. Nicholas' parish, Ipswich, Suffolk, although he practiced law in London. Documents record his involvement in many suits during the 1650's, including work for both his brother and his brother's in-laws, the Powells.

With the Restoration Christopher's fortunes further improved. He was called to the bench of the Inner Temple on November 25, 1660, and numerous data indicate his work there as reader, committeeman, and member of the Parliament in later years. He was a member of the Parliament in 1674, 1676, and 1679 (and presumably in intervening years), but not in 1673 and 1680. Records also exist of his legal activities in Ipswich, where he was justice of the peace and deputy recorder. He was taxed for nine hearths in 1674 in Suffolk, but was listed as living (probably in error) in St. Margaret's parish. He was a frequent visitor to his brother after the Restoration and was the main deponent in court proceedings concerning Milton's nuncupative will* and the settlement of inheritances for Milton's daughters. He was in an excellent position to supply John Aubrey* with information about his brother, but details that he did not know (for example, his grandfather's first name) and the apparent errors he made are curious.

In April 1686 he was elevated by James II to sergeant-at-law (on the twenty-first), baron of the Exchequer (on the twenty-fifth), and knight (on the twenty-sixth). The next year (April 16, 1687) he was appointed justice of common pleas, but on July 6, 1688, he retired or was dismissed, though retaining his salary. He retired to Rushmere in Suffolk, not far from Ipswich; he was buried at St. Nicholas, Ipswich, on March 22, 1693. Rushmere remained the home of two of his daughters for a short while thereafter. He was reputed to be a Roman Catholic, largely on a comment by Dean William Binckes of Lichfield in *A Sermon Preach'd . . . Novemb. 5. 1704* (London, 1705). He is often listed in library catalogues and bibliographic volumes as the author of *The State of Church Affairs* (London, 1687), which shows Roman Catholic bias and which includes material from *Brit.*

The children of Christopher and Thomasin Milton were: Christopher, born perhaps in 1637–1638; an unnamed infant, buried at Horton on March 26, 1639; Sarah, baptized at Horton on August 11, 1640; Anne, baptized at St. Laurence's Church, Reading, on August 27, 1641; John, baptized at St. Clement Danes, London, on June 29, 1643; Thomas, baptized at St. Clement Danes, on February 2, 1647; Thomasin, born perhaps in 1648–1649; Richard, born perhaps within the period of 1648–1652; Mary, baptized at St. Nicholas, Ipswich, on March 29, 1656; and Catherine, born a year or so before or after 1656. Christopher was admitted to the Inner Temple on June 30, 1661, and called to the bar on February 9, 1668. He is named the

eldest son. He died, however, shortly thereafter and was buried at St. Nicholas' on Marsh 12, 1668. Sarah may have been married to a John Younger; but nothing further is known of her, including her date of death. Anne became the wife of John Pendleberry of Enfield, Middlesex, on February 20, 1683. She was then living in the parish of St. Dunstan in the West, London, where her brother Thomas was also residing. Perhaps she lived with him and his family. Her parents are said to be deceased, in the marriage allegation, which also cites her age as 22, although she was 41. Pendelberry gave his age as 24, although he was probably around 30, some years younger than his bride. He was a Protestant clergyman—which may account for the alienation from her parents—who became vicar of Farmingham, Kent, around a year later. He died on December 9, 1719, leaving bequests in his will to his sisters-in-law Mary and Catherine. Anne died on February 20, 1721, also leaving bequests to her sisters.

John was a student of Pembroke College, Cambridge, from January 29, 1668; the records give his age as 15, an error for 25. But he was soon dead and buried at St. Nicholas', on December 29, 1669. Thomas was admitted to the Inner Temple on November 27, 1670, on special request of his father; he was called to the bar on November 29, 1677. On July 22, 1672, he married Martha Fleetwood, daughter of Sir William Fleetwood (1603–1674) of Aldwinkle, at St. Mary le Bone, London. She was the niece of Charles Fleetwood*, a friend of John Milton's and an important member of the Council of State* who was the leading contender to succeed Oliver Cromwell* shortly before his death. Thomas and Martha Milton's children were: Thomas, baptized on June 26, 1679, at St. Dunstan's in the West and buried there a few weeks later on July 1; Margaret, baptized on March 7, 1681, and buried on June 25, 1685, in the same church; Charles, baptized on January 20, 1684, at the same church, but about whom we know nothing more; and Elizabeth, born around 1690 and alive on July 26, 1769. Elizabeth was living on Grosvenor Street in 1753, where she was housekeeper to Dr. Thomas Secker (1693–1768), the Archbishop of London from 1758 onward.

Thomas Milton may have had some connection with Chancery prior to the death of his uncle Thomas Agar*, whom he succeeded as Deputy Clerk of the Crown in November 1673, a post he held until his death. Documents connected with his position exist for December 15 and 16, 1679; April 28, 1680; June 15, 1683; May 22, 1693; and 1694. He also mortgaged his father's property at Rushmere to Sir Henry Felton on October 1, 1688. He died in October 1694 in the parish of St. Dunstan in the West; he was buried out of Fleet Street on October 17. His widow moved to St. Margaret's parish, Westminster, but married Dr. William Coward in Ipswich some time later. Lawsuits continued to involve them in Thomas's financial affairs. Coward, a graduate of Oxford in June 1677, received his medical degree in July 1687. In 1682 he published a Latin translation of Dryden's* *Absalom and Achitophel,* a poem variously indebted to *PL.* His own *Abramideis . . . An Heroic Poem* (1705) shows Milton's influence also, and he discusses the epic* in *Licentia Poetica Discuss'd* (1709). He was author of other books, including medical works. His will was proved on April 20, 1724. We do not know the death date of his wife Martha.

Christopher and Thomasin's daughter Thomasin was buried at St. Nicholas' on July 6, 1675. Nothing else is known of her. Richard, however, is important in his uncle's biography, although mentioned only by John Aubrey among the early biographers*, because of probable legal work that he handled for John Milton and his descendants. His father was able to have Richard admitted to the Inner Temple under special admission procedures on November 24, 1667. He was still resident at the Inn in 1674, although he was also taxed for two hearths in Cockfield, Babergh, in Suffolk, for the year ending March 25, 1674. Documents in which he had a hand exist from February 13, May 10, May 13, and December 2, 1674. He aided his father in working out the legacies for Milton's daughters in 1675, witnessed their releases, and signed Anne Milton's name for her. For some reason, however, he was not called to the bar until November 26, 1676. Around this time he moved to Ipswich, where documents relating to his legal practice have been discovered, dated 1677, 1686, 1687, and 1688. In March 1688 he was named to a commission to investigate fines levied on recusants and dissenters. This is probably an indication that he espoused Roman Catholicism, apparently like his father. His brother Thomas seems to have been Protestant. With his father's retirement in 1688 he went to Ireland where he died, the date unknown. On August 12, 1713, John Taylor, a gardener of Highgate, where Richard's sisters Mary and Catherine lived, was granted part administration of his estate. Mary and Catherine, neither of whom ever married, lived together at Highgate, in the parish of Hornsey, for many years, although in December 1695 they were at Rushmere, Clopton, in Suffolk. Mary was buried on April 26, 1742, in Farmingham, where her sister Anne had lived and was buried. The administration of her estate was given to Catherine, who then went to live with her cousin Deborah's daughter, Mrs. Elizabeth Foster* in Lower Holloway, Middlesex. She died in April 1746 and was buried in Farmingham with her sisters. The registers oddly reverse Mary's and Catherine's names. She is said to have been around ninety when she died, making her date of birth before or after 1656, which was the year of Mary's birth. [JTS]

**MILTON, JOHN (Senior):** *see* MILTON FAMILY.

**MILTON FAMILY.** Here will be cited only those members of Milton's immediate family: his father, his mother, his sister, brother, and other siblings, his wives, and his children. But see the following separate entries: CHILDREN, MIL-TON's; MILTON, ANNE; MILTON, SIR CHRISTOPHER; MINSHULL, ELIZABETH; POWELL, MARY; and WOODCOCK, KATH-ERINE. For other family members, see RELATIVES, MILTON's as well as cross-references listed in that entry.

Milton's father was born around late 1562 in Stanton St. John, Oxon, to Richard Milton, a yeoman and Roman Catholic, and his wife (unnamed). Richard Milton, a churchwarden in the Anglican parish, was excommunicated in 1582 for his Catholic beliefs. Around this time John Milton, the poet's father, quarreled with his father over religious principles and his reading of an Anglican Bible, and left home apparently never to be reconciled. His disinheritance was often mentioned in later years. He proceeded to London where perhaps around 1583 he became an apprentice scrivener, establishing his own business around 1590. A scrivener is one who prepared documents such as deeds and wills, served as notary public, and engaged in real estate transactions, largely mortgages. Milton's father was admitted to membership in the Company of Scriveners in 1600; his place of business and his home were The Spread Eagle, on Bread Street. *See* RESIDENCES, MILTON's.

Whether he had some education at Christ Church, Oxford, or only some musical training, as early biographers have reported, is not really known. He did, however, become a song composer of some significance. In the course of some twenty years, he wrote twenty-one madrigals, anthems, motets, and other choral works characteristic of the British school and largely in the tradition of William Byrd. One of his most notable compositions is an *In Nomine* in forty parts for voices and viols. The high regard in which he was held by leading contemporary composers is indicated by his inclusion in their published collections: Thomas Morley's *The Triumph of Oriana* (one madrigal); William Leighton's *The Tears or Lamentations of a Sorrowful Soule* (four anthems); Thomas Myriell's *Tristitiae Remedium* (a motet and five anthems); Thomas Ravens-croft's *Whole Book of Psalms* (three settings). Though most of his music, sacred and secular, was written for voices, he occasionally employed consorts of instruments. Ernest Brennecke, *John Milton the Elder and His Music* (1938) gives a complete list of Milton's known compositions, and reprints forty-six pages of scores.

John Milton married Sara Jeffrey some time well before 1601, when he was already established in his home and shop on Bread Street, in the parish of All Hallows, where the poet and his siblings were born. The marriage may have been as early as 1590, when Sara would have been eighteen. A child, perhaps their first, was buried unbaptized ("crysome") at All Hallows on May 12, 1601. Perhaps other children, unrecorded in the registers, were also born before the birth of John on December 9, 1608, but only Anne survived. The exact place and date of her birth are unknown. She married Edward Phillips in 1623; two of their children survived into adulthood, Edward and John Phillips. In 1632 she married Thomas Agar; only one of their children, Anne, grew to adulthood. The date when the poet's sister died is unknown as well: suggested has been the period during Milton's continental sojourn (1638–1639) or at least prior to his taking over the education of his nephews (1640). A legal document dated December 29, 1639, in which she is named, has suggested to some that she was alive at that time.

John and Sara's second surviving child was the poet, John. Two other births are recorded before that of Christopher in November 1615: Sara, baptized on July 15, 1612, and buried a month later on August 6, and Tabitha, baptized on January 30, 1614, and buried on August 3, 1615. Christopher became a lawyer in 1639, having married Thomasin Webber a year or so before; they had ten children, not all of whom lived past infancy. Christopher, knighted in 1686 and appointed justice of common pleas in 1687, was buried at St. Nicholas, Ipswich, Suffolk, on March 22, 1693.

Milton's father retired from active

business around 1635 when the family moved to Horton*, Bucks, although some legal matters continued to require his attention after that date. With his wife's death in 1637 and his son John's intended leave-taking from the parental home for his continental tour in April 1638, John Milton, senior, brought his younger son and new wife to live with him at Horton until around the end of 1640 or beginning of 1641, when the family group moved to Reading, Berks. The change in domiciles may have been forced by the encroachments of the Civil War. In April 1643 he went to live with his older son at Aldersgate Street. With the return of Mary in 1645 and soon the extended visit of her family, the Miltons took up residence in a large house on the Barbican around September 1645, at which residence the elder John Milton died on March 13?, 1647. He was buried in St. Giles, Cripplegate, two days later.

Milton's mother, Sara, was born to Paul and Ellen Jeffrey around 1572 in the parish of St. Swithin's, London. We know little about her, although John Aubrey* did note that she had weak eyes and used spectacles. She died on April 3, 1637, at Horton, and was buried in the church there three days later. Her death altered family matters most meaningfully for her son. Some months later his life seems to have undergone considerable change : he took steps to remove himself from his "studious retirement*," considering moving to London and finally making an extended trip to the Continent. Perhaps the health of both his parents in 1632, but especially that of his mother, was a major reason for his removal to the parental suburban home in Hammersmith* and then to Horton rather than a pursuit of a career in London.

Milton's marriages were to Mary Powell in May? 1642, to Katherine Woodcock on November 12, 1656, and to Elizabeth Minshull on February 24, 1663. Mary bore him four children : Anne, July 29, 1646; Mary, October 25, 1648; John, March 16, 1651; and Deborah, May 2, 1652. Anne was married around 1675 and

died around 1677; of Mary little is known, but she was alive in 1678, apparently unmarried; John died in June 1652; and Deborah married Abraham Clarke in 1674, had a family, and died in 1727. Their mother died as a result of childbirth on May 5, 1652. Katherine Woodcock had a daughter Katherine on October 19, 1657. Milton's second wife died on February 3, 1658, and their daughter on March 17, 1658. There were no children by Betty, his widow, who died in 1727. [JTS]

**MILTON GALLERY:** see FUSELI, HENRY.

**MILTONIAN, MILTONIC, MILTONIST.** These terms may be differentiated in certain ways; and their occurrences are more numerous than the entries in the OED would suggest. The ending -ian, as a noun, means "one who is somehow related to" Milton and "one who is skilled in or specialized in" the study of Milton and his works, and as an adjective, "of or belonging to," "characteristic of," "resembling" Milton or his works. Its first use, as noun, appears in a manuscript notebook by Sir John Finch in 1680, when he calls Thomas Coke "a perfect Miltonian." His meaning would seem to be that Coke was in favor of republicanism and against monarchy as tyranny. The adjective is found in John Philips's* *Cyder. A Poem. In two Books,* line 1, published in 1708; it means in a style* associated with Milton, that is, in blank verse* and sublime, high-flown language. It is repeated in *Milton's Sublimity Asserted: In a Poem, Occasion'd by a late celebrated piece, entitled, Cyder, a poem; in blank verse, by Philo-Milton* (1709).

The ending -ic, as an adjective, means "in the manner of" or "associated or dealing with" Milton or his works; that which is *Miltonic* has the character or form of whatever is associated with Milton. While it might imply Milton's sonorous and stately line, his language and syntax, or even his ideas and attitudes, it frequently came to mean blank verse. It thus transforms into a noun, meaning a poem in blank verse (the lexical movement like that for Anacreontic); and as lines of poetry in blank verse, it also appears in the plural *Miltonics* (like Sapphics). The adjective occurs in John Gay's *Wine a Poem* (1708), line 15, and in such items as E. C.'s *Gin, a poem, in Miltonick Verse* in *London Magazine* 3 (December 1734):663, and William Lilly's "Psalm 8, Paraphras'd in Miltonick Verse" in *London Magazine* 4 (December 1735): 683. Sir Richard Steele in *The Spectator*, no. 396 (Wednesday, June 4, 1712), used the term as a quasi-substantive : "and unfortunately stumbles upon that Mongrel miscreated (to speak in Miltonic) kind of Wit, vulgarly termed, the Punn*." An early use of the term as substantive is in the anonymous poem *Lucifer's Defeat: or, The Mantle-Chimney. A Miltonic* (1729). In its plural form it described the verse of *PL* for William Cowper* in his incomplete commentary on the poem in 1792 (published in 1806 by William Hayley*). The first entry of *Miltonically* in the OED comes from the July 1905 issue of *The Quarterly Review*, page 8. *Miltonize*, to import a Miltonian dignity to or to imitate the literary style of Milton, is listed from *The Athenaeum* of February 25, 1893, page 254. *Miltonism*, a form or expression imitating Milton, occurs in one of Charles Lamb's* letters (1888 ed., 1 : 190), dated 1802.

The ending -*ist*, as a noun, means "one having the character or nature of," "one who adheres to or advocates a doctrine or system," "one belonging to or associated with." The two earliest uses of *Miltonist* on record specifically refer to a follower of Milton in his views on divorce* : Christopher Wasse in *Electra of Sophocles* (The Hague, 1649) (sig. E8r), says, "While like the froward Miltonist,/We our old Nuptiall knot untwist"; and Charles Symmons in his edition of Milton's works (1810), page 250, uses it the same way (written 1806). Today the term is employed academically to mean one devoted to the study of Milton and his

works; *Miltonian* occurs in the same context. [JTS]

**MILTON, OTHERS OF THE SAME NAME.** Because the surname Milton is derived from a place (one living in or near a mill town), it is very common; at the same time it is variously spelled as Melton, Millton, Miltoun, Mylton, and so on. Accordingly, a number of people with the name Milton, and specifically the name John Milton, appear in records in the sixteenth through eighteenth centuries. Whether any of these people, aside from those who were close relatives, were related to the poet is unknown, but it is possible that among these people were cousins and the like, some of whom resided near him at times. For example, a John Melton lived in the parish of St. Martin in the Fields in 1629–1632, a period when at least the poet's sister also lived there. See Parker, *Milton*, pp. 1365–80, for a list of these "mute inglorious Miltons," who have sometimes been discussed as relatives and some of whom have even been advanced as being the poet himself. [JTS]

**MILTON SOCIETY OF AMERICA, THE,** has formally existed since December 1948, though earlier meetings of students of Milton had taken place on a regional basis and in Philadelphia in 1934 on a national basis. In concert with the annual meeting of the Modern Language Association, the Society assembles on one evening every year for dinner and an address by a distinguished Miltonist. It has also frequently recognized on these occasions a "Distinguished Scholar of the Year" and from time to time a foreign scholar as well. Membership requirements are limited to an interest in Milton and payment of nominal dues. The Society prints an annual booklet, which is distributed to all members and which includes the dinner program, a bibliography of the writings of the scholar if one is being honored, a list of research projects being undertaken by members of the Society, and a list of members, of whom there are currently nearly five hundred located worldwide. It has financially supported the restoration of the church of St. Giles, Cripplegate, and it regularly contributes to the publication of *Seventeenth-Century News* and the *Milton Quarterly*. [WBH]

**MILTONIS EPISTOLA AD POL-LIONEM:** *see* ATTRIBUTIONS.

**MINERALOGY.** The earliest recording of the term in *OED* is dated 1690. But interest in the subject was widespread in the sixteenth and seventeenth centuries, as one would expect, if for no other reason than the reports and discoveries of subterranean riches in the lands being settled in the New World. The evidence is in the number and popularity of books on the subject. The German iatrochemist Paracelsus (1493–1561) makes frequent reference to various aspects. Georg Bauer, a German who Latinized his surname as Agricola, published in 1546 his *De Natura Fossilium*, which has been characterized as "the first textbook of mineralogy" (the Latin *fossilis*, adj.= dug out, dug up, here includes metals and minerals); but his chief work, actually a compendium of his studies and observations, was issued the year after his death, in 1556, under the title *De Re Metallica, Libri XII.* Agricola became a source for Lazarus Ercker's treatise on assaying, published in German, in Prague, 1574 (4th printing, 1629). This, more than a century later, was translated by Sir John Pettus, a deputy governor of the Mines Royal under Charles I and II as well as Cromwell, while temporarily confined for political reasons in Fleet Prison, under the punning title *Fleta Minor,* the subtitle being a translation of Ercker's original: *The Laws of Art and Nature, in Knowing, Judging, Assaying, Fining, Refining and Inlarging the Bodies of confin'd Metals* (1683).

These men made their practical observations in European mines. The Spanish priest Alvaro Alonso Barba was for many years "curate of *St. Bernards* Parish in the Imperial City of *Potosi*, in the Kingdom of Peru in the *West-Indies*,"

and the practical knowledge that bolsters theory in his *El Arte de los Metales,* Madrid, 1640, was transoceanic in origin. Interestingly enough, the book was kept a secret in Spain until a copy was obtained in 1660 by Edward Montague, the first Earl of Sandwich, when he was ambassador extraordinary to Spain; his translation of two of Father Barba's five books was published in London in 1670: *The First Book of the Art of Metals, In which is Declared the Manner of their Generation. . . . The Second . . . Wherein is Taught the Common Way of Refining Silver by Quicksilver. . . .* Gabriel Plattes is the first English author to appear in this mineralogical company. His book is a small quarto issued in London in 1639: *A Discovery of Subterraneall Treasure, viz. of all manner of Mines and Mineralls from the Gold to the Coale. . . .* There was a second edition in 1653, a third in 1679. Plattes is particularly apt for the present purpose since he was an acquaintance of Milton's friend Samuel Hartlib*. In turn, another of Hartlib's acquaintances, the Moravian educational reformer J. A. Comenius*, published in Antwerp in 1643 a *Synopsis* of the subject in Latin, which was translated into English with the title *Naturall Philosophie Reformed by Divine Light: or, A Synopsis of Physicks,* London, 1651. Ten years later another exponent of educational reform, the Anabapist preacher John Webster, published his *Metallographia or An History of Metals,* dedicating it to Prince Rupert, who became in 1668 governor of the Society of Mines Royal. Both Comenius and Webster include approving chapters on alchemy. The latter modestly disclaims being an expert metallurgist, declaring that his knowledge has been "gathered forth of the most approved Authors that have written in *Greek, Latine,* or *High Dutch.* With some Observations and Discoveries of the Author himself." A second edition was issued in 1671. The year before this, Sir John Pettus, whose translation of the German Ercker has been mentioned, brought out his own work: *Fodinae Regales, Or the*

*History Laws and Places of the Chief Mines and Mineral Works in England, Wales, and the English Pale of Ireland,* London, 1670.

Along with these treatises dealing principally with minerals and metals must be listed three that are much broader in subject, being in fact cosmological in scope. The first two are by Englishmen, the third by a learned German who was a Jesuit priest and whose collections are still preserved in the Jesuit College in Rome. By each of these three mineralogy is presented in its proper place in a system that undertakes to explain the cosmos. The most learned of the three was Robert Fludd*, who took an M.D. at Oxford in 1605, became a Fellow of the Royal Society of Physicians, 1609, and practiced medicine until his death in 1638 in his rooms on Fenchurch Street, later Coleman Street, London. His chief work, which employs, among others, Cabalistic and abstruse Neoplatonic* sources, was published in Latin in two handsomely illustrated folio volumes of nearly 800 pages each in Oppenheim, 1617–1619; its title may be Englished as *A History, Metaphysical, Physical, and Technical, of Both the Greater and the Lesser Cosmos,* with a separate title page to the second volume that may be translated : *On the Ape of Nature, or Technical History of the Macrocosm.* Much more modest in size and appearance, though as unabashedly broad in the scope subsumed in its title, is the quarto of some 500 pages by John Swan, *Speculum Mundi or a Glasse Representing the Face of the World . . . Whereunto is joyned an Hexameron, or a Serious Discourse of the Causes, Continuance, and Qualities of Things in Nature. . . .* "Printed by the Printers to the University of Cambridge," 1635, with new editions in 1643 and 1671. The third, like the first, in Latin and never translated, is Athanasius Kircher's *Mundus Subterraneus In XII Libros digestus,* Amsterdam, 1665, 2nd ed. 1668. These two folio volumes are, like Fludd's, handsomely illustrated. They have the additional distinction of

containing a vigorous criticism (amounting to a disclaimer) of the alchemists' claims of metallic transmutation, a position not adopted even by Robert Boyle in *The Sceptical Chymist,* 1661.

Evidence that Milton was not unaware of, nor uninterested in, the mineralogical branch of science* survives from his university days. In his final academic prolusion, the *Oratio pro Arte,* on the happiness to be derived from learning, he finds occasion to mention the delight that comes from understanding "all vapours and gases which earth and sea exude; then to know the secret powers of plants and minerals. . . ." That he sustained this interest during the decade of his continued self-education in Hammersmith*, Horton*, and London seems probable. The curriculum of studies followed with his nephews in the years 1640–1644 includes, for one year, introductory readings in natural science, followed the next year by texts in meteorology, mineralogy, the arts of warfare, and so forth. But the surest evidence of his interest in, as of the comprehensiveness of his knowledge of the mineralogical science of his day, on its theoretical side, is Milton's incidental use of that knowledge in constructing his imagined version of the universe in which his imagined version of the fall of angels and the creation and Fall of mankind is set.

There are in *PL* six passages of from ten to more than forty lines that adumbrate mineralogical theory and allusively depict activities of mining and metallurgy, besides several other briefer ones, occasional or supportive of the main statements. The theories and practices assumed in these passages are in general accord with those contained in the mineralogical literature of the time and they yield their fullest meaning when examined against the background that literature affords. Furthermore, the details of mineralogy and alchemy in the poem are fully integrated into the overall cosmological system that gives the poem its scenic and ideological unity. In 1. 670–712, are described the fallen angels'* mining operations in Hell* and preparations of the metallic substances used in their building of Pandemonium*. In 2.927–38, Satan's flight through Chaos* is described by means of a trope that employs a mineralogical-meteorological explanation of lightning and thunderbolt. Satan's visit to the sun in Book 3 gives the poet occasion to portray that orb (572–612) in minerological and alchemical terms as the arch-chemist of the finite universe. In the retrospect of the War in Heaven*, Book 6, Lucifer delivers a mineralogical lecture to the revolting angels (472–83) and proceeds with them (507–19) to mine the heavenly mold for materials with which to fashion engines of artillery. Finally, in Book 11, Michael includes in his preview of the history of Adam's progeny a scene (564–73) of primitive prediluvian metallurgical activity. Perhaps it should be noted that, wherever the location, Milton regularly uses conceptions properly associated with terrene mineralogy to body forth those of the celestial and infernal regions, in this respect following the practice of his own Raphael who, in his conversation with prelapsarian Adam, "lik'ning spiritual to corporal forms" measures "things of Heav'n by things on Earth."

In the following sketch of mineralogical theory and its application to PL, space permits only limited reference to a few sixteenth- and seventeenth-century authorities. (For full discussion, see Edgar H. Duncan, Osiris 11 : 386–421.)

Aristotle's Meteorologica is the starting place of mineralogical theorizing in Western culture. In Bk. 1 of that treatise are posited two exhalations, one vaporous, the other dry and smoky (in themselves combinations of the four elements : air, water, earth, and fire), which are the material cause of all vegetation on the surface of the earth and of metals, gems, and minerals beneath its surface. These are the "materials dark and crude / Of spiritous and fierie spume" of Lucifer's lecture in PL 6, which, in turn, recall the allusion in the Pro Arte quoted above. It seems to have been the Arabian natural philosopher Avicenna who, in the era of

Islamic appropriation and modification of ancient science, identified Aristotle's two exhalations in their proximate subterranean manifestations with mercury and sulphur. Translated into Latin probably by the tenth century, Avicenna's treatise became attached to the Latin version of the Metorology as its book four and, as such, introduced the "sulphur-mercury hypothesis" into the literature of medieval European alchemy, where it is generally and variously expounded as the material cause in the natural generation of metals. In the thirteenth century, for example, the Summa Perfectionis of Geber devotes several chapters to it, and it is explained in the Speculum Alchemiae attributed to Roger Bacon. According to the theory, each of the six solid metals known to the Middle Ages—from the lowest to the highest, from lead to gold—is a combination in varying degrees of quality or quantity of mercury and sulphur. The fearful and wonderful elaborations, explanations, and theorizings that the hypothesis spawned, wherein the "sulphur" and "mercury" are treated as hypostatical essences that bafflingly are and are not subject to sensible experience and are variously related to the common varieties of those substances, became the inheritance of Renaissance mineralogical treatises such as those listed above.

How thoroughly the hypothesis maintained its ground is indicated by the manner in which Alonso Barba's Art of Metals disposes of a possible contrary view, mineralogy by divine fiat :

Many, to avoid difficult disputes of this nature, do hold with the vulgar; that at the Creation of the world God Almighty made the veins of the Mettals in the same condition, as we now find them at this day; herein doing nature a great affront by denying her (without reason) a productive vertue in this matter, which is allowed unto her in all other sublunary things; moreover, that experience in divers places hath manifested the contrary.

Here is John Webster's statement of the hypothesis :

Aristotle makes the humidity of water and the dryness of earth, to be the matter of all Minerals: the dryness of earth to participate with fire, and the humidity of water with air; as *Zabarella* interprets it: so that to make a perfect mixt body, the four Elements do concur: and to make the mixture more perfect, these must be resolved into vapour or exhalation, by the heat of fire, or influence from the Sun and other Planets, as the efficient cause of their generation. . . . The ancient chymical philosophers [called them] Sulphur and Mercury.

Not surprisingly, the sulphur-mercury hypothesis lies in the background of the universe of *PL* as providing the material cause of metals and minerals.

For the efficient cause, the situation is not so simple as the quotation from Webster seems to imply. The fact is that an important development of Avicenna's sulphur-mercury hypothesis in medieval natural science, carried over into the Renaissance, was the differentiation of mercury as the passive, material cause of metallic substances and sulphur as the active, efficient cause; or, alternatively, two sulphurs were identified, one passive and material, the other active and efficient. The latter seems to be in the background of the description in *PL* 1. 674, of metallic ore as "The work of Sulphur." It is in keeping with the statement of Barba, who writes that sulphur "is esteemed to be nearest of kin to the element of fire, of any compound substance. The chymists call it the Masculine seed, and Natures first agent in all generation." To this add the opinion expressed in William Johnson's *Lexicon Chymicum,* published in England in 1652, that "sulphur is . . . a vapor hot and dry, the cause and father of metals . . . burning, hot, and most pure"; that variety by means of which nature makes gold Johnson denominates "pure fire." And this must have been the variety responsible for the ore mined in Hell, for when the crew "Op'nd into the Hill a spacious wound/[They] dig'd out ribs of gold" *PL* 1. 599–600.

On the other hand, Sir John Pettus contends in *Fodinae Regales* that when

God breathed upon the "Face of the Waters" the "boisterous waters" turned into hills and mountains, the spaces between into valleys, and that in both "the Seminal *Virtues* of all *Sublunary* things being locked up, [have been] more durably *preserved* . . . ; and yet from thence they are transmitted through *Terrene Pores,* either from their own *Exuberancies,* or the *Sun* or *Stars Extractions* into *various* and *visible Forms."* Satan's statement of efficient causes in the mineralogical lecture in Heaven, "touch't / With Heav'ns ray," "pregnant with infernal flame" (6. 479–80, 483) seems closer to Pettus's than to Barba's or Johnson's.

That the conflict between these two accounts of efficient causes is apparent rather than real may be demonstrated by an examination of the cosmogony of Robert Fludd. For Fludd as for Pettus and for Milton, the active principle used by God in the creation of the universe was light or fire, identified with the Spirit of God, which brooded over the Mosaic waters and thus created the world. It worked by thrusting downward and toward a center the shadows of the primordial substance, forming thus on the first day the empyrean, at whose center was the earth; and on this and the two succeeding days the *corpus solare,* the *corpus vegetabile,* and the *corpus minerale,* using in turn as aid the portions of light remaining over from each preceding day's operations. The two latter lights, which Fludd denominates secondary and tertiary, are weaker than the primary light, being infected by the *tenebrae* against which they have had to struggle. Some portions of them were even held captive, as it were, in the respective *corpora,* along apparently with some of the primary light as well. Fludd graphically describes the condition of the tertiary light captured in the *corpus minerale,* or the interior of the earth :

thus a residual part of that other mass proper to this lowest region embraced in its very viscera some quantity of this accompanying light. . . . But because the disposition of light is naturally to attenuate . . . , the portions of tertiary light are not sufficient to subtilise and purify the dense and rebellious spirits of the lowest shadows. Whence it happens that matter conquers . . . and the form of light is miserably . . . incarcerated in the womb of this matter on account of the too great constriction of the pores in its body.

Thus Fludd accounts for the grossness of body and "unagility of spirit" of the proximate materials of minerals and metals that make them seemingly devoid of life. This though is not the end:

> But because the desire of any corporeal thing is toward perfection, and since no perfection can be acquired except through that motion which some portion of light produces, so the little light . . . though weak, as (so to speak) only a spark, desires to perpetuate its body, and in the mode of fire to survive its earthy and watery disposition; its own spirit mediating, it struggles to subject that whole rebellious matter to its will and nature. . . . For the spark of light in the mineral body does not cease to labor, and, gradually proceeding as conqueror, it reduces the whole mass of its body into its own nature, active quality, and splendor, as is openly demonstrated in the generation of gold.

That the little spark does not do all this without outside help is made clear when we are told that it "draws to its aid virtues of lucid influences which penetrate even to the centre of the earth." For these "lucid influences" we have to thank the *corpus solare* which, created on the first day, became in the fourth day the Sun as we know it in Milton, both the repository of primary light and the source whence that light sheds its beneficent beams on and into the earth. Small wonder that such a sun became for Milton the imagined seat of the Philosopher's Stone.

So the "sulphur" in Hell is identical with the "infernal flame" beneath the soil of Heaven, and both in turn are ultimately of the same essence as the "ray" that emanates from the Sun; for all are but manifestations of the "light" that God originally breathed upon the primordial waters. With this conclusion

no mineralogical theorist of the Renaissance would seriously disagree. Paracelsus, for one at least, went even further, fully to identify material and efficient causes. In his *Short Catechism of Alchemy* the question is put: "What is actually the living gold of the Philosophers?" And the answer:

> It is exclusively the fire of Mercury, or that igneous virtue, contained in the radical moisture, to which it has already communicated the fixity and the nature of the Sulphur, whence it has emanated, the mercurial character of the whole substance of philosophical sulphur permitting it to be alternately termed mercury.

Sulphur is mercury; mercury, sulphur; all is one. Thus can mineralogical-alchemical theory of the seventeenth century accommodate itself to the monistic world view of *PL*. [EHD]

**MINISTRY OF REDEMPTION.** The classic definition of Christian redemption, the deliverance of man from sin, suffering, and death by the incarnation and death of Jesus Christ, appears in the first chapter of Paul's epistle to the Ephesians. Even though Milton claimed the doctrine, the sincerity of his adherence to the Reformation formula of reconciliation with God solely through faith\* in the redemption has been questioned by advocates of E. M. W. Tillyard's statement in 1930; few would now challenge C. A. Patrides's 1966 defense of Milton's whole-hearted avowal. (*See* ATONEMENT; JUSTIFICATION.) In his discussion in the fourteenth, fifteenth, and sixteenth chapters of the first book of *CD*, Milton defines redemption as "that act whereby CHRIST, BEING SENT IN THE FULNESS OF TIME, REDEEMED ALL BELIEVERS AT THE PRICE OF HIS OWN BLOOD, BY HIS OWN VOLUNTARY ACT, CONFORMABLY TO THE ETERNAL COUNSEL AND GRACE OF GOD THE FATHER." Milton continues to stress the humiliation of both Christ's human and divine persons while he was earning man's exaltation. (*See* INCARNATION; MESSIANIC HUMILIATION AND EXALTATION.)

Milton emphasizes Christ's ministry of

redemption throughout his prose defenses of personal, political, and spiritual freedom from his statement in the earliest pamphlet, *Ref,* that all Christians, having been "wash'd with *Christs* blood," have freedom of belief. He extends the ministry of redemption to include personal Christian liberty* in the divorce tracts of the mid-1640s and to include political freedom in thes regicide pamphlets of the late 1640s and the defenses of the English commonwealth in the 1650s. The sense of freedom he derived from redemption culminates in the magnificent prayer that magistrates not bereave Christians "of that sacred libertie which our Saviour with his own blood purchas'd for them" (*CivP*).

Milton founds much of his poetry on his sense of the ministry of redemption. The early series of poems on events in Christ's life are based on Christ's redemption of John Milton with Christian mankind : *Nat* celebrates the fact that the incarnate Word "Our great Redemption from above did bring"; the unfinished *Passion* was to have dwelled on the crucifixion; and *Circum* describes the first physical pain of Christ's infancy as an emblem of his compassionate satisfaction of that penalty divine justice exacted for man's sins.

*PL* is a poem of salvation in its stress on the redemptive pattern established by the Father's* request and the Son's* offer for sacrifices after God's definition of the redemption of mankind during the dialogue in heaven opening Book 3. Michael describes the ministry of redemption in detail for Adam as he recounts the history of humanity as one of human sins and God's legal exactions until Christ's sacrificial life and death, "Proclaiming Life to all who shall believe / In his redemption, and that his obedience / Imputed becomes theirs by Faith," recovers bliss. Adam is both prepared for descent to the world beneath Paradise and ultimately is saved by his recognition of Christ's ministry of redemption, "Taught this by his example whom I

now / Acknowledge my Redeemer ever blest."

*PR* does not substitute the temptation in the wilderness for the atonement, as was first suggested by eighteenth-century editors. Rather it portrays Milton's sense of the ministry of redemption, which occurs throughout Christ's entire lifetime on earth, and Christ's preparation for the final and most severe requirement, as the angelic choir imply in conclusion : "Now enter, and begin to save mankind." [IC]

**MINSHULL, ELIZABETH,** Milton's third wife. She was baptized in Wistaston, Cheshire, on December 30, 1638. Her father was Randle Minshull, a yeoman farmer of Wistaston and Nantwich; her mother was Anne Boote Minshull. Through the negotiations of Dr. Nathan Paget*, her grandmother's nephew and an old friend of Milton's, she became acquainted with the blind poet. On February 24, 1663, in the Church of St. Mary Aldermary, the 54-year-old widower took as his bride the 24-year-old spinster. Unlike Milton's marriage to Katherine Woodcock, over whose wedding a Justice of the Peace had been required to officiate in compliance with Cromwell's Marriage Act of 1653, that to Elizabeth had the services of a clergyman, probably Dr. Robert Gell*, a Fellow at Christ's College*, Cambridge, during Milton's school years there. In 1661 Milton had moved to Jewin Street, and to this home he brought his young wife. They moved to the house in Artillery Walk, Bunhill Fields, around 1669.

Little is known about the domestic situation as it now existed, with three teen-aged daughters and a step-mother in her early twenties. According to interviews with Milton's granddaughter, Elizabeth Foster, in 1737–1738 and 1750, and other early biographical materials, the new mother and her step-daughters did not get along. It was perhaps she who arranged for them to learn skills like embroidering. Another unsympathetic report, as recorded by Jonathan Richardson*, describes her as "a Termagant" (*Early Lives*, p. 280). However, when John Aubrey* visited her in 1681 to collect biographical materials on her late husband, he found her "a gentle person," of "a peaceful and agreeable humour."

Whatever her relationship to the daughters may have been, she was apparently a suitable helpmate to her now very dependent husband. He was not able to appreciate the personal beauty of his "Betty" (reportedly she had golden or red hair), but he enjoyed her singing. She had "a good voice but no ear," he was fond of saying. Although she was probably not well educated, they may have discussed English poetry together, since she asserted later with authority that her husband's favorite English poets had been Spenser*, Shakespeare*, and Cowley*; Dryden*, who had visited them, was a mere rhymist rather than a poet. There is no reason to believe other than that she brought into the household an element of calm and understanding that Milton needed in the difficult years of the Restoration when he was struggling financially and artistically. The only jarring note in their relationship may have been her alleged attempt to induce him to accept an unfounded and unlikely offer from Charles II* to become Latin Secretary.

Shortly before Milton's death in 1674 he stated to his brother Christopher that Elizabeth, his "loving wife," was to have all his goods upon his death, the daughters to receive only their mother's unpaid dowry. When this nuncupative will* was held invalid on technical grounds, Elizabeth paid each daughter £100 to relinquish further claims to their father's estate. In addition to the small amount of goods and money that Milton left her, Elizabeth inherited some of his papers and letters, which she told Aubrey she gave to Phillips. In 1680, perhaps under financial stress, she sold to Samuel Symmons* for £8 all her rights to *PL*. Seven years after Milton's decease, his widow retired to Nantwich, where she lived frugally until her death on about August 23, 1727. She may have been buried near the chapel of the Anabaptists in Barker Street. On August 22 she had made out her will, leaving her possessions to various nephews and nieces in Nantwich. [AA]

## MINTURNO, ANTONIO SEBASTIANI

(1500–1574), Italian humanist and cleric. Son of Antonio Sebastiani and Rita Magistra, he was called Minturno after either the ancient name of his birthplace or his maternal uncle. He studied philosophy, classics, and Hebrew at Traetto (now Minturno), Naples (under Agostino Nifo), Sessa, Aurunca, Pisa, and (after a stay at Rome) again at Naples, where he was elected to the Pontanian Academy in 1526. After serving the Pignatelli family in Naples and Sicily and the Duke of Nocera (1538–1551), he was called to the University of Pisa and also taught at Florence and Rome. Through Pope Julius II, he was named Bishop of Ugento in 1559, in which dignity he participated in the Council of Trent, and in 1565 became Bishop of Crotone, a post retained until his death. Though an author of poetry and of minor treatises on literature and ecclesiastical matters, Minturno is best known as an interpreter of Aristotle*. His *De poeta* (1559), which he revised in Italian as *L'arte poetica* (1563) to conform to the spirit of the Counter-Reformation, is a major Cinquecento commentary on the *Poetics*, which was known and used by critics such as Ben Jonson* or Sir Philip Sidney*. When in *Educ* (4 : 286), Milton speaks of Tasso*, Castelvetro*, Mazzoni*, and "others" as authorities on the "sublime Art" of poetry, he may have Minturno in mind, though he never mentions him explicitly. The homeopathic analogy between psychology* and medicine in the Preface to *SA* has sometimes been thought to have followed Minturno's "ethico-medicinal" interpretation of catharsis*, but one cannot conclude that the two critics think of catharsis in the same way. Medicinal analogies notwithstanding, Minturno views catharsis as an extirpative purgation of emotions, not a tempering or setting of passions in "right tune" as stated in *RCG* (3 : 238) or the Preface to *SA*. Moreover, the emotions purged are undesirable passions other than pity and fear, not Milton's pity, fear, and such "like" passions. [PRS]

**MIRABEAU, HONORE GABRIEL RIQUETI, COMTE DE** (1749–1791), French revolutionist. After a rather dissolute youth marked by family difficulties but wide reading, the revolutionary developments in the later 1780s gave him a ready forum for his forceful writing and speeches. His unpublicized position seems to have favored a constitutional monarchy somewhat on the model of England, but circumstances forced him for a while to represent the cause of the people against that of the court. Beginning in the early summer of 1790 he became a private political adviser to Louis, who in turn paid off Mirabeau's large personal debts. In January 1791 he was elected to the National Assembly, which he served briefly as president before his death that spring from natural causes.

It is clear that Mirabeau read Milton attentively and enthusiastically in 1788, finding especially in his prose works support for the revolutionary principles then being argued in France. His plea for freedom of the press, *Sur la Liberté de la Presse,* appeared late in 1788, asserting that a sound Estates-General could not be established without free exchange of ideas. In *Areop* he found the arguments that he needed; his book paraphrases or directly translates much of Milton's pamphlet. In particular, he concludes that in England a free press as Milton had defined it had become a reality and to this fact the country owed its political strength.

The next year there appeared anonymously the *Théorie de la Royauté, d'après la Doctrine de Milton,* for which he probably wrote the prefatory material, followed by a free translation or paraphrase of *1Def* in which he may have collaborated with J.-B. Salaville. The former is a wholly appreciative if sometimes factually erroneous life. Following Toland's* biography, it stresses especially Milton's prose works, examining them in some detail so as to show how over a

century earlier Milton had arrived at sound political principles. Thus its author strongly approved of his arguments to abolish tithes, to reduce church power, and to permit divorce* on less rigorous terms than the church or state had permitted. Long quotations from *Areop* again appear, together with excerpts from most of the other prose treatises. The contemporary influence that these books had has not been examined; indeed, no full study exists of Milton's influence upon the Revolution. For a preliminary investigation see Don M. Wolfe, *Publications of the Modern Language Association* 49 : 1116–28. [WBH]

**MIRACLES.** In *CD* Milton expresses the traditional Christian view of miracles, as a manifestation of "the extraordinary providence of God . . . whereby God produces some effect out of the usual order of nature, or gives the power of producing the same effect to whomsoever he may appoint. . . . God alone is the primary author of miracles, as he only is able to invert that order of things which he has himself appointed" (15 : 95). Miracles are used "to manifest the divine power, and confirm our faith," as well as "to increase the condemnation of unbelievers by taking away all excuse for unbelief" (pp. 95–97). Faith in miracles enables one either to be "endued with the power of working miracles in the name of God," or to believe "that another is endued with this power" (pp. 363–65). Milton insists that miracles should not always be expected in the visible church, nor do they possess "inherent efficacy in producing belief." He commends those who believe without miracles (16 : 227).

In *PL, PR,* and *SA* Milton exploits the inclusion of miracles for epic* and tragic* effect, by creating wonder and marvel as an element of the epic marvelous. Events of miraculous nature are usually signaled by some form of the words *wonder* or *amazement.* The proof texts cited in *CD* encouraged this connection, since Psalm 122 : 18, translated "who only doeth wondrous things," refers to God as sole source of miracles, and 2 Thessalonians 2:9 identifies the anti-Christ "whose coming is after the power of Satan, with all power and signs and lying wonders" as capable of performing limited acts that only *seem* miracles but are in fact "false wonders" and far inferior to God's true miracles. In *Mask* Comus works a variety of apparently miraculous works, perhaps better called magic: he changes into animals those who drink from his cup, and he fixes the Lady in her chair. But he cannot touch her mind, and magic responds to magic in the boys' employment of haemony* and in Sabrina's counter charms. *PL* exhibits both the "wondrous things of God" and the "lying wonders" of Satan. The changes of shape by Satan and of size by the devils, and the bridge constructed by Sin and Death, are examples of the "lying wonders" performed within the designated power of devils. The crucial instance is Satan's deception of Eve, whose acceptance of Satan's lying report is based on false information and evidence that she takes as report of the miraculous, though her resulting actions only *seem* to be an appropriate response to belief in true miracles. Ironically, the nearest reference to miracle in the sequence is Satan's address to Eve as "sole Wonder" (9.534), a tribute to the true miracle of God's creation of man, subverted here for flattery rather than evidencing belief.

Of true miracles in *PL,* examples appear in Christ's defeat of the rebel angels* and the creation* of the world and of man. Adam wonders greatly at the account of the War in Heaven*. Satan as well as Adam and Eve marvels at creation, though it does not lead Satan to worship its Creator as it does Adam and Eve. *PR* is in some respects unified by the use of miracles as evidence of deity. The signs accompanying Christ's baptism precipitate Satan's attempts to force Christ to act miraculously as evidence of his self-identity. The fast in the wilderness is miraculous because Christ feels no hunger, a violation of natural law and therefore no example supporting Lent (2.247–

55). Satan's disguises, the banquet in the wilderness, the storm, the transportation from place to place, concluding on the temple pinnacle, are allowed instances of his power within the limits set "from above" (1.496). In the final test, Christ miraculously *does* stand on the pinnacle "with Godlike force endu'd" (4.602) as evidence of his divinity, while Satan "smitten with amazement" falls (4.562). In contrast to Satan's banquet, Christ is then miraculously fed by angels; Satan is advised to "learn with awe / To dread the Son of God" (4.625–26). Thus the brief epic begins and ends with miracle, but only as God allows and not by temptation or challenge from Satan. Appropriate wonder attaches to Christ as the champion of God, in this poem as in *PL*.

In *SA* Milton adjusts his use of miracles to fit the requirements for another "faithful Champion" (1751), a tragic hero "with might endu'd / Above the Sons of men" (1294–95), who falls from "the top of wondrous glory" to "lowest pitch of abject fortune" (167–69). He regains his heroic stature in his final heroic deed, which he himself announces to the gathered Philistines: after performing feats of strength for them "not without wonder or delight beheld," Samson promises a feat "as with amaze shall strike all who behold" (1642–1645), ironically fulfilling literally the intent to "strike" by pulling down the roof, through restored faith in his God of miracles. His whole life has been miraculous, that is, out of the order of nature, so that when his father recounts the miracle of his birth and his miraculous hair, symbol of his "gift of strength" (47), he accurately labels his son the "miracle of men" (363), for the exploits have been performed by "Divine impulsion" (422). The climax is anticipated throughout, as when Manoa reminds Samson that God must plan to use him further:

> why else this strength
> Yet remaining in these locks?
> His might continues in thee not for naught,
> Nor shall his wondrous gifts be frustrate thus.
> (586–89)

Harapha laments that Samson's reputation for "wonders" (1095) cannot be tested against his own giant strength, and suggests "some Magician's Art" (1133) responsible for Samson's exploits. The Chorus anticipates the marvelous outcome as Samson leaves for the feast, by reminding him that

> never was from Heaven imported
> Measure of strength so great to mortal seed,
> As in thy wond'rous actions hath been seen.
> (1438–40)

Finally, the delayed explanation of the cause of the tremendous shouts heard in the distance allows speculation that Samson's eyesight has been "by miracle restor'd." The actual event demonstrates a miracle of even greater persuasion to belief in Israel's God, yet enabling Samson to finish heroically . . . a life Heroic" (1710–11). Thus even while maintaining orthodox Christian beliefs regarding miracles, Milton adapts miraculous events to suit his epic and tragic requirements. [JLH]

**MOLOCH,** whose name, signifying "king," derives from *Malach,* meaning "to reign," was usually thought to subsume all kinds of idols, since he was the first idol invented by superstition and thus the source of all idolatry*. This recognition caused Milton to alter the usual infernal hierarchy, which presents Beelzebub* as prince of the first rank, by making Moloch the chief representative of "false gods . . . adored as idols" and by having him represent as well the third rank, the vessels of anger and fury (usually associated with Belial), the fourth rank, the "malicious revenging Devils" (usually associated with Asmodaeus), and the seventh rank, the destroyers who cause war, tumult, and uproar (usually associated with Abaddon). (See Robert Burton*, *Anatomy of Melancholy* [1621], I. II. i. 2, and Henry Cornelius Agrippa, *Three Books of Occult Philosophy* [1651], pp. 397–400.) A god of fire, notorious for demanding the sacrifice of children (Lev. 18 : 21, 20 : 2-4; Jer. 32 : 35) and for leading men into whoredom (Book of Jubilees 30 : 10; Lev. 20 : 5), Moloch or Molech is "the abomination" of the Ammonites and Moabites to whom Solomon built a temple "in the valley of the children of Hinnom" (1 Kings 11 : 7; 2 Kings 23 : 10; Amos 5 : 26). He is associated in Scripture with Malcham and Milcom (Zeph. 1 : 5; 1 Kings 11 : 5, 33; 2 Kings 23 : 13) and also with Remphan (Acts 7 : 43) which, John Diodati* explains, is the basis of the commonplace opinion that Moloch, Saturn, and the devil are one. The identification of Moloch with Remphan is also behind the incidental tradition that associates Moloch with Mars.

Cognizant of both these traditions, Charles Dunster* remarks that Milton preserves the connection between Moloch and Mars in his depiction of the devil in Book 2 of *PL*; but Dunster also contends, with reference to the usual association of Moloch and Saturn, that Milton did not "suppose it" to be a valid one, or "at least did not attend to the supposition" (Henry John Todd*, *Poetical Works* [1809], 2 : 329). *Nat* and also *PL* suggest otherwise. While no specific connection is drawn between Moloch and Saturn in *Nat,* Milton mentions Moloch in the context of a host of solar deities who are routed by Christ's coming. He is clearly aware of the traditional connection between Moloch and Saturn and of their association with time and destruction. The same is true of Milton's depiction of Moloch in the council scene as "Scepter'd King" (2. 43), an epithet that recalls the association of Moloch and Saturn with pride, malice, and destruction (see Alexander Ross*, *Pansebeia* [1672], p. 519, and *Mystagogus Poeticus* [1672], pp. 378–82).

However much Milton's portrait of Moloch may owe to "the Aristotelian concept of rashness" or to Dante's* Amata (see Robert C. Fox, *Die Neueren Sprachen* [1962], pp. 389–95), to Shakespeare's Hotspur (Marjorie Nicolson, *John Milton: A Reader's Guide to His Poetry* [1963], p. 205), to descriptions of the statue of Kronos at Carthage (see Thomas

Keightley, *Account of Milton* [1855], p. 471), or to Oliver Cromwell (see James Holly Hanford*, *A Milton Handbook* [1946], p. 198), the best gloss on Moloch is a passage from George Sandys, *A Relation of a Journey* (1615). (But John Selden's* account in *De D[i]is Syris* (1617) 1. 6 and 2. 1 is also illuminating.) In *Nat*, Milton writes:

And sullen *Moloch* fled,
Hath left in shadows dred,
  His burning Idol all of blackest hue;
In vain with Cymbals ring,
They call the grisly King,
  In dismal dance about the furnace blue;
The brutish gods of *Nile* as fast,
*Isis* and *Orus*, and the Dog *Anubis* hast.
                                         (205–12)

If Milton did not have Sandys's account in mind, he as least drew upon the tradition it records:

> we descended into the vally of Gehinnon [where] . . . the Hebrews sacrificed their children to *Molech,* an Idoll of brasse, having the head of a calfe, the rest of a kingly figure, with arms extended to receive the miserable sacrifice, seared to death with burning embracements. For the Idoll was hollow within, and filled with fire. And lest their lamentable shreeks should sad the hearts of their parents, the Priests of *Molech* did deafe their eares with the continuall clangs of trumpets and timbrels; whereupon its was called the valley of *Tophet*. But the good Josias brake the Idoll in peeces, hewed downe the groves, and ordained that place (before a Paradise) should be for ever a receptacle for dead carcasses and the filth of the citie. Gehenna, for the impiety committed therein, is used for hell by our Saviour. (Sandys, p. 186)

Milton has selected those materials "most susceptible of poetical enlargement" and "most interesting to the fancy" (Thomas Warton*, *Poems Upon Several Occasions* [1785], p. 283). The "cymbals," customarily used to "out-sound" the "lamentable cries" of dying children (John Diodati, *Annotations* [1657], gloss on Lev. 18 : 21), are used in Milton's poem by the "brutish gods" to call for the return of their "grisly King." The ironies implicit in Milton's allusion to Moloch

are underscored by Blake* in his depiction, *The Flight of Moloch* (one of six designs for *Nat*). The god who exacted from parents the sacrifice of children is shown fleeing as the Christ-child stands miraculously, triumphantly, before the idol.

This and other traditional associations stand behind the depiction of Moloch in *PL* who, according to C. S. Lewis*, is "the simplest of fiends; a mere rat in a trap" (*A Preface to Paradise Lost* [1942], p. 102). In the catalogue of the pagan deities in *PL,* Moloch is mentioned first; he is a "grim Idol," a "horrid king besmear'd with blood / Of human sacrifice" (1. 392–96), whose temple was built "right against the Temple of God" in "The pleasant Valley of *Hinnom* . . . the Type of Hell" (1. 400–405). In this "Grove of . . . homicide" lustful Orgies were held that turned "lust hard by hate" (1. 415–17). Moloch's speech (2. 51–105) to the infernal council is in line with the character here delineated and, unlike others' speeches, reflects his "true Ethos" (John M. Steadman, *"Ethos and Dianoia*: Character and Rhetoric in *Paradise Lost," Language and Style in Milton,* ed. Ronald David Emma and John T. Shawcross [1967], p. 200). It is also neutralized by the recollection that for all his ferocity "*Moloc* furious King . . . with shattered Armes / And uncouth paine fled bellowing" when "pierc'd" by Gabriel (6. 354–62).

The "first" to come in the epic catalogue, Moloch is also the first to speak in the epic debate. Holding tenaciously to the politics of force, having learned nothing from the Battle in Heaven, the "Scepter'd King / Stood up, the strongest and fiercest Spirit / That fought in Heav'n; now fiercer by despair" (2. 43–45), to propose "open Warr" (2. 51). Rather than being less than God, Moloch prefers "not to be at all" (2. 46–48) and thus urges the devils to use "force" and with it to turn their "Tortures into horrid Arms / Against the Torturer" (2. 60–64). This speech reveals Moloch as an integral part of Satan—"the Satan of the 'fixt' mind and absolute courage, unafraid of Death" (Arnold Stein, *Answerable Style* [1953], p. 51).

Forming a splendid contrast with the speech by Belial (which immediately follows), Moloch's sentiments are "rash, audacious, and desperate" (*Paradise Lost,* ed. Thomas Newton\* [1751], 1 : 90) and if, in them, he resembles any other Miltonic character, it is Milton's Samson (see Irene Samuel, *Calm of Mind,* ed. Joseph Wittreich [1971], pp. 235ff.), not Milton's God (see Moncure Daniel Conway, *Demonology and Devil-Lore* [1880], 1 : 163). Moloch's preference for annihilation to shame and misery and his proposal of open war are in perfect accord with his violent, impetuous nature, and so too is the form of his speech, which defies the first rule of oratory. The orator, Milton insisted, should begin by eliciting the good will of his audience. Not even in the treatment of an ordinary subject should he be so hasty as to forgo an appropriate introduction. This counsel Moloch ignores, as does Satan, who "all impassioned" and with "no delay / Of Preface" (9. 675–76, 678) proceeds with the temptation of Adam and Eve. And if Moloch's speech defies the rules of rhetoric\*, it also ignores those of logic\*. Moloch speaks of an inner principle of motion that propels the devils upward of their own accord; but as Frank Manley observes, "anyone at all familiar with the traditional Platonic-Aristotelian cosmos would have seen the error at once and delighted in the irony. For the motion Moloch is talking about comes only from the love of God" (*Modern Language Notes* 76: 110–16).

Concerned with character apart from rhetoric, Robert Fox focuses attention upon Moloch as a reflection of "the wrathful side of Satan's soul," Moloch's countenance revealing the desire for "desperate revenge" (*Texas Studies in Language and Literature* 2 : 275). In Fox's scheme, the triad of vices—pride, envy, and wrath—point to the infernal trinity composed of Satan, Beelzebub, and Moloch, who individually embody the

vices gathered together in the figure of Satan. It is more probable, however, that Milton's scheme, drawing upon the tradition of the three-headed Beelzebub and upon the Cabala, which identifies Moloch and Satan, intends for Moloch, Belial, and Mammon to represent the three faces of evil, identified with the three master categories of sin and with the threefold temptation process, which is at the the thematic and dramatic center of Milton's poem. [JAW]

**MONARCHY, MILTON'S VIEWS ON:** *see* POLITICS, MILTON'S.

**MONBODDO, JAMES BURNETT, LORD** (1714–1799), author of *Of the Origin and Progress of Language* (1733–1792, 6 vols.), a comprehensive discussion of the history of language. Monboddo states : "I . . . quote [Milton] oftener than any other English writer, because I consider him as the best standard for style, and all the ornaments of speech, that we have in our language" (3 :68). His huge work consists in part of a comprehensive analysis of Milton's language, which Monboddo sees as heavily influenced by Latin and Greek, yet still a combination of the best English, these classical languages, and others, like Italian. For example, Milton uses Latinate words for sweetness or for smoothness, as in describing the opening of the gates of heaven, while he uses "Saxon" words to express the harshness of the opening of the gates of hell (2 : 405–6).

In his critical evaluations of Milton, Monboddo attacked Samuel Johnson\*: "Dr. Johnson certainly has not genius enough to comprehend even the beauties of Milton, who I think is the only poet in English that can be compared with Homer" (letter to Sir George Baker, 2 October 1782, in *Lord Monboddo and his Contemporaries,* ed. William Knight [1900], p. 214). He disliked the subject of *PL;* rather, the subject of *Mask* is better chosen, and therefore it is the better poem, although the "rhetoric" of the epic is greater and nearer to Homer) [ibid.].

Yet he describes *SA* as "the last and most faultless" of all of Milton's poetical works (3 : 71). [WM]

## MON(C)K, GEORGE

**MON(C)K, GEORGE** (1608–1670) military leader. He was born at Potheridge, in Devonshire. He entered military service in 1625, campaigning abroad until the Bishops' Wars. After service in Ireland, he joined the king's forces in England in 1643. Taken prisoner by Fairfax* at Nantwich in 1644, he was released in 1646 on condition that he employ his military talents solely in the Irish wars. In July 1650, however, Monk took part in the invasion of Scotland and in 1651 Cromwell* made him commander-in-chief of the forces in Scotland. With the death of Oliver Cromwell, and the abdication of Richard Cromwell, the Commonwealth threatened to develop into a military dictatorship. To forestall this, Monk led his army from Scotland to London, first in support of the existing Rump Parliament, then in the revival of Parliament as it had been in 1648, and finally in the restoration of the Stuarts to the English throne.

Milton, trusting in Monk's dedication to the Commonwealth, supplemented his final Republican pamphlet, *Way,* with a letter addressed personally to Monk (according to John Toland* in 1698), entitled *The Present Means and Brief Delineation of a Free Commonwealth, Easy to be Put in Practice and that Without Delay* (March or April 1660). In this letter Milton repeated, substantially, the recommendations contained in *Way.* His special appeal to Monk was that the General use his prestige and, if necessary, his army to impose a free Commonwealth upon the English people. Monk did not respond to Milton's appeal.

After the Restoration, Monk was created First Duke of Albemarle (July 7, 1660) and captain-general of the army for life (August 3, 1660). He died on January 3, 1670. [JLG]

**MONISM:** *see* METAPHYSICS.

**MOORE FAMILY:** *see* AGAR, THOMAS.

## MORE, ALEXANDER

**MORE, ALEXANDER,** Latinized as Morus (1616–1670), was the son of a Scottish Presbyterian clergyman and a French mother. He was born at Castres, Languedoc, where his father served as pastor of a French Protestant church. After preliminary education at home, he went to Geneva for the study of theology. There, in open competition, when he was only twenty-three, he was appointed to the professorship of Greek in the University, a post previously held by such distinguished scholars as Casaubon, Scaliger*, and Beza*. After three years, 1639–1642, he was elected to the chair of theology, vacated by Frederick Spanheim*. After he became Rector of the University in 1645, he held both offices and served as pastor in the city until 1649, when he left Geneva under attack for unorthodox teaching and immorality. The personal problem of More is very difficult to assess. It appears beyond doubt that he was a scholar of great ability and an eloquent preacher. Yet, wherever he served, questions of his orthodoxy were raised and charges of sexual improprieties became current. Positive evidence indicates that he was the object of personal animosities, particularly jealousies, that were bitter and relentless. On the other hand, documents on file at Geneva (Affaire Alexander Morus, MS. Fr. 468, Bibliothèque Publique et Universitaire) show conclusively that charges of specific acts of fornication were certified by officials of the church, and that he was forced publicly to affirm his belief in fundamental doctrines of Christian faith. (Among his improprieties was an affair with Claudia Pelletta, named by Milton; see Yale *Prose* 4 : 565, n80; 566, n83.) And there is evidence that he manifested contemptuousness of manner toward colleagues. The two points of attack that Milton presses most steadily against him in *2Def,* however, grew out of the poet's uncritical acceptance of rumor. They were (1) that More, under promise of marriage, seduced a maid to Madame Salmasius named Elizabeth Guerret, variously called Bontia and Pontia, a charge of which More was completely exonerated in court action brought by More himself; and (2) that he was the author of *Regii Sanguinis Clamor ad Coelum Adversus Parricidas Anglicanos.* Though More was not the author, he contributed to it some very gross and abusive prefatory material, which he induced the printer Adrian Vlacq* to sign, and he was, in effect supervising editor of the tract. The actual author, Peter du Moulin*, sent his text to Salmasius, who entrusted it to More for transmittal to Vlacq, the printer. Under the circumstances, it is not difficult to understand why Milton and many others accepted the rumor of More's authorship. Though given impressive testimonials, More left Geneva in July 1649 under a cloud of suspicion as to his orthodoxy and his character, and proceeded to Holland, where he was warmly received and admired as a preacher. He was desired in Lyons, London, and Edinburgh, but he accepted a call, arranged for him by Salmasius, to become co-pastor and theology lecturer in the Walloon Church at Middleburg in Zeeland Province. He remained there for three years (1649–1652) and became an important officer in the Walloon Synod. But personal problems came to the fore, and in July 1652 he received, at his own request, letters of dismissal. He had actually left in April and gone to Amsterdam, where he accepted an invitation, rejected before he went to Middleburg, to be professor of Sacred History. He spent most of 1652 in Leyden as a guest in the household of Salmasius, his faithful admirer and friend. With Madame Salmasius, however, he developed a bitter feud, resulting largely from his alleged affair with Elizabeth Guerret, her maid. He delayed assumption of his duties at Amsterdam in order to travel in Italy, which he believed was a fertile field for the propagation of evangelical religion. He appears, however, to have devoted his visit more to cultural pursuits than to religion. Ironically, he became acquainted with Lucas Holstenius*,

Librarian of the Vatican and Milton's mentor in Rome, and with Carlo Dati*, dearest of Milton's Florentine friends. Under pressure of the magistrates of Amsterdam he finally, in 1656, assumed the duties to which he had been appointed in 1654. He served there until 1659, when he was called as pastor of the Protestant church at Charenton in suburban Paris. His appointment was not arranged without difficulty, for, though the French Consistory and Synod approved him, the Walloon Synod persisted in firm opposition for some time. He visited England in 1661–62 in the hope, it appears, of obtaining a pastorate there. With admiration but doubt John Evelyn* heard him preach ("harangue" is his word) first in Geneva and later, during his English visit (*The Diary of John Evelyn,* ed. E. S. de Beer [1955], 2 : 527–29; 3 : 310–11). More died at Charenton in 1670. Two of his tracts, prepared in his own defense against Milton's attacks in *2Def,* and *3Def* are *Alexandri Mori Ecclesiastae Sacarumque Litterarum Professoris Fides Publica, Contra Calumnias Ioannis Miltoni Scurrae* (The Hague, 1654), and *Supplementum Fidei Publicae* (The Hague, 1655), both published by Vlacq. In view of the fierceness of Milton's attack, More wrote these with a measure of restraint. In his characterization of Milton as a rogue and a liar and in his use of coarse vilification, he revealed his anger, but, more often, he expressed pain for the hurt to his good name and for what he considered a distortion of his motives. He sought to present himself as a martyr. In an attempt to dignify his defense and to justify himself, he quoted in full several impeccable testimonials to his innocence in the *Clamor* matter. He was also the author of a book of verse entitled *Poemata* (Paris, 1669). [DAR]

**MORE, HENRY:** *see* CAMBRIDGE PLATONISTS, THE.

**MORISOT, CLAUDE BARTHELEMY:** *see* ANTAGONISTS.

**MORLAND, SIR SAMUEL** (1625–1695), diplomatist, mathematician, and inventor. He was born at Sulhampstead-Bannister, Berkshire, and attended Winchester School and Magdalene College, Cambridge. A zealous supporter of the Parliamentary party, Morland traveled to Sweden in 1653 as part of Whitelock's* embassy to Queen Christina* and, on his return, took service under John Thurloe*, General Secretary to the Council of State* of the Commonwealth. In May 1655, Cromwell, outraged by the massacre of the Vaudois, or Waldenses*, of the Piedmont Valley, sent Morland as his special Commissioner to King Louis XIV of France and to Carlo Emanuele II, Duke of Savoy and Prince of Piedmont, to stimulate the reaction of the former and to remonstrate with the latter about the massacre and the restrictions placed on the religious liberty of the persecuted minority. While performing these offices and helping with the distribution of relief funds sent from England in behalf of the Waldenses, Morland collected material for his book *The History of the Evangelical Churches of the Valleys of Piedmont,* which was published in 1658. Eight state letters concerning the massacre, written to various governments by Milton, are given in *The History,* in Latin and English. Six are dated ca. May 25, 1655, and two on May 26, 1658, the latter dealing with renewed prosecutions of Protestants by the Duke of Savoy. Morland's formal speech of protest to the Duke on behalf of Cromwell is usually dated May 25, 1655. It has been attributed to Milton at times, apparently only through association with the above state letters. It is found in the Public Record Office, SP 96, Vol. VI, part 2, ff. 264–265v, and in *The History.* An extant letter to Geneva, dated June 7, 1655, introduced Morland as Cromwell's envoy, but attribution to Milton rests on no evidence. Details of the massacre cited in *The History* were probably reported to the Council of State in May 1655 and may have furnished information used by Milton in *Sonn* 18.

Some time in 1658 Morland became a Royalist. He was at Breda in May 1660, and returned to England with King Charles*. In July 1660 he was created a baronet and spent the rest of his life in the king's engineering service, working particularly in hydraulics and hydrostatics. He died on December 30, 1695. [JLG]

**MORLEY, GEORGE:** *see* PURITANISM, MILTON'S.

**MORRELL, THOMAS:** *see* ADAPTATIONS.

**MORTALISM** denotes the belief that the human soul as well as the body is mortal; that is, the soul dies with the body. After the orthodoxy of his early poetry (the Latin elegies and *Lyc,* for example), Milton became a staunch advocate of this doctrine, which is opposed to the more usual Christian belief that the soul is immortal and survives the death* of the body. When professed by Christians, including Milton, mortalism is usually accompanied by the affirmation that both soul and body will be resurrected at the day of judgment.

Milton states the doctrine of mortalism explicitly in *CD*: "Inasmuch as the whole man is uniformly said to consist of body, spirit, and soul . . . I shall first show that the whole man dies, and secondly, that each component part suffers privation of life" (15:219). Man's soul, Milton asserts, "is subject to death, natural as well as violent" (15:229). The philosophical basis of this doctrine is Milton's belief that the body and soul are not separable entities, but are inseparable aspects of one unified being: "Man is a living being, intrinsically and properly one and individual, not compound or separable, not according to the common opinion, made by and framed of two distinct and different natures, as of soul and body, but that the whole man is soul, and the soul man . . ." (15:41). This concept of body-soul unity logically entails mortalism, and so Milton attacks "those who assert that the soul is exempt from death, and that when divested of the body, it wings its way . . . directly to its appointed place of reward or punishment, where it remains in a separate state of existence to the end of the world . . ." (15 : 237). Through the emphasis on unity in his ontology, Milton's mortalism is related to some of his other distinctive ideas : 1) traduction*, the belief that the human soul as well as the body is passed from father to son at the moment of conception (*CD* 15 : 47–51); 2) *creatio ex Deo,* the notion that God did not create all things out of nothing, but out of Himself, thus emphasizing the unity of creation* (15 : 15–27); 3) the scale of nature* or being, in which Milton imagined that prelapsarian man (the whole body-soul unit) would "by gradual scale sublim'd" move up from corporeal to a spiritual existence (*PL* 5. 469–503).

Milton cites numerous biblical prooftexts in support of mortalism, and he is correct in his interpretation of the Hebrew word *nephesh* as referring to the whole man rather than to a separate soul; nevertheless, he also seems to be working from a philosophical tradition that began with Aristotle*. In his *Metaphysics* Aristotle insists that all existents are composed of matter and form, but that matter and form never exist independently of each other except as logical concepts. In *De anima* Aristotle then proposes that in man the soul is form and the body is matter*, with the implication that neither exists independently. Later philosophers, such as Alexander of Aphrodisias and Averroes, built on this foundation. Thomas Aquinas* was the first important Christian theologian to discuss the soul-body relation in terms of form and matter, but he balked at drawing the conclusion of mortalism. A spirited defense of mortalism by Pietro Pomponazzi in the early sixteenth century also draw upon the Aristotelian concept and renewed the controversy in the Renaissance. Sixteenth-century opponents of mortalism included Thomas More in *Utopia* and John Calvin*, whose first book was an elaborate defense of the usual position. Two important expositions of mortalism appeared in the seventeenth century : Hobbes's*, in *Leviathan,* and

Richard Overton's, in *Mans Mortallitie.* Milton reveals his debt to Aristotle when he says, for example, that "The rational soul is the form of man, since through this man is man and is distinguished from all other natures" (11 : 61). He also asserts "that every form, to which class the human soul must be considered as belonging, is produced from the potentiality of matter" (15 : 48 retranslated). Thus Milton's mortalism, although heretical in the eyes of some, was firmly grounded in philosophical and theological tradition. [WBH]

**MOSCHUS,** the poet, was born in Syracuse and wrote about a hundred years after Theocritus*, in the second century B.C. He was a grammarian and an acquaintance, perhaps a pupil, of the librarian and scholar Aristarchus. He appears to have lived in the East, probably in Alexandria or Cyprus.

Four poems and a few fragments are commonly ascribed to Moschus, including the *Lament for Bion* and *Europa,* an elegant account of the way Zeus in the form of a bull lured Europa to climb on his back and then carried her across the sea to Crete. The *Lament for Bion* is now thought to be the work not of Moschus but of an Italian pupil of Bion*, who was himself younger than Moschus. The poem had great importance for the subsequent development of the pastoral* elegy because it was the first to lament the death of a real person. The author used techniques of Theocritus's first idyll and Bion's *Lament for Adonis* to mourn the death of his friend Bion, presented in the poem as a shepherd, thereby establishing the pastoral elegy as a vehicle for personal grief.

The influence of the *Lament for Bion* can be seen, among other places, in Virgil's* tenth eclogue, Spenser's* *Astrophel* (on the death of Sidney*), and both *Lyc* and *EpDam*. Milton's account of the mourning of nature in *Lyc* seems to echo a similar passage in the *Lament for Bion*. The opening lines of *EpDam* refer explicitly to the memory of Bion, and Milton's initial gesture of invoking the nymphs of Himera (a Sicilian river) recalls the refrain of the *Lament for Bion*: "Begin, Sicilian Muses, begin the dirge." [JRK]

**MOSELEY, HUMPHREY:** *see* PUB-LISHERS.

**MUSE, MILTON'S.** Although Milton's muse has traditionally been identified with the Holy Spirit*, many scholars have found this interpretation controversial. For some it is the Logos-Christ and the inspiration of Moses; Tillyard* concludes that it is a "mystery that is inscrutable." Differing opinions as to the identity leave the muse as a Trinitarian* godhead or as its individual components. Hughes's* edition of the poems and major prose lists ten different conjectures. Possibly Milton can appeal without sense of contradiction to both orthodox and unorthodox concepts of the godhead.

The identity and nature of the muse or muses will be found in five invocations in *PL* (1. 1–26, 376; 3. 1–13; 7. 1–12, 40). In addition, the muse in *PR* (1. 8–16) is invoked as "Thou Spirit . . . inspire / As thou art wont, my prompted Song else mute." This Spirit seems identical with the "Heav'nly Muse" of *PL*.

The tradition of the muse develops from Homer* to Milton. In the *Iliad* it is unnamed but addressed variously as "goddess," "muse," or "muses." In the *Odyssey* the invocation at the beginning is merely "O muse." All Homeric muses are unnamed, bare and primitive by standards of Renaissance ornateness or by the standards of the Homeric Hymns, which are addressed to Apollo, Aphrodite, Pan, Artemis, and Calliope; or by the standards of Pindar's* odes to Zeus, Olympia, Aphrodite, and the Daughter of Cadmus.

Lucretius's* *De Rerum Natura*, though not an epic* in the Homeric sense, continues the practice of long, serious poems of introducing materials by invocations, though the muses are named: Venus in 1. 49 and Calliope in 6. 93. Seemingly dual invocations appear in the *Aeneid*.

In 1. 8, a muse is invoked (*O musa*); no name appears. In 7. 37, Virgil* invokes Erato. Then in 9. 77, he invokes plural muses (*musae*). The invocation of Hesiod* (*Theogony* 73, 79) and Ovid* (*Metamorphoses* 24. 60) of Calliope as the muse of epic poetry seems not to have been very influential, for the poets of the Renaissance do not confine themselves to one muse. Calliope is only one of many invoked, and her prominence in heroic verse itself is not above that of other muses. Dante* has nine invocations in the *Divine Comedy*, only one to her. Spenser in the proems to 1 and 6 of the *Faerie Queene* invokes several: "Venus," Cupid, Elizabeth, "Virgin, Chief of Nyne," and "all ye impes that on Parnasso dwell." In 3. 3, 4, he invokes Clio by name.

In Book 7 of *PL* Milton clearly states that he is invoking "the meaning, not the name," of Urania*, the ninth muse of Greek mythology, the muse of astronomy, whom he also calls Heav'nly Muse, Spirit, Holy Light, Offspring of Heav'n first-born, and Celestial Patronness; but his semantic intent is made explicit only in the words quoted from 7. Milton's overall plea seems to be directed to the Christian Godhead; whether he is referring specifically to God the Father*, Son*, or Holy Spirit seems relatively unimportant, for all three persons seem to be reflected. Neither Trinitarian nor anti-Trinitarian will find sure evidence to disabuse him of a conviction that Urania is a Christian muse reflecting three parts of the godhead.

The muse as Urania had been used by DuBartas*, Drayton, and Drummond of Hawthornden before Milton employed the name, which can generally be said to be that of the muse of Protestant poetry. [NH]

**MUSES, THE.** Patronesses of humane learning and especially of music and poetry, the nine daughters of Zeus and Memory (Mnemosyne) are frequently associated with different literary modes or diverse branches of learning: Calliope, foremost of the nine, with heroic epic; Clio with history; Euterpe with lyric poetry; Erato with amatory verse; Melpomene with tragedy; Terpsichore with choral song and dance; Thalia with comedy; Polyhymnia with sacred poetry; Urania* with astronomy. Nevertheless, as Renaissance mythographers as well as twentieth-century classicists have recognized, the traditions concerning them are ambiguous and sometimes contradictory. In Curtius's opinion (*European Literature and the Latin Middle Ages*), their "image was vague even in ancient Greece," and in Greek and Latin literature alike they have varied widely in name, number, and function.

Though the Hesiodic* nomenclature is best known, recurring in Apollodorus's *Library* and in Spenser's* *Teares of the Muses,* alternative names were not uncommon in antiquity (*see Paulys Real-Encyclopädie, s.v. Musai*), and Renaissance mythographers recorded variant traditions as to their total number: two, three, four, five, seven, eight, as well as the customary nine. Epithets for the Muses as a group also varied widely. They were invoked as "Nymphs," "Virgins," and "Daughters of Memory"; as "Camenae" (native Italian divinities whom the Romans later identified with the Muses); as "Pierides" (an allusion to Pieria in Macedonia or to Mount Pierus, which was often regarded as their birthplace; to a semi-legendary tribe, the Pieres or to their victory over the daughters of the Macedonian king Pierus); as "Heliconian" (after Mount Helicon in Aonia, the site of the sacred fountains Aganippe and Hippocrene); and as "Olympian." As companions of Apollo Musagetes (leader of the Muses) or of Dionysus, they were also associated with Parnassus and the nearby Castalian spring—another fountain of poetic inspiration. Sicilian poets, in turn, associated them with their own countryside. In invoking the *"Sicilian Muse"* (*Lyc*) Milton followed the example of Moschus* and Virgil*, both of whom had called on the "Sicilian Muses." In *EpDam,* where he invokes the *"Himerides nymphae,"* bidding them sing a Sicilian song beside the Thames, he is alluding to the river Himera (or Himeras), mentioned by Theocritus*. According to Charles Estienne, there were actually *two* Sicilian streams bearing this name, but the ancients believed that these arose from the same spring.

The specific functions of the Muses sometimes varied widely with different poets and mythographers. According to H. J. Rose (*Handbook of Greek Mythology*), the convention of assigning a specific branch of learning to a different muse belongs to late classical antiquity, and in two such poems in the Palatine Anthology he finds significant disagreement on "nearly every Muse."

Among various sons and daughters of the Muses—Linus, Rhesus, Hyacinth, the Sirens—the most famous was the Thracian musician Orpheus*, son of Calliope.

Allegorical* interpretations of the Muses ranged from the organs of speech and the several arts or sciences to the celestial spheres and the principal musical tones and modes. Nevertheless, the Sirens also had been allegorized in terms of the music of the spheres; and as a result the two groups of sisters, in spite of their mythical rivalry, sometimes became identified. Plato's* myth of Er had assigned a siren to each of the celestial spheres; together they sang to the three singing Fates, while Necessity turned the spindle of the cosmos. Milton's *Prol* 2 (12:150–55) interprets the Muses, the Sirens, and Apollo's lyre as interchangeable symbols for the music of the spheres*, observing that "from the very beginning of things the story has prevailed about the Muses dancing day and night around the altar of Jove" and that "hence from remote antiquity skill with the lyre has been attributed to Phoebus. . . ." Plato*, the "most skilful interpreter of Mother Nature," has followed Pythagoras* in his doctrine of "the harmony of the spheres," since he had affirmed that "certain sirens sit one upon each of the circles of the heavens and hold spell-bound gods and men by their most honey-sweet song." In *Arc* Milton's account of the heavenly sirens—that is, Muses—is again heavily indebited to the myth of Er :

> . . . then listen I
> To the celestial *Sirens* harmony,
> That sit upon the nine enfolded Sphears,
> And sing to those that hold the vital shears,
> And turn the Adamantine spindle round,
> On which the fate of gods and men is wound.

The sirens are clearly equated with the Muses in Milton's *RCG*; in a passage that foreshadows the contrast between the classical Muses and the heavenly Muse of biblical poetry in *PL*, Milton declares that his future *opus* is "not to be obtained by the invocation of Dame Memory and her Siren daughters, but by devout prayer to that eternal Spirit, who can enrich with all utterance and knowledge. . . ." A variant on the Siren-Muse parallel also occurs in *SolMus* where the poet hails the "mixt power" of music and poetry as a "Blest pair of *Sirens*, . . . Sphear-born harmonious Sisters, Voice, and Verse. . . ." These are not (it should be noted) among the conventional sacred nine; but Milton has availed himself of the license afforded him by the conflicting mythical traditions of the ancients themselves concerning the names and number of the Muses, introducing his own pair of celestial sisters and emphasizing their twinship as a metaphor for the interdependence of sound and sense—a theme that would recur in his sonnet to Lawes*. (It has also been suggested that Milton may be referring to Polyhymnia and Erato, though in generic rather than mythological terminology.)

With the notable exception of Urania, Milton's Muses usually display attributes traditional in both classical and Renaissance poetry and mythography. He conceives them as dancing or singing "in a ring round about *Joves* Altar" (*IlP*; cf. *Prol* 2), describes them as "Sisters of the sacred well, / That from beneath the seat of *Jove* doth spring" (*Lyc*), and associates them with Mount Helicon and the company of the Graces and goddesses of delight (*Prol* 6). In *Idea* he invokes them

as guardian-goddesses of sacred groves and hails Memory herself as the blessed mother of the "ninefold divinity." His *El*6, addressed to Charles Diodati*, portrays them as a "ninefold throng" who mingle with a Bacchic chorus on the Aonian hills shouting "Evoe !" In contrast to the Orphic mysticism of Pico and Ficino, Milton treats the Dionysian affinities of the Muses lightly in this passage. In this sportive rejoinder to Diodati's letter they perform a rhetorical function, reinforcing his arguments that poetry and revelry, wine and song are not incompatible (as Diodati had asserted) but interrelated ("Carmen amat Bacchum, Carmina Bacchus amat") and that his friend's poetic genius has surely been stimulated, rather than curbed, by the festival cheer of the Christmas holidays : "you pour out your meters from the wine-jug itself." Cf. Horace*, *Epistles* 1. 19 on wine as a source of poetic inspiration.)

In this passage, as frequently elsewhere in his poetry, Milton follows a traditional conception of the Muses, but adapts it to the theme and tone of the particular poem—elegy* or epic*, hymn or pastoral*—that he is writing. In considering his treatment of the Muses, accordingly, we must bear in mind his distinction between the "meaning" and "name" of his Patroness (*PL* 7), and the relationship between the poet's mythical language and the concepts he really intends it to signify. We can best understand this relation between allegorical figment and actual reference (or between "vehicle" and "tenor") by examining his allusions to the Muses in a dual context—against the background of Renaissance mythography and in terms of the logical or rhetorical strategy of the individual poem or prolusion.

Like other mountain and water nymphs and like the majority of Olympian deities themselves, the Muses had once been the objects of a religious cultus, had possessed their own shrines and temples, and had been accorded both worship and belief. Though belief and cult decayed, reducing them to the status of literary fictions, their rhetorical value remained. Like other obsolete divinities, they remained an important part of the poet's inherited vocabulary and his store of literary conventions, or served as allegorical symbols for physical or metaphysical* doctrines that still commanded assent. Even though the principal characteristics of Milton's Muses are for the most part traditional, the use he makes of them is often conditioned by theme and genre or by the particular points he is making at certain stages in his argument. His allusions to the sacred sisters not only underline his command of the *stilo antico* and the mythological* idiom of the ancients, but also call attention to his imitation of particular authors or emphasize the continuity of classical and Renaissance tradition within a particular genre. Thus the particular Muses he invokes or the particular aspects that he selects frequently give greater emphasis to his fidelity to, or departure from, the conventions of heroic poetry or pastoral.

Even within the same work, moreover, he may employ the word *Muse* (or *Muses*) in a variety of senses: as humane learning in general or, more narrowly, as poetry or music* in general; as a specific literary genre or mode or style; as the distinctive quality or genius of a particular poet, or as a synonym for the poet himself; as the source of poetic inspiration or as its effect. In *Lyc,* for instance, he uses this word on one occasion to signify another poet ("So may some gentle Muse/ With lucky words favour my destin'd Urn"). In other instances it can signify a particular genre or kind of verse, as in his *Scazons to Salsilli* ("O Muse, who of choice dost trail a limping foot") or (in the same poem) his own poetry as distinguished from that of other poets ("Salsilli, who takes my Muse so warmly to his heart, preferring her . . . to the truly mighty poets."). Similar examples of his use of *Muse* in this sense occur in *Vac* ("But fie my wandering Muse how thou dost stray!"); *Passion* ("Ere-while of

Musick, and Ethereal Mirth . . . My muse with Angels did divide to sing"); *Mansus* ("you will not spurn a Muse that comes from afar, a Muse that, though nurtured but hardly 'neath the cold Bear, unthinkingly dared, recently, a flight through the cities of Italy"); *El* 6 ("But why does *your* Muse seek to lure forth *mine?* Why does your Muse not suffer mine to court the obscurity she craves"). In *El* 1, similarly, he refers to Roman poetry (and perhaps the poetry of Ovid* in particular) through the phrase *Tarpeia Musa.* All of these usages are traditional (cf. *OED* and Estienne's *Thesaurus, s.v. musa*) and can be paralleled in both classical and Renaissance verse; Milton would have encountered a variety of senses of *Muse* in Spenser's* poetry.

*Lyc* derives much of its power from such variations in the meaning of an important term. Like the "false surmise" of the flower-passage, the Virgilian or Theocritan echoes in this poem call attention to the differences as well as the similarities between their original contexts and the "real" situation thinly disguised under the veil of pastoral allegory. The Dorian garments of the uncouth swain do not quite fit, and occasionally the Sicilian Muse lets her veil slip to reveal not a Mediterranean but a northern tragedy. The British landscape is distinctly visible through the mirage of classical nomenclature; and the brutal realities—King's death and weltering corpse, the corrupted clergy—break through the conventions of the Theocritan and Virgilian mode. These discrepancies between the "real situation" and the fictional pastoral conventions function, on the whole, as a subtle yet powerful variant on the "inexpressibility-topos" (cf. Curtius). They emphasize, more effectively than a severer decorum, the inadequacy of language—even the idioms and conventions of poetry—to express the full reality of grief. This itself is a poetic convention—and it is to Milton's credit that (like other Renaissance artists, who had depicted their subjects as stepping *out* of the painting and through the picture-frame) he could enhance the illusion of reality by skillfully undercutting his poetic fiction.

There is a significant difference between Milton's classical echo ("meditate the thankles Muse") and its models in Virgil's* "silvestrem tenui musam meditaris avena" (Eclogue 1) and "agrestem tenui meditabor harundine Musam" (Eclogue 6). In the former instance the phrase is applied to a shepherd (allegorically, Virgil himself) who has been saved from exile by imperial favor and, reclining at ease under a beechtree, is : piping the praises of Amaryllis. In the second case, the Muse whom the poet "meditates" is the sportive Thalia, and it is an amusing tale of a prank played on the drunken Silenus that the poet pipes on his pastoral reed. Milton adapts this Virgilian phrase to a strikingly different dramatic situation and a different line of argument—to the untimely death of a scholar poet, the seeming injustice of his lot, and the apparent fruitlessness of the labors he had expended on his literary and academic studies. In his second elegy Milton had similarly complained that Death is "cruel to the Muses."

This complaint against the "thankles Muse" complements the argument of the previous stanza, with its unmistakable echo of Theocritus's "Thyrsis" (Loeb Classical Library translation) :

"Where were ye, Nymphs, when Daphnis pined? ye Nymphs, O where were ye?
Was it Peneius' pretty vale, or Pindus' glens? 'twas never
Anapus' flood nor Etna's pike nor Acis' holy river."

Unlike Mount Etna and the Sicilian rivers Anapus and Acis, Mount Pindus and the river Peneus belong to Thessaly; this is the region of the Vale of Tempe. Through the antithesis between this rhetorical question and the comment that immediately follows it—deliberately contrasting the Sicilian haunts of the Muses with their older and more traditional Thessalian habitat—Theocritus gives additional stress to the Muses' absence from the scene of Daphnis's death; had they been present,

they might have saved their beloved poet. In imitating (or adapting) this passage, Milton raises the same rhetorical question and ostensibly for the same purpose. Had the Nymphs remained at their ancient haunts on the Welsh coast, they might have preserved their "lov'd *Lycidas*." Nevertheless, instead of diverting attention from the scene of King's tragedy by suggesting remote localities where the Nymphs *might* have been, Milton stresses the British setting, replacing the Sicilian and Thessalian streams and mountains of Theocritus's idyll with their counterparts close by the Irish Sea—the "wizard stream" of the Dee and the "shaggy top of *Mona* high." Here lie the ancient British bards; had the Muses themselves remained faithful to these their former abodes, Lycidas might not have died. Through these specifically British allusions, introduced into a passage modeled on Theocritus, Milton establishes a link between the ancient bardic tradition of Britain and the Doric lays of Sicily, heightening the analogies between the two dead shepherds—both beloved of the Muses—and between the pastoral techniques of the two surviving poets who celebrated them.

Milton's chief innovation on Theocritus at this point, however, is to introduce the Orpheus-Calliope allusion, in answer to his own complaint to the Nymphs. This addition places the Theocritan borrowing in a distinctly different light, and prepares directly for the next stage in the argument—the complaint against blind fate* and the "thankles Muse" in the following stanza. For learning and poetry and academic promise are apparently of no avail against death; even if they *had* been at hand, the Muses would have been powerless to protect their favorite. After these complaints—first against the absence of the Muses and secondly against their impotence—the argument takes still another, and more dramatic, turn as Apollo himself—leader of the Muses and god of vatic illumination—intervenes directly to defend the "thankles Muse" and (as on a very different occasion in Virgil's Eclogue 6), to touch the poet's ears, admonishing and instructing him.

The Muses of *Lyc* are at home in Sicily and Arcadia in Italy and northern Greece and Britain—and they are decidedly more than mere literary conventions. The river Mincius, which flows from Lake Garda to Mantua and into the Po, had long been associated with both Virgil and Catullus*. In Theocritus's first Idyll, Daphnis bids farewell to the Syracusan fountain Arethusa, and the legend of this spring and the Arcadian river Alpheus appears among poems attributed to Moschus. Like the invocation of the Sicilian Muse, Milton's allusions to these streams function virtually as metaphors for the pastoral genre, establishing the continuity of his own elegy with Sicilian and Virgilian tradition.

His initial invocation, calling upon the "Sisters of the sacred well" under Jove's throne to begin and "somewhat loudly sweep the string" presents a different problem. Traditionally the pipe was a far humbler instrument than the lyre, and the contrast between them had played a significant role in the musical contest between Marsyas and Apollo. Milton's conscious distinction between the oaten flute of his uncouth swain and the harps of the Muses emphasizes the fact that he is composing the lowly pastoral, in contrast to more lofty poetic genres. Nevertheless it also serves as a humility-*topos,* suggesting his deference to the divine powers he is invoking and his dependence upon them for inspiration. The identity of the "sacred well" may have been deliberately left ambiguous. Though this term frequently applies to the Hippocrene fountain on Mount Helicon or the Castalian spring on the lower slopes of Parnassus, Milton's allusion to the "seat of *Jove*" (which is traditionally Mount Olympus) suggests that he is referring to the "Pierian spring." It is possible, however, that like many other Christian poets, he may be exploiting the Jove-Jehovah parallel to introduce a veiled allusion to the Christian heaven, with its

river of life and the groves and "streams" (174) that, in the final lines of the poem, so delight the soul of the dead Lycidas.

Like Cicero*, who associated the sacred sisters with *litterae humaniores* ("cum Musis, id est, cum humanitate et doctrina"; Curtius, *European Literature,* p. 228), Milton exploits the imagery of the Muses to praise humanistic studies, whether at home or in the university or at centers of Renaissance learning like Florence. Conversely, in denouncing the enemies of humane learning—scholastic barbarism or the violence of war and riot—he depicts them as foes to the Muses. In *Prol* 1 he describes dawn as "friend of the Muses," since daybreak "summons you again to the more gentle Muses, from whom the disagreeable night has separated you"; and he concludes his address to his fellow collegians with the wish "that the Muses may bless your studies" (12 : 139, 149). In *Prol* 3 he thinks it "not likely that the charming and elegant Muses preside over these shrivelled and obscure subjects [i.e., scholastic philosophy], or that the silly followers of these lay claim to their patronage" (12 : 185). In *Prol* 6 he flatters his audience by suggesting that there was "hardly any need for me to beseech and implore aid of the Muses" since he was already surrounded by men "full of all the Muses and Graces"; indeed it would be "vain to seek anywhere on earth for the Muses and Graces and Goddesses of delight, except in this place"—the halls of Cambridge (12 : 213–15). In *Prol* 7 he again associates medieval scholasticism with barbarism, declaring that "the presiding Muses had abandoned all the universities of that age" (12 : 259). In his ode to John Rous*, written during the turbulent winter of 1646–47, Milton associates Oxford with the "groves of the Muses," expressing his desire that some god or hero may recall "the Muses, now without their proper seats, banished now from well nigh every nook and corner of the land of England's sons."

He frequently speaks of his own devotion to the Muses—that is, to poetry or to all humanistic learning. Either "my Fate or my Genius did not wish me to depart from my early love of the Muses" (12 : 251). Rusticated from Cambridge, he rejoices that "I am privileged now to give here hours free of all else to the calm Muses, and my books—my true life—sweep me off with them, mastering me utterly." The "sweet love of the Muse" had detained him in Tuscany (a region that Milton extolled as a center for the study of *humanitas* and all the arts of civilization) among other "youths busied with the Muses" at the time of Diodati's death. Even in old age and blindness he does not cease "to wander where the Muses haunt/Cleer Spring, or shadie Grove, or Sunnie Hill, Smit with the love of sacred Song"—a passage reminiscent of Virgil's declaration that he had been smitten by great love of the Muses ("ingenti percussus amore"; *Georgics* 3. 475ff.)—and Milton compares his own fate with that of other blind bards or prophets : Thamyris and Homer, Phineus and Tiresias (*PL* 3).

Since the sweetness of eloquence was frequently described in terms of nectar or honey (just as the flow of eloquence was often represented through the metaphor of a stream), it was only natural that the Muses should be associated not only with sacred well but also with bees. Theocritus (Idyll 7) relates that the goatherd Comatas, whom a tyrant had confined in a coffer and left to starve, had been fed by the bees inasmuch as he was a poet whose "lip was free O' the Muses'" nectar (Loeb). Hesiod declares (*Theogony*, Loeb) that "whomsoever of heaven-nourished princes" the Muses honor and behold at birth, "they pour sweet dew upon his tongue, and from his lips flow gracious words." Horace alludes to "Poetica mella" (poetic honey), and Varro refers to bees as "birds of the Muses" ("Musarum . . . volucres"). Pausanius related (Book 9) that when Pindar once fell asleep by the wayside "bees alighted on him and plastered his lips with their wax. Such was the beginning of Pindar's career as a lyric poet" (Loeb). Citing all of these

examples of the close association between eloquence, Muses, and honey, Valeriano (*Hieroglyphica*) interprets the bees as a hieroglyph of "Grata Eloquentia" and "Poeticae Amoenitas"—grateful eloquence and the pleasantness of poetry. This tradition underlies Milton's observation (*1Def* 7 : 281) that bees "belong to the Muses" and therefore hate and "confute such a beetle" as Salmasius.

Of the traditional nine Muses, Milton mentions five by name—Thalia, Clio, Calliope, Erato, and Urania. Like his earlier allusion to the "ninefold throng, mingling with the Thyonean troop," his references to Thalia and Erato in the same poem (*El* 6) serve as arguments rebutting Diodati's complaint that poetry flees wine and feasting. On the contrary (Milton argues), music and dance should inspire Diodati to poetry. Thalia herself (mirth, conceived either as the Muse of comedy or as one of the three Graces) will inspire him through the eyes and music of a young girl. Moreover, the gods themselves (Erato, Bacchus, Ceres, and Venus) assist the light Elegy. The association of love and music is conventional in medieval and Renaissance literature and iconography (cf. Venus's cithara, the music of the Sirens, and the songs of temptresses in allegorical gardens of delight); the association between Bacchus, Ceres, and Venus in Milton's elegy recalls a familiar proverb (*Sine Cerere et Baccho friget Venus*—i.e., Love grows cold without food and wine). (Cf. the allusion to Thalia in *Culex*, in the Virgilian Appendix.)

Clio appears more frequently in Milton's poetry. In *El* 4, addressed to Thomas Young*, Milton declares that under his tutor's guidance he had first traversed "Aonia's retreats" and the lawns of twin-peaked Parnassus, drinking "Pieria's waters" and springling his lips with "Castalia's wine" through Clio's favor. In *AdP* he declares that he possesses no wealth "save what golden Clio has given me, what slumbers have begotten for me within some grot sequestered, and the laurel-thickets in the holy wood, shady dells on Parnassus." The reference to sleep in some distant grotto (*semoto . . . sub antro*) probably springs from classical accounts of the dreams experienced through incubation rites in caverns. Milton may have had in mind the "cave of the nymphs called Leibethrides" (Strabo [Loeb], 5 : 107, 109); in *Prol* 3 and 6 he alludes to vaticination in the cave of Trophonius. The allusion to Clio is especially appropriate in the light of Milton's interest in historiography* and his wide reading in ancient, medieval, and modern history. In a later poem he hails Manso* in the name of Clio and Apollo, praising him for writing the lives of Marino* and Tasso* and comparing him to Herodotus*, who had allegedly composed a biography of Homer*.

In both of Milton's epics, Urania displaces the traditional Muse of heroic epic (Calliope), and his allusions to this Muse center primarily on the fate of her son, the poet Orpheus. In *TM* of *Lyc* Milton initially wrote the lines "what could the golden hayrd Calliope / for her inchaunting son," but subsequently altered this passage to read : "What could the Muse her self that *Orpheus* bore, / The Muse her self, for her inchanting son. . . ." In *PL* (7) he returns to the same theme—the mutilation of "the *Thracian* Bard" and the Muse's powerlessness to save him : "nor could the Muse defend / Her Son." In both instances the example of Calliope and her son reinforces the theme of the poet's vulnerability to sudden and violent death in spite of his skill. In the first passage the victim is a young man dead before his prime, in the second case it is Milton himself in old age. The force of this argument lies not only in its personal application but also in its apparent violation of a mythographical commonplace —that the Muses are *ex officio* the protectors of poets as well as their sources of instruction and inspiration. Natale Conti had described them as *poetarum praesides,* "protectors of poets" as well as "authors of all songs." Like Calliope, who had failed to rescue Orpheus, the local nymphs were unable to save Lycidas. In

*PL,* Milton hopes for securer protection from his celestial patroness than Calliope —the conventional patroness of epic poetry but actually no more than a mythological figment—has been able to give her disciples.

The allusions to Orpheus's tragedy in *Lyc* and *PL* may not be altogether pessimistic, for the Thracian poet was believed to be living still after death. Nor had the Muses abandoned him entirely. According to Eratosthenes, the Muses themselves had gathered his scattered limbs and buried him; his head (in Philostratus's account) reached Lesbos, where it became famous for its oracles. In *Rhesus* (a tragedy of uncertain date and authorship, though sometimes attributed to Euripides), Orpheus is described as living under Mount Pangaion (or Pangaeus) in Thrace. The Muse who is the mother of Rhesus, bearing away the dead body of her son, foresees a similar existence for him in some underground cavern through the favor of Demeter.

Of all the Muses, the "heavenly Muse" Urania appears most frequently in Milton's poetry. She owes this prominent role, however, not to her classical association with astronomy but to her identification (by DuBartas and other late Renaissance Christian poets) with "divine poetry" based on the Judeo-Christian revelation. (For a study of this tradition and its relationship to the Urania of Spenser's *Teares of the Muses,* the "greater Muse" of his Mutability cantos, the invocation of the Holy Spirit in his *Hymne of Heavenly Love,* and to Milton's own celestial patroness, see Lily Bess Campbell, *Huntington Library Bulletin* 8). Milton's first invocation of the "Heav'nly Muse" occurs in *Nat,* where he calls on her "sacred vein" to afford a "Present to the Infant God. . . ." In *Mask* he refers to the hidden significance underlying the fables of "sage Poets taught by th' heav'nly Muse. . . ." Such allusions are few and dispersed, however, in his early poetry, and it is not until his epic on the Fall that his Muse* Urania reaches her maturity. [JMS]

**MUSIC, MILTON AND.** Musical references, ideas, and images permeate the works of John Milton. The poet came by his musical interests naturally, for his father, John Milton the Elder, was one of England's professional musicians, whose reputation might have been higher today had it not been for the greater fame of his son.

According to Aubrey* (Helen Darbishire, *The Early Lives of Milton*, p. 1), the elder Milton was a student at Christ Church, Oxford; and on the basis of this statement, Brennecke pictures him trained as a chorister under the organist William Blitheman, who was Master of the Choristers in 1573, when Brennecke assumes Milton to have been at Oxford (Ernest Brennecke, *John Milton the Elder and Music*, pp. 3ff.). Illustrating his musical prowess, Edward Phillips (Darbishire, p. 51) states that "he Composed an *In Nomine* of Forty Parts : for which he was rewarded with a Gold Medal and Chain by a *Polish* Prince, to whom he presented it." Although Milton became a scrivener by profession, he was highly enough regarded as a composer to be invited to contribute a madrigal to Thomas Morley's collection in honor of the aging Queen, *The Triumphs of Oriana* (1601), apparently the words as well as the music for his five-part "Fair Orian." He also left a number of anthems, some of them printed during his lifetime in important collections to which the leading composers of the century—Byrd, Bull, Dowland—also contributed.

How much of his musical training young Milton owed to his father, to his "domestic Teachers" mentioned by early biographer John Toland* (Darbishire, p. 86), and to the teachers at St. Paul's*, there is no way of knowing. Aubrey writes of him (ibid., p. 6), "He had a delicate tuneable Voice & had good skill : his father instructed him : he had an Organ in his house : he played on that most." One assumes that the lad received instruction in music at St. Paul's School, well known for its emphasis on music in the days of Mulcaster—although even in his own treatise *Educ* where he highly recommends singing and keyboard performance for recreational purposes, Milton does not outline any system of musical instruction.

At any rate, young Milton's musical talents, mentioned by all his early biographers*, continued throughout his life and comforted him in old age. "Hee had an excellent Ear, and could bear a part both in Vocal & Instrumental Music," says the anonymous biographer (Darbishire, p. 32). This and Aubrey's remark are echoed by Anthony à Wood* : "He had a delicate tuneable voice, an excellent ear, could play on the Organ, and bear a part in vocal and instrumental Musick" (ibid., p. 48). All of the early biographers praise him as a scholarly musician—Richardson, for example, reporting that "his Voice was Musically Agreeable" and that "Musick he Lov'd Extreamly, and Understood Well. 'tis said he Compos'd, though nothing of That has been brought down to Us. he diverted Himself with Performing, which they say he did Well on the Organ and Bas-Viol" (ibid., pp. 202, 204). There is a persistent legend that he played the organ (now in Tewkesbury Abbey) for Cromwell*; and there are several paintings and engravings still in existence memorializing this performance (French, *Life Records*, 3 : 69—70).

Certainly influential in the poet's formative years was the fact that his father was very much at home in London with an Italian colony of professional musicians of great prominence—Alfonso Ferrabosco, Giovanni Coperario, Thomas Lupo—as well as leading English composers—Nicolas Lanier, the Lawes* brothers, Thomas Ravenscroft. The girl for whom the poet wrote his Italian sonnets may have been a daughter of someone in this circle, friendly with the Milton and the Diodatis*.

During his "retirement" at Hammersmith* and Horton* after his Cambridge years, Milton kept up his musical interests. He himself states in *2Def* that during this time he sometimes exchanged "the country for the town, either for the purchase of books, or to learn something new in mathematics, or in music, which at that time furnished the sources of my amusement" (8 : 120–21). The Italian journey* must have further enhanced his musical experiences. One of the highlights of his visit to Rome was attendance upon a musical entertainment put on with "truly Roman magnificence" at the palace of Cardinal Francesco Barberini* and being personally greeted by the Cardinal (12: 40–41). Toland mentions this (Darbishire, p. 93), stating that Holstenius "presented him to Cardinal *Barberini*, who at an entertainment of Music, perform'd at his own expence, look'd for him in the Croud, and gave him a kind Invitation." In Rome, too, Milton heard Leonora Baroni*, the famous soprano, as witness his three Latin poems "To Leonora singing at Rome." Passing through Venice a little later, he shipped home, states Phillips (Darbishire, p. 59), "a Parcel of curious and rare Books which he had pick'd up in his Travels; particularly a Chest or two of choice Musick-books of the best Masters flourishing about that time in *Italy,* namely, *Luca Marenzo, Monte Verde, Horatio Vecchi, Cifa,* the Prince of *Venosa,* and several others."

Living in London later and having taken his nephews "into his tuition," according to Aubrey (ibid., p. 12), "he made his Nephews Songsters, and sing from the time they were with him." Music continued to divert and comfort him through his later troubled years. As Aubrey notes (p. 5), "he would be chearfull even in his Gowtefitts; & sing." Toland reports that "when Blindness and Age confin'd him, he play'd much upon an Organ he kept in the House" (p. 194). Richardson, noting how "his Ears Now were Eyes to Him," says that "in relation to his Love of Musick, and the Effect it had upon his Mind, I remember a Story I had from a Friend I was Happy in for many Years, and who lov'd to talk of *Milton,* as he Often Did. *Milton* hearing a Lady Sing Finely, *'now will I Swear'* (says he) *'This Lady is Handsom'* " (p. 204). In summing up Milton's character and

talents at the end of his life, Richardson puts it very neatly (p. 283) : "Only Musick he Enjoy'd."

Long before his trip to Italy Milton had come to know well one of England's leading composers, Henry Lawes, who, as music tutor to one or more of the Egerton* children, may have asked the young poet to submit verses to be set to music by Lawes and used as "part of an entertainment" for the Dowager Countess of Derby ca. 1631–1634. A monologue and three songs in this pastoral minidrama known as *Arc* were probably "set in Music by Mr. Henry Lawes," as the 1645 title page reports. He also, it is thought, sang the lines of the Genius of the Wood and assisted some of the Egerton children in the songs. *Mask* was similarly written for performance by the three Egerton children and their music tutor. Its musical portion included five songs set by Lawes : "From the heavens now I fly," "Sweet Echo," "Sabrina Fair," "Back, shepherds, back," "Now my task is smoothly done"—all sung by Lawes except "Sweet Echo," sung by the Lady. The music has survived in Lawes's autograph collection and in a transcription; it is conveniently available in Andrew J. Sabol, *Songs and Dances for the Stuart Masque* (1959). Gretchen Finney has found in *Mask* many analogues with early music drama in Rome, especially with *La catena d'Adone* by Ottavio Tronsarelli and Domenica Mazzochi, 1626 (*Musical Backgrounds for English Literature* [1962], pp. 175–94). She considers it significant that Milton chose to write "a musical drama in the Italian style . . . , a crystallized dramatic form, with which he must have been acquainted before his Italian journey" (p. 194).

Despite the fact that he and Lawes were to differ on political issues, music seems to have sustained their friendship, commemorated in Milton's sonnet *"To Mr. H. Lawes, on his Aires,"* written February 9, 1646. It will be considered below with the other minor poems.

Musical imagery is, of course, paramount with Milton, to be found in greater or lesser degree in most of his poetical works and in many prose passages. Such references cover the whole range of music, both *musica speculativa* and *musica practica*. In the earlier seventeenth century, these two branches of music, the "speculative" and the "practical," were still recognized. The latter is quite analogous to what is called "applied music" today, but the former is scarcely similar to modern musical "theory" or "history" in that it was based upon an ancient tradition tracing especially through Boethius to ancient Greek mathematics, ethics, and cosmology. It is no accident that the scales (or modes) of Western civilization consist of seven different notes, that there are seven days in the week, and that the seven visible "planets" were thought to govern men's lives. *Musica speculativa* understood its subject on such a cosmic scale. More details will appear in the discussions of individual works, of which we turn first to the minor poems.

While still a student at Cambridge, Milton delivered a Latin address on an important aspect of *musica speculativa* that was to be a favorite topic throughout his life : *Prol 2, On the Harmony of the Spheres*. Light and gently mocking in tone, the oration nonetheless contains most of the musical ideas found later in the poetry : the Pythagorean theory of the harmony of the spheres, Plato's* addition of a Siren seated upon each of the celestial orbs (*Republic* 10), Aristotle's* statement (*De Caelo* 2. 9) that the music of the spheres* is unheard by mortals (Milton's address is actually an answer to this view), the ecstatic effects of music, the song of the lark and nightingale "according" with the celestial harmony, the Muses dancing before Jove's altar, the attribution of musical skill to Apollo, the ability of Pythagoras* to hear the sphere-music, the return of the Age of Gold if humans were pure and chaste enough to hear the music.

The Pythagorean idea of a universe composed of music, to which humanity may respond, infuses several of Milton's youthful poems. This idea is central to *Nat,* which describes the music of creation (cf. Plato *Timaeus* 35) with an echo of Job :

Such Musick (as 'tis said)
Before was never made,
    But when of old the sons of morning sung,
When the Creator great
His Constellations set,
    And the well-ballanc't world on hinges hung.

The fusion of classical with Christian is evident throughout. The "ninefold harmony" of traditional Pythagorean/Platonic tradition is here supported by Milton's favorite musical instrument, the organ (in its metaphorical sense, of course) :

Ring out ye Crystall sphears
Once bless our humane ears,
    (If ye have power to touch our senses so)
And let your silver chime
Move in melodious time;
    And let the Base of Heav'ns deep Organ blow,
And with your ninefold harmony
Make up full consort to the' Angelike symphony.

If one can attune to this music, "Time will run back, and fetch the age of gold" —that perfect time before the Fall*. Laurence Stapleton (*University of Toronto Quarterly* 23 : 217–26) sees a reflection here of "the new music" of the early Christian Platonist, Clement of Alexandria*—praised by Milton in *RCG*—in his *Exhortation to the Greeks*. Clement identifies the new music with Christ; Milton "describes it, like the coming of Peace, as an announcement of a change in human history." Through the symbol of the music of the spheres, Milton is thus able "to achieve in the centre of his composition a masterly focus, making the present moment both revive man's best capacity for perfection and prophesy its future realization."

In *Arc* the Genius of the Wood (an immortal) is able to hear the music of the "nine enfolded Sphears," each with its Siren, in a passage reflecting Plato's description of the music "which none can hear / Of human mould with gross un-purged ear" (cf. *Republic* 10). The poem *SolMus* is actually an exhortation that the "Sphear-born Harmonious Sisters, Voice, and Vers" wed their "divine sounds" to bring back "That undisturbed Song of pure concent" so that "we on Earth" may hear and respond. Here however, an important change has taken place : the sphere-music is now the angelic music; the "Song of pure concent" is "sung before the saphire-colour'd throne"

Where the bright Seraphim in burning row
Their loud up-lifted Angel trumpets blow,
And the Cherubick host in thousand quires
Touch their immortal Harps of golden wires.

The music itself comprises "Hymns devout and holy Psalms," and the wish is

That we on Earth with undiscording voice
May rightly answer that melodious noise;
As once we did, till disproportion'd sin
Jarr'd against natures chime, and with harsh din
Broke the fair musick that all creatures made
To their great Lord, whose love their motion sway'd
In perfect Diapason.

*Diapason,* literally the interval of the octave, here means harmony or concord in general, like the metaphorical organ of the Nativity poem.

In *Mask* the sphere-music, significantly, is seen as the dance of the heavenly bodies, to which earthly rhythms respond:

We that are of purer fire
Imitate the Starry Quire
Who in their nightly watchful Sphears,
Lead in swift round the Months and Years;
The Sounds, and Seas with all their finny drove
Now to the Moon in wavering Morrice move.

Expression of sphere music by way of the dance ("wavering Morrice") was a well-established figure, elaborated, for instance, in Sir John Davies's *Orchestra: A Poem of Dancing* (1596). The opening lines of the song *May* reflect the same convention. Milton's association of music with purity of heart or chastity* (the general subject of *Mask*) is based on Revelation 14, where

heavenly music can be heard only by those undefiled by women.

Not until *PL* does Milton return to the cosmic music and dance. But a rather different type of musical rhetoric, based on "practical" as well as "speculative" ideas, infuses several other of the minor poems. Music is a most essential element, for example, in *L'Al* and *IlP*; Nan C. Carpenter (*University of Toronto Quarterly* 22 : 354–67) has shown that music is "indispensably related to form, content, and meaning in the lyrics." References to the music of nature in its many forms as well as to more sophisticated musical attractions underline the cyclic form of each poem. In *L'Al,* secular music predominates, climaxing in "soft *Lydian* Aires, / Married to immortal verse"—allusion to the most beguiling of the eight Greek modes (each of which was thought to have its own particular effect upon the emotions) and possibly to the Italian aria as well, often a dramatic piece; for the lines describing this music call to mind the florid Italian solo with its virtuoso passages, trills, roulades :

with many a winding bout
Of lincked sweetness long drawn out,
With wanton head, and giddy cunning
The melting voice through mazes running;
Untwisting all the chains that ty
The hidden soul of harmony.

In *IlP* with its religious overtones, the "pealing Organ" and "full voic'd Quire . . . / In service high, and Anthems cleer" of the Anglican ritual dissolve the soul into ecstasies. The figure of Orpheus*, found in both poems, symbolizes the poet-prophet-seer idea, important to the young Milton, and also resolves the action/contemplation dichotomy basic to the poems; for in the active poem Orpheus is a passive listener, whereas in the contemplative poem he is an active creator of music.

*Lyc,* lamenting the early death of a young poet, contains no typical Miltonic passages on musical ideas. Yet it is hung on a frame of musico-poetic rhetoric that subtly underlines the idea of the union of music and poetry in ancient times: "Who would not sing for *Lycidas*? He knew / Himself to sing, and build the lofty rhyme / . . . Begin then, Sisters of the sacred well / . . . Begin, and somewhat loudly sweep the string." Orpheus figures again, the prototype of all serious poets. Here, fittingly enough, the story of his death is told. Gretchen Finney considers the influence of the "new" Italian opera upon *Lyc*, suggesting recitatives, arias, and choruses, and reflecting the musical style of Caccini and Peri (*Musical Backgrounds*, pp. 195–219).

The opening lines of Milton's first sonnet—

O Nightingale, that on yon bloomy Spray
Warbl'st at eeve, when all the Woods are
    still—

are almost identical with lines 25–26 from the fifth elegy :

Iam Philomela tuos foliis adoperta novellis
    Instituis modulos, dum silet omne nemus.

The "liquid notes" of the sweet sad bird, found many times in Milton's verse, bring associations of music's power and of chaste, romantic love, whether youthful passion as in *IlP* or wedded bliss as in the epithalamion ("Haile wedded Love") in *PL* 4.750ff. There is an echo of this in *Sonn* 2 to Aemilia, where the young singer is praised in terms of the old idea of the power of music to move men, beasts, and even trees. In the sonnet to Diodati* (4), Milton describes her gift of song as able even to draw the moon from its course.

The sonnet to Lawes, already mentioned, praises the musician in terms of *musica practica* : for having been the first to teach "our English Musick how to span / Words with just note and accent, not to scan / With *Midas* Ears, committing short and long." That is, Lawes has subordinated his music to the rhythmic needs of his text, suiting the notes to the syllables. Thus he will be remembered, says the poet, as "the man, / That with smooth aire couldst humor best our tongue." With the sestet comes a shift in thought : Lawes has honored verse by

setting it properly; now poets honor him and Fame will set him higher than Dante's* musical friend Casella. Lawes's original printing of the sonnet contains a marginal note on the word *story* : "The story of Ariadne set by him in Music." The poem referred to is a complaint or lament, William Cartwright's *Ariadne Deserted by Theseus*, in recitative style, modeled upon Monteverdi's *Lamento d'Arianna*.

Nan Carpenter (*English Literary Renaissance* 2 : 237–42) explains that Milton's double comparison of Milton and Dante, Lawes and Casella reflects his wit and humor; for the *Purgatorio* passage (2 : 106ff.) that describes the meeting of Dante and Casella begins with the words, "If a new law," giving Milton the opportunity to pun (unheard) in two languages, with multiple wordplay on Henry's name.

The *ayre* figures again in a sonnet (20) written much later to another friend: "*Lawrence* of vertuous Father." Here the poet includes music—specifically, lute music and the Italian *aria parlando* (the model for the English *ayre*)—among life's greatest pleasures. When will he and Lawrence, Milton asks, be able to enjoy a "neat repast" and afterwards

hear the Lute well toucht, or artfull voice
Warble immortal Notes and *Tuskan* Ayre?

In conclusion to this consideration of musical elements in the minor poems, mention should be made of Milton's translations of the Psalms, at least two groups of which he almost certainly wrote for performance, accompanied by the traditional tunes of the church. The first two, Psalms 114 and 136, "done by the Author at fifteen years old," were perhaps a by-product of his father's contributions of musical settings to the Ravenscroft Psalter (1621). No. 136 appears regularly in modern worship services. Again, in 1648, he translated nine more, all designed for Protestant congregational singing to well-known tunes. Finally, in 1653 he translated eight more, but their varying meters prove that they were not conceived for church performance. If Milton ever thought of them as being sung, they would have required unique and quite untraditional musical settings. In any case, his profound devotion to this kind of musical performance remained constant to the end of his life, since Jesus testifies to the power of the Psalms in *PR*.

In the major works, musical imagery takes many forms, especially in *PL*. Like Dante, Milton describes heaven in terms of music and light, and the greatest number of musical allusions occur in Books 3 (the scenes in heaven) and 7 (the Creation). After the Fall (9), musical images tend to lessen, and there are very few in the last four books. The sphere-music of the early poems is now the angelic music; the orders of angels constantly praise God with harps and song. Whenever God speaks, angelic choirs praise him—as in 3. 347–49: "Heav'n rung / With Jubilee, and loud Hosanna's fill'd / Th'eternal Regions." Heaven, indeed, *is* harmony: "No voice exempt, no voice but well could joine / Melodious part, such concord is in Heav'n" (3. 370–71). Songs of triumph, too, are part of the angelic role: as in 6. 885–86, when Messiah returned victor, "each order bright, / Sung Triumph, and him sung Victorious King." Even in Satan's realm, music never loses its power to enrapture. The fallen angels await their master's return after the Great Consult and sing "With notes Angelic to many a Harp" (2. 548) with Milton's comment:

Thir Song was partial, but the harmony
(What could it less when Spirits immortal
  sing?)
Suspended Hell, and took with ravishment
The thronging audience.
(552–55)

Like heaven, which it echoes, the Garden is described audibly in terms of music: here "The Birds thir quire apply" and "aires . . . attune / The trembling leaves" (4. 264–66); in this chaste spot, the nightingale "all night long her amorous descant sung" (4. 603); over the "blissful Bower," "heav'nly Quires the *Hymenaean* sung" (4. 711). Adam, indeed, comments

on the music audible in the Garden (4. 682–88), noting how often he and Eve have heard

Celestial voices to the midnight air,
Sole, or responsive each to others note
Singing thir great Creator; oft in bands
While they keep watch, or nightly rounding
  walk
With Heav'nly touch of instrumental sounds
In full harmonic number joind, thir songs
Divide the night, and lift our thoughts to
  Heaven.

Book 7 is musical throughout, for the Creation* takes place to music (as in Plato's *Timaeus* 35). From the first day's creation (when the Celestial Quire "touch't thir Golden Harps, and hymning prais'd / God and his works, Creatour him they sung," 258–59) to the relaxation on the Sabbath (when "the Empyrean rung, / With *Halleluiahs*," 633–34), the hierarchies praise God in song and symphony. After the sixth day, in Raphael's words, God rode up (7. 557–62):

Followd with acclamation and the sound
Symphonious of ten thousand Harpes that
  tun'd
Angelic harmonies: the Earth, the Aire
Resounded, (thou remember'st, for thou
  heardst)
The Heav'ns and all the Constellations rung.

Raphael's statement to Adam ("thou remember'st, for thou heardst"), reminds use once more that before the Fall, man was able to hear the heavenly music, as Adam has earlier stated (4. 682ff.).

This harmony often takes the form of the heavenly dance—sometimes in a description of the turning heavens (cf. *Timaeus* 40), as the "Starry dance" of the constellations, "in numbers that compute / Days, months, & years" (3. 80–81), echoed in the Garden where "universal *Pan* / Knit with the *Graces* and the *Hours* in dance / Led on th'Eternal Spring" (4. 266–68); or as "wandring Fires that move / In mystic Dance not without Song" (5. 177–78). The cosmic dance is reflected on earth at the Creation, where, on the third day, "Rose as in Dance the stately Trees" (7. 324). Angelic dance fuses with cosmic dance in heavenly scenes—for example, as the angels (5. 620–24) spend their time in song and

Mystical dance, which yonder starrie Spheare
Of Planets and of fixt in all her Wheeles
Resembles nearest, mazes intricate,
Eccentric, intervolv'd, yet regular
Then most, when most irregular they seem.

Milton's verse abounds with allusions to musical instruments—and there are many such references in his prose works as well. Most of these allusions are quite traditional with the exception, perhaps, of his strong emphasis upon the organ. With a few exceptions (the "jocund rebeck" of *L'Al,* always associated with rustic song and dance; the golden lyre of Apollo, a much-used symbol for the charm and power of music to sway man's soul), these instruments all have a place in *PL.* The trumpet (a favorite with Milton, even in his prose works) is many times associated with warlike activities or to herald great events—whether in heaven, where it activates the "Powers Militant" (6. 61), proclaims victory over the rebels (6. 203) or over death (11. 73–74), and ordains God's law (12. 229); or in the realm of Satan, where it heralds the Council in Pandemonium (1. 754), and proclaims the results of the Council (2. 515). Golden harps, associated constantly with angels throughout the heavenly scenes, swell to a hyperbolic ten thousand as Creation ends (7. 559). At the human level, however, the harp seems to be related to the lute, mentioned only once (5. 151) to describe human hymns in the Garden—"More tuneable than needed Lute or Harp." Flutes and recorders, playing music in the Dorian mode, accompany Satan's hosts as they quietly march in battle formation (1. 549–53)—a reference to the Greek system of *ethos,* in which the Dorian mode was thought to make one strong and manly. On the seventh day, God is praised with all instruments suitable for celestial rejoicing : harp, pipe, dulcimer, organ, and voice (7. 595ff.). One of the most striking metaphors in all *PL* is the description of Pandemonium

(1. 705–30) in terms of the baroque organ. Helen and Peter Williams, *Musical Times* 107 : 760–63, observe that Milton's organ is not an English church organ—"none had pillars or fretted gold"—but an Italian organ such as he had seen during his travels abroad.

Musical imagery in *PR* is similar, in its heavenly vein, to that of its companion epic, but there is far less of it (none at all in Book 3) and the few references are, significantly, more concise. Decisions in heaven are celebrated with angelic song and dance, described more compactly than in *PL* :

So spake the Eternal Father, and all Heaven
Admiring stood a space, then into Hymns
Burst forth, and in Celestial measures mov'd,
Circling the Throne and Singing.
                              (1. 168–71)

The Nativity music is mentioned to emphasize the Son's* special status, as the Father* explains (1. 242–44),

At thy Nativity a glorious Quire
Of Angels in the fields of *Bethlehem* sung
To Shepherds watching.

This is echoed by Satan (4. 505–6) when he recalls to Jesus the "Angelic Song in *Bethlehem* field, / On thy birth-night." And heavenly music at the banquet enhances Jesus' triumph near the end of the epic (4. 593–99) :

    and as he fed, Angelic Quires
Sung Heavenly Anthems of his victory
Over temptation, and the Tempter proud.

As part of the intellectual joys of "Plato's retirement," the "Olive Grove of *Academe,*" Satan tempts Jesus with ideas from *musica speculativa*—Pythagorean ideas of music as the science of numbers, with its power over man's emotions :

There thou shalt hear and learn the secret
    power
Of harmony in tones and numbers hit
By voice or hand.
                              (4. 254–56)

Music allied with poetry is then presented ("*Aeolian* charms and *Dorian*

*Lyric* Odes")—again with reference to the ethos of the Greek modes. Rejecting these delights, Jesus praises "our native Language," hymns, psalms, "Our Hebrew Songs and Harps in *Babylon*" (4. 331–36) as being superior to those of Greece in religious inspiration. Thus Jesus finds philosophical ideas and practical music effective for weighting his arguments against prideful intellectual attractions.

Aside from the "warbling charms" of Dalila (934) who, she says, will be among famous women "sung at solemn festivals" (982–83), and brief reference to trumpets proclaiming the festival, pipes, timbrels, and "sweet Lyric song" to memorialize the fallen hero, *SA* is devoid of musical allusions. Its ancestry, however, is strongly musical. Milton in his Preface cites the German Calvinist David Paraeus* (whose work on the Apocalypse was translated into English in 1644) as having divided the Book of Revelation "into Acts distinguisht each by a Chorus of Heavenly Harpings and Son between" just as Milton had earlier written (*RCG*) when describing a tragedy based on the Apocalypse ("shutting up and intermingling her solemn Scenes and Acts with a sevenfold *Chorus* of halleluja's and harping symphonies," 4 : 815) and just as Milton divided his own scenes in heaven in *PL*.

Mrs. Finney (*Musical Background,* pp. 220–37) offers cogent evidence that in composing *SA* Milton was strongly influenced by the Italian oratorio, "one of the most popular musical attractions in Rome when Milton was there," especially *Il Sansone,* by Benedetto Ferrari. The resemblance of the chorus in some of the Italian *drammi per musica* to that of *SA* (see pp. 224–27) sheds light on William R. Parker's question (*Milton's Debt to Greek Tragedy,* pp. 140–41) as to why the choruses in *SA* are generally longer than those in the classical models. Mrs. Finney finds the answer in the Italian models, where length of chorus is based on musical considerations. She finds closest parallels with Alessandro Striggio's *La favola d'Orfei,* set by Monteverdi (1607), "not only in the contemplative function

of the chorus, but in the length of the choral speeches" (p. 227).

Brief musical references occur fairly often in Milton's prose works, sometimes direct and sometimes metaphorical. Two longer prose passages, however, are especially significant in summing up his ideas about music, both speculative and practical. The first, from his treatise *Educ,* runs the gamut from Platonic ideas of the effects of music on man's soul to mention of the later forms (the fugue, not fully developed during Milton's lifetime), instruments (organ, lute), and their combinations ("the whole Symphony"), as he describes the beneficial effects of music upon young students (4 : 288–89) :

> The interim of unsweating themselves regularly, and convenient rest before meat may both with profit and delight be taken up in recreating and composing their travail'd spirits with the solemn and divine harmonies of Musick heard or learnt: either while the skilful *Organist* plies his grave and fancied descant, in lofty fugues, or the whole Symphony with artful and unimaginable touches adorn and grace the well studied chords of some choice Composer: sometimes the Lute, or soft Organ stop waiting on elegant Voices either to Religious, martial, or civil Ditties; which if wise men and Prophets be not extreamly out, have a great power over dispositions and manners, to smooth and make them gentle from rustick harshness and distemper'd passions.

The other statement appears in *Areop.* Eloquent in making his point against censorship, Milton here (4. 317) reaches heights of lyricism as he includes music in "all that is delightfull to man" and again roams from Grecian ideas of *ethos* to modern instruments and vocal forms (the solo air, the multivoiced madrigal), aware of the difference between the courtly instruments (lute, violin, guitar) and the rustic ones (bagpipe, rebec), and always connecting music and poetry :

> If we think to regulat Printing, thereby to rectifie manners, we must regulat all recreations and pastimes, all that is delightfull to man. No musick must be heard, no song be set or sung, but what is grave and *Dorick.* There must be licencing dancers,

that no gesture, motion, or deportment be taught our youth but what by their allowance shall be thought honest. . . . It will ask more then the work of twenty licencers to examin all the lutes, the violins, and the ghittarrs in every house; they must not be suffer'd to prattle as they doe, but must be licenc'd what they may say. And who shall silence all the airs and madrigalls, that whisper softnes in chambers? . . . The villages also must have their visitors to enquire what lectures the bagpipe and the rebbeck reads ev'n to the ballatry, and the gammuth of every *municipal* fidler, for these are the Countrymans *Arcadia's* and his *Monte Mayors.*

In conclusion, Milton was deeply concerned with music throughout his life. In his Cambridge days, he seems to have been more interested in Platonic-Pythagorean ideas about music than in his later years. But from his early works through the long epics, Milton consistently equates motion, harmony, cosmic order, and divine love with the music of the spheres. His poem *SolMus* contains, perhaps, the most perfect statement of this. Only in *SA* is there no universe of music. In commenting on this lack, Mrs. Finney suggests (*Musical Backgrounds,* p. 178) that "Milton here reflects at last the changing ideas of the century that discovered music to be nothing but air, nothing but physical motion": the old tradition of the "speculative" disappeared. Perhaps this is true. Actually, there is no evidence in Milton's works of any knowledge of new theories of accoustics so important to Baroque* musicians (culminating, finally, in Rameau's treatise on harmony, 1722). Nor is there the slightest anticipation of the trivialization of music that set in with Restoration poets, when music's chief end was thought to be entertainment, the arousing of the passions, and when the old sphere-music concept became more rhetorical than real. [NCC]

**MUSIC OF THE SPHERES**. A theory of macrocosmic harmony, attributed originally to Pythagoras*, in which the stars and planets are harmonically ordered on mathematical principles. The music of the spheres was not considered to be audible

to human beings, but could be heard by God. In *PL,* speaking about the movement of the planets, Milton says: "And in their motions harmonie Divine / So smooths her charming tones, that God's own ear / Listens delighted" (5. 625–27). Milton's *Prol* 2, delivered while he was a student at Cambridge, briefly summarizes the theory of heavenly harmony, and concludes that the reason man cannot hear the music is that "we remain brutish and overwhelmed by wicked animal desires" (12 : 157). *See also* MUSIC, MILTON AND.

The idea of the existence of the music of the spheres has an interesting progression in the centuries between Pythagoras and Milton. The concept was generally held by ancient writers, although Aristotle* is notable for not accepting it (*On The Heavens,* trans. W. K. C. Guthrie, Loeb ed., pp. 195–97). Plato*, however, in *Timaeus,* agrees with Pythagoras, and concludes that the creation of the universe occurred as harmonic intervals and that each planetary soul possessed a musical tone that was in harmonic relationship with every other planetary soul (trans. R. G. Bury, Loeb ed., pp. 63–73). Further, in the same dialogue Plato suggests that human beings have souls that also revolve in harmony with planetary souls (p. 109). In *De re publica,* Cicero pursues much the same argument, focusing on the actual cause of the sound. He postulates that sound is produced "by the onward rush and motion of the spheres themselves; the intervals between them, though unequal, being exactly arranged in a fixed proportion, by an agreeable blending of high and low tones various harmonies are produced; for such mighty motions cannot be carried on so swiftly in silence" (trans. C. W. Keyes, Loeb ed., pp. 271–73).

In ancient discussions on music of the spheres it is evident that much of the interest in the subject stemmed from a desire to understand man's relationship to the music produced by heavenly bodies. In the early Middle Ages, Boethius made an attempt to define this relationship in *De institutione musica.* He divided music as a whole into three categories: *musica mundana,* the music of the planets themselves; *musica humana,* the corresponding harmony of the human soul; and *musica instrumentalis,* the sound produced by musical instruments.

If there was an actual connection between the music of the planets and the music of man's soul, as Boethius attempted to show, then perhaps it was possible for the human soul to come into contact with the celestial harmony by somehow reproducing it on earth. To the Renaissance, such was the meaning of the myth of Orpheus*. Orpheus, it was argued, was able to play the tones and intervals of planetary music, and thus bring down this harmony to earth, even to the extent of using it to restore life. (Gretchen Finney, *Musical Backgrounds for English Literature: 1580–1650* [1962], p. 102).

Milton's awareness of the Orpheus myth shows up in various places in his poetry, particularly in his early work: "Untwisting all the chains that ty / The hidden soul of harmony. / That *Orpheus* self may heave his head / From golden slumber on a bed / Of heapt *Elysian* flowres, and hear / Such streins as would have won the ear / Of *Pluto.* . . ." (*L'Al* 143–49). And as Finney has observed, *Lyc* is filled with references to the Orpheus legend, as in this passage reflecting on Orpheus's power to restore life: "What could the Muse her self that *Orpheus* bore, / The Muse her self for her inchanting son / Whom Universal nature did lament, / When by the rout that made the hideous roar, / His goary visage down the stream was sent, / Down the swift *Hebrus* to the *Lesbian* shore" (58).

In addition, there were several attempts made in the Renaissance to prove that the connection between the soul of man and the music of the spheres was more than merely a myth or metaphor. Easily the most noteworthy of these attempts was made by Marsilio Ficino. Ficino drew a great deal of inspiration for his views from Pythagorean mysticism, as characterized by Plato's *Timaeus,* which Ficino himself translated, and from the

collection of works attributed to Hermes Trismegistus, particularly the *Asclepius.* As Herbert Agar points out, Ficino's Platonism was a strong influence in the sixteenth and early seventeenth centuries in England, and thus no doubt influenced Milton's early work. Later, however, Milton appears to have read Plato in Greek, and drew his own conclusions from it (*Milton and Plato* [1928], pp. 25–31).

It is doubtful if Milton ever took the idea of the music of the spheres as literally as did Ficino. The closest he came, perhaps, is in the poem *SolMus* (1633) where the actuality of heavenly harmony forms the major metaphor. In this poem Milton argues that our fall from obedience* has caused us to be deaf to the music of the spheres. Achieving again the state of obedience is the Christian equivalent of Ficino's union with celestial harmony: "Or may we soon again renew that Song, / And keep in tune with Heav'n, till God ere long / To his celestial consort us unite, / To live with him, and sing in endless morn of light" (25–28).

The bulk of internal evidence indicates that Milton's interest in the idea of music of the spheres occurs in his earlier works. By the time that Milton was middle-aged, scientific discoveries concerning the actual nature of the heavens made it difficult to hold such a theory in any serious way, perhaps even as a metaphor. And as Gretchen Finney comments, the treatment of heavenly harmony in *SA* "reflects at last the changing ideas of the century that discovered music to be nothing but air, nothing but physical motion" (*Musical Backgrounds,* p. 137). [RCR]

**MUTSCHMANN, HEINRICH** (1885–1955), German scholar who received his doctorate from Bonn with a dissertation upon Scottish phonology. His linguistic interests led him later to compile a *Glossary of Americanisms* (1931) and an English grammar for German students. Most of his professional life was associated with the University of Dorpat. In the 1920s he ventured into Milton scholarship by arguing the remarkable theories that

Milton was an illegitimate child and an albino, the last being an explanation for his blindness (see *Der Andere Milton* [Bonn, 1920] and *The Secret of John Milton* [Dorpat, 1925]), but the ideas were never widely accepted. His next book on Milton, *Further Studies Concerning the Origin of Paradise Lost* (Dorpat, 1934), sees the poet as having conceived originally an epic on the Spanish Armada, which he later changed and adapted to one on the Fall of Man, finding parallels in it to descriptions of the Armada by Ubaldini and Camden, a subject to which he returned in his *Milton's Projected Epic* (Dorpat, 1936). The theory has been no more widely accepted than that of the supposed albinism. [WBH]

**MYLES, MATHER:** *see* INFLUENCE ON AMERICAN LITERATURE, MILTON'S.

**MYLIUS, HERMANN** (1600–1657). In July 1651, Mylius arrived in London on a diplomatic mission to secure for his master, the Duke of Oldenburg*, a written safeguard that would permit him to travel without hindrance in areas controlled by the British. This minor incident in the affairs of the Commonwealth is of interest because Mylius was in the habit of keeping a diary in which he wrote a detailed account of his activities and because he retained the letters, sixteen by himself and seven by Milton (all in the hand of an amanuensis), that passed between him and the Secretary for Foreign Hongues* during the lengthy negotiations. In addition, the collection includes one of Milton's State Papers and several copies of the Oldenburg Safeguard itself. The papers were discovered by Alfred Stern* in the Staatsarchiv in Oldenburg and were published in his *Milton und seine Zeit* in 1877–1879. The *Tagebuch* gives an intimate insight into the day-to-day activities of Milton in his government post, some details on his blindness*, and valuable information concerning the functioning of the Council of State* and its relationship with Parliament.

The negotiations were frustratingly long, probably because the government was preoccupied with the aftermath of the Battle of Worcester, the reorganizing of the Council of State* and its committees, and diplomatic matters of more weight, such as the negotiations with the Dutch. Mylius had to write three letters to Milton before the busy Secretary could find time to reply. Finally, on October 20, he presented a draft of the safeguard at an audience presided over by Bulstrode Whitelocke*, Lord Commissioner of the Great Seal, with Milton in attendance. More delays and correspondence followed, until December 31, when through Milton's personal intercession with Whitelocke, then acting President of the Council, the matter was scheduled for debate. There followed a seven-week interval during which the safeguard was first entrusted to an *ad hoc* committee for consideration, returned to Council, then referred to the Committee for Foreign Affairs, returned again to Council, and finally, on February 17, 1652, approved. Milton saw Mylius frequently during this period (a practice for which he was reprimanded by some members of Council) and kept him informed of the various obstacles that arose during the debate, particularly the questions of Oldenburg's hostility to the English allies in Bremen and his alleged friendship with Royalists, and the Duke's insistence that the benefits of the safeguard be extended to his heirs, which the Council was reluctant to concede. When all of these questions were resolved, there was a delay of two more anxious weeks while the whole matter was reconsidered by Parliament. It was not until March 2, 1652, eight months after his arrival in London, that Mylius, with the approved safeguard in hand, was granted a farewell audience with the Council of State, where he saw once more the now-blind Milton, presumably for the last time.

The correspondence reveals a very gracious and considerate Milton, generous with his time and counsel in behalf of the often discouraged envoy, using his inffluence to guide a routine diplomatic agreement through the tangle of the

Commonwealth government at a time when he was deeply involved in other matters, such as the Dutch negotiations, which were of greater importance to England. It is a picture of a very active Secretary for Foreign Tongues, in frequent attendance at the Council of State, using the last days of his sight in the performance of a variety of demanding tasks for his country. [RTF]

**MYRIELL, THOMAS.** A person of this name (spelled also Merrill, Merrills, Meryell, and Muriell) plays a part in Milton's life in two ways. One was a collector of music, whose six-volume *Tristitiae Remedium* (British Museum, Additional MSS 29372–29377) contains 192 songs, of which ten were composed by Milton's father. These are: "Fair Orian in the Morn," "Precamur, Sancte Domine," and eight anthems (six not previously published). Myriell's collection was ready for publication in 1616, but it has never been printed. Perhaps this man knew Milton, Sr., personally and visited his home on Bread Street. The other was rector of St. Stephen, Walbrook, 1616–1625, where he officiated at the marriage of Milton's sister Anne to Edward Phillips on November 22, 1623. Myriell (1577–1625) was a B.A. from Corpus Christi College, Cambridge, 1601, and ordained on April 5 and May 16, 1601. He was the author of three published sermons. Although there is no evidence to link these two Thomas Myriells, it is generally considered that they were the same, which fact would account for Anne's marriage outside her own parish and in one that seems to have no other connection with the Miltons or Phillipses.

Myriell was probably the father of Henry (1610?–1643), who had been a student at St. Paul's School* when Milton was, and who went up to Corpus Christi College shortly before Milton went to Christ's*. [JTS]

**MYTH AND MYTHOGRAPHY.** Milton's learning* was so extensive, his poetic demands so all-consuming, that no one

critical approach to his uses of mythology is sufficient. The modern reader is most likely at a disadvantage through his lack of direct knowledge of the classical tradition. The stories of the gods and goddesses, their customary interpretations through the ages, and the language of some of the best-known sources are required knowledge for one who would go past mere mythological adornments to an appreciation of the richness of word-play, thematic shifts, and other reverberations central to Milton's purpose. This article in brief scope sets a contemporary context in which Milton used the myths, describes some of these uses in the poems, and then reviews criticism of Milton's myth over the past three hundred years.

The classical myths, like so many other traditions and institutions in the seventeenth century, suffered a sharp change in Milton's lifetime, declining from a position of high seriousness to one of scorn and crude humor (Douglas Bush documents this decline in *Mythology and the Renaissance Tradition in English Poetry* [1963]). We can see in publications from two years, 1632 and 1667, the kind of conflict surrounding the myths in the period. Scholars give 1632 as the approximate date for Milton's *L'Al* and *IlP* and for the masque, *Arc\**, all three poems that draw on a classically pure form of mythology. The same year saw George Sandys's translation and commentary on Ovid's* *Metamorphoses,* one of the last and most popular of many such efforts in the Renaissance to explain the moral wisdom contained in the pagan poet. Henry Reynolds's *Mythomystes* was also published in 1632, a throwback to the mystical-allegorical theories of the Italian Neoplatonists* a century and a half before. Reynolds draws on Orpheus*, the Cabala, the poetry of Zoroaster, and the art of numbers of Avenzoar the Babylonian, among other esoteric sources, to reveal the mystical knowledge hidden in the fables. And finally, 1632 is also the date of the sharpest attack on the myths yet, the Puritan William Prynne's* massive *Histriomastix*. A syllogism Prynne constructs to expose stage plays and the myths should give something of the book's tone: "1. Plays which give stories of rape-adultery, etc. of Heathen-Gods are odious. 2. But such are most plays. 3. Therefore, they are odious and unlawfull" (p. 75).

It is an understatement after this mixture of Sandys, Reynolds, and Prynne all in the same year to say that this was a time of transition for the myths. At this stage in his poems the young Milton seems oblivious to any controversy, yet that would not long be the case, as we shall see. By the time of the Restoration, mythology is no longer vital as a serious tradition for poetry; Milton's epic appears anachronistic in that it employs it. The year 1667 would be better represented by Thomas Sprat's *History of the Royal Society* than by *PL*. "The Wit of the Fables and Religions of the Ancient World is well-nigh consum'd," Sprat proclaims. "They have already serv'd the poets long enough" (ed. Jackson I. Cope and Harold Whitmore Jones [1958], p. 414). There was little room in the clear light of scientific rationalism nor in the inner light of Puritan faith for the shady bowers of Olympian fable. How far the myths had fallen is obvious in Dryden's judgment of those who admire Ovid's wit:

> The Things they admire are only glittering Trifles, and so far from being Witty, that in a serious Poem they are nauseous, because they are unnatural. Wou'd any Man who is ready to die for Love, describe his Passion like Narcissus? ("Preface" to *Fables Ancient and Modern, The Poems of John Dryden,* ed. James Kinsley [1958], 4:1451)

There were, however, several lines of recourse for the seventeenth-century poet who shared some of the Puritan* convictions about the myths and yet did not want to cut himself off from the great classical traditions that had inspired poetry in the past. First, Puritan or not, he would from his earliest school days likely have been trained in a curriculum heavily weighted toward the classics, and

he would have learned the myths from handbooks that accompanied exercises in rhetoric* and Latin versification. Donald Clark describes how Ovid was started at St. Paul's School* in the Third Form, with verses from the *Metamorphoses* analyzed and stories "in Heathen-Gods" turned into Latin in the Fourth Form (*John Milton at St. Paul's School* [1948], pp. 110–13). So the poet might then turn quite instinctively to Ovid for language and imagery as he began to write his own poetry.

Furthermore, since translations and interpretations of mythological texts were best sellers all through the period, Milton and his contemporaries would constantly update their school learning with these popular sources. Sandys's *Metamorphoses* and Arthur Golding's version, first published in 1567, were probably the most influential, and both were careful to reconcile Ovid with Christian doctrine. But there were many other mythographers, most of them claimed over the years as likely sources for Milton's allusions as if it were possible to pin someone of his learning and inventiveness to a one-for-one borrowing): Boccaccio*, Giraldus, Comes, Robert and Charles Stephanus, and Cartari all wrote handbooks before 1560; Bacon*, Ralegh*, Selden*, and Ross* allegorized the myths in the seventeenth century, Ross as late as the 1650s. Although the Greek and Roman fables received most attention, we know from the catalogues in *Nat* and Book 1 of *PL* that Milton knew the mythologies of several cultures. Because many of these pagan gods—Thammuz, Rimmon, Dagon, Baal, and others in the lists—are actually in the Bible, their impact in passages describing the fallen angels* is all the more powerful.

Another influence that served to counteract a strict prohibition against the myths was a recognition even by extremists like Prynne of the need for rhetoric, poetry, music, and other "inventions of Infidels, and Pagans, which may further Gods glory, or the good of men" (p. 18). Interest continued in finding among the pagan writers intimations of Christian truth, what Puritan minister John Bulkley sees in Ovid's *Metamorphoses* as "the Footsteps of the Sacred History" (in *The Puritans,* ed. Perry Miller and Thomas H. Johnson [1938], p. 682). Convinced of God's presence in historical events and of the imminence of His shining forth again to Englishmen, Puritans were receptive to the ancient tradition of Christian typology*, the interpretation of persons and events in the Old Testament as prefigurations of New Testament persons and events. It was even possible to extend these divine connections in history to Puritan England, as in the use of David as a type for Cromwell*. In the last two books of *PL*, Milton has Michael explain "types and shadowes" of the Old Testament to Adam (12. 232–33, 303). In the Middle Ages several of the figures and events of classical myth were extended this typological interpretation, and it was not a far step to continue this tradition for Orpheus, Hercules, and a few others, with proper qualifications, in the Puritan period.

The ambivalence that Milton and his age felt increasingly about the classical myths made them ideally suited for use as a major source of imagery in his poems. It would take some experimenting for him to get the right balance, and this process we shall see in the minor poems. There is a definite tension between the feelings evoked over the centuries through the sense imagery of the myths and a "right reason*" demanding control of these feelings and acknowledgment of the myths' pagan source. This tension is a major element in the theme and dramatic action of Milton's poems. He makes of the myths a perfect correlative for his own predicament and for the human struggles —be they expressed as body and soul, nature* and grace*, pagan and Christian—that must be resolved to justify God's ways to men. In Milton's time the Ovidian tradition had decayed for enough to allow an imaginative objectivity, but not so far that it was beyond use. Milton is able to hold in suspension that moment

in the tradition when one could look back to the glories of the golden age and ahead to the rejection of the ancient fables—in Milton's case for a greater glory.

All the uses of myth found in the later poems are developed in Milton's earlier ones. Just as he was experimenting with different styles* and genres in these poems, so was he varying his subject matter and the structure of his imagery. There is little need to stop over the early Latin poems or even *L'Al* and *IlP*. The former are unabashedly Ovidian in their use of myth, consonant with the practice of Renaissance elegies in Latin. Sometimes they contain personal accounts of the young poet's yearnings and high poetic calling (see *El* 1, 4, 5, and 6, for example), but the myth is primarily decorative. *L'Al* and *IlP* are closer to the spirit of these Latin poems than to any of the English ones. We can agree with Bush's observation that "nowhere in these serene and lovely poems is there a hint that the classical deities which adorn them are of the tribe of Satan; 'yet there was no fear of Jove' " (p. 271).

In *FInf* Milton uses mythological figures to describe both "the sordid world" and "sheenie Heav'n." Stanzas 1–4 are an allegory* at the level of nature of winter's rape of the child. Winter, classicized as one of "the wanton gods," wants to free the child, but he is powerless even to metamorphose her to "a purple flower," as Apollo had done with Hyacinth (see Hugh Maclᴇan (*Milton: Modern Essays in Criticism,* ed. Arthur E. Barker [1965], pp. 21–30).

But things are little better in "sheenie Heav'n." Milton blurs the distinction between "the hated earth" and "heav'n-lov'd innocence," at least within those stanzas of classical material which make up a large part of the poem, by confounding his image of the mythological heaven with doubts and strife. In stanza 6 the possibility that the child might have gone to a classical heaven is undercut by a Puritan conditioner—"the Elisian fields (if such there were)," a doubt that by *PL* would be put to positive use in comparisons: "Hesperian Fables true, / If true, here only." Then in stanza 7 it seems clear that there is little difference between the uncertainty of earthly existence and the disorder of things above:

Wert thou some Starr which from the ruin'd roofe
Of shak't Olympus by mischance didst fall;
Which carefull *Jove* in natures true behoofe
Took up, and in fit place did reinstall?
Or did of late earths Sonnes besiege the wall
Of sheenie Heav'n, and thou some goddess fled
Amongst us here below to hide thy nectar'd head.

No cause is even given for Olympus's "ruin'd roofe," the siege of the Titans having come "of late," later, we assume, than the shakeup of the first lines of the stanza. And for a goddess to seek sanctuary in nature from the wars of heaven is a full reversal of the distinction elsewhere in the poem between heaven and earth.

Other difficulties Milton has in the poem, such as the change in the child's role to that of savior at the end, are surely compounded by Milton's inability to subordinate the material from classical mythology to his overall theme of the division between heaven and earth. In the lines on the Elysian Fields and Jove's Olympus he has allowed his concern to emphasize the difference between the pagan and Christian heavens to take priority over the main theme of the poem.

No such difficulties are found in the ode *Nat*, where Milton's greater control over his imagery* and theme results in a more sophisticated treatment of mythical material within the levels of nature and grace. The last third of the poem is about the flight of the pagan gods with the entry into the world of "the Heav'n-born-childe." The catalogue of the gods, a shortened version of the one in *PL*, anticipates the link between the Olympians and the fallen angels in the kingdom of "th'Old Dragon," Satan. Apollo, Dagon, Thammuz, Moloch, Osiris, and the others "troop to th'infernal Jail" in a reverse of events in the epic where the devils come from Hell to Earth to live among the sons of Eve.

A second and quite different anticipation in the ode of Milton's use of myth in his later works is the figure of the young Hercules throttling the snakes in his cradle as a prefiguration of the infant Christ:

Nor all the Gods beside,
Longer dare abide,
    Not *Typhon* huge ending in snaky twine:
Our Babe to shew his Godhead true,
Can in his swadling bands controul the damned crew.

(224–28)

The imagery of *Nat* is, in fact, organized typologically, anticipating Milton's use of this method in the treatment of pagan myths and other material in later poems. Here the realm of nature participates in the nativity by prefiguring in the activities of its personified characters the events to come from God's grace.

Hercules appears again as a type in *Passion*, where he is used for Christ's temptation and labors, but not for the Crucifixion itself:

Most perfect Heroe, try'd in heaviest plight
Of labours huge and hard, too hard for human wight.

(13–14)

Indeed, Milton is never able to address the subject of the Passion directly in the poem. After bemoaning in several extravagant conceits the difficulties he has with his "plaining verse," he breaks off after eight stanzas, "nothing satisfi'd with what was begun." The use of Hercules or Orpheus as types for Christ's suffering on the Cross might have provided the images the poet so desperately needed. But Milton seems to follow the conviction laid down by Justin Martyr* and other Church Fathers that the Crucifixion was the one act that the pagans had never imitated in their mythmaking. Elsewhere Milton portrays the deaths of Hercules and Orpheus five times, but never specifically as types of Christ's death on the Cross. This is the more remarkable when we recognize how common the practice was in the Renaissance : Spenser*, for example, had used Hercules' death as a type for the Crucifixion in *The Faerie Queene* (1. 11. 27), and D. C. Allen reports of the use of Orpheus for Christ that "by Milton's time it was such a part of the symbolic fabric of Christianity that one had only to think of 'lyre' to say 'cross' " (in Barker, p. 182).

The imagery of *Mask* is organized as allegory, which works on a moral level, rather than the typology that we have seen Milton developing in his previous poems. Appropriately for the masque form, Milton relies almost entirely on classical mythology for his imagery. But all the imagery has a Christian reference through the poem's themes and explicitly through occasional Christian metaphors : "sainted seats," "hovering Angel," "Saintly Chastity," and the like.

As in *FInf*, the myths in *Mask* are lined up on both sides of the struggle between nature and grace (these two terms for the split were first given prominence by A. S. P. Woodhouse*; see *A Maske at Ludlow: Essays on Milton's Comus,* ed. John S. Diekhoff [1968], pp. 17–42), here represented by the "wilde Wood" that is the setting for the conflict between Comus and the Lady and "Joves Court," the home of the attendant Spirit. But unlike the confusion of realms that develops in the earlier poem, the imagery in *Mask* is sharply split between nature and grace, or in mythological terms between the world of Comus, Bacchus, and Circe and that of Sabrina, "Celestial Cupid," and Psyche. Bush and others detail a passage in the attendant Spirit's opening speech that Milton deleted from the 1634 acted version of the text, no doubt because it depicted an Edenic scene in heaven, complete with "scalie-harnest dragon," that was too earthly in its sensuous distractions (Bush, pp. 276–77). Milton realized this and so sacrificed it, in contrast to his failure of editorial nerve in *FInf*.

Additions to the 1637 printed edition of *Mask* only widened the split between the Spirit's "strange removed climes" and "this pinfold" earth, especially the Lady's speech on "the sage and serious doctrine of Virginity" (778–805). Milton may have intended a resolution in the lines added to the epilogue about Venus and Adonis, and on a higher level, the wedded bliss of Cupid and Psyche :

Beds of *Hyacinth,* and Roses
Where young *Adonis* oft reposes,
Waxing well of his deep wound
In slumber soft, and on the ground
Sadly sits th'*Assyrian* Queen;
But far above in spangled sheen
Celestial *Cupid* her fam'd Son advanc't,
Holds his dear *Pysche* sweet intranc't
After her wandring labours long,
Till free consent the gods among
Make her his eternal Bride,
And from her fair unspotted side
Two blissful twins are to be born,
Youth and Joy; so *Jove* hath sworn.
                                    (997–1010)

The variety of critical interpretations of these thirteen lines points up the difficulty they present as a convincing resolution to the conflict in the poem. E. M. W. Tillyard*, to take one example, claims that the passage is such a clear reference to Spenser's Gardon of Adonis in Book 2 of *The Faerie Queene* that all the moral force of Spenser's allegory is easily transferred to Milton's masque— "(List mortals, if your ears be true)": Comus's palace is the Bower of Bliss and the Lady must trade her role of Belphoebe for Amoret (in Diekhoff, pp. 45–47, 52–54). There are, however, some differences between Spenser's garden and Milton's. If Milton were counting on an immediate identification by the reader of the garden in his epilogue, he would surely expect him to recognize that all was not as well here as it had been in Spenser's much expanded version. Notably, though Adonis is "waxing well of his deep wound," he still has it, and consequently while he sleeps on the bed of flowers Venus sits sadly on the ground. In *The Faerie Queene*, Adonis is well enough recovered to be "ioying his goddesse, and of her enioyd," and any threat of further harm is gone with the secure imprisonment beneath the mountain of the wild boar that had attacked him (3. 6. 48). So too, Spenser has Cupid and Psyche in the Garden of Adonis with their child, Pleasure. In *Mask* Cupid is "far above in spangled sheen," his marriage to Psyche awaiting "free consent the gods among." The material was at hand, in the Adonis myth made popular by Spenser, for a reconciliation between the extreme positions of Comus and the Lady. But Milton chose instead in his 1637 revisions to make even more emphatic the Lady's defense of virginity with "sacred vehemence." And he rearranged Spenser's Garden of Adonis scene so that it too would be separated into two spheres.

*Lyc,* too, is concerned with the separation between a natural scene devastated by Lycidas's death and the "blest King-doms meek." But now with the subject the death and resurrection of a poet-priest rather than the rewards of virginity, a convincing resolution is achieved. The poem moves, as Rosemond Tuve says, "entirely on a metaphorical plane," and so a study of the ordering and the inter-connection of the imagery is the only way to understand the poem (in *Milton's Lycidas: The Tradition and the Poem,* ed. C. A. Patrides [1961], p. 179). Figures and events from the classical myths are used at key points along the way to anticipate or prefigure the resolution at the end. The typological relation between the myths and Christian imagery had been used, as we have seen, in various instances in previous poems, but never had these two sources been so fully integrated into the basic structure of a poem.

No figure from the myths would more correspond to Lycidas or, indeed, to Mil-ton himself, as we conclude from his frequent use of the myth, than Orpheus. We know that Milton rewrote the Orpheus section more than any other in the poem, and the most important change was surely from "goarie scalp rowl downe the Thracian lee" to the final version, "goary visage down the stream was sent / Down the swift *Hebrus* to the *Lesbian* shore" (62–63). The crude and unneces-sarily startling "scalp" is amended to a more refined and abstract "visage" ("divine head" was an intermediate emendation), embodying more closely the sense of a face singing. But also the entire image takes to the water from the lee and the story is carried through as far as Lesbos, to be suspended there for the time. The Orpheus myth, like most of the other imagery of the poem, is consummated in Lycidas's salvation "through the dear might of him that walk'd the waves" (173). We discover that Orpheus was a type to be fulfilled by the soothing of Lycidas's head

Where other groves, and other streams along,
With *Nectar* pure his oozy Lock's he laves,
(174–75)

much as Orpheus's head was comforted on Lesbos in the legend. And like Orpheus in his charmed position on Lesbos, Lycidas becomes "Genius of the shore."

Of course, much of the working of these images and sounds is implicit, such as any connection between the "Miter'd locks" of St. Peter and the "oozy Lock's" of Lycidas. We must heed Tuve's warning that the imagery in any of Milton's poems is too complex and derivative to be analyzed apart from a general treatment of traditions and of his other poems (pp. 188–89). The passage of Orpheus, for example, is given its proper place in the meaning of the poem only after the reader knows something of the weight this figure had accumulated through the centuries. But with this approach, we can see that "all-judging *Jove,*" who follows Orpheus, is substituted in the first third of the poem as a type for the Last Judgment, so that the explicitly Christian images of resolution can be kept for the St. Peter passage and even more fully for Lycidas's resurrection. Milton had now perfected the method of typology that enabled him to include all the rich imagery and powerful drama of the clas-sical myths within his Christian frame-work.

With this understanding of the basic structure of the poem, other images assume new, dramatic meaning. The invocations to Arethuse and Alpheus, taken together, follow a movement of imagery similar to the Orpheus passage. None of the story of Arethuse's efforts to flee the river god Alpheus as a stream is presented in *Lyc*. But Milton appropriately addresses the nymph as "Fountain *Arethuse*" and the god as "*Sicilian* Muse," fixing the attention of the knowing reader on the resolution of the myth, Arethuse's rising as a fountain in Sicily, her waters mingled peacefully with Alpheus's. Thus, in addition to signaling the return of the pastoral* voice at two points in the poem, after the pronouncements of Phoebus and St. Peter, these two classical figures anticipate the rising of the sun and Lycidas from the sea.

We know from autobiographical* passages in both his poems and prose that Milton's plan for an epic on the Fall of Man* had evolved slowly :

Since first this Subject for Heroic Song
Pleas'd me long choosing, and beginning late.
(*PL* 9. 25–26)

Neither his original plan to write an Arthuriad* nor his detailed outlines for a tragedy, "Adam unparadiz'd," would provide Milton with a tableau broad enough to contain the wealth of classical imagery that he had come to understand in all his previous shorter poems would be essential for the flesh on the bones of his major work. In his elegy to Diodati*, Milton explains the Spartan life required of the epic poet if he "sings of wars, of Heaven controlled by a Jove full grown, of duty-doing heroes, of captains that are half gods, if he sings now the holy counsels of the gods above, now the realms deep below wherein howls a savage hound" (63–66). Certainly a young man whose poetic vision sweeps from "the holy counsels" to "the realms deep below" would attempt to find a subject and an approach that would allow him to follow the tradition of Homer* and Virgil* rather than the pattern of Puritan epic soon to be set by Davenant* and Cowley* in which the classical myths were banished.

The answer, of course, was to be an epic where for nine of its twelve books Milton could freely apply his classical imagery in an unfallen world to Satan and the devils and to Eden. He also evolved a special role for the narrator that made it possible for Milton to be the classical poet telling his Christian story. In *Milton's Epic Voice* (1963) Anne Davidson Ferry gives full treatment to the narrator, the blind bard, singing in the fallen world with "mortal voice," yet illuminated by "sovran vital Lamp," and soaring above human flight. There is an important distance in both time and space between Adam and a narrator who is aware historically of the move of the tribe of Satan to Olympus. And there is also a great difference between the angel Raphael and a narrator who, like his reader, needs to liken "spiritual to corporeal forms." Almost all the rich detail supplied by references to myth and history comes through the narrator (there are a few exceptions, like the implicit Narcissus myth in Eve's description of herself); without the narrator, Milton would have lost most of his descriptive power and the means of anticipating the action of his story, which is the most important function of his imagery.

The narrator explains early that the fallen angels are to be identified with the pagan gods, a traditional view espoused since the Church Fathers to discredit the pagan religion :

Nor had they yet among the Sons of *Eve*
Got them new Names, till wandring ore the
   Earth,
Through Gods high sufferance for the tryal
   of man,
By falsities and lyes the greatest part
Of Mankind they corrupted to forsake
God thir Creator, . . .
. . . . . . . . . . . . . . . . . . . . .
Then were they known to men by various
   Names
And various Idols through the Heathen World.
(1. 364–75)

Because of their awesome size and their proclivity for rebellions, these pagan gods, especially the Titans, were ideal for depicting both the stature of Satan and his crew and the revolt in Heaven. And they also worked to anticipate the rebellion on earth that would make their identification with the heathen gods historical fact.

If we understand Milton's view of the origins of the pagan gods and his double use of them for description and anticipation, then several key passages that have caused the editors and critics trouble might be clarified. For example, the standard interpretation of the famous passage relating Mulciber's fall at the end of Book 1 is that a chastened Milton undercuts his own obvious relish in the lines with a concluding "thus they relate, Erring" (738–51). The pagan error, however, was not in the myth's fictitiousness, but in the chronology of the event. For the next lines explain that "he with this rebellious rout / Fell long before," a historical fact that pagans with only partial knowledge of history would not be expected to know. The subtle choice of words to describe Mulciber's fall —"from Morn / To Noon he fell, from Noon to dewy Eve, / A Summer's day"— is an implicit anticipation of Eve's fall at noon, the ruin of another summer's day.

Myths used to depict Eden and its inhabitants from the other chief cluster of mythological imagery in *PL,* and these too have a double purpose. Here, however, there are definitely no authentic historical links as there were between the devils and the pagan gods, so these highly sensual myths must be quite self-consciously labeled as fictions : "If true, here only, and of delicious taste" (4. 251). The only exceptions to "feign'd" myths in this section of the poem are those used unqualified in descriptions of Eve. Here the anticipations are also explicit, as in this comparison with Pandora :

More lovely then *Pandora,* whom the Gods Endowd with all thir gifts, and O too like In sad event.

(4. 714–16)

Most editors and critics have recognized Eve's precarious position in the epic, and William Empson in *Some Versions of Pastoral* (1947) has gone so far as to put her in the devil's camp from the start. The association between Eve and Satan is most explicit in Book 10 when the narrator describes

how the Serpent, whom they calld *Ophion* with *Eurynome,* the wide-Encroaching *Eve* perhaps, had first the rule Of high *Olympus.*

(580–83)

The eighteenth-century editor Bentley* excised the passage as indecorous, and indeed the crucial "perhaps" that qualifies Eve seems a very thin lifeline to the "paradise within" that she had been promised. However, Milton has a few lines earlier in Book 10 represented Eve as a type for Mary, "second Eve." The tension in Eden because of Eve's ambivalent character, reflected largely through mythological imagery, is central to the poem's dramatic action. But in these passages in Book 10 and in earlier sections, as in 4. 456–76 where Eve hears a voice as she gazes Narcissus-like into a pool in Eden—quite different from the terrifying voice Sin hears in her Narcissus episode (2. 759–89), Milton carefully controls Eve's character so that the Christian reader will understand her final role as "Mother of human Race."

After the Fall the myths describing Paradise would be out of place since Adam and Eve speak "bland words at will." But with the descent of "Prevenient Grace" in the last two books, Milton turns to those special myths that could be used as prefigurations of the Christian history to come. Now Adam and Eve are compared to Deucalion and Pyrrha, who were, in turn, widely recognized as types for Noah and his wife (11. 9–14). And as the Archangel Michael comes to escort Adam and Eve out of Eden, he is escorted by cherubim described as having four faces, "like a double Janus," in an emblematic passage that combines the myths with the biblical visions of Ezekiel and Revelation (11. 128–36).

Three references to myth in *SA* are noted by Bush, as well as a surprising

range in *PR,* given its subject and theme
(Bush, pp. 293–96). Those concluding too
simplistically that Christ's denunciation
of classical learning in Book 4 of *PR* is
Milton's own opinion in his later years
should look again at the ironic reference
in the middle of the passage to the cloud
by which Jove deceived Ixion on Olympus :

> Who therefore seeks in these
> True wisdom, finds her not, or by delusion
> Far worse, her false resemblance only meets,
> An empty cloud.
> (318–21)

It is, of course, an apt illustration of the
frustrations due false seekers, but it is
surprising, to say the least, in a passage
that goes on twenty lines later to a
rigorous censure of "thir Gods ridiculous."

Near the end of the poem Milton
uses the myth of Hercules vanquishing
Antaeus, a traditional type, as a simile
for Christ's victory over Satan (4. 563–68).
General critical opinion has held that
Milton followed the trend in his age,
becoming increasingly antagonistic toward
the classical myths in his later poems. But
his sustained use of myth in *PR,* especially the Hercules passage that takes us
back to the early use of Hercules in *Nat,*
should prove that the myths remained
vital material for poetry throughout his
life.

From the start Milton's uses of myth
have been a subject of interest and controversy among critics, editors, scholars,
and other poets. The body of criticism in
any period about a major writer is often
more of a clue to the literary sensibilities
of that age than it is an increase in
understanding of the writer. This is true
of Milton and particularly true of his
uses of the myths, since each age has had
to consider for itself the role myths should
play in literature, both past and present.

The 1674 edition of *PL* has a commendatory poem by Andrew Marvell*
that marks the first time the epithet
*sublime* is attached to the epic. Yet Marvell confesses his early fears that Milton's
"vast design" encumbers sacred themes
with all the pagan trappings :

> the Argument
> Held me a while misdoubting his Intent,
> That he would ruine (for I saw him strong)
> The sacred Truths to Fable and old Song.
> ("On Paradise Lost," 5–8)

Farther on in the poem Marvell affirms
that all the elements of *PL,* even, we
assume, Milton's heavy use of the classical
myths, are subordinated to the overruling
theme and tone :

> That Majesty which through thy Work
>    doth Reign
> Draws the Devout, deterring the Profane.
> And things divine thou treatst of in such state
> As them preserves, and thee, inviolate.
> (31–34)

But Marvell's statement of his own
early doubts about Milton's use of the
pagan myths is a forecast of the controversy that would persist through the
next century. Although Addison's* papers
in the *Spectator* in 1712 constituted the
most thorough and appreciative critique
of Milton to date, he does explain that
among the defects of *PL*

> is his frequent allusion to heathen fables,
> which are not certainly of a piece with the
> divine subject of which he treats. I do not
> find fault with these allusions, where the
> poet himself represents them as fabulous,
> as he does in some places, but where he
> mentions them as truths and matters of
> fact. (in *Milton Criticism: Selections from
> Four Centuries,* ed. James Thorpe [1951],
> p. 52)

Dr. Richard Bentley was not nearly so
generous in his notorious 1732 edition of
*PL.* "Fierce Bentley," as he became
known, simply eliminated most material
from the myths, including the comparisons
between the "fair fields of Enna" and
Eden in Book 5 and Scylla and Sin in
Book 2. The latter, Bentley scorned, only
"contaminate[s] this most majestic poem
with trash," giving "idle and dangerous
stories to his young and credulous Female
Readers" (in R. J. White, *Dr. Bentley*
[1965], p. 218).

Bentley's harshness stirred Milton
defenders to a new reading of the epic
in search of justifications. In the first
variorum edition of *PL* in 1749, Thomas

Newton* pauses at the Deucalion and Pyrrha passage in Book 11 to note:

> Milton has been often censured for his frequent allusions to the heathen mythology, and for mixing fables with sacred truths: But it may be observed in favour of him, that what he borrows from the heathen mythology, he commonly applies only by way of similitude; and a similitude from thence may illustrate his subject as well as from any thing else, especially since it is one of the first things that we learn at school, and is made by the ancients such an essential part of poetry, that it can hardly be separated from it; and no wonder that Milton was ambitious of showing something of his reading in this kind, as well as in all other. (in *The Poetical Works of John Milton,* ed. Henry John Todd [1801], 3:336–37)

Samuel Johnson* seems to accept Milton's uses of myth in *PL,* but turns instead, in his celebrated Milton essay in 1779, on the mingling of "trifling fictions" with "the most awful and sacred truths" in *Lyc.* Not only are the pagan deities indecorous, but they are boring: "Nothing can less display knowledge, or less exercise invention, than to tell . . . how one god asks another god what is become of Lycidas, and how neither god can tell" (in Thorpe, p. 67). Yet until the structure of the poem has been better understood in recent times, the best that Milton's defenders, like editors Warton* and Todd*, could come up with was the excuse that Spenser and the Italians had set the example of such minglings in pastoral for Milton obligingly to follow.

The enthusiasm for Milton and his epic among the Romantics is well known, and it surely extends in a poet like Keats* to the language and imagery of poems heavily mythological, especially *Hyperion.* Shelley* anticipates a broader, modern view of myth when in *A Defence of Poetry* (1821) he credits Milton with molding and thus helping to preserve the Christian myth as well as those from other cultures: "The *Divina Comedia* and *Paradise Lost* have conferred upon modern mythology a systematic form" (in Thorpe, p. 359).

In the first half of the twentieth century, at the same time that attacks on Milton's "grand style" were mounting, the kind of thorough, scholarly studies of the previous century continued, contributing several books on Milton's uses of mythology that deserve mention, if only briefly. In 1900 Charles Osgood* catalogued Milton's allusions to classical mythology and traced their sources in the classics, Renaissance and medieval texts, and among Milton's own works. His long introductory essay, though a bit didactic on Milton's moral vision, makes the case convincingly that the "organ voice" is always in perfect tune and capable of the most subtle touches:

> His treatment of mythology is throughout characterized by firmness and control. It is felt in his compression of myths, and in the freedom with which he moves among them and groups them. It is felt more distinctly in the subjection to which he reduces every myth. Frequently as they occur, it is impossible to find one of them which is not in some way subordinate to a ruling idea or truth. (*The Classical Mythology of Milton's English Poems,* p. xlv)

Douglas Bush has only a chapter on Milton in his impressive *Mythology and the Renaissance Tradition in English Poetry* (1932; 2nd ed. rev., 1963). But we learn much from seeing Milton in context in the book: as the culmination of the mythological tradition, at once both more learned and more individualistic in his uses of the tradition than any English poet, yet writing at a time when the myths were being reduced to travesty. Bush gracefully combines broad strokes for general themes with the finely chosen, striking detail. As a result, we can trace the course of poetry generally in the Renaissance through his survey of the single traditional element of the myths.

Finally, of this kind of scholarship exploring classical backgrounds of Milton's myths, two books by Davis P. Harding* should be noted. While his *Milton and the Renaissance Ovid* (1946) too often pushes literary influences from Ovid and his Renaissance editors to claims of actual verbal borrowing by Milton, always a hazard with a poet that inventive and well read, it does give us a full appreciation of thee ubiquitous "Christian Ovid." *The Club of Hercules* (1962) is more restrained in working with the "ghost influences" of *PL*. Harding shows in implicit and open allusions and verbal echoes (he explains the use of the Narcissus myth to link Sin and Eve; Osgood had missed it) how much a gloss on the classics, especially the *Aeneid, PL* is.

The effect of the challenges by Eliot*, Pound, Leavis, and others to Milton's reputation has been, like the earlier charges by Bentley and Johnson, an invigoration of Milton studies, where attention is turned primarily to the texts themselves and to the poems' meanings. The burden of these books and articles is that Milton's "grand style" does stand up under close scrutiny, and that the imagery and themes, including the myths, are remarkably unified and relevant, the verse ingenious and subtle. In many of these studies Milton's mythology is analyzed not for its sources as much as for its contribution in particular passages to the larger meanings of the poems.

One of the earliest of this new wave of Milton studies and still the most important for our purposes is Isabel MacCaffrey's *Paradise Lost as "Myth"* (1959). Drawing on Jung, Cassirer, and the view of comparative mythology we saw expressed in Shelley, MacCaffrey describes how *PL* embodies not just the theme of the Christian myth or "one true history," but also the structure of verse and imagery necessary for the kind of cyclic pattern common to all myths. The classical legends are from this perspective useful in reflecting the true myths: "a broken image is reconstituted by fitting together the fragments that fallen man has been able to collect in his myths, and at the same time the status of the image as the original of and superior to all the fragments is established" (pp. 122–23). MacCaffrey pursues her subject with finesse and good judgment and the result of the new context she sets is a genuinely new treatment of mythological passages. [JHC]

**NALSON PAPERS:** *see* PAPERS, STATE.

**NATURAL HISTORY.** Until recently, when natural history came to refer simply to the description of animal life in a relatively nonscientific and popular form, the term encompassed the systematic description of "all natural objects, animal, vegetable, and mineral" (*OED*). Writers of the sixteenth and seventeenth centuries could draw on a long tradition of accumulated lore by referring to the work of encyclopedists such as Stephen Batman, John Maplet, and Peter de la Primaudaye or upon separate works: lapidaries, herbals, and bestiaries. The Encyclopedia tradition is discussed at length by Svendsen* in the opening chapter of *Milton and Science* (1956). The sources the encyclopedists could draw upon included classical science (especially Aristotle*), Arabic science, biblical writings, the work of medieval scientists, and reports of travelers such as Marco Polo and Mandeville.

Milton's understanding of science* is old-fashioned and bookish, deductive and authoritarian rather than inductive; he has read in the classical and medieval writers, but he is unaware of contemporary experimenters. Lawrence Babb asserts in *The Moral Cosmos of Paradise Lost* (1970), "there is no indication . . . that [Milton] understood Bacon's scientific method or its philosophical or social significance. . . . Although he eventually waked up to the meaning of the new discoveries in astronomy, he remained, on the whole, unaware or unconcerned while one of the most consequential developments in intellectual history was in rapid progress" (p. 42). Facing the medieval world rather than the modern, Milton holds that for fallen man to tamper with the elements of nature* is to engage in the work of the devils. Natural history must be subservient to moral philosophy and ethics* and is not studied for its own sake, just as all learning must eventually produce virtuous action and is not an end in itself.

In *Educ* Milton recommends that students read "all the historical physiology of Aristotle and Theophrastus" as well as "Seneca's *Natural Questions*" and Pliny. (Edward Phillips records that Milton made his nephews read "a great part of Pliny's *Natural History*.") "And in natural philosophy they may proceed leisurely from History of Meteors, Minerals, plants and living Creatures, as far as Anatomy" (4 : 283). In *Prol 3* he speaks of the satisfactions of learning*, including "to investigate and to observe the natures of all living creatures; and from these to plunge the mind into the secret powers of stones and plants" (12 : 171). In *Prol 7* he refers to some beast fables from Plutarch's* *Moralia*.

Milton's use of natural history goes beyond providing merely colorful or descriptive images to enforcing a moral statement. He states : "Can we suppose that there is nothing more in fruits and herbs that grow so abundantly than their frail green beauty? If we are to value these things so unworthily as to perceive nothing more in them than brute sensation reveals, we shall seem to act not only vilely and basely, but unjustly and wickedly toward that gracious spirit whom our indifference and ingratitude rob both of much of His glory and of the veneration due to His power" (*Prol 7*). Milton's use of the animal simile as compared with that of other epic poets carries significantly greater "associative force."

We may consider three of the segments of the scale of nature* that constitute the study of natural history, "minerals, plants and living creatures," in that ascending order and begin with the mineral* lore. The "ever-burning Sulphur" (*PL* 1. 69) or brimstone is one of the main minerals* in hell, but there are other ores as well, as the mining scene in *PL* 1. 670ff. indicates. Milton introduces gold into Hell* not for the sake of imagery alone but to enforce a moral statement :

> Let none admire
> That riches grow in Hell; that soyle may best
> Deserve the precious bane.
> (1. 670ff.)

When the scene shifts to heaven, it is

again Satan's crew who are mining, this time the ingredients for gunpowder, "Deep under ground, materials dark and crude, / Of spiritous and fierie spume" (6. 478–79).

Then they dig veins of "Mineral and Stone" to make the cannon and balls. Raphael points out the moral to Adam that such mining is "mischief," "inspir'd / With dev'lish machination" (503–4).

Living in an age when many were "well skill'd / In every vertuous plant and healing herb / That spreds her verdant leaf to th' morning ray" and could show "simples of a thousand names, / Telling their strange and vigorous faculties" (*Mask,* 602ff.), it is not surprising to find Milton displaying a great deal of botanical lore in the pages of his work. Many herbals have been suggested as being Milton's sources : Le Comte cites John Gerard's *Herball or General Historie of Plantes* (1597, 1633, 1636), and Harrison prefers Henry Lyte's *A New Herball* (1578, 1586, 1595, 1619), but as Le Comte points out "there is no such thing in John Milton as a single influence." Svendsen succinctly surveys (pp. 127–36) a great deal of this material as it appears in Milton's prose and poetry. Again, out of an image Milton derives a moral statement, as in the famous passage in *Mask* (619–56) that centers on the magical plant Haemony*. Le Comte has suggested a relationship of its name with Haemonia or Thessaly, a land of magic, and with "blood-red," which suggests a myth associated with the plant Moly, which grew at the spot where a giant was slain by the Sun to save his daughter Circe. He further associates it with the plant "Christes Thorne," reputed for its magic and ability to neutralize enchantments. *Haemony* may represent divine grace* in the allegory* of the poem.

Of the image of the elm and the vine (*PL* 5. 125–219), Svendsen writes, "No bit of botanical lore was better known—it occurs in Horace, Virgil, Columella, Spenser, Shakespeare, Bartholomew, Batman, and Maplet—yet how strikingly Milton uses it" (p. 133). It becomes not only an image of Adam and Eve's careful tending of the garden and the harmonyl within it, but an image of prelapsarian marriage and the couple's harmony with the rest of nature. Some of the effects of the Fall are symbolized in the image of the "Figtree" (*PL* 9. 1099–1115), which provides huge leaves out of which the pair fashion crude clothes to cover their nakedness.

In *PL* 11.414–18, Michael removes the film over Adam's eyes placed there by sin. Thus Adam was enabled to see the vision of the future prepared for him by Michael. Euphrasy and rue, as well as fennel, were known as restoratives of sight, and may well have been tried by Milton for his own blindness*. It is ironically significant that here Adam uses them to achieve that inner "mental sight" that Milton felt he had achieved in compensation for his blindness. Svendsen notes that Milton avoided referring to fennel in this context because of its association with snakes and Satan, so that as always we find Milton preserving the integrity and moral content of his images.

With respect to Milton's sources for his zoological references, it is almost impossible to pin down any one source, for his reading was so wide and animal lore so popular and widespread that the same images may be found in dozens of places. As with his use of mineral and vegetable lore, Milton makes the image subservient to the moral statement he wishes to make. Animals all are lower than man on the scale of being, and the ones Milton singles out are especially perfidious, unpleasant, stupid, or lazy. "Owles and Cuckoes, Asses, Apes and Doggs," as well as "Hinds, Froggs, and Hoggs" are all listed in *Sonn* 12, and the prose is filled with scores : pythons, monsters, serpents, foxes, horses, seagulls, vultures, caterpillars, dormice, ferrets, wild beasts, whales, bees, hornets, wolves, cocks, magpies, sheep, worms, beetles, and more.

Not all of Milton's use of animal lore is pejorative. In *Areop* one of the noblest passages compares England to an eagle, which was thought to be able (like the phoenix) to renew itself. Samson in his glorious death is like the phoenix that dies in flames and is reborn from the ashes.

Milton's most extended passage of natural history is the description of the creation of the beasts of the sea, air, and land on the fifth and sixth days of Creation in *PL* 7. 388–504. The overall impression is one of intense vigor and activity as the sea and air fill, and the animals burst forth from the teeming earth. Svendsen, without even pretending to be complete, discusses seventy-two creatures of sea, air, and land. A total catalogue of Milton's beasts would be a very long one indeed, yet, while his sources are many and difficult to pin down, they strike one as having been drawn mostly from books, rather than from experience. [JWF]

**NATURAM NON PATI SENIUM.** This sixty-nine line Latin poem appeared in both the 1645 and 1673 editions of Milton's works but with no indication as to its date of composition. Miltonists have traditionally assumed that it is the poem that Milton enclosed in a letter to his former teacher, Alexander Gill*, dated July 2, 1628, but this is only an assumption. In his letter, Milton wrote that the poem that he was enclosing was one that he had composed for a Fellow of his College "who had to act as Respondent in the philosophical disputation in this Commencement" : the Fellow "chanced to entrust to my puerility the composition of the verses which annual custom requires to be written on the questions in dispute, being himself already long past the age for trifles of that sort, and more intent on serious things" (*Epistol* 3). The date of the letter has been questioned, however, and 1631 has been suggested for it and *Naturam*. Unfortunately, Milton did not include or further identify the poem when he published his correspondence; thus, it cannot be ascertained which, if any, of Milton's published poems is the one in question.

In support of the traditional assumption that it was *Naturam,* we may note that its subject—that nature is not getting any older—would have been very popular in 1628. Only the year before, George Hakewill* had published a substantial book on the same topic, *An Apologie of the Power and Providence of God in the Government of the World.* In his book, Hakewill reached the same conclusions that Milton reached in his short poems. Indeed, Milton's alleged indebtedness to Hakewill has been one of the principal reasons for the traditional dating of the poem. Milton's poem, however, resembles Hakewill's book only in a general way. Its date, then, remains conjectural, although it no doubt belongs to the poet's Cambridge period.

The issue that Milton treated in *Naturam* is difficult to understand. Through a variety of images embellished with classical allusions, he asserted that the universe is eternally young : the heavenly bodies follow the same course that they always have; the elements of wind and ocean are as powerful as they ever were; the earth itself is as fertile as it ever was. The difficulty lies in grasping the view that Milton, like Hakewill, opposed—that the world was growing old and decaying just as the individual human body did. Modern readers are likely to find that view quaint even when they are familiar with it through the writings of John Donne. The idea, however, was a very old one and also a very popular one with Protestants during the Reformation. It had been espoused by the Church Father Saint Cyprian, and had been recently and vigorously restated by the Bishop of Gloucester, Godfrey Goodman, in his work *The Fall of Man,* 1616.

The issue, then, was a vital one to Milton and his contemporaries. Furthermore, as Joseph Allen Bryant, Jr., has observed, "there is nothing . . . in any other work by Milton which precludes our regarding the description of the universe in *Naturam non pati senium* as an accurate and adequate statement of Milton's mature opinion . . ." (*SAMLA Studies in Milton* [1953], p. 6). This being so, *Naturam* must be considered a significant minor poem in the Miltonic canon. [ERG]

**NATURE.** While readily granting the existence of evil within the created order, Christianity has never conceded that any segment of nature is either purposeless or deprived of the constant supervision of God. The sum total of creation, it is affirmed, lives and moves and has its being under the Shadow of the Most High : nature is God's "vicaire" (as Chaucer had maintained) or—to use some of Donne's metaphors—"Gods immediate commissioner," "foreman," "Lieutenant," and "Vicegerent." Hence Dante's* statement that "natura lo suo corso prende/dal divino intelletto" (*Inf.* 11. 99ff.)—a conviction that during the English Renaissance was rephrased by Richard Hooker as follows : "it cannot be, but nature hath some Director of infinite knowledge to guide her in all her wayes. Who the guide of Nature, but onely the God of Nature? *In him we live, move, and are* [Acts 17 : 28]. Those things which nature is said to doe, are by divine Arte performed, using Nature as an instrument: nor is there any such Arte or Knowledge divine in Nature her selfe working, but in the guide of natures worke" (*Of the Lawes of Ecclesiasticall Politie* [1617], p. 8). In sum, by differentiating sharply between God and nature, the Renaissance perpetuated the traditional distinction between God as *natura naturans* (nature "naturing" or creative) and the created order as *natura naturata* (nature "natured" or created).

The thesis that nature it totally subordinate to the Divine Purpose has inevitably led Christianity to an emphatic denial that we are the slaves of change and flies of every wind that blows. The Reformers could always turn to Calvin* for a lucid statement : "nothing commeth by chaunce, but what soever commeth to passe in the world, commeth by the secrete providence of God" (*Com-*

mentaries . . . upon the Prophet Daniell, trans. Arthur Golding [1570], fol. 65). This and similar affirmations were finally directed against the Renaissance obsession with "the ever-whirling wheele of Change," which Christian apologists viewed with mounting alarm and which resulted often in such passionate denunciations as the following by Justus Lipsius: "Thinkest thou that CHAUNCE or FORTUNE beareth any sway in this excellent frame of the world? Or that the affaires of mortall men are caried headlong by chance-medley? I wot well thou thinkest not so, nor any man els that hath either wisdome or wit in his head" (Two Bookes of Constancie, trans. Sir John Stradling [1595], p. 32). Instead of "chance-medley," the expositors of the faith maintained that the universe is pervaded by an order which—in the words of Sir Thomas Elyot—"lyke a streyghte lyne issueth oute of provydence, and passethe directly throughe all thyngs" (Of the Knowledge which maketh a Wise Man, ed. E. J. Howard [1946], p. 103).

The Renaissance belief in cosmic order has been made abundantly clear by many scholars. A statement by Thomas Wilson summarizes the standard thesis: "al things stande by order, and without order nothing can be. For by an order we are borne, by an order we live, and by an order we make our ende. By an order and rule as head, and other obey as members. By an order Realmes stande, and Lawes take force. Yea, by an order the whole worke of Nature, and the perfite state of all the Elements have their appointed course" (The Arte of Rhetorique [1553, rev. 1560], ed. G. H. Mair [1909], pp. 156–57). As may be expected, such statements multiplied to an intimidating degree in the innumerable treatises directed against atheism. But the essential point of their prolonged arguments was best—and at any rate most economically—set forth in Milton's CD as follows: "There can be no doubt that every thing in the world, by the beauty of its order, and evidence of a determinate and beneficial purpose which pervades it, testifies that some

supreme efficient Power must have pre-existed, by which the whole world was ordained for a specific end" (14 : 27).

Milton is to be numbered among the principal Renaissance thinkers who expounded the concept of universal order in all its glory. In PL the principle is maintained in Uriel's account of God's imposition of order on the "formless mass" of chaos* (3. 708–20), but especially in Raphael's account of creation* (Bk. 7). In fact, however, PL in its entirety illustrates Lancelot Andrewes's* belief that order is "highly pleasing" to God. The efforts of the Godhead are constantly bent toward creation, in direct opposition to the activities of Satan, for whom "Save what is in destroying, other joy / . . . is lost" (9. 478ff.). The first adverse interference of Satan with the natural order occurs as early as the War in Heaven*, when the rebellious angels, in order to secure the necessary materials to build their instruments of destruction,

> up they turnd
> Wide the Celestial soile, and saw beneath
> Th' originals of Nature in thir crude
> Conception.
>
> (6. 509–12)

This rape of the created order may have been intended as a parallel to the excavation of "the quiet wombe" of nature in The Faerie Queene, which Sir Guyon, not surprisingly, regarded as a sacrilege (2. 7. 17). In any case, the express violation of nature by the rebellious angels and the subsequent havoc created by their uprooting of the hills are set in striking contrast to the action of the Son of God*:

> At his command th' uprooted Hills retir'd
> Each to his place, they heard his voice and went
> Obsequious, Heav'n his wonted face renewd
> And with fresh Flourets Hill and Valley smil'd.
>
> (6. 781–84)

Milton indeed emphasizes on countless occasions God's endless efforts to prevent the cosmic structure from collapsing into discord. Early in the War in Heaven, for example, the embattled angels would have spread destruction far and wide

Had not th' Eternal King Omnipotent
From his strong hold of Heav'n high over-
rul'd
And limited thir might.
(6. 227–29; cf. 671–74)

In still another instance, this time in the sublunary world, the fearful combat between the mightly Gabriel and Satan would have confounded both heaven and earth

had not soon
Th' Eternal to prevent such horrid fray
Hung forth in Heav'n his gold'n Scales.

(4. 995–97)

Satan, fully aware of the sign's import, promptly retired murmuring. Yet neither this incident nor the others conclude Milton's concern with the larger theme of God's constant preservation of the universal order. The apex of that theme is not reached until the restoration of man by the incarnate God.

In one of his most influential statements, St. Paul affirmed that even pagans cannot pretend to be unaware of God's ways, since "that which may be known of God is manifest in them; for God hath shewed it unto them. For the invisible things of him from the creation of the world are clearly seen, being understood by the things that are made, even his eternal power and Godhead" (Rom. 1 : 19ff.). This sanction of the study of nature as revelatory of God, which later ages termed "natural theology," manifested itself during the Renaissance in a variety of related ways : in some instances quite simply through a reiteration of the idea that the world is nothing other than God revealed; on other occasions, through an affirmation of the divine "signatures" and "hieroglyphics" said to be engraved on the created order; and at last through an appeal to the popular metaphor of "the book of nature." As Milton avers in *PL*, the heavens "speak / The Makers high magnificence" (8. 100ff.), and indeed the totality of the created order comprises

"the Book of Knowledge fair" (3. 47). In Raphael's statement to Adam,

Heav'n
Is as the Book of God before thee set,
Wherein to read his wondrous Works.

(8. 66–68)

This is not to say that orthodox Christian thinkers have ever maintained the self-sufficiency of natural theology. St. Paul, indeed, made it quite clear that we can never know God perfectly this side of Heaven; for, as he wrote, "now we see through a glass, darkly; but then face to face : now I know in part; but then shall I know even as also I am known" (1 Cor. 13 : 12). For the best summary statement of this point of view we may turn to Donne : "Certainly, every Creature shewes God, as a glass, but glimmeringly and transitorily, by the frailty both of the receiver, and beholder : Our selves have his Image, as Medals, permanently, and preciously delivered. But by these meditations we get no further, then to know what he *doth,* not what he *is*" (*Essays in Divinity*, ed. E. M. Simpson [1952], p. 20). Donne's attempt to balance the book of nature with the written one of the Scriptures is a Renaissance commonplace.

Behind the Renaissance persuasion that the natural order reveals the purposes of God stands the Judeo-Christian view of nature. The Hebrew and early Christian attitude to nature was conditioned by the conviction that the omnipotent Most High has absolute jurisdiction over every aspect of creation. This belief, magnificently phrased in God's address to Job out of the whirlwind, was stated as poetically, if more briefly, by Amos :

Seek him that maketh the seven stars and
Orion,
And turneth the shadow of death into the
morning,
And maketh the day with night:
That calleth for the waters of the sea,
And poureth them out upon the face of the
earth:
The Lord is his name.
(Amos 5 :8)

From this belief the Hebrews advanced

to the conclusion that in some way all of nature's "singularities and discontinuities" are vitally important in the gradual revelation of the Divine Purpose in history. Hence the righteousness of God was related to the joys of nature (e.g., Ps. 96: 11–12), and the divine wrath to the convulsion in the created order (e.g., Hab. 3 : 10–11). The same attitude is characteristic of the early Christians. Throughout the New Testament, the terms of total reference appropriate to the omnipotent God are employed again; and again we find nature reacting benevolently or adversely, in either case reflecting the purposes of the Most High. The most striking manifestation of this attitude is, of course, nature's violent reaction upon the Crucifixion, beginning with the darkness at the height of noon, and progressing through an earthquake to the resurrection of the dead.

The continuity of tradition throughout the age of Milton is testified by countless treatises of the Renaissance. Most frequently—almost habitually—nature's reaction to contemporary events was said to have been parallel to incidents recounted in the Scriptures. But even when the reference was not directly to a specific biblical event, the language used was often largely, and at times exclusively, derived from the Old Testament. Here is George Wither's typical description of the angry Lord, in *Britain's Remembrancer* (1628; fol. 17v) :

from about

His eye lids, so much terror sparkled out,
That ev'ry circle of the Heav'ns it shooke,
And all the World did tremble at his looke;
The prospect of the *Skie,* that earst was cleare,
Did with a lowring countenance appeare:
The troubled *Ayre,* before his presence fled;
The *Earth* into her bosome shrunke her head;
The *Deeps* did roare; the *Heights* did stand amaz'd;
The *Moone* and *Stars* upon each other gaz'd;
The *Sun* did stand unmov'd in his path;
The Hoast of Heav'n was frighted at his wrath.

Yet the Renaissance held not only that God's attitude is revealed through nature during a given incident or shortly after it,

but also that God employs nature to divulge occurrences of the future. Here, it may be thought, we touch upon Renaissance astrology, whose capital rule —to quote Francis Quarles—was that "Heav'ns seldome shine / With idle fires; like Prophets they devine / Stupendious events" (*Hosanna,* ed. John Norden [1960], p. 6). But the disciples of astrology were not the only ones to attach significance to nature's "singularities and discontinuities." In the 1580s, to quote John Harvey, this view was shared by "the common people" no less than by "the learneder, and wiser sort," while in the next generation, according to George Hakewill, the "common opinion" was still that comets and similar disturbances in the heavens "have allwayes prognosticated some dreadfull mishaps to the world, as outragious windes, extraordinary drought, dearth, pestilence, warres, death of Princes and the like" (Harvey, *A Discoursive Probleme* [1588], p. 1; Hakewill, *An Apologie* [1627], p. 119). That such convictions were widely spread is not necessarily surprising; for if nature is indeed the book of God, may it not be that disorders in the skies and on earth are "signes of his wrath" over "our sinnes"? Calvin was by no means the only one to reply that this is so (*Sermons . . . upon the Booke of Job,* trans. Arthur Golding [1574], p. 707); this was repeatedly proclaimed by the vast majority of Christians, Protestants as well as Catholics, who held that comets and eclipses and earthquakes are "not to be thought trifles," being rather significant events that "foreshewe somewhat to follow" (Abraham Fleming, *A Bright Burning Beacon* [1580], sig. D4$^v$). Although the apologists of the faith by the early seventeenth century fully aware that "unnatural" phenomena could be explained scientifically, they insisted that "though some naturall reasons may bee probably rendered, yet being extraordinarie, they do proclaime, in their kinde, Gods anger, and threaten some judgment" (Thomas Jackson, *Judah must into Captivitie* [1622], pp. 22–23).

The Christian view of nature was

upheld by Milton in *Nat* as well as in *PL*. Nature participates in the happiness of Adam and Eve upon their marriage :

> all Heav'n,
> And happie Constellations on that houre
> Shed thir selectest influence; the Earth
> Gave sign of gratulation, and each Hill;
> Joyous the Birds; fresh Gales and gentle Aires
> Whisperd it to the Woods, and from thir wings
> Flung Rose, flung Odours from the spicie Shrub,
> Disporting, till the amorous Bird of Night
> Sung Spousal, and bid haste the Eevning Starr
> On his Hill top, to light the bridal Lamp.
> (8. 511–20)

When Eve eats the forbidden fruit, however, the violent reaction of nature, set forth by Milton in a preponderance of monosyllables, indicates all too clearly the attitude of God's "vicaire" :

> Earth felt the wound, and Nature from her seat
> Sighing through all her Works gave signs of woe,
> That all was lost.
> (9. 782–4)

Likewise, the moment that Adam shared the disobedience of his wife,

> Earth trembl'd from her entrails, as again
> In pangs, and Nature gave a second groan,
> Skie lowr'd and muttering Thunder, some sad drops
> Wept at compleating of the mortal Sin Original.
> (9. 1000–1004)

The theory underlying these lines reappears in two other instances in *PL*. The first occasion is during the passage of Sin and Death through the constellations on their way to our world after the Fall, when

> the blasted Starrs lookt wan,
> And Planets, Planet-strook, real Eclips
> Then sufferd.
> (10. 412–14)

The second forms part of the War in Heaven "accommodated" to our understanding. When Lucifer's rebellion aroused the divine wrath,

> Clouds began
> To darken all the Hill, and smoak to rowl
> In duskie wreaths, reluctant flames, the signe
> Of wrauth awak't.
> (6. 56–59)

Milton approached cautiously the other Renaissance view that "unnatural" phenomena "foreshewe somewhat to follow." In *Brit*, admittedly, he reports a series of portents—eclipses, comets, and even midnight "barbarous noises" and "hideous howlings"—but these were dictated by the practice of Renaissance historiographers. Otherwise, there is no evidence to suggest that Milton was so uncritical as to believe with Comenius* that comets and all other apparent disorders in the heavens "indeed are wont to portend no good" (*Orbis sensualium pictus,* trans. Charles Hoole [1659], p. 304). In *PR* Milton even more cautiously indicated that some "signs" are instigated not by God but by Satan (1. 393ff.; 4. 489ff.), though in other instances, when it was certain that they had been caused by God, he accepted them as forerunners of the Divine Purpose. Thus after the Fall in *PL,* when Eve naively thinks that she is to remain with Adam in the Garden, Milton intervenes to observe that

> Fate
> Subscrib'd not; Nature first gave Signs, imprest
> On Bird, Beast, Aire; Aire suddenly eclipsd
> After short blush of Morn; nigh in her sight
> The Bird of *Jove,* stoopt from his aerie tour,
> Two Birds of gayest plume before him drove:
> Down from a Hill the Beast that reigns in Woods,
> First Hunter then, persu'd a gentle brace,
> Goodliest of all the Forrest, Hart and Hinde;
> Direct to th' Eastern Gate was bent thir flight.
> (11. 181–90)

Adam, no longer able to read the book of nature as infallibly as he used to (cf. 8. 273–9), now resolves to await a direct revelation from God. His observation to Eve, therefore, though seemingly a restatement of Raphael's earlier assurance that the natural order is "the Book of God," is distinctly more cautious :

O *Eve*, some furder change awaits us nigh,
Which Heav'n by these mute signs in Nature
  shews
Forerunners of his purpose . . .

(11. 193–95)

[CAP]

**NEEDHAM, MARCHAMONT** (1620–1678), pamphleteer for both the Royalists and Parliament. Needham had been chief author of *Mercurius Britannicus,* an opposition newspaper to the Royalist *Mercurius Aulicus*; it ran from August 16–22, 1643, through August 4, 1645; Needham seems to have been the author of the last eighty issues. For remarks against Charles I*, he was arrested but soon released. In 1647 he changed allegiance, publishing *Mercurius Pragmaticus* in defense of the king. Under an order of the Council dated April 26, 1649, he was arrested on June 18, and Milton was requested to examine his various papers and report back to the Council. Needham escaped from Newgate but was rearrested on August 14. The Council ordered his release on November 14, possibly through the intervention of Council members William Lenthall (Speaker) and John Bradshaw* and possibly through a favorable report from Milton. Needham was apparently persuaded to the cause of the Parliamentarians again, and from this point forward he and Milton seem to have been good friends. He elaborated his new governmental attitudes in *The Case of the Common-wealth of England Stated,* published on or before May 8, 1650. He was awarded a gift of £50 for this volume on May 24 and given a probationary pension of £100 a year for further journalistic assistance. This assistance three weeks later on June 13, 1650, took the form of a new weekly paper, entitled *Mercurius Politicus**. The leading articles of nos. 16–69 were sections from his aforementioned book. *The Excellencie of a Free-State* (1656) is a compilation of articles in *Mercurius Politicus;* it was reprinted by Richard Baron in 1757 and translated into French by T. Mandar (Paris, 1790) in two volumes.

Needham was also employed as a translator and as editor of the *Public Intelligencer,* another Parliamentarian news sheet. He was not, however, in favor with Parliament as the years moved toward the Restoration, and on April 9, 1660, he was removed from the editorship of both *Mercurius Politicus* and the *Public Intelligencer.* He was not excepted under the Act of Oblivion (August 1660). In later life he practiced physic as well as pamphleteering. [JTS]

**NENNIUS,** eight-century Welsh historian, reputed author of *Historia Britonum,* cited in Holinshed*, Ussher*, Camden*, and Speed*, and from them by Milton in *Brit*—or from manuscripts, of which two were at Cambridge (the *Historia* was not printed until 1691). (See Constance Nicholas, *Introduction and Notes to Milton's History of Britain* [1957].) In any case, "Nennius" is frequently cited as an authority on the earlier years covered by *Brit.* [WBH]

**NEOPLATONISM IN MILTON.** In the case of Milton it is more accurate to speak of a Neoplatonic tradition than Neoplatonism, since the latter implies immediate debts, borrowings, and influences. That Milton's works are composed and assimilated in the wake of a long, widespread, and eclectic tradition is indisputable. But the imputation of immediate and specific appropriations of Neoplatonism, especially where his alleged heresies* are concerned, is hazardous hypothesizing. What follows, then, undertakes to survey components of the Neoplatonic tradition that are clearly perceivable in Milton's works, in particular *PL.*

As metaphysicians Neoplatonists in all periods base their ontology on a concept of emanation by which there is a progression of the One to the many, of form to matter*, of the incorporeal to the corporeal. Ultimately all things return to their source. Plotinus's* cosmology*, for instance, describes an emanation of the One to the many in three stages. From the One, which is the first cause, infinite, transcendent, above being itself, come two opposing spiritual energies, attraction and repulsion; the first level of being occurs when these two are brought into balance, for in the imbalance is chaos. This is true in that infinite attraction draws everything together into a point while infinite repulsion results in total expansion. The first level of being is *Nous* or Mind, which is multiple and contains the archetypal ideas. From Mind emanates *Psyche* or Soul, which is also multiple and contains reason. Soul is subdivided into two parts: the higher soul which looks back to Mind, and the lower soul or nature*, which looks forward to the phenomenal world. Soul creates the phenomenal world by combining form and matter or, in Platonic terms, by impinging ideas upon matter that cannot exist alone, a planting of ideas in matter. But matter does not come from the One; it is nothing, not-being, and as such the source of evil*. Matter is the principle of absolute form-lessness and indeterminateness. By its absolute lack of all form, matter is at the opposite extreme to things intelligible, and is in its own nature ugly and evil.

Though Milton has many points of similarity, his ontological position is fundamentally different from that of Plotinus. Milton's ontology is monistic, like that of Proclus* and before him Origen* (182–254), who had clearly defined and defended ontological monism. Matter is that which underlies bodies and has an existence in its own right apart from qualities. When souls fall, they become embodied in this prime matter; bodily creation is thus a punishment. When bodies have suffered sufficient penance and purgation, they once again become souls. While in the body these souls are joined to matter by a third agent, the intermediary spirit or luciform body. (*See also* METAPHYSICS, MILTON'S.)

The writings of Proclus (411–85) present a reinterpretation of Greek myths in a monistic way. The gods descend from the One in a process of emanation in a supernatural hierarchy. More stages would make emanation more probable. There are six stages bridging the gulf between the One and the phenomenal world. Emanation is a necessity of the One and is eternal, deteriorating, and cyclical. The One does not elect to emanate; it is part of its nature. The levels of being deteriorate as they achieve distance from the One until the emanation reaches the farthest deterioration in matter. Then it begins a retracing of its course back to the One; hence it is cyclic and the power of the One flows in a circle back to its origin. *See also* PHILOSOPHY.

The system is a strict monistic emanation. Matter as well as spirit comes from the One, and the intervening stages are simply bridges for the gulf. The One is all and in all and is the only principle, hence a monad. Therefore evil is inextricably united with good and the essence of evil is preference of the free will for evil over good. Proclus always asserts that evil is a deviation from good, a tending downward.

Proclus's monism leads him to accept matter as part of the divine. In his system it is the last and lowest stage of emanation. In the treatise *On Evil* he gives considerable attention to proving that matter is not evil in itself as the dualists have asserted. All things including matter proceed from the one principle, which is the Good. To justify his contention that matter is good, Proclus equates it with infinity or repulsion, while form is bound or attraction and body is the mixture of the two.

Continuing the monastic ontology developed by Proclus were such Christian thinkers as his probable contemporary and disciple Pseudo-Dionysius* the Areopagite, the early scholastic John Scotus Erigena (815–877), and the later scholastic Duns Scotus* (1265–1308). Following the Jewish philosopher Avencebrol, Duns postulates three species of prime matter. *Materia primo prima* is the common substratum of all created beings. It is that which is absolutely indeterminate with regard to all forms whatsover, its only reality being that which it receives immediately from God. *Materia secundo* *prima* is that which is the substratum of generation and corruption, coming into being and passing away. It is that which is transformed by created agents, that is, forces of nature. *Materia tertio prima* is the matter of every particular natural agent.

Though it is untenable to maintain that Milton specifically derived his monistic ontology from any one of these thinkers, it is sound to conclude that clearly he is in the Proclean tradition. And he is insistent on his monism in both *CD* and *PL*:

> With regard to the original matter of the universe, however, there has been much difference of opinion. Most of the moderns contend that it was formed from nothing, a basis as unsubstantial as that of their own theory. . . . That matter should have been always independent of God . . . that matter, I say, should have existed of itself from all eternity, is inconceivable. If on the contrary it did not exist from all eternity, it is difficult to understand from whence it derives its origin. There remains, therefore, but one solution of the difficulty . . . namely, that all things are of God. (*CD* 15:17–21)

Since matter is from God, it is therefore good, another point on which Milton is insistent:

> For the original matter of which we speak, is not to be looked upon as an evil or trivial thing, but as intrinsically good, and the chief productive stock of every subsequent good. It was a substance, and derivable from no other source than from the fountain of every substance, though at first confused and formless, being afterwards adorned and digested into order by the hand of God. (15:23)

No thing can finally be destroyed:

> Since . . . God did not produce everything out of nothing, but of himself, I proceed to consider the necessary consequences of this doctrine, namely, that if all things are not only from God, but of God, no created thing can be finally annihilated. (15:27)

In *PL*, the clearest statement of ontological monism and emanation is the important scale of nature* passage in which Raphael explains to Adam the material but not the formal oneness of all existence:

> *O Adam,* one Almightie is, from whom
> All things proceed, and up to him return,
> If not deprav'd from good, created all
> Such to perfection, one first matter all,
> Indu'd with various forms, various degrees
> Of substance, and in things that live, of life;
> But more refin'd, more spiritous, and pure,
> As nearer to him plac't or nearer tending
> Each in thir several active Sphears assignd,
> Till body up to spirit work, in bounds
> Proportiond to each kind.
>
> (5. 469–79))

Clearly Milton here articulates a process of emanation that is descending and deteriorating but cyclical. Further, it is a monistic emanation like that described by Proclus and later by Scotus when he postulated the three degrees of prime matter. In fact Milton himself so divides matter in *Logic* (11 : 53) : "Matter is commonly divided into primary and secondary; the secondary into proximate and remote." Primary matter subsists in the spiritual existence of God, the metaphysical subsistence of highest divinity. Secondary-remote matter in *PL* is chaos*, which is matter fitted for the reception of forms (2. 910–16). This matter is nevertheless part of God's essence, though a lower part that has been withdrawn from His higher part, as He Himself states to the Son (7. 168–73). Secondary-proximate matter is matter formed and created (7. 232–40). It is here that the "various forms, various degrees of substance" are realized.

If for Milton matter is not in itself evil, what is the source of evil? Raphael explains the return of all things to God "if not deprav'd from good." Conversely, nearest to God is best ("more refin'd, more spiritous and pure, / As nearer to him plac't or nearer tending"). Evil, then, is a tendency away from God, the relative lack, deficiency, privation of being. Like Proclus Milton believed that there is "no unmixed Evil, no evil thing that does not participate in some vestige of Good. And in this sense we may hold that Evil is from God, as being in some measure a good" (*On "The Republic,"* 358). Evil, therefore, is a deviation from good. Milton says,

> Strictly speaking indeed it is neither matter nor form that sins; and yet having proceeded from God, and become in the power of another party, what is there to prevent them, inasmuch as they have now become mutable, from contracting taint and contamination through the enticements of the devil, or those which originate in man himself? It is objected, however, that body cannot emanate from spirit. I reply, much less then can body emanate from nothing. (*CD* 15:25)

But if matter is not evil, it is at least corruptible and farthest from God. Most important of all Milton's uses of material submergence is Satan's entrance into folds of the serpent:

> O foul descent! That I who erst contended
> With Gods to sit the highest, am now constrained
> Into a Beast, and mixt with bestial slime,
> This essence to incarnate and imbrute . . .
> (9. 163–66)

But there is, as an alternative to the emanation into matter, a higher place in the emanative scheme: "But more refin'd, more spiritous, and pure / As nearer to him plac't or nearer tending . . . Till body up to spirit work. . . ." And Raphael, a moment later, specifically postulates a spiritous existence for Adam: "Your bodies may at last turn all to wingd ascend / Ethereal as well . . . (5. 497–99). Milton turns this postulation into part of Eve's temptation. In her dream the voice had already instructed her:

> Taste this, and be henceforth among the Gods
> Thy self a Goddess, not to Earth confind,
> But sometimes in the Air, as wee, somtimes
> Ascend to Heav'n, by merit thine, and see
> What life the Gods live there, and such live
> thou.
> (5. 77–81)

In the actual temptation Satan shrewdly manipulates the notion of ascent to Eve's destruction:

> Ye shall be as Gods,
> Knowing both Good and Evil as they know.

That ye should be as Gods, since I as Man,
Internal Man, is but proportion meet,
I of brute human, yee of human Gods. . . .
And what are Gods that Man may not become
As they, participating God-like food?
(9. 708–17)

Milton had entertained the monistic concept of the ascent into the divine essence and the descent into matter as early as *Mask* (1634). The elder Brother vividly moralizes to the Younger concerning their lost sister:

> So dear to Heav'n is Saintly chastity,
> That when a soul is found sincerely so,
> A thousand liveried Angels lacky her,
> Driving far off each thing of sin and guilt,
> And in cleer dream, and solemn vision
> Tell her of things that no gross ear can hear,
> Till oft converse with heav'nly habitants
> Begin to cast a beam on th' outward shape,
> The unpolluted temple of the mind,
> And turns it by degrees to the souls essence,
> Till all be made immortal: but when lust
> By unchaste looks, loose gestures, and foul talk,
> But most by leud and lavish act of sin,
> Lets in defilement to the inward parts,
> The soul grows clotted by contagion,
> Imbodies, and imbrutes, till she quite loose
> The divine property of her first being.
> (452–68)

Also in *Mask,* articulated by the same philosophical speaker, is the notion of the self-genesis of evil:

> But evil on it self shall back recoyl,
> And mix no more with goodness, when at last
> Gather'd like scum, and setl'd to it self,
> It shall be in eternal restless change
> Self-fed, and self-consum'd, if this fail,
> The pillar'd firmament is rott'nness,
> And earths base built on stubble.
> (592–98)

In addition to these crucial implications of monistic emanation, other features of the Neoplatonic emanation may be mentioned here. One is that ominous couple of *PL* 2, Chaos and Old Night. W. C. Curry maintains that they are to be found in Proclus's scheme of monistic emanation: "Chaos may be identified with the second divine principle of the 'intelligible triad,' and Night with the first or summit of the so-called 'intelligible and at the same time intellectual triad' of the Neoplatonic system." Proclus had described the supercelestial place as maternal, the receptacle for the paternal causes; it is the first manifestation of space. Neoplatonists had identified matter with darkness, on the face of the deep in Genesis or the Hermetic "downward-tending darkness terrible and grim." Ancient Night, then, is a fit emblem for the "Womb of nature and perhaps her Grave" (2. 911), the "wide womb of uncreated night" (2. 150).

Another Neoplatonic commonplace involved in emanation, originally argued by the stoics, is the concept of the seeds of individual beings, the *semina*. Again W. C. Curry has devoted most attention to this motif, applying his findings to both Shakespeare and Milton. In *PL* 7, when the Son creates, he does so by planting seeds in matter, implied in the statement "vital vertue infus'd, and vital warmth / Throughout the fluid Mass, . . . (7. 236–37) These seeds are the *logoi spermatikoi* or *rationes seminales,* pale reflections of exemplars in the mind of God. Curry believes that both Shakespeare and Milton are here following the Augustinian* doctrine of exemplarism. After Augustine, Ficino was to use the same notion to describe how Nature plants her seeds in matter to produce the forms of the *corpus mundi.* Augustine and Ficino are dualistic, but among the monistic Neoplatonists like Iamblichus one meets both the term and the notion. Whatever his source, whether dualistic Augustinian* exemplarism or monistic Neoplatonic occultism, Milton makes effective poetic use of the tradition. The semina are sown in matter when the vital virtue and warmth is infused throughout the fluid mass (7. 236–37). They are germinated throughout the six days of creation, especially on the last, when beasts are said to spring fully grown from earthly soil like plants (7. 463–73).

Like Plotinus, Ficino conceived of Soul as having two parts : one that looked back to God and was purely spiritual; another that looked forward to matter and was generative. To Ficino Nature was not chaotic, indeterminate, and transitory, but a great animal and the active faculty of Soul, its outer life. It is the lowest spiritual substance and adds substantiality to matter. In this respect Nature is like the garden of Adonis, a joyous paradise, as fair a place as nature could create, "the first seminary / Of all things that are borne to live and dye, . . ." (*Faerie Queene* 3. 6. 30). Milton himself was aware of the usage of the symbol and had used it himself in *Mask* to describe in terms that anticipate the destruction of Eden the garden "where young Adonis oft reposes . . ." (999).

A final aspect of the Neoplatonic tradition of emanation is its tendency toward mysticism. This mysticism is theocentric in that it is the aspiration to ascend to the vision of God and a state of unity with Him. Almost all the early Neoplatonists display the tendency, chiefly Plotinus, whose mysticism seems near that of Plato*. In the main, Neoplatonic mysticism is the ascent, vision, and unity requiring purgation and contemplation. The law or force that binds all creation is love (Plotinus, *Ennead* 4. 4. 40 and Proclus, *Commentary on the Timaeus* 2. 85). The ascent is by means of love through the various levels of emanation to behold the One. Adam's response to Raphael's description of the scale of nature is a statement of the ascent :

Well hast thou taught the way that might direct
Our knowledge, and the scale of Nature set
From centre to circumference, whereon
In contemplation of created things
By steps we may ascend to God.
(5. 508–12)

Love is the law of creation, the force binding all things, and the power by which the soul rises in mystic ascent. So Raphael instructs Adam :

In loving thou dost well, in passion not,
Wherein true Love consists not; love refines
The thoughts, and heart enlarges, hath his seat
In Reason, and is judicious, is the scale,
By which to heav'nly Love thou maist ascend. . . .
(8. 588–92)

Love, Adam states to Raphael, "Leads up to Heav'n, is both the way and guide . . ." (8. 613).

But there is another technique, practiced by the Neoplatonists, and by Milton, for setting forth the spiritual and accommodating it to human sense. This device is the cosmic symbol of correspondences, which holds that each level of being corresponds to another both below and above it in the scale of emanation. The macrocosm or material phenomenal world corresponds to the noumenal world of heaven, the mind of God, and is made in imitation of it as though by a pattern. Corresponding to the macrocosm and cunningly made in imitation of it is the microcosm or little world of man. Finally there is the state, which men create on the model of the microcosm. God rules Heaven, the sun rules the macrocosm, reason rules the microcosm and the king rules the state. These correspondences are frequently made explicit in *PL* as, for instance, Satan's apostrophe to the earth in Book 9:

O Earth, how like to Heav'n, if not preferr'd
More justly, Seat worthier of Gods, as built
With second thoughts, reforming what was
    old!
For what God after better worse would build?
Terrestrial Heav'n, danc't round by other
    Heav'ns
That shine, yet bear thir bright officious
    Lamps,
Light above Light, for thee alone, as seems,
In thee concentring all thir precious beams
Of sacred influence: As God in Heaven
Is Center, yet extends to all, so thou
Centering receav'st from all those Orbs; in
    thee,
Not in themselves, all thir known vertue
    appears
Productive in Herb, Plant, and nobler birth
Of creatures animate with gradual life
Of Growth, Sense, Reason, all summ'd up
    in Man.
                    (9. 99–113)

In Satan's passionate address the three main components of the universe are assimilated in equivalence, similarity, analogy, and correspondence: heaven, earth, and man.

If the material of Neoplatonic symbolism is frequently made explicit in the poem, so is the method as a device. In a succinct and articulate statement that virtually defines the cosmic symbol, Raphael declares the difficulties that face him in his forthcoming narration:

            what surmounts the reach
Of human sense, I shall delineate so,
By lik'ning spiritual to corporal forms,
As may express them best, though what if
    Earth
Be but the shaddow of Heav'n, and things
    therein
Each to other like, more then on Earth is
    thought?
                    (5. 571–76)

Earth—the phenomenal, material, corporeal, empirical—is a shadowy imitation of Heaven—the noumenal, spiritual, incorporeal, divine. Furthermore, symbolism is a means of accommodating these high realities to man's limited facilities. It is, like language itself, a device for perceiving, embodying, and conceptualizing into finite vehicles and forms the mysteries of the infinite (8. 176–79). [JDA]

**NESTORIANISM:** *see* INCARNATION.

**NEVE, PHILIP,** who flourished at the end of the eighteenth century, is important in Milton studies for two books. Aside from them little is known about him. The anonymous *Cursory Remarks on Some of the Ancient English Poets, Particularly Milton* (London, 1789) devotes the longest section and the final section, pp. 109–46, to an examination of *Arc, Lyc, IlP*, foreign language poems (very briefly), Milton's language (primarily through the two epics), Milton's fame, and Milton's genius. "The genius of *Milton*, the contemplations, the powers of intellect in invention and combination," he wrote, "are above example, or comparison. In proportion to the terror excited by the sublimity of his design, is the delight received by his wonderful execution. His subject, and his conduct of it, exalt him to a supreme rank; to a rank, with which all other poets compare but as a second class."

Also anonymous was *A Narrative of the Disinterment of Milton's Coffin, in the Parish-Church of St. Giles, Cripplegate, on Wednesday, 4th of August, 1790; and of the Treatment of the Corpse, During That and the Following Day* (London, 1790), 1st ed., pp. 5–34. This macabre event was reported in a number of newspapers of the day and provoked William Cowper's* poem on the subject. Neve's volume sold out rapidly, for soon after a second edition appeared with additions, covering pp. 5–50. It is a most detailed account of the way in which relics were sought and treasured and the desecration that follows on riot. There has been doubt that the remains disinterred were Milton's, but Allen W. Read's examination of the question, based on Neve's volume (*Publications of the Modern Language Association,* 45 : 1050–68), concludes that they were. [JTS]

**NEWCOMB, THOMAS:** *see* PRINTERS.

**NEWCOMEN, MATTHEW.** One of the Smectymnuans* Newcomen (1610?–1669) attended St. John's College, Cambridge, 1626–1633 (B.A., 1629; M.A., 1633). He began to preach in Colchester, Essex, in 1636 and soon became the leader of the church reform group there. He married the sister of Edmund Calamy's* first wife in 1640. He was a member of the Westminster Assembly* from 1643 onward. He refused the office of chaplain to Charles II* at the Restoration, but was created Doctor of Divinity on October 10, 1661. Still he would not accede to the Act of Uniformity and was thus ejected. He became pastor of the English church at Leyden, where he died around September 1, 1669, of the plague. [JTS]

**NEWTON, THOMAS** (1704–1782), Bishop of Bristol, biographer* and editor* of Milton's poetry. After a number of minor posts and disappointments in not receiving clerical preferments, Newton became Bishop of Bristol through Lord Bute at the end of 1761. Further advances were also denied him, although he was made Dean of St. Paul's in October 1768. He completed his autobiography shortly before his death in February 1782.

His edition of *PL* with variorum notes collected from printed and unprinted sources, along with his own remarks and annotations, came out in two volumes in 1749. The remaining poems were published three years later in a corresponding one-volume edition. *PL* was illustrated* with George Vertue's engraving from the Onslow portrait, the bust of Milton by Jonathan Richardson*, engraved by Vertue, and the designs of Francis Hayman, executed by S. F. Ravenet or C. Grignion. Besides the new life written by Newton for the edition, it included a Postscript on the charges of plagiarism made by William Lauder* and examples of Lauder's interpolations, an index of descriptions, similes, and the like, and a verbal index. Newton's important biography pulled together the materials known to date, made corrections, and reflected his own interview with Elizabeth Foster, Milton's granddaughter, as well as others' interviews with her. It was repeatedly reprinted in the British Isles and the Colonies, and was the source of numerous shorter biographical notices. The volume containing *PR, SA,* and the *Poems Upon Several Occasions* used a medallion portrait* by Richardson, engraved by Vertue, and illustrations by Hayman, engraved by T. Miller, Grignion, and Ravenet, for *PR,* Book 1, *SA, L'Al, IlP,* and *Mask.* Two sonnets are given non-Miltonic, though ubiquitous and erroneous, titles; no. 7 is "On His Being Arriv'd to the Age of 23" (derived from a title given in Tonson's* 1713 edition), and no. 19 is "On His Blindness." Reprinted are the plans and subjects from *TM.* The Latin poems include the spurious verses to Queen Christina*, which Charles Gildon* had published as Milton's in *Chorus Poetarum* (1696), p. 19, and which had been noticed by Toland (1 : 38–39). The volume contains a brief word-list. Both editions were frequently reprinted, but many were not new editions (despite their title pages) but rather reissues with new title pages. [JTS]

**NICETAS ACOMINATE (or CHON-IATES),** late twelfth century historian of the Eastern Empire, whose *Imperii Graeci Historia* Milton cites from the Paris, 1647, edition, concerning "Navigation and Shipwrecks" in the last entry in *CB.* He is also recognized as an authority on Byzantine history in *Eikon* (5 : 84). [WBH]

**NICKOLLS, JOHN, JR.** (1710?–1745), the editor of *Original Letters and Papers of State, Addressed to Oliver Cromwell; Concerning the Affairs of Great Britain. From the year MDCXLIX to MDCLVIII. Found among the political collections of Mr. John Milton* (1743). These were papers kept by Milton, perhaps simply because they did not get thrown away or because he thought they might be important in later years. According to the preface, Milton turned them over to Thomas Ellwood*, but this does not agree with the title page statement, "Found among the political collections." If Milton did give them to Ellwood, he would have received them, in all probability, in the middle sixties. Why Milton would simply dispose of them to Ellwood is unexplainable. After Ellwood's death in 1713, the papers passed into the possession of his close friend Joseph Wyeth, who died in 1731. His widow gave them to Nickolls to publish. None of the items, of course, are of Milton's composition. The manuscript is now owned by the Society of Antiquarians in London. [JTS]

**NOVAE SOLYMAE LIBRI SEX:** *see* ATTRIBUTIONS.

**NUMEROLOGY.** Recent scholarship has made much of the philosophical and religious symbolism traditionally attached to certain numbers. Ultimately derived from Pythagorean* interpretations of the significance of number, particularly one and the intervals of the octave, number symbolism had its adherents through most of Western history. The World Soul in Plato's* *Timaeus* is structured according to numerical proportions. After him, Cicero*, Augustine*, Capella, Boethius, Isidore, Dante*, Cusanus, Pico, Ficino, Giorgio, and a host of others all attach great significance to the arcane symbolism of numbers. Yet besides a truly extensive body of commentary on the mystical and theological meanings inherent in certain numbers, it occurred to many theoreticians that their written compositions should make structural use of the numerical patterns they found so significant : thus the 33 books of Augustine's *Contra Faustum manichaeum,* the 33 sections of Dante's letter to Can Grande, the 33 chapters of the first book of Milton's *CD* (33 recalling the number of years in Christ's life), Pico's seven-fold interpretation of the seven days of Creation* in his *Heptaplus,* and many more. As it was commonly held that certain numbers and their combinations were sacred (3, 9, 27, etc.) and that God had disposed the universe according to numerological symmetries, there were powerful reasons for poets, as proper imitators, to construct their poems numerologically. The technique was usually to determine the number of lines, stanzas, or books, etcetera, according to a preconceived pattern. Many Latin and vernacular works, like some works of Virgil*, Donne, Jonson*, and Herbert, clearly evidence this technique. Dante arranged his *Comedia* into three sections of 33 cantos each which, plus the first, add up to 100 cantos, a number commonly taken to signify cosmic unity. By evidencing such kinds of structure certain works acquire an added symbolic meaning by virtue of the arrangement of their parts.

Readers who confront Milton's explicit statement in *CD* rejecting any inherent power in numbers would, on the face of it, seem to be discouraged from attempting numerological analyses of Milton's works. In arguing against holding the Sabbath on the seventh day, Milton says

> It ought also to be shown what essential principle of morality is involved in the number seven; and why, when released from the obligation of the Sabbath, we should still be bound to respect a particular number, possessing no inherent virtue or efficacy. (17 : 183. See also 15 : 19–21)

In response to these statements, critics have pointed to Milton's prolusion on the music of the spheres [12 : 149–57] as proof that he was acquainted with Pythagorean ideas about the symbolic value of harmonious numbers. But because this is so clearly a witty school exercise, prefaced by Milton's injunction that we should take it in jest, that argument is not wholly convincing. Yet in the face of considerable evidence that he does use numerological patterns in *Nat, Lyc, Mask,* and *PL,* it would seem that Milton's comments in *CD* refer, perhaps, to his views on the magical potency of numbers rather than to their usefulness as symbols and structural devices in his poetry.

It has been claimed (Maren-Sofie Røstvig, *The Hidden Sense and Other Essays* [1963]), that Milton adapted the mystical *lambda* of Plato for the structure of *Nat.* The *lambda* is generated by doubling and tripling from one until one gets two series of numbers, 1, 2, 4, 8, and 1, 3, 9, 27. Hence the 27 8-line stanzas of the poem represent the two impulses from the One, God. The introduction has four seven-line stanzas, numbers that connote the world of time, appropriate for Christ's Incarnation*. The Hymn itself is composed of 27 eight-line stanzas, numbers expressive of perfection appropriate to Redemption, justification*, and the completion of the divine plan. Douglas Bush has questioned the significance attached to these numbers, when similar numbers and stanza patterns are used frequently in other poems of the period where the symbolism discussed by Røstvig is singularly inappropriate [*Studies in English Literature* 6 : 1–6].

In a similar way, Røstvig finds provocative symbolism in the length of Comus's first speech in *Mask,* 52 lines corresponding to the 52 weeks of the year, which suggests his accord with the world of time and mutability. The 25 lines of the second part of the speech correspond to the square of 5 which, appropriately for the character of Comus, represents the world of sense. As Comus begins his great speech at line 666, the reference to the

Beast of St. John's Revelation seems reasonably clear.

Alastair Fowler in *Silent Poetry* (1970), maintains that many of the supposed structural irregularities of *Lyc* are in fact numerologically explainable. For instance, the ten unrhymed lines of the poem break up every stanza except the third, eighth, and tenth. Hence there is an appropriate parallel between the unbroken stanzas and the scenes of harmony, apotheosis, and immortality pictured there. As six-syllable lines likewise break every stanza except the tenth, Milton creates a structural analogy to the return to unity and reconciliation with the divine suggested there. The concluding eight lines of the poem suggest the octave and its associations with harmonious unity and reconciliation. The ten stanzas and the 24 decasyllabic couplets connote the ten spheres and the 24 hours, and the 179 lines of the poem are half the number of days in the 359 yearly degrees in the diurnal orbit of the sun. *Lyc,* of course, ends at nightfall.

Numerological analyses of *PL* are predictably far more complex than those above. It has been maintained that the epic is Christocentric both thematically and numerologically. In the first edition (1667), Christ mounts his chariot in the exact center of the poem, an episode framed by two 23-line speeches, 23 representing the fullness of his deity: 3 (Trinity) + 10 (New Covenant) (see Gunnar Qvarström, *The Enchanted Palace* [1967]). In the second edition, though the center line has shifted (perhaps inadvertently), Milton seems in other ways to have continued to manifest his concern for numerologically balanced patterns. The poem may be divided thus: Invocation (1) + 1 (2) + Invocation (3) + 3 (4, 5, 6) // Invocation (7) + 1 (8) + Invocation (9) + 3 (10, 11, 12).

Fowler (*Triumphal Forms* [1970]) computes the duration of the epic to be 33 days of direct and narrated action. The Creation* by the Messiah occurs halfway through the action (7). The week of Creation is likewise accented in the center, for on the fourth day Christ created the sun, an event described with the word *crowned,* a term commonly placed in the numerical center of crucial parts of baroque* poems and usually signifying sovereignty. Fowler, then, divides the time of the poem to illustrate that Milton consciously conceived the epic as Christocentric and used a numerological structure to accent the idea: 13 + 3 + 1 + 3 + 13, with the sequence of days 3 + 1 + 3 covering the week of Creation with the creation of the sun at the center.

Throughout the poem numerological considerations seem apparent. Adam and Eve appear in 4, the number of Earth and Man; the perfect harmony of the Trinity is reflected by the Council in Heaven's being placed in 3; the hebdomad of Creation appears appropriately in 7; Death first appears at 2. 666 (the number of the Beast in Revelation); and Adam falls precisely at line 999 in the original Book 8—999 being 666 upside down.

The analyses above are typical of numerological criticism. The vexing problem of the relation of such numerical patterns to meaning and literary value has been considered by some, though the problem has by no means been settled. Scholars have determined to some extent numbers that had established, denotative meanings to Milton and his contemporaries. Yet, as with many symbols, numbers or number sequences have been used in a myriad of kinds of works with many different purposes and effects. Asking for dictionary codification of exact meanings in light of this is, perhaps, asking for a consistency history does not offer. [GHS]

# CONTRIBUTORS TO VOLUME 5

| | |
|---|---|
| AA | Arthur Axelrad. California State University, Long Beach, Calif. 90840. |
| ACL | Albert C. Labriola. Duquesne University, Pittsburgh, Pa. 15219. |
| BR | Balachandra Rajan. University of Western Ontario, London, Ontario, Canada. |
| CAP | C. A. Patrides. Langwith College, University of York, Heslington, York, England. |
| DAR | Donald A. Roberts. Vineyard Haven, Mass. 02568. |
| DBC | David B. Carroll. California State University, Los Angeles, Calif. 90032. |
| EFD | Edgar F. Daniels. Bowling Green State University, Bowling Green, Ohio. 43614. |
| EHD | Edgar H. Duncan. Vanderbilt University, Nashville, Tenn. 37235. |
| ERG | E. Richard Gregory. University of Toledo, Toledo, Ohio. 43606. |
| ESD | Elizabeth Story Donno. Columbia University, New York, New York. 10027. |
| FBY | Frank B. Young. University of Tennessee, Nashville, Tenn. 37203. |
| GHS | Gerald H. Snare. Newcomb College, Tulane University, New Orleans, La. 70118. |
| HS | Howard Schultz. Late of Southern Illinois University, Carbondale, Ill. 62901. |
| IC | Ira Clark. University of Florida, Gainesville, Fla. 32607. |
| JAW | Joseph A. Wittreich, Jr. University of Maryland, College Park, Md. 20742 |
| JCB | Jackson C. Boswell. District of Columbia Teachers College, Washington, D.C. 20009. |
| JDA | Jack Ashley. University of South Carolina, Columbia, S.C. 29208. |
| JGD | John G. Demaray, Rutgers University at Newark, Newark. N.J. 07102. |
| JGH | John G. Halkett. Syracuse University, Syracuse, N.Y. 13210. |
| JHC | Jonathan H. Collett. New York State University College, Old Westbury, N.Y. 11568. |
| JLG | John L. Gribben. Kent State University, Kent, Ohio. 44242. |
| JLH | James L. Hedges. Azusa Pacific College, Azusa, Calif. 91702. |
| JMS | John M. Steadman. Huntington Library and Art Gallery, San Marino, Calif. 91108. |
| JRK | John R. Knott, Jr. University of Michigan, Ann Arbor, Mich. 48104. |
| JS | Joy Schultz. Southern Illinois University, Carbondale, Ill. 62901. |

| | |
|---|---|
| JTS | John T. Shawcross. City University of New York, New York, N.Y. 10031. |
| JVM | James V. Mirollo. Columbia University, New York, New York. 10027. |
| JWF | James W. Flosdorf. Russell Sage College, Troy, New York. 12180. |
| MCP | Mother M. Christopher Pecheux. College of New Rochelle, New Rochelle, N.Y. 10801. |
| MF | Michael Fixler. Tufts University, Medford, Mass. 02155.    z |
| NCC | Nan Cooke Carpenter. University of Georgia, Athens, Ga. 30602. |
| NH | Nathaniel Henry, 200 East Horne Ave., Farmville, N.C. 27828, |
| PEB | Purvis E. Boyette. Tulane University, New Orleans, La. 70118. |
| PMZ | Paul M. Zall. California State University, Los Angeles, Calif. 90032. |
| PBR | Philip B. Rollinson. University of South Carolina, Columbia, S.C. 29208. |
| PRS | Paul R. Sellin. University of California. Los Angeles, Calif. 90024. |
| PS | Philip Sheridan. Carleton College, Northfield, Minn. 55057. |
| RBR | Roger B. Rollin. Clemson University, Clemson, S.C. 29631. |
| RBW | Roger B. Wilkenfeld. University of Connecticut, Storrs, Conn. 06268. |
| RCR | Richard G. Rierdan. Pepperdine University, Los Angeles, Calif. 90044. |
| REH | Ralph E. Hone. University of Redlands, Redlands, Calif. 92373. |
| RHW | Robert H. West. University of Georgia, Athens, Ga. 30602. |
| RRC | Robert R. Cawley. Late of Princeton University, Princeton, N.J. 08540. |
| RTF | Robert T. Fallon. La Salle College, Philadelphia, Pa. 19141. |
| SSt | Stanley Stewart. University of California, Riverside, Calif. 92502. |
| SW | Susanne Woode. Brown University, Providence, R.I. 02912. |
| WBH | William B. Hunter. University of Houston, Houston, Texas. 77004. |
| WJO | Walter J. Ong S.J. St. Louis University, St. Louis, Mo. 63103. |
| WM | Willis Monie. P.O. Box 105, Hartwick, N.Y. 13348. |